Changing World Order

Changing World Order

India, EU and US—A Trialogue

Editors
B. KRISHNAMURTHY
GEETHA GANAPATHY-DORÉ

SHIPRA

ISBN: 978-81-7541-535-5

First Published in India in 2009

Changing World Order: *India, EU and US—A Trialogue*

Published by :
SHIPRA PUBLICATIONS
115-A, Vikas Marg, Shakarpur, Delhi-110092 (India)
Tel. : 91-11-65277210, 22500954, Fax : 91-11-22458662
Email : info@shiprapublications.com
www.shiprapublications.com

Preface

> "By and large the literature of a democracy will never exhibit the order, regularity, skill, and art characteristic of aristocratic literature; formal qualities will be neglected or actually despised. The style will often be strange, incorrect, overburdened, and loose, and almost always strong and bold. Writers will be more anxious to work quickly than to perfect details. Short works will be commoner than long books, wit than erudition, imagination than depth. There will be a rude and untutored vigor of thought with great variety and singular fecundity. Authors will strive to astonish more than to please, and to stir passions rather than to charm taste."
>
> —*Alexis de Tocqueville*

The present volume deals with current developments in international political order which is witnessing unprecedented changes and as its sub-title suggests, is Eurocentric in its scope and approach. The initial ambition of establishing a United Europe, with the intention of assuming the 'responsibilities in the world of tomorrow' and making a 'contribution commensurate with its traditions and mission', has got tremendous relevance in today's world "more than ever before". It is believed that the EU with its value system, civilisational strength, democratic experiments and experiences, trials and tribulations, achievements and failures, will be able to guide, moderate and correlate both India and the US together in the noble attempt to establish a new world order. The articles presented in this volume try to honestly, accurately and critically present the changing world order and the legal, political and strategic considerations that are weighing on it.

The editors hope that this joint publication from the University of Paris 13 and Pondicherry University will make interest in this field of enquiry endure and joint academic efforts in this area expand. This volume aims to be but a harbinger of the idea of an *Indo-French Journal of Studies in*

International Law and Politics put forward by Professor J.A.K. Tareen, the Vice-Chancellor of Pondicherry University. They thank authorities of Pondicherry University, especially the Vice-Chancellor, for the financial assistance for conducting the international colloquium on this topics of immense contemporary relevance in March 2008. Special thanks are due to the staff and students of the Department of Politics and International Studies, Pondicherry University. The editors are highly indebted to the Faculty of Law, Political and Social Sciences and the CERAP (Centre for Research on Administrative and Political Sciences) of the University of Paris 13 for their financial and intellectual support to the project and to those who, from near and far, helped make this little collective dream of a book come true.

Geetha Ganapathy-Doré would like to specially thank Professor Jean-Loup Salzmann, President of the University of Paris 13, Dr. Robert Etien, Dean of the Faculty of Law, and Professor Pierre-Yves Monjal, Head of CERAP, for their help in getting her the sabbatical leave without which collecting, translating and collating some of the articles would have taken more time.

Pondicherry/Villetaneuse
August 2009

B. Krishnamurthy
Geetha Ganapathy-Doré

Contents

SECTION II
Institutional and Constitutional Questions

SECTION III
External Relations

SECTION IV
Post-colonial Approach

SECTION V
Human Rights

Introduction

B. KRISHNAMURTHY and GEETHA GANAPATHY—DORÉ

To 'war' is 'human'. History suggests that war, and not peace, is the "normal" condition of "civilized" human society and that in about 5,600 years of recorded human history there have been around 14, 500 wars, or 2.6 a year and of 185 generations of man's recorded experience ... only ten have known unsullied peace. Europe's contribution to this infamous record of mankind was quite substantial. It always sat on the powder-keg and was always ready to burst into flames. In the post-war period and especially after the onset of the Cold War era, the Europeans have realised that if they were not going to hang together they would be hanged separately. As such, the driving motivation of the Eropean Union's (EU's) founders was a stable and united Europe with long-lasting peace. Economic integration, it was hoped, would lead to greater understanding, underpinned by the myriad interactions that inevitably flow from commerce and increased interdependence would make conflict unthinkable. They envisioned «an ever closer union» of the states and peoples of Europe.

The EU is a novel experiment in international politics. It is, on the one hand, outcome of history and history made, on the other. It is an association of sovereign nation states, who have voluntarily parted with certain extent of their sovereignty to the supranational entity, which some times acts supranationally and some times intergovernmentally. It is an enigma to those who practice it and form part of it and even to those pundits who spent their life time in studying it. To be precise, the EU institutional set up is a successful attempt to do justice to both the intergevernmental and supranational concepts. The EU has emerged as a post-sovereign polity that, despite its imperfections, has firmly established a new form of governance at an intermediate level between the global and the national. Here lies its significance in international politics.

The integration process is likened to the pilgrimage of Lourdes, where the pilgrims move forward slowly, but, steadily. Though the onward march of the

EU is staggering, its achievements are quite substantial and worth pondering over. The EU experiment has proved as well as disproved certain assumptions and presumptions of international relations which are lessons to comity of nations and peoples who aspire for global peace and prosperity. The speedy rapprochement initially between France and Germany and subsequently among the countries of Western Europe and the consequent creation of a zone of democratic peace were powerful confirmation of the liberal thesis that States were not fixed things bound to collide, but rather active entities able to negotiate a new set of cooperative relationships. Liberalism also worked economically and one of its most significant triumphs was the creation of a zone of prosperity in the West that by 1989 had totally exposed the economic pretensions of Soviet-style Communism in the East. In this way, the theory of Liberalism, when put into practice, did more than military pressure spear headed by the Atlantic alliance, in winning the Cold War hands down and consequently in overcoming the division of Europe and of the world.[1]

Critical theorists have made some of their most important contributions through their explorations of the meaning of emancipation. For the first generation of critical theorists, emancipation had to be conceived of in terms of a reconciliation with nature. European environmental policy which is progressive in nature and content; the positive reaction of the European countries to the present day environmental and ecological problems like climate change and global warming and their proactive policy of supporting Kyoto Protocol as well as going beyond Kyoto clearly proves that the EU citizens are really emancipated on the face of the present global environmental catastrophes and ecological disasters. It is noteworthy that the Europeans are ready to extend all possible financial and technical assistance to third countries to emancipate their own citizens, thus proving the fact that not only environmental problems but also the solutions are borderless.

Jürgen Habermas, one of the famous Critical theorists, stresses on the centrality of communication and dialogue to these processes of emancipation. He argues that the promise of a better society lies in the realm of communication. His central point is that the route to emancipation lies in radical democracy. It is through a system in which the widest possible participation is encouraged not only in word (as in the case in many Western democracies) but also in deed, by actively identifying barriers to participation—be they social, economic, or cultural—and overcoming them. For Habermas and his followers, participation is not to be confined within the borders of a particular sovereign state. Rights and obligations extend beyond state frontiers. EU is a practical and ongoing experiment in this direction.

Under the Westphalian system, the state borders have acted as an ethical boundary. They denote the furthest extent of our sense of duty and obligation, or at best, the point where our sense of duty and obligation is radically blurred, proceeding further only in a very attenuated form. This situation is simply indefensible to critical theorists like Andrew Linklater, who argues that emancipation in the realm of international relations should be understood in terms of expansion of the moral boundaries of a political community. He equates emancipation with a process in which the borders of the sovereign state lose their ethical and moral significance. The goal is therefore to move towards a situation in which citizens share the same duties and obligations towards non-citizens as they do towards their fellow citizens.

To arrive at such a situation would entail a wholesale transformation of the present institutions of governance—a transformation which most of us would find very unlikely at present. But an important element of the critical theory method is immanent critique—the process of identifying, encouraging, nurturing and consolidating tendencies that exist within the present conjuncture that point in the direction of emancipation. On this basis, Linklater identifies the development of the European Union as representing a progressive or emancipatory tendency in present day world politics. He suggests that an important part of the international system is entering a post-Westphalian era in which the sovereign state, which has for so long claimed an exclusive hold on its citizens, is beginning to lose some of its prominence and preeminence. The fact that Art. 1 of the European Convention for Human Rights and Fundamental Freedoms of November 4, 1950, which has been signed and ratified by most of the EU member states, stipulates that human rights of the non-nationals too would be protected[2]. This may very well be taken as an illustration where the state as well as its citizens share the same duties and obligations towards non-citizens as they do towards their own as well as fellow citizens. As such, the nuances and intricacies of the Union polity and the human rights regime that the European try to project through their example are worthy of identification and encouragement.

The EU has realized the dream of the founders and much more. It has ensured uninterrupted peace and prosperity to the continent, and thereby to the world, by putting a premium on international organizations, multilateralism and multipolar world order. As such, the European Project has been an enormous success, not only for Europe, but also for the world.[3] The lesson to be learnt is to keep the narrowly defined national interest under control and to work for the broadly based international altruism.

India is emerging as a major player in international affairs and advocating a just and democratic multipolar world order, with itself as one of the poles and it is maintaining close and fruitful relations with the European Union since its inception and at present, the latter is a major trade partner, donor and economic collaborator of India. Quite expectedly, the policies and programmes of the European Union are influencing India in a big way. Of late, India has succeeded in unfettering the traditional hangovers and is on the road to foster a close relationship with the US. Some believe that this new cosiness between India and the US has minimized India's commitment to the multipolar world order.

The US, on the other hand, stands for unilateralism and has least regard for international law/organization. It relies on the military power and brooks no opposition. It tends to treat allies as satellites and difference of opinion as blasphemy. It does not display patience for diplomacy and magnanimity for correction of the course that it is following without remorse. It is for democratisation and national interest even with the use of force, if need be.

The central theme of the present volume is to suggest a trialogue among these three powers—India, EU and US—so as to enable them to face and solve problems of present day international politics. As of now, there are so many hurdles, both inbuilt and extrapolated. However, it is believed that the EU, with its strengths and experiences, will be able to rope in the two other powers together and keep them engaged between them as well as with other powers, especially China and Russia, for the sake of a new and equitable global order. While elaborating on the power of the EU to lead and to ensure stability to the future of international politics, Joseph Nye points out that one of the political determinants of the future will be the «evolution of European policies and power».[4]

Section I of the book deals with the experiments and experiences in the creation of a democratic set up of the European Union. It opens with Robert Etien's «United States, India and France: Three Different Political Regimes for One Common Conception of Democracy» which, combining constitutional law and political science in the right proportion, proposes a comparative analysis of the political regimes of three major democracies in the world and their common concern for the sovereignty of the people, freedom of opinion, competition among political parties and the protection and defence of citizens' rights. The examples he has chosen—the presidential regime of the US, the parliamentary regime of India carrying the unmistakable imprint of the British system and the mixed regime of France, also called 'presidentialism', which sometimes results in a curious situation of cohabitation—are historically significant because each constitutes a distinct moment in the democratic experiment of the modern world. Using the concept of balance of power as a touchstone, Robert Etien demonstrates how opposition is a structural ingredient of democracy and alternance a necessity for its renewal. Robert Etien does not shy away from discussing recent debates on affirmative action in France, which are bending its republican conception of integration into a democratic one of accommodating diversity largely under the influence of America and the devolution of power through the revision of the French Constitution. He also alludes to forms of local democracy practised in Indian *panchayats* which makes the rapprochement[5] between France and India easier.

Pierre-Yves Monjal's «European Union in the 21 Century World: A Successful Example of Regional Organization» shows how the European Union, which comprises twenty-seven member states that share totally different cultures and languages, has become a successful example of regional political, economic and especially juridical integration. He attributes the success of this international organization primarily to the conception of the very powerful institutional and political framework which has enabled its members to be united in diversity and confront the challenges of globalization. According to him, the three mainsprings of this success are: common ethical values, powerful legal principles that are technical in nature and a dynamic institutional framework. In spite of the serious crisis that the EU has been undergoing since 2005, it will bounce back ever stronger, he concludes, once the new Lisbon Treaty modifying its mode of functioning will have entered into force.

Claudine Moutardier's «Policy of Access to European Union Documents: The End of Opacity» retraces the Swedish origin of the principle of transparency and its crucial role in the European Union today through a documentary angle. The Maastricht Treaty introduced the principle of openness of community institutions by giving the public the possibility to write for access and the Treaty of Amsterdam explicitly enshrined the right of all European citizens to have access to documents of Community institutions (EC Art 255). Transparency is fast becoming the hall mark of democracy in the EU. Claudine Moutardier explicates how EC Regulation 1049/2001 obliged EU institutions to modify their access to documents in order to comply with the requirements of good governance. She scrutinizes European Commission's proposals to revise the regulation in order to set right its lacunae so that the European Union could get rid of its image as an opaque and secret institution. The EU example certainly holds lessons for India which ranks 85th in the Transparency International Index of 2008[6].

Charles Reiplinger's «It's Fun to Comply with the FCPA» deals with the problem of fighting corruption with a preventive legal tool in order to preserve the stability of liberal democracies based on market economy and free trade. As such, his article is thematically linked to the question of transparency discussed above by Claudine Moutardier. The US Congress passed in December 1977, the Foreign Corrupt Practices Act, which according to Reiplinger, is a good example of legal imperialism. One of its main provisions, making the corruption of a foreign public official a crime, became an international rule thanks to four major international conventions[7] signed in the period between 1996 and 2003. It is interesting to note that emerging economic powers like Russia, India and China have signed the Merida Convention. Corrupting foreign public has thus become a crime twice punishable, as an offence under national law in the country where it took place, but also as an offence in the country where the concerned company is registered. In the era of increased competition between companies and countries, this rule is being implemented with varying efficiency in the regions of the world as the example of the French company Total's activities in South Pars (Iran) shows.

In this context, it is easy to understand Poland's fascination for the US. Hugo Pouillaude turns the tables and presents us with the picture of «The European Union in Poland». A fervent member of the European Union since 1 May 2004, Poland has adopted a peculiar behaviour which sets it apart from other EU member states. Its military co-operation with the United States, its intransigence concerning the values of Europe and its zeal in implementing laissez-faire European economic policies constitute this singularity which is making even the European Union feel uncomfortable. Poland has never before managed to foreground its national sovereignty as much as in its current capacity as a member state, observes Pouillaude. Marked by its peculiar history, Poland is making individual choices. Poland is defending its self-interests, sometimes thanks to the European Union particularly with regard to its democratic and economic development, sometimes without the EU, indeed even against it. More than its peculiarity, what strikes us in this behaviour is the significance that can be drawn from it. It shows how it is difficult for the EU to override the member states. Questions arise as to what it can credibly offer to the new member states today. If Poland sides with the United States in military affairs, Pouillaude opines, it is because it does not find the EU convincing in this regard. Poland leans heavily on its own values, in the absence of a unique European culture that prevails over all its regions. In order to overcome this shortcoming, the active drive of all the member states is needed.

Pierre-Yves Monjal's «Implementation of EU Policies: Remarks on the Exercise of Economic Competences by the Union» proposes an overview of EU's economic policies, legal principles and system of competences. The European Union has the ability to implement a whole series of public economic policies which originally fell under the purview of the member states. Around thirty action areas such as competition, free movement of goods, persons and services could thus be identified. These action plans or policies are deployed at the internal level, i.e., among the member states. But the Union is also developing a full-fledged foreign policy which is simultaneously economic and diplomatic, says Monjal. These policies are implemented thanks to Union institutions and juridical principles that support it: principle of primacy and direct effect of European economic law on national law; complex system of power sharing between the member states and the Union. Monjal's fine legal reasoning tries to convincingly counter the criticism of democratic deficit in the functioning of EU institutions.

Section II deals with the Constitutional and Institutional questions that come to haunt the EU time and time again. Concerns that the enlarged Union, if not reformed substantially, would find it difficult to take decisions and maintain a reliable legal framework led to several attempts to reform the treaties. The most wide-ranging proposals, and the most significant step—change in the language of integration, came with the Treaty for a Constitution of the European Union which was signed by EU Heads of State in 2004. During the course of the ratification process, the people of France and the Netherlands gave a body blow to the EU with their 'No' votes. While Dominique Moisi maintains that since May 29, 2005 (the day that French voters rejected the EU constitution treaty), there has been less France in Europe and probably less Europe in the world[8], relying on the bedrock of constitutional theory, Julien Sterck's «The Referendum on the Treaty Establishing a Constitution for Europe: The Constitutionalization of Europe despite the 'Non' to a Treaty» argues that the French rejection of the constitutional treaty has not really impeded the long term goal of the institution of a European constitution that will override national constitutional law. While acknowledging the fact that the French 'No' to the referendum maintains juridical pluralism in the European space, Sterck sustains that it cannot be taken as the final outcome of the many encounters between French constitutional law and the Treaty establishing a Constitution for Europe. The French vote, which is an expression of its sovereign people, no doubt reveals the difficulties in building a political Europe. It particularly underscores the legal problems relating to the absence of a specifically European sovereignty without which the notion of the constitution cannot stand. The decision of the French Constitutional Court dated 19 December 2004, which gave reasons for revising the French constitution to comply with the European Constitution, had recognized the compatibility between the two legal instruments with regard to essential matters. This decision created a new dynamics in which legal dialogue takes precedence over the increased participation of national and European parliaments. This dynamics, which has been forgotten in the silence of the referendum, points out Sterck, makes it possible to envisage a constitutionalization of Europe where the notion of constitution is understood differently.

When the French '*Non*' was followed by the Dutch '*Neen*', President Sarkozy and other leaders of Europe engaged in damage control and came up with the Lisbon Reform Treaty. Patrick Griffin's «The European Union and its Issue with Democracy: A Closer Look at the Irish Rejection of the Lisbon Treaty» updates our knowledge of the reticence of the Irish voters, who are not known to be Eurosceptics, with regard to the Lisbon Treaty. On 13 June 2008, they plunged the European Union into crisis rejecting the Lisbon Treaty and forcing the organization to put on hold supposedly vital institutional reforms considered indispensable to handle the enlarged Union. Griffin first considers the place and role of the Lisbon Treaty before analyzing in greater detail the effect of the Irish «No» vote on the future direction of the Union. The Irish «No» vote is symptomatic, he contends, of a far greater problem at the heart of the EU, namely the democratic deficit resulting from continued attempts by EU leaders to hoodwink and foist increasing integration through backdoor on an unconvinced citizenry, thereby provoking the alienation of a disenchanted European public. He is quite critical of the 'integrationists' who fail miserably to offer correct and convincing answers to the issues—factual or imaginary—raised by the anti-integration block.

External relations of the EU form the subject of study of Section III. B. Krishnamurthy maintains that the Europeans have contemplated the Common Foreign and Security Policy so that Europe will be able to speak in a single voice on any international issue, and eventually develop into one among the poles in the ensuing multipolar world order. Europe's genuine commitment to multilateralism (in sharp contrast to the unilateralism practiced by the US) is capable of bringing a new and welcome change in international political and economic order, thus far dominated and frustrated by the sole Super Power, the US. The general perception is that this plausible paradigm shift might be favourable to the cause of developing world in general and of India, in particular.

Scott Erb in his article on the German-American Relations in the 21st Century convincingly argues that the difference of opinion on the use of force to achieve perceived national interest is not a new but decades old phenomenon and that the Americans shocked the German non-military norm even during the Cold War era. He explains the circumstances and developments that created a wedge between Germany and the US, mainly due to the vainglory and wrong policy priorities of the Bush administration and even warns that if the Americans fail to embrace a more wholly multilateral approach, «the Atlantic alliance might well be seen as primarily a 20th century Cold War phenomenon which slowly crumbled as the global economy transformed the world in the 21st century».

The objective of the Fourth Section is to construct a real bridge between India and Europe by attempting a comparative study on their post-colonial historical developments and problems. An Indian turned European citizen, Geetha Ganapathy-Doré draws parallels between the construction after decolonization of the multiethnic and multireligious nation state that is the Union of India and the post-and supranational community of the European Union, both born after the Second World War. Her essay does not purport to be an exercise in reverse Orientalism, but highlights how Nehru's prescience of a supranational state prefigures the European Union. Both the Unions are spurred by the perpetually deferred dream democracy. Though each is marked by a great religion, each Union has the obligation to protect religious minorities by practicing the principle of secularism. Secularism is interpreted as neutrality of the state in Europe, while in India it is read as tolerance for all religions. Both the Unions have had to grapple with the principle of federalism at one point. India is consolidating its national territory by reorganizing it on a linguistic basis, while Europe continues to enlarge. But separatist claims based on ethnic origin, language, social class, religion or nationalism threaten the peace brokered by political will. India is often brandished as a political rival to Europe because of the increasing size and dynamism of its economy. But India has much to gain by working hand in hand with the European Union to fight against terrorism on the one hand and ensure, on the other hand, an equitable and sustainable growth of human life in the increasingly globalized economy.

Shazia Aziz-Wülber's «Comparison of Indian Muslims and Muslims Living in the European Union Countries» tackles the sensitive issue of the condition of Muslims in India and the European Union. It is well known that secular democracies better tolerate Muslim culture than Islam as a political force. The uneasy co-existence of a religion that Naipaul considers as one making «imperial demands»[9] and democracy in two different parts of the world is difficult to study, though it may prove useful. There exist a lot of differences between the condition of Muslims in India and EU. Islam is more deeply rooted in India and has almost a thousand year old history, whereas Islam, which was driven away from Mauresque Spain in the 15th century, has become visible in Europe after the Second World War mostly due to the number of Muslim immigrants from the Afro-Asian continents, especially from North Africa, settled in European territory. In India, the Hindu Muslim divide after partition has definitely taken a violent turn in the form of communalism. The integration of Muslim minorities in EU member states has become a political preoccupation only recently. Whatever the divergence, there is one common feature, i.e., the impoverished state of the Muslims. If terrorist attacks have lead to an identity crisis in India and Europe where the 'Muslim' is seen as the menacing 'Other', a form of moderate European Islam is emerging which resembles the form of Islam acclimatized by Indian culture. The socio-economic uplift of these minorities in India and the European Union could certainly prevent their recourse to Islamic radicalism.

During his campaign for presidential elections, Nicolas Sarkozy had proposed a Mediterranean Union in relation to his policy of chosen immigration as opposed to the chain and illegal migration that is happening in France and other European countries and his reticence about the admission of Muslim Turkey as a member in the European Union. As soon as he was elected, he gave an Atlanticist turn to the French foreign policy. His idea of the Mediterranean Union was intended to signal a break with France's Africa policy which was undermining the Barcelona Process. Having had to assume the presidency of the European Union from 1 July 2008, Nicolas Sarkozy had to accept to make concessions to his European partners in order to bend his original idea of the Mediterranean Union into the Union for the Mediterranean. The Summit held on 13 July 2008 in Paris gathered forty-two representatives coming from European Union as well as Northern Africa and the Middle East. Geetha Ganapthy-Doré's «Is the Union for the Mediterranean a Postcolonial Political Contract?» describes the genesis of the idea since the days of the Roman Empire, delineates the road map of this new international organization and weighs the pros and cons of this project before concluding on the pragmatic aspect of this postcolonial experiment which implements the idea of co-management by the North and the South. The success or failure of this new regional organization will hold valuable lessons for South Asia.

The Europeans consider that human rights concept and its protection and promotion are the products of their historical tradition, political culture and civililzation. They claim that they lead other countries and regions in the human rights front by their stellar example. They believe in the universality of human rights and maintain that their inquisitiveness on the third countries' human rights record should not be taken as intervention in their internal matters, contravening their sovereignty. They claim that it is their regard for human rights that makes them different from others. As such, Section V concentrates on Human Rights and consequently the heritage of Renaissance which put Man at the centre of the universe.

P. Marudanayagam's «Thou Shouldst Be Living at This Hour! Milton as a Champion of Human Rights» takes us back to the Republican debate in 17th Century England. Many ignore that the great Epic poet Milton was a champion of Human Rights ahead of time. Marudanayagam draws extensively from the prose and poetical works of Milton to drive home this fact. The conception of liberty was the central theme of his prose work and the emancipation from the tyranny of kings and priests his major preoccupation. Milton divides liberty into three categories, religious, private and civil. His pamphlet entitled *Doctrine and Discipline of Divorce* is a plea for the freewill of the couple against the restrictions imposed by law and religion which held that the bond between the couple was permanent. *Areopagitica* is a vigorous and a stunningly modern defence of the writer's freedom of speech and protests against the arbitrary power of the censor appointed by the king and bishops. In his *Second Defence of the People of England* Milton vindicates the rights of the English nation and liberty itself. When Cromwell's Commonwealth floundered, Milton recommended setting up of a Grand Council of Able Men elected by the public to safeguard civil and religious liberty. He had the courage and vision to propose a sort of federalism based on county assemblies subordinated to national parliament. All these ideas resonate in his poetry. Indeed, Milton depicts Satan's revolt in *Paradise Lost* in such an enthusiastic light that it could be interpreted as a heroic struggle for liberty. Marudanayagam finally proposes a very original reading of *Samson Agonistes* in which the protagonist can be seen as an allegory of the selfless passion for the extension of human rights.

Iver Neumann's «Redefining the European Balance between Sovereignty and Human Rights in Kosovo» is built on two premises: The monopoly of violence does not any more belong to sovereigns but to the international community. Human rights form part of universal principles that transcend national borders and claims of sovereignty. Interpreting war as an extension of political violence, Neumann's article tries to basically answer three questions: Who are the legitimate actors of war? What causes can be said to justify a war? What are the legitimate means of waging a war? In the new post-national order, we are moving away from the Hegelian idea of war where one law is opposed to another to come closer to the Catholic notion of war as the struggle of the good against the evil. In the Islamic world, such a conception has resulted in the holy war. In the case of Kosovo, the position of Serbia which tried to legitimize its violence by invoking the notion of defence of sovereignty of the nation state was perceived as anachronistic. Even if the term «humanity» exists in a political and legal sense, it is not sufficiently solid, deems Neumann, to carry the weight that the NATO countries have conferred on it because there does not yet exist a political body which can legitimately speak in the name of humanity. He concludes his contribution with a couple of quintessential questions: Are somebody's human rights more valuable than others? and whether it is worthy to sacrifice thousands of 'lesser mortals' of the Western Balkans in order to prevent loss of life of a few 'noble' Americans in the name of humanitarian intervention?

Section VI of the book focuses on the trialogue proper. Etien's article brings forth the fact that democracy, respect for human rights, rule of law and good governance are the common values that tend to bind the three powers—India, the EU (as represented by France, in his article) and the US—together. Situating his presentation on the base thus created by Etien, B. Krishnamurthy builds up his case for a trialogue among India, EU and US. The central theme of his paper and of course, of the present volume, is that the US continues to need Europe as much as Europe needs the US and both need India as much as the latter needs them, whatever may be the past prejudices and the present pretensions.

NOTES AND REFERENCES

1. John Baylis and Steve Smith, *The Globalization of World Politics—An Introduction to International Relations*, OUP, New Delhi, Indian Edition, Third Impression, 2007, p. 148.
2. The wordings of Art. 1 are quite significant: «The High Contracting Parties shall secure to *everyone within their jurisdiction* the rights and freedoms defined … (in) this Convention» (emphasis added).
3. Joseph E. Stiglitz, «The EU's Global Mission», http://www.project-syndicate.org/print-commentry/stiglitz85/English. (18/6/2008).
4. Joseph S. Nye, «Europe's Power to Lead», February 2008, http://www.project-syndicate.org/commentary/nye54.
5. Jacques Weber, *Pondichéry et les comptoirs de l'Inde après Dupleix. La démocratie au pays des castes*, Paris: Denoël, 1996.
6. http://www.transparency.org/news_room/in_focus/2008/cpi2008/cpi_2008_table
7. The Inter-American Convention against Corruption of March 29, 1996, the OECD Convention on Combating Bribery of Foreign Public Officials in International Business Transactions of November 21, 1997, the African Union's Convention on Preventing and Combating Corruption of July 12 2003 and the Merida Convention of December 9, 2003.
8. Dominique Moisi, What is France's Place in the World?, September 24, 2007. http://www.atlantic-community.org/index/Open_Think_Tank_Article/What_Is_France's_Place_In_The_World%3F
9. V.S. Naipaul, *Beyond Belief: Islamic Excursions Among the Converted Peoples*, London: Vintage, 1999, p. X1.

1

United States, India and France:

Three Different Political Regimes for One Common Conception of Democracy

ROBERT ETIEN

"Globalization and Westernization which are seen today essentially in their economic dimension can only be realized with the help of the States and a political and legal dimension". This adage is becoming increasingly significant these days. It underscores the profound transformation of the international community, the new power balances that exist between Western countries gathered around Europe and the United States and the emerging nations like India, China, Brazil and Africa tomorrow.

As in the case of European construction, the economic dimension and the legacy of an economy founded on free trade constituted a contributing factor in promoting solidarity and market economy which fostered a certain form of development of States. Even if today this development is far from beneficial to all the protagonists, no one any more questions the formidable economic development of India, China and Brazil which appear to be the countries to contend with in the future: their economic weight compared to other States makes them stand out as the dominant countries of tomorrow.

However, along with the economic dimension, what appears more and more prominent is the political and legal dimension[1] which includes the place of democracy in modern societies, particularly in emerging nations and the requirement that any economic development be parallelly accompanied by political and legal development or emergence. Such development or emergence is no longer measured in economic terms simply but also in relation to the evolution of democracy and the protection of rights and fundamental liberties.

The comparison of political regimes shows a big difference with regard to these points as far as India, USA and France are concerned. Their three political regimes represent a whole gamut of Western forms of political regime: presidential regime for the United States, parliamentary regime for India and semi-presidential or mixed regime for France[2]. Nevertheless, the inspiration for democracy and the practice of democracy remain very close.

I. THREE DISTINCT POLITICAL REGIMES: PRESIDENTIAL, PARLIAMENTARY AND SEMI-PRESIDENTIAL

The purpose of this article is not to describe in detail the political regimes of the United States, France and India[3], but simply point out the particularities of these regimes in order to compare them and show their diversity and specificities. These three regimes, despite their difference in nature, are, each in their own way, political regimes that maintain separation of powers among the executive, legislative and the judiciary. If in all the three instances, the executive is dominant, the legislative is either reinforced given its independence—this is the case of the American political regime; or remains the fountainhead of all power—this is the case in India; or assumes, with difficulty, its competition with the executive, which is the case in France. In the three cases, the judiciary is the guardian of the rule of law and plays a determining role in the protection of rights and fundamental liberties.

(A) The American Presidential Regime[4]

Studies which have often explored[5] this presidential regime are unanimous about its three distinctive features: preponderance of the American President, maintenance of the power of the Congress and the Supreme Court as a balancing power in judicial matters.

Preponderance of the American President

The President of the United States is at the centre of the American political system. He exercises fully and in its entirety the set of regalian prerogatives that are vested in him by the constitution as well as by political convention and which give him a pre-eminent position as much within the United States as in the whole planet. He owes his major strength to the fact that he is elected by universal suffrage. Even if this election is indirect, he is elected by all American citizens and he has the support of the whole nation thanks to the federal vote of the States in the Union.[6] His prestige is, of course, due to this democratic competition, but at the same time he is the President of the most powerful State in the world which internationally wields an uncontested domination as much in the diplomatic domain as in the economic and military domains. He cumulates all the powers of the executive. Surrounded by advisers and secretaries, he solely occupies the regalian functions in their totality. The American presidential role simultaneously consolidates the unity of the nation and determines America's position in the world[7]. Federalism and the personalization of power further strengthen him in his position. Faced with the Congress and the judicial power of the Supreme Court, he not only benefits from preponderance but also the tools of power that the constitution and political convention give him to be able to exercise his power fully.

Maintenance of Congress

The American Congress[8] comprising the Senate and the House of Representatives fully exercises the legislative function which consists in making and enacting laws which are fundamental rules that bind all American citizens. The representativity of the American parliament is flawless as, elected by the people, the Senators represent the States—besides they are two per State whatever the population of the State, the Representatives being elected in proportion to the population of each State. The principle adopted for the representation of American parliamentarians is again brought into play for the election of the President of the United States. The Congress has its own autonomy with regard to its organization and functioning. The separation of powers is clearly affirmed; the American executive does not have the initiative for law making with regard to the Congress and cannot interfere in the law making and voting procedure. Representative democracy functions particularly well in the United States because the legislature enjoys full legislative power. The role of the Republican and Democratic political parties is crucial, but the notion of majority has only a relative significance as in this case, contrary to parliamentary regimes, the executive cannot be overthrown by the legislature. The relations between the President and the Congress depend first of all on the political situation. It will be much easier for the President to get his proposals passed in Congress, if he has a large majority. In any case and in reality, the relations between the Congress and the President are balanced. If the principle of interdependence between them is the rule, the President can use the majority party totally to make it support his programme. He can address the Congress. He can use his veto to put pressure on the Congress after a law which he does not favour has been adopted. For its part, the Congress has a right to control the nominations for the Presidential team. It can facilitate the President's tasks while implementing his political programme or on the contrary render them more difficult. It is then up to the President to reach a compromise with a reticent Congress.[9]

The Supreme Court as Righter of Wrongs[10]

The American Supreme Court fully exercises its judicial power. The nine justices of the court are nominated for life by the President after the consent of the Congress. Once nominated, their independence is total. It has often been remarked that the American President's choices in this regard were more political than legal. Because they are nominated for life, this institution remains a bench composed of aged judges who are independent vis-à-vis the ruling party. The date of renewal of its members is unknown because "a justice has to die" or resign for him/her to be replaced. In spite of the diversity of American law within the Federal States, the Supreme Court guarantees coordination of American law and a certain uniformity in the application of this law. Besides, it ensures national unity by its protective action. As the court of last resort for all American courts with regard to a series of major political and moral topics, it has kept a general line of orientation where the rule of law has to be maintained and federalism safeguarded, when dealing with issues such as abortion or racial segregation. The Supreme Court is solidly there against the localism of the federated States to assume national unity and see to it that law remains at the service of democracy.

In fine, the American political regime is in principle a regime of separation of powers where each institution fully exercises its function and adheres to the values of the Union. A true continent involved in external actions, the American political regime fosters presidential authority and in practice has been able to adapt itself to the multiple situations that it has witnessed since independence.

(B) The Indian Parliamentary Regime[11]

India is without doubt the world's largest democracy. The Indian political system is based on a parliamentary democracy inspired by the British model. A parliament that determines the political majority and the formation of the Council of Ministers headed by the Prime Minister, who is the true Number One and nominated by the President. The latter has but an honorific role. A complex judicial system helps maintain a certain unity in the federal State where diversity and specificities are numerous.

Importance of Parliament

The Indian Parliament is a bicameral parliament set up after the independence of the Union of India by the Constitution of India promulgated on 26 January 1950. It comprises a lower House of the People (*Lok Sabha*), the quasi totality of whose members are elected by direct universal suffrage and the higher Council of States (*Rajya Sabha*)[12] which represents the States and territories. Bicameralism is total in India. The two chambers have the same power except in financial matters where the House of the People has the power of final decision. The Indian Parliament is very keenly attached to its legislative prerogatives. Debates within it are noisy. The verbal exchanges with the Council of Ministers entail very heated discussions. The Parliament fully exercises it legislative role. As for any other parliamentary regime, it is the fountainhead of all powers. The parliamentary majority at the House of the People determines the formation of Council of Ministers and the nomination of the Prime Minister by the President of the Republic. The House of the People can call into question the responsibility of the Council of Ministers by passing a vote of no confidence and the President of the Republic in turn can dissolve it. The Indian Parliament must represent all the political currents in India in order to respect the diversity of opinion as it must draw a majority which shall help safeguard national unity far and above the federal nature of the Indian State[13].

The Prime Minister as Leader of the Majority

The true executive power of the nation belongs to the Prime Minister[14] who heads the Council of Ministers. Nominated by the President, the Prime Minister has a majority in the House of the People. The Indian Council of Ministers with the Prime Minister as its head possesses classical powers that belong to any council of ministers under parliamentary regime. The Indian Premier has nothing to envy with regard to the British Prime Minister or the German Chancellor. Veritable leader of the majority, he must both assert his authority and be capable of gathering together divergent opinions, which, in a country of more than one billion inhabitants, is a complex matter to say the least. The constitution gives him necessary powers to react, should a crisis arise. He can declare a state of emergency. He could, in certain cases, directly administer a federal state according to the principle of President's rule[15]. His essential task consists in coordinating an overall and general policy for the whole of India and maintaining the balance while taking into account the multiple political opinions, the cultural diversity of Indian citizens and the immensity of the territory. The central government exercises extensive prerogatives, especially administrative ones. It has the added mission of exercising a large control over the federated states.

As in any parliamentary regime, the executive is two-headed. The President and the Vice President are elected through indirect suffrage by a special electoral college whose composition takes into account the disparities in the Indian State. The federal states are largely represented therein.

Justice Reinforced

The very elaborate judicial institutions in India[16] resemble those of and have been influenced by the Anglo-Saxon system and more particularly the British, not only with respect to the general organization and functioning of the judicial system in India but also with respect to procedure. The principle of the rule of law has been safeguarded in spite of the influence of traditions, local customs and the vast size of India. The Supreme Court sits at the apex of the Indian judicial power. All its judges, as their American counterparts, are designated by the President in accordance with the recommendations of the Prime Minister. By being at the top of the whole Indian judicial system, the Supreme Court plays a decisive role in unifying case law, defending fundamental rights and harmonizing decisions taken by lower courts, especially those in the federated states.

In fine, the Indian political regime is parliamentary, which is very different from the presidential regime. It has naturally been inspired by the British parliamentary regime. In order to accommodate the vastness of India and its political pluralism, it has learnt to adapt itself by taking into account what is practised in the American presidential regime.

(C) The Mixed French Regime

The French political regime[17] which is the outcome of the constitution of 4 October 1958 is neither presidential like that of the US nor parliamentary like that of India. It combines characteristics of both the parliamentary and presidential regimes. This basic information is verified in practice. The President of the Republic exercises an omnipotent power. The decline of parliament is expected to lead to its re-enhancement. Constitutional justice deserves to be strengthened. The constitutional revision of 23 July 2008 on the modernization of the institutions of the Fifth Republic reinforces presidential authority while re-enhancing the role of the legislative and strengthening the role of the judiciary.

Omnipotence of the President

At the heart of the two-headed executive comprising the President of the Republic and the Council of Ministers with the Prime Minister as its head, the President exercises a veritable leadership. The constitution allows him to enjoy this omnipotence because he is the embodiment of the power of the people, having been elected on the basis of direct universal suffrage and enjoying, in addition, prerogatives at the pinnacle of the State which often endow him with an uncontested power. Practice has considerably reinforced this situation because the President of the Republic while exercising his function enjoys immunity from both the political and penal points of view. There is no authority above him to whom he must report. He depends directly on the people. Hence, the importance of voter turnout, public opinion, media and opinion polls![18] Truly Number One, he can rely on the Council of Ministers and indeed even put it into difficulty. The President enjoys full freedom in the choice of the Council of Ministers as well as its revocation. In the Fifth Republic, the Council of Ministers headed by the Prime Minister always finds itself in a delicate situation. The Prime Minister conducts and determines the nation's policy under the President, torn as he is between the parliamentary majority to whom he should render accounts for his actions and the President of the Republic whose action he must support. As a remnant of the parliamentary regime, the Council of Ministers can be overthrown by a challenge to its political responsibility. The National Assembly might be dissolved by the President. The exercise of power under the Fifth Republic resembles rather the power exercised in the presidential regime than that exercised in the parliamentary regime. Political power seems personalized with the President who acts as a symbol of reinforced national unity. The constitutional revision of 23 July 2008 seems to again show that France has doubts as to presidentialization[19], that it is not ready to call into question the architecture of the Fifth Republic, even if this revision was meant to re-enhance the power of the French parliament.

Decline of Parliament

The French parliament is bicameral. The Members of the National Assembly are elected by direct universal suffrage. The National Assembly represents the French people and national unity, the Senate represents the French people's territorial diversity. The experience of the Fourth Republic had reinforced the need for the decline of the French parliament[20]. Everything is done so that the last word rests with the Council of Ministers and that the latter governs. Legislative powers are limited as much in the area of law, procedure of discussions and vote as in the area of executive control. The Council of Ministers is in control and its actions take precedence.

The Council of Ministers possess a whole range of techniques within the framework of the legislative procedure, which allows it to put forward its point of view, cut the discussions short and prevent the parliament from correctly exercising its legislative and controlling power. Besides, the discipline of the majority is a very strict one in France. Due to the electoral system, the parliamentary majority is strong. It supports the Council of Ministers. A transfer of power is set in motion which favours the Council of Ministers to the detriment of Parliament. Parliament has thus become a simple recording office of the political projects defended by the President and the Prime Minister. We have been witnessing an effective decline of the French Parliament since the setting up of the Fifth Republic. The constitutional revision of 23 July 2008 seems to want to remedy this existing state, but we can afford to be rather sceptical about the realization of this goal of enhancement. The content of the reform is disappointing to say the least. The practice of the Fifth Republic is undoubtedly not ready to wither away as long as a political regime ambivalent in the texts but coherent in reality is preserved bearing the mark of the leadership of the President of the French Republic.

Reinforced Constitutional Justice

The setting up in 1958 of a veritable control of the constitutionality of laws[21] in France with the creation of the Constitutional Council was one of the major events of French political life. Even if this check is far from taking the proportions it takes in the Anglo-Saxon systems, it was a true little revolution at that time in France. It is *a priori* a control in principle, because the final legislative text cannot be controlled, even if the 2008 revision indeed allows the Final Court of Appeal and the Council of State to take the matter to the Constitutional Council, when a legal dispute arises. The Constitutional Council comprises nine members nominated by the President of the Republic, the Presidents of the National Assembly and Senate and the ex-Presidents of the Republic. The Council's jurisprudence is very rich. It has been able to render itself credible in spite of some periods which were difficult, or during which there was alternance or cohabitation[22]. It has reinforced the conception of the rule of law, which is a corollary to constitutionalism. Its action has been particularly efficient in defending fundamental liberties. It has helped give priority to the constitution and reinforce law.

In fine, the French political regime is a synthesis of the parliamentary and presidential regimes. It has lead to a marked presidentialization, a strengthening of the executive which must lead to the reinforcement of the legislative.

The three political regimes: those of the Unites States, France and India are very different from each other. Nevertheless they manifest one and the same conception of democracy.

II. ONE COMMON CONCEPTION OF DEMOCRACY

Democracy resides in "the government of the people as a body[23]" which involves three consequences: the sovereignty of the people, competition among political parties and the protection and defence of rights of citizens.

(A) Sovereignty of the People

People are sovereign which means that there is nothing above this power. This principle constitutes the very foundation of democracy. The people hold, as Machiavelli says, "the power of powers".

Democracy: Elections the Basis of People's Sovereignty

Elections disputed constitute the basis of democracy. People express themselves directly through free elections. In the three States under study, this principle is in effect. In the United States, it goes back to the formation of the States of the Union. It is a strong principle that is expressed at all the levels of the State because one has to be elected by the people to be able to accede to major political offices, whether it is the office of the President of the United States, Senator or Representative or at the local level, State Governors or members of local parliament. Indeed other offices like those connected to justice or police can be occupied only by elected officers[24].

In India, the principle of general elections has been laid down as the basis of its democracy from the dawn of its independence[25]. British colonialism had facilitated the importance of elections in its own way. The quasi totality of Indian parliamentarians is elected, the Council of Ministers is chosen from the majority which is drawn from the *Lok Sabha,* the House of the People. At the local level, the executive and parliamentary authorities are also elected.

In France, the President of the Republic is directly elected by universal suffrage and this election conditions and marks the French political life in a decisive manner. Parliamentarians, members of local governments, Municipal councillors, General and Regional Councils as well as local executive officers such as the Mayor, the President of the General Council, and President of the Regional Council are also elected by the people. The tradition was formed during the course of time. The principle of election was enshrined at the time of the French Revolution. Universal suffrage triumphed during the Second Republic in 1848. The evolution of the political regime born out of the Constitution of 1958 led to the President being elected in 1962 by direct universal suffrage. It was the law of 2 March 1982 that regulated the elected status of members of other local authorities.

The electoral method can be different in each of the countries under study, but most of the time it is direct universal suffrage. The elections are controlled and the results respected[26]. The authority of sovereign people is manifest in the reinforcement of the representative regime. Elections take place at regular dates and are occasion for a regular competition among political parties.

Local and Participative Democracy

The United States and India have a federal structure[27]. France is a decentralized republic. This difference deserves to be underscored. The vastness of American and Indian territories and the diversity of their populations are doubtless particularly conducive to the structure of a federal State. Localism is very pronounced, local identity is also recognised. In France, decentralization or devolution has occurred rather late. Implemented truly in 1982, it was confirmed in 2003. These three countries practise effective local democracy each in their manner. There can be no true democracy without a functioning local democracy. People participate directly in decision-making at the local level either through local representatives they elect or by the fact that people are consulted or by people intervening in big local decisions. Participative democracy finds all its meaning at the local level. It allows people to show they are there, express their opinion and directly influence decisions taken, considering that they are the most apt to let their will known. Local democracy seems reinforced in a federal State where the federated states have the power to make law and manifest their specificities and originality as opposed to common interests developed by federal authorities. Local governments in India have less autonomy compared to American States. A certain form of local democracy is expressed thanks to multiple techniques. In India, states are trying to revitalise village councils or *panchayats* which enable democratic participation at the rural level. A decentralized unitary State, with a form of intense decentralization, can have the same results. Even if France is a little bit shy with regard to this aspect, given the fact that historically its tradition is a centralizing one, it has been able to develop a new form of decentralization which gives significant powers to local and devolved institutions. France has not reached the state of devolution that is practised in Spain or Italy[28], it has finally recognized the originality, customs, history of its overseas territories and the culture of their peoples and even their languages.

Inter-communal Peace

Communal diversity implies that this diversity be integrated and recognized. Accepted and recognized pluralism is without doubt one of the characteristics of democracy. Each of the three countries studied possesses a big diversity in terms of peoples and communities. This diversity can vary according to the origin, culture, religion or attachment to such and such way of life.

In the United States, recognition of communities is pronounced. The Anglo-Saxon solution consists in taking into account the specificities of groups. Each one is thus recognized by considering the specific features of his/her identity. A system of quotas is in place, a sort of positive discrimination, in order to improve the situation of minority communities[29]. It is not by chance that the current President is black. A woman has been the candidate of one of the two big political parties in this election.

In India, the diversity is very large. According to its constitution, India is a "sovereign, socialist, secular and democratic republic"[30]. Officially castes do not exist in India, but in reality castes constitute one of the determining elements of Indian political life. Casteist framework continues to perpetrate corporatist or clientalist relations or traditions forbidding certain things in matters of employment or marriage. Numerous efforts have been made to restrict the influence of castes. A veritable system of positive discrimination comparable to what is practised in the United States exists. Quota systems have been implemented in Indian administrations and universities similar to the principle of affirmative action. It is not surprising to learn that a Sikh is the head of the Indian government and a woman, the head of the State.

The French system is quite contrary with its principle of secularism (understood as state neutrality toward religion) which is based on equality between human beings, a State that is religiously neutral and accepts all beliefs. French equality and the necessity to accommodate neutrality and the French regulations have not always been efficient. There is a big temptation to develop a form of positive discrimination which will allow for the recognition of minorities derived from immigration in terms of employment and social visibility. France's colonial past has resulted in a significant mixing of populations. There exist but only people: The French. But very recently the constitution has recognized the existence of distinctive peoples by taking into consideration the population of France's overseas territories[31].

The Anglo-Saxon and French solutions differ but their objective is the same: integrating minorities.

(B) Competition between Political Parties

In the three states under scrutiny, competition between political parties exists. It gives rise to peaceful struggles which allow for a majority power resulting from elections to be set up and recognition of the opposition parties.

Multi-party System, Pluralism of Opinion

Opinions are multiple and diverse. The vastness of American and Indian territories has naturally resulted in the existence of pluralism of opinion.

In the United States, there are numerous political parties but political pluralism centres around two big political parties, the Republicans and the

Democrats. These two political parties are formidable machines for electing the president and congressmen[32]. The African-American and Latin-American minorities have to be taken into account without neglecting the Jewish or Asian-American minorities. They constitute significant stakes independently of the choice of the federated States in the presidential elections.

Indian diversity is expressed in its more than two hundred political parties[33], its many religions, its separatist movements which demand independence. The question of religion is at the heart of the debate. The Hindu tradition is opposed to Islam which is the cause for multiple conflicts, especially with neighbouring countries like Pakistan. The question of the frontier is very important especially in Kashmir. Tensions are rife with Myanmar, Bangladesh and of course Pakistan. The Tamils and the Sikhs constitute the numerically most significant minorities in India. It is not always easy for a veritable majority to be drawn. One single party i.e., the Congress Party, which had been present during all the stages of struggle for independence has been dominating the Indian political scene. It was in power from 1947 to 1977, then from 1980 to 1989 and again from 1991 to 1996. Ever since the general elections that took place in May 2004, it has been the leading party in the House of the People (*Lok Sabha*) in terms of number of seats (one hundred and forty-five out of five hundred and forty-three). It heads the governing coalition. It enjoys the support of local political parties.

The other political party which is important in India, the Bharatiya Janata Party (BJP—the Party of the Indian people) founded in 1980 is a party whose orientation is Hindu and nationalist. Its electoral base is in the North and West of India. Numerous state governments are headed by the BJP. With the support of regional parties, it formed the National Democratic Alliance which ruled India from 1998 to 2004.

In France, there are numerous political parties. The Fifth Republic has enabled the Gaullist right-wing party to regularly come to power, the left-wing and the Socialist parties occupying power only temporarily. The idea of the majority is very significant[34]. Today everything has been done to see to it that the presidential majority and the parliamentary majority be one and cohabitation avoided.

The Relationship between the Majority and Opposition: Recognized Alternance

In all the three countries under scanner, alternance exists. In the United States, between the Democrats and the Republicans, in France between the Gaullist Right and the Socialist Left, and in India between the Congress Party and the BJP. But it must be said that this alternance is not perfect. In the

United States, we approach near equality, even if the Republicans have been more often in power than the democrats. In India, outside the ephemeral periods of 1977-80, 1989-96 and 1998-04, the Congress party dominates the scene. It has to nevertheless find a compromise; it is difficult for it to obtain the majority all alone. Opposition in each of the countries studied is a recognized political force. In the United States, opposition is represented by the second biggest political party and in France by the Socialist party which wants to reconquer power. In India, things are more complex, even if the commitment of the Congress Party to secularism and centrism, and the support of the BJP for upper casts and Hinduism, help us understand the split between the two big Indian political parties. In France, outside the presidential periods of François Mitterand (1981-88 and 1988-95) and the ones during cohabitation (1986-88, 1993-95 and 2002-07), the Socialist party has never been a majority party during the Fifth Republic. The UNR, URD and UMP have always been at the apex of power outside the aforementioned periods. Opposition is present at the heart of federated American States. In France, the Socialist Party holds power in almost all the regions. In India, the sharing of power is more equitable in the federated states. Recognized opposition is completely accommodated within the power structure[35]. It symbolizes political change by complying with democratic rules.

(C) Protection and Defence of Citizens' Rights

The protection and the defence of citizen's rights are primordial goals in democracy. All the three states studied assert this principle.

Freedom of Speech

Freedom of speech constitutes the kernel of the democratic system. It is not by chance that it forms part of the first amendment of the American Constitution. Freedom of speech is repeatedly referred to in the Indian Constitution. It is mentioned in the Declaration of the Rights of Man and of the Citizen of 1789. Each citizen must enjoy unfettered freedom of expression. This freedom is multiple and diversified. It consists of fundamental liberties that each citizen can exercise in total freedom. They are universal[36] and are obviously found in the three States under study. Limits to freedom of expression arise when democratic rules of the game are not respected. "No liberty for the enemies of democracy". Each of these three States condemns in its own way any form of violent action, and punishes attacks on democracy perpetrated in the name of freedom of expression. Terrorism is severely fought against whether it is internal to the nation or external[37]. Freedom of expression takes many and varied forms and must allow all currents of thought to express themselves. Freedom of the Press and the Media is without doubt one of the key elements of the existence of democracy. The struggle for its maintenance is crucial. The ruling party should, under no pretext, challenge freedom of expression. It must accept contestation and diversity of opinion which, in the countries under scrutiny, are varied. The struggle for the maintenance of freedom of expression is a continuous one. It ought to be remembered for ever that the fight for the defence of freedom of speech is never over and that it has to go on for ever[38].

Recognition and Defence of Individual Rights

There are numerous constitutional texts that enshrine the defence and protection of individual rights[39]. In the United States, the amendments to the constitution contain the whole system of recognition of individual rights and liberties. The historical formation of the United States has favoured a certain concept of freedom which includes the individual feeling that each American citizen has of belonging to a nation where individual liberty goes very far, to the extent even of including the right to posses arms without true control. In France, the preamble to the constitution includes three different texts: The Declaration of the Rights Man and of the Citizen of 1789, the preamble of 1946 and the Charter for Environment of 2004. These three texts are complementary. They are about individual rights and liberties, collective rights and environmental rights. In India, the beginning of the constitution tarries on the protection of rights and fundamental liberties in order to give more leeway for custom. The tradition of habeas corpus and protection of rights persists. The Indian judicial system favours the protection of persons subject to trial. Decisions concerning copyright and the protection of intellectual property have been taken to reinforce efficient judicial control with regard to freedom. As in the United States, at each level, the constitutionality of measures taken that go against fundamental liberties may be questioned. In France, the supervision of administration by the administrative court is an original feature.

The American Supreme Court and the French Constitutional Council ensure the protection of rights and fundamental liberties within their respective and different frameworks. The ruling party may be put into difficulty by judicial checks. But the implementation of the protection of rights and liberties is achieved by a day-to-day behaviour that concerns the exercise of citizenship[40].

Protection of Minorities

This is without doubt one of the key elements of the existence and relevance of a real democracy. Each State must envisage the protection of minorities. There minorities are multifarious. These have to be particularly protected. The context is different in each of the States under study. The United States has to find solutions for problems concerning African-Americans and Latin-Americans. In India, there are several ethnic groups that belong to different religions and social classes. France has had to confront its history of immigrants. Basically Italian and Spanish, then Polish, the source of immigration today is African and is the outcome of its colonial past. The French gamble based on secularism, national unity and egalitarianism has yielded controversial results[41]. Apparently migrant minorities, originating especially from the Maghreb countries, seem to find it difficult to integrate in the French society and effectively benefit from the same rights. The American solution founded on the protection of communities leaves out those who do not take advantage of the benefits of capitalism. India finds it difficult to ensure what is known as inclusive development. The caste system is in reality an entrenched one. The gap between the rich and the poor is wide. The minorities belong to the latter category and must be protected in a pacified democracy that practises constitutionalism. These minorities are often territorial minorities such as Corsica or the overseas populations in the case of France, Kashmir in the case of India or Mexican border regions in the case of the United States. As a result, repressive measures might be encouraged, population movements controlled and nationality might become more difficult to obtain[42]. The protection of minorities in a pacified democracy and the rule of law are ensured by integrating these minorities. Political institutions must defend the rights demanded by minorities and courts play a considerable role in controlling the action of public authorities.

Conclusion

The place of the political and legal dimension in the community of States is primordial. In spite of the diverse contexts, cultures and traditions that have made them adopt different types of political regimes, the three countries studied benefit from a significantly historical experience in the functioning of democracy and protection of rights and fundamental liberties despite the difficulties faced. The principles are the same for the three States: The Unites States since its inception has upheld democracy, in spite of its tendency to impose a certain idea of freedom not only in its territory but all over the planet. India since its independence has practised parliamentary democracy and remains an example for other emerging nations, even if the hurdles are still huge and minorities not completely integrated. France is considered as the land of liberties, even if the reality is less and less commensurate with its reputation and the integration of minorities derived from colonization proves to be complex. The equilibrium is precarious. Social and economic development based on the law of supply and demand has naturally resulted in a disparity of treatment between those who benefit from growth and those who are excluded from it. Vigilance must be maintained with regard to each of the citizens in order to foster, develop and reinforce democratic rule which can never be taken for granted.

Translated from French by
Geetha Ganapathy-Doré

NOTES AND REFERENCES

1. To borrow Marxist terminology and distinguish between "economic and social" infrastructure and "legal and political" superstructure.
2. This choice is particularly significant because it represents a gamut of political regimes founded on the principle of separation of powers.
3. Bibliographical resources for this topic are abundant. Many a work on political regimes in general, the American political regime and the political regime of the Fifth Republic has been published by French constitutionalists. American publications on this issue are numerous. In France, there exists an interest for the contemporary political regime of India. Journals and websites contain a mine of data.
4. Walter Bagehot used the expression « presidential regime » to describe Abraham Lincoln's experience.
5. Considering the large number of works available on the American political regime, please confer R. Aron, *La république impériale*, 1973; R. Dahl, *Pluralist Democracy in the United States*, 1967 and the classical works of Tocqueville, Kaspi, Tunc and Mathiot.
6. The election of the American President is a skilful compromise which gives the new president a considerable force and one whose first satisfaction is first of all having been able to successfully win the elections.
7. This formidable alchemy makes the American President Number One in the most powerful country in the world which dominates the whole planet
8. Consult M.F.Toinet, *Le Congrès des Etats-Unis,* 1972 on this topic.
9. Cf the time honoured techniques of checks and balances that enable the American society to find a balance in spite of the independence and autonomy of the different branches.
10. On this topic, consult E. Lambert, *Gouvernement des juges*, 1921.
11. Some books in French that could be consulted: J. Assayag, *L'Inde désir de nation*, Odile Jacob, 2001; C. Bardot, *L'Inde au miroir du monde, démocratie, géopolitique et développement de 1947 à nous jours*, Ellipses, 2007; Ch. Bettelheim, *L'Inde indépendante*, Colin, 1962; F. Doré, *La république indienne*,

LGDJ, 1969; C. Jaffrelot, *La democratie en Inde, religion, caste et politique*, Fayard, 1998; M.J. Zins, *Inde destin démocratique, La documentation française*, 1999.

12. Out of the 250 members of the Council of States, 12 members are nominated by the President as experts in sciences and arts. In the House of the People, 20 out of 530 MPs represent the Union territories and 2 are nominated to represent the Anglo-Indian community.
13. India thus has known the tradition of classical parliamentary regimes which is very close to the British political regime.
14. Among the Indian Prime Ministers figure the prestigious names of Nehru, Indira and Rajiv Gandhi, or currently Manmohan Singh.
15. Principle according to which the Central Government can directly administer a state in case of conflict.
16. The court at the top is the Indian Supreme Court. But state courts are numerous and diversified according to a pattern which copies both the British and American systems.
17. Literature on the political regime of the Fifth republic is multiple and varied. Obviously I would like the readers to consult my own book on "General Public Law", Editions Foucher, 2nd reprint (the third is expected to be out in October 2009).
18. This immunity is often considered as one of the characteristics of the French political regime, which thus differs from other Western political regimes.
19. Constitutional reform is at the heart of political debate with two alternatives: reinforce the powers of the President and make the Fifth Republic a presidential regime or come back to the parliamentary tradition. Successive reforms seem to reinforce the idea that the Constitution of 1958 revised and rectified has stood the test of time. The constitutional revision of 23 July 2008 has given the occasion for numerous discussions which have not lead to the effective reinforcement of the internal functioning of the French Parliament.
20. The Fourth Republic (1946-1958) was a parliamentary regime which was very much criticized for its political instability especially by the Gaullists.
21. The control of the constitutionality of laws in France has the originality of reinforcing the authority of the law as expression of the general will of the people according to the democratic principle that once it has been made a law can be unmade only by another law.
22. Alternance comes from the fact a new majority comes to power. Cohabitation in the French system consists in distinguishing between a presidential majority and a parliamentary majority which naturally must get along with each other.
23. Noteworthy definition which marks the importance of the power of the people.
24. Principle of sovereign elections which has spread naturally without challenging democracy in any way.
25. It is interesting to note that the principle of elections has been reinforced since the independence of India. If this is a principle that has been generally accepted in the newly independent nation States for presidential elections, it has, on the contrary, been badly applied in the case of parliamentary elections.

26. Democratic rules demand free and uncontested elections.
27. India comprises twenty-eight states and seven union territories.
28. The Italian and Spanish examples show that a decentralized state has nothing to envy from most of the federal States in matters of local democracy.
29. The Anglo-Saxon people are very much attached to the idea of the community which is directly opposed to the principle of secularism.
30. If state neutrality toward religion is real in the Indian constitution, it corresponds, in practice, to a form of secularism. The system of preferential choices practised is a proof of this, while in France egalitarianism is a basic principle.
31. Obviously France is looking for solutions to integrate minorities. This is an important issue for its future.
32. We tend to forget that in the United States there are numerous little political parties that exist apart from the two big political parties.
33. India is characterised as a State where there is a multi-party system. The diversity of opinion and the staggering number of political parties entail difficulties in the formation of a majority. If the Congress party plays a key role, it is necessary to foresee alliances to form stable governments. Such alliances could be constructed around a political leader.
34. The idea of the majority is crucial in the Fifth Republic. The institutions and the electoral methods favour the formation of a stable majority, even if alternance has been rare in the Fifth Republic.
35. In order to understand the importance of the notion of opposition to assess democratic regimes, see my thesis on *The Institutionalization of Opposition in Western Democracies*, University of Paris 1, 1981.
36. The idea of universality with respect to liberties and especially freedom of speech is fundamental.
37. In a democratic structure, terrorism cannot be tolerated. Nevertheless, there must be full freedom and terrorism should not become a pretext for strengthening the authority of the State to the detriment of individual rights and fundamental liberties.
38. The civil society and the role played by associations that defend civil liberties need to be mentioned here.
39. National texts are fundamental. But we have to bear in mind the importance of the United Nations and especially the 1948 Universal Declaration of Human Rights.
40. It is not enough to have texts. They need to be enforced. The control in this regard is clearly ensured by the highest court in each of the three States under scrutiny.
41. The principle of secularism (understood as neutrality toward religion) has undoubtedly proved its worth. It has to be maintained and adapted to suite the new French reality.
42. The temptation to favour repressive measures ill-suited for the demands of democracy is strong for the State.

2

European Union in the 21st Century World:
A Successful Example of Regional Organization

PIERRE-YVES MONJAL

Introduction

Did Europe have a chance of being united or unified one day? The answer seems to be self evident today. The twenty-seven states, who are currently members of a regional economic union, are quite specific, but they have succeeded in establishing peace among themselves thanks to law and economy. This combination of law and economy is in itself a political project. Without a political will, without a political motivation, the European Union would not have seen the light of day.

The Europe of 2009 is a Product of Singular History

First of all, historians like to explain, with examples to back up this idea, that out of the two thousand years that the Christian era comprises, there have been nineteen hundred years of murderous war among most of the European States. Indeed the expression "European civil wars" is some times used to bring out the fact that in spite of the multifariousness of states, powerful cultural links exist which bind them over and above their differences. Out of the hundred years of peace, two periods could be clearly distinguished: a discontinuous period of about fifty years which are dispersed and sixty years of uninterrupted peace since 1950. Around 1950, two international organizations emblematic of today's Europe were born: the Council of Europe set up by virtue of the Treaty of London of 5 May 1949 entrusted with ensuring the protection of the fundamental rights of persons and the European Coal and Steel Community instituted by the Treaty of Paris of 18 April 1951, which forms the basis of the European Union. There has indeed been a meeting of at least two factors, an unquestionable relation between the institutionalization of the European Union and the pacification of the continent.

Secondly, Europe is composed of a significant number of States (forty-three including Russia) all of which possess the common characteristic of being culturally very dissimilar. These differences could be traced back to their peculiar history, their language, their culture and life form, their traditions etc. The constant challenge to be united in diversity was therefore immense. The absence of a territorial, linguistic, historical, legal unity did not favour such a rapprochement. One had to wait until 1 January 2007 to see the Union grow from six (1951) to twenty-seven members. This having been said, the cultural question needs to be relativized. France does not certainly resemble Germany. Nor is the Roman law (written and constructed around principles) the equivalent of Common Law. It is no doubt difficult to convince a Swedish citizen that he is as European as a Cypriot. It is absolutely necessary to grasp the fundamental point that a common cultural basis that is much more powerful than one would have us believe sustains all European states: Christianity, Greek and Roman philosophy, the idea of liberty, democracy, fundamental rights as expressed in the 18th century, art, commerce, state intervention in favour of social and redistributive justice... In other words, even if it appears simplistic, the four hundred and ninety-three million Europeans who form part of the twenty-seven member states more or less agree on common values concerning good and evil, justice, equality, democracy. This common basis is doubly fundamental. It is the cement of a Union that is being built. It constitutes the very identity of the Union. That is the reason why the question of Turkey's accession to the European Union is being effectively raised, in terms that may appear hypocritical but remain very clear all the same. Does Christian Europe want to admit seventy million Muslims at its heart? Is Jewish Christian Europe ready to open herself to another great religion of the Book? There are two possible answers to this culturally decisive question: No, because Islam is not culturally dissolvable in the Jewish-Christian heritage. Besides, Western values such as liberty, democracy, gender equality, economic liberalism constitute as many counter values to be fought against from the point of view of a non-negligible part of the followers of Islam. Yes, because the values of the Union are the values of a life together built around common universal principles (democracy, human rights...). The European Union has the innate ability to make dissimilar peoples live together. The gamble is immense and the stakes decisive for the history of humanity.

The European Union is a Product of a Conjoining of Specific Principles

The European Union of 2009, whatever people say, is alive and well. To be precise, it has been functioning for over fifty years, though the European Union as such was created in 1992 by virtue of the Maastricht treaty (entered into force on 1 November 1993). Initially three distinct international bodies were set up: ECSC, Euratom, EEC. Two of them still exist (Euratom and EC). The European Union heads and completes these two international organizations by adding a common foreign and security policy and cooperation in justice and home affairs relating to criminal matters. The Union is not a legal entity. Nor does it have the status of an international organization.[1] In all likelihood, the Treaty of Lisbon, when it enters into force in 2009, will confer this status on the EU. But, what makes the European Union run? What are the principles, what are the engines that make the twenty-seven member states not only unite in the course of time but also collaborate and develop their economy? Three series of principles could be discerned some of which are projections of identity values of European Union member states.

Common Ethical and Political Values

This question should not be underestimated. The European Union is not something to be taken for granted or something shallow. It is the very opposite. Its values have been defined in Article 6 of the Treaty on European Union. Indeed these values are but those of the states, of Europe projected in the Union:

1. The Union is founded on the principles of liberty, democracy, respect for human rights and fundamental freedoms, and the rule of law, principles which are common to the Member States.
2. The Union shall respect fundamental rights, as guaranteed by the European Convention for the Protection of Human Rights and Fundamental Freedoms signed in Rome on 4 November 1950 and as they result from the constitutional traditions common to the Member States, as general principles of Community law.
3. The Union shall respect the national identities of its Member States.
4. The Union shall provide itself with the means necessary to attain its objectives and carry through its policies.

Article 6 of the Treaty on European Union plays a significant role in the legal and political system of the Union. To some extent, it acts as a substitute for the Charter of Fundamental Rights that the Union has not yet endowed itself with. Indeed, it consecrates a certain number of values and principles that are vital to the regulating institutions of the European Union, much in the way the constitutional rules and principles of a state are essential for the legislator. So much so that even if the debate on the democratic deficit in the Union regularly crops up, Article 6 gives to both the normativity of the Union and its legislation (regulations and directives) a legal legitimacy which is hardly questionable.

At another level, it must be underscored that Article 6 of the Treaty on European Union also plays a filtering role before admitting new states in the Union. In fact, apart from the geographic criterion which is difficult to systematize and has to be fulfilled by candidate countries (be a European state according to Article 48 of the EC treaty), a whole series of basic factors have to be fulfilled by the said candidate before seeing its candidacy result in membership. These fundamental factors are enumerated precisely in Article 6. To put it simply, the candidate for membership must respect human rights, be a democracy and a state where there is rule of law to ensure liberty. Article 6 also plays the role of censor or controller of member states' compliance with the values of the Union. Thus, if a member state does not comply with the principles formulated in the aforementioned article, sanctions can be pronounced against it by virtue of Article 7 of the Treaty on European Union:

1. On a reasoned proposal by one third of the Member States, by the European Parliament or by the Commission, the Council, acting by a majority of four fifths of its members after obtaining the assent of the European Parliament, may determine that there is a clear risk of a serious breach by a Member State of principles mentioned in Article 6(1), and address appropriate recommendations to that State. Before making such a determination, the Council shall hear the Member State in question and, acting in accordance with the same procedure, may call on independent persons to submit within a reasonable time limit a report on the situation in the Member State in question. The Council shall regularly verify that the grounds on which such a determination was made continue to apply.
2. The Council, meeting in the composition of the Heads of State or Government and acting by unanimity on a proposal by one third of the Member States or by the Commission and after obtaining the assent of the European Parliament, may determine the existence of a serious and persistent breach by a Member State of principles mentioned in Article 6(1), after inviting the government of the Member State in question to submit its observations.

3. Where a determination under paragraph 2 has been made, the Council, acting by a qualified majority, may decide to suspend certain of the rights deriving from the application of this Treaty to the Member State in question, including the voting rights of the representative of the government of that Member State in the Council. In doing so, the Council shall take into account the possible consequences of such a suspension on the rights and obligations of natural and legal persons. The obligations of the Member State in question under this Treaty shall in any case continue to be binding on that State.
4. The Council, acting by a qualified majority, may decide subsequently to vary or revoke measures taken under paragraph 3 in response to changes in the situation which led to their being imposed.
5. For the purposes of this Article, the Council shall act without taking into account the vote of the representative of the government of the Member State in question. Abstentions by members present in person or represented shall not prevent the adoption of decisions referred to in paragraph 2. A qualified majority shall be defined as the same proportion of the weighted votes of the members of the Council concerned as laid down in Article 205(2) of the Treaty establishing the European Community. This paragraph shall also apply in the event of voting rights being suspended pursuant to paragraph 3.
6. For the purposes of paragraphs 1 and 2, the European Parliament shall act by a two-thirds majority of the votes cast, representing a majority of its Members.

In a larger perspective, the question of integration of a true catalogue of fundamental rights specific to the European Union in its basic treaty is being raised. Currently, it is the text of a convention dated 4 November 1950 that is extraneous to the Union which is applied: The European Convention on Human Rights. Whereas, even if the Court of Justice has ensured its enforcement in the legal order of the Union. Nevertheless, keeping in mind the need for coherence, the Union has got its own instrument of fundamental rights. The Lisbon Treaty which should enter into force in 2009 and replace the prevailing 1957 Treaty of Rome is going to render this contribution possible. In fact, the Charter of Fundamental Rights, which dates back to 7 December 2000, constitutes an updating and reinforcement of rights guaranteed in the 1950 text. In addition to the inclusion of labour rights (right to strike, freedom to join trade unions...), new rights make their entrance, especially those relating to new technology (Internet) and biomedicine.

This basis of common values which is going to be strengthened in a few months constitutes what might be called the criteria for measuring the Europeanness of the member states. To the question of knowing what a European state is, the answer is that it is above all a state which adheres to, assumes, promotes and protects liberty, democracy, rule of law and fundamental rights.

An Institutional Framework Adapted to Common Ethical and Political Values

The institutional framework that allows the EU to make its decisions and enact unilateral community law whose reach far exceeds the classical international law rests on four well-designed cornerstones, in addition to being the projection of the ethical and political values of member states. The languages of the member states enjoy respect (twenty three official languages translated verbally and orally). The crux of the matter is to know whether the institutional framework of the European Union reflects the ethical and political values that form the basis of the Union and its member states. It is on the area of democratic representation that the critical lens had to be focussed.

The European Parliament is the Democratic Basis for the Union

The European Parliament is a fundamental institution of the Union. It constitutes the "guarantee" of the Union. Indeed, its current seven hundred and eighty-five members (seven hundred and fifty-one in the framework of the Lisbon treaty) are elected by universal suffrage for a term of five years renewable by the populations of member states. The voting procedure is nowadays uniform as it has been decided to elect MEPs through a proportional list system. The role of representing the populations of the states and not one people or an identified European nation would not have any immediate relevance, if the institution of European Parliament was not endowed with effective legal prerogatives. The analysis of the treaties tells us that the European Parliament exercises two important functions.

The first is a regulating role. With the Council, Parliament codecides, colegislates (Art 252 of the EC Treaty) in thirty-three areas (environment, equality of treatment, services, harmonization of legislation ...). It can refuse any draft regulation or directive, if it is not amended in the way it wants. In other words, a project initiated by the Commission, defended or sustained actively by the Council (member states) will not see the light of day, if the European Parliament is opposed to it. Instances of rejection are very rare. But in practice, what one remarks is the incontestable effort by the Council to take into account, the amendments proposed by Parliament at the time of debate and the shuttling of bills. So, it might be said, without grossly exaggerating, that a regulation or a directive that will have been approved by the European Parliament and the Council symbolizes the accord between the represented populations and the states (two pillars of the Union's legitimacy). On the contrary, when Parliament opposes or imposes its veto on the Council, it can be reasonably said that it is the represented people who have the last word against the representatives of the states. This aspect of the issue should not be underestimated.

The second role that is available to the Parliament of the Union is the role of political control. It consists in controlling the action of the European Commission. This control is first exercised at the time of the Brussels panel's taking office. The Commission cannot be legally and validly "set up", if it has not obtained a vote of confidence from the Parliament which should approve it by an absolute majority of its members. Without this Parliamentary moment, which is decisive as we know in our European democracies, the Commission cannot exercise its duties. The European Parliament continues to exercise its control through out the term of office of the Commissioners (and of the Commission). In fact, at any given time, in view of circumstances that justify it, the European Parliament can adopt a motion of censure against the Commission, if the latter does not comply with its initial political commitment: the very commitment that made Parliament grant its confidence. In 1999, owing to embezzlement and a rather disastrous management by the Commission of certain community programmes destined for the Mediterranean, the Commission headed by the Luxemburgher Jacques Santer was obliged to tender individual resignation of all its members in order to avoid parliamentary censure. In fact, the no-confidence motion which was under way had all the chances of being voted. In order to avoid a veritable political crisis, which would have marked the institutional victory of the Parliament over the Brussels executive and which was not found suitable by the member states, little inclined to engage in a fight with a European Parliament in a politically stronger position, the Commissioners chose to resign collectively. With regard to these two aspects—regulating and politically controlling—it could be said that the European Parliament is an institution that faithfully represents the values of representative democracy.

The Council is the Guardian of Governmental Legitimacy in the Union

At first sight, the Council of Ministers, which is composed of representatives from the governments of member states having a ministerial rank does not appear as an institution, which by itself, would entertain great links with democracy. It would be more appropriate to categorize it as one of those executive and intergovernmental bodies which we might be tempted to think purports to impose the will of the states, either on Parliament or on the Commission. This analysis, though not completely false, is nevertheless not totally convincing. Such an analysis relies on a very organic and superficial conception of the Union institutions. The issues at stake are more subtle than what a quick analysis would have us believe. It is necessary to integrate the place of the Council of Ministers in the Union's general institutional system and ask whether its legitimacy, if not quantifiable, is appreciable and verifiable. From this point of view, several remarks may be made.

First, to the question of knowing whether the Council is an institution endowed with democratic legitimacy, it seems to me that the answer is self-evident. Basically, its composition cannot be called into question. The ministers who make it up are all either democratically elected or nominated (in rare cases). In instances where the ministers are not elected, it is clearly established that all the governments of the twenty-seven member states of the Union are collectively and politically responsible before the assemblies, the representative chambers of the people. The well-known mechanism of engaging governmental responsibility, typical of parliamentary regimes, is a constant and verifiable datum of European democracies. If we take up the case of France, the current government whose Prime Minister is François Fillon, we can notice that that many of its members, including its chief, are either members of parliament or local governments. Those rare members who have not been elected or re-elected, it should be noted that in any case it is the President of the Republic, Nicolas Sarkozy, who nominates them. The Head of the State is elected by direct universal suffrage in France. In these circumstances, notably by taking into consideration the French example, it appears rather tenuous to deny the Council of Ministers its legitimacy. This legitimacy is twofold. On the one hand, its existence has been foreseen by the EC Treaty itself which we know has been approved by all member states (formal legitimacy) and on the other, its composition does not leave any space for doubt concerning its democratic legitimacy (material legitimacy). Seen from this angle, the arguments for contesting it, which by harping upon the democratic deficit of the Union appear to be contesting its very basis and denying its legitimacy to make decisions become more nuanced. Indeed when one knows that it is the Council which is the major decision maker in the Union, it is legally and rhetorically very complicated to deny what is obvious: The Council is a democratic institution.

Secondly, one might examine whether in its mode of functioning, the same argument as above could still be valid. By mode of functioning, the following three things are meant: the voting procedure in the Council, the representative nature of its members and the control of its action. As regards the voting procedure, the treaty lays down that the ministers can approve acts they adopt by either a unanimous vote or a qualified majority vote. In the latter configuration, each state is given a number of votes corresponding to its demographic weight (29 for Germany, France and Italy; 27 for Spain, 3 for Malta and so on). The total number of votes is 345. If the total number of votes of the states is equal to 258, which represents about two thirds of consent by the member states, the act will be adopted. Let us underscore the fact that neither the big states nor the smaller ones will be able to reach 258 votes all alone. It means that for each vote with qualified majority, the big and smaller states are associated. The blocking minority stands at 91 votes. If unanimity is found to be reassuring by the states in the sense that it gives the feeling of maintaining their sovereignty, which can be understood in this case as the power to oppose, refuse, it is beyond doubt that the majority vote results out of a more democratic process. The rule of law by majority vote forms one of the major improvements in terms of democracy. Let us add that in the case where a member state abstains from voting, or even opposes it, it is under obligation to apply the community regulation or directive that will have been adopted by other partners.

The representativeness of the Council is an aspect which is rarely discussed. The question is simple. Does the Council represent only the governments of the states? It is obviously yes. But if we look deeper, we have to nuance the answer a bit more. Indeed the ministers are first of all members of national governments responsible before their respective parliaments. It must therefore be admitted that the ministers are not the only representatives of the states in their capacity as members of the government to which they belong, but are also representatives of the policies supported by the representatives of the people consisting of the members of parliament to whom they are accountable. But more interesting is the role of representing the people that the Council plays at the time of vote. Indeed, the Treaty of Nice has added in its Declaration no. 20 that the member states can ask at the end of each vote to check that the famous 258 votes out of 345 represents three fourths of states sitting at the Council and 62 per cent of the population of the European Union, i.e., 305.6 million (out of a total of 493 million population). In other words, when the Council, a governmental and representative body decides, it functions at the same time as a body representing the peoples. Of course, this representation is highly indirect, but the legitimacy of the ministers and their bond with the peoples of member states cannot be questioned.

Last, the action of ministers does not escape critical review. It is to their national parliaments that the ministers are accountable first. We might deplore in France that at no time in the history of the Fifth republic, parliament had engaged the government's political responsibility on European issues or the government asked for a vote of confidence to the National Assembly. But the case stands that the European action of governments and ministers must be and is controlled by the peoples in the framework of the fundamental mechanisms of parliamentary regimes. It should moreover be noted that the European citizens also depend on EU's justice. It means that they can institute legal proceedings before the Court of First Instance and before the Court of Justice against the acts adopted by the Council. This control is, of course, jurisdictional and technical, but it is done by the people, i.e., the appellant citizen. One should not underestimate this aspect. It is a form of democratic control.

The Commission Ensures the Promotion of Common Interest

The European Commission is an independent institution which represents neither the peoples of the member states nor the states. Its members, the twenty-seven Commissioners in all, are not elected. Entrusted with the task of promoting European general interest, the Commission has a rather bad reputation in public opinion, which is largely shared by a major part of the political class. The complaint against it is that it is not legitimate. Indeed its omnipotence and its regulating activity give the impression that the member states and economic actors are the victims of an uncontrolled institution of doubtful legitimacy.

This idea, rather this belief, needs to be doubly corrected. On the one hand, it is not easy to sustain that this institution is not legitimate in so far as its existence has been laid down in a treaty (Rome) approved by all the member states according to their constitutional procedures. Besides, we ought to remember that the Commissioners are nominated after common agreement among Heads of States, Governments and MEPs. The setting up of the Commission becomes effective only after the Parliament has granted its confidence in the framework of the investiture procedure and after a special vote which should gather an absolute majority of members of European Parliament. All along its term, the Commission is placed under the political control of Parliament which can bring it down with a motion of censure. When all these elements are added up, it is preposterous to sustain that the Heads of States and Governments have no legitimacy, the MEPs are devoid of it and in fine the Commission is not legitimate.

In a different angle, the prerogatives of the Commission, it is to be remembered that it has but a power of initiative. It is up to the Council and the European Parliament to adopt in the last resort the regulations and directives of a binding legislative nature. When the Commission adopts regulations and directives, what is very frequent is that it is based on an act adopted by the Council and/or the Parliament which authorises the Commission to do so. Its action is neither independent nor uncontrolled.

The Court of Justice is the Guardian of Rights and Liberties

The rôle of the Court of justice is decisive in the system. It is the Court which ensures the protection of rights and liberties of individuals, by enforcing the treaty, it goes without saying. The point to be remembered especially is that it ensures the protection of fundamental rights as they are defined in the European Convention on Human rights of 1950. As the European Community is a party to the ECHR, it was difficult to enforce it in the community legal order. Nevertheless, it is this task that the Court of Justice will devote itself to by integrating provisions of the ECHR through the general principles of community law. Like all other courts, the judge in Luxembourg is able to create, discover general principles that could be enforced with out a text. These case law principles have the same value as the treaty and are mandatory on the Union institutions and the acts they adopt. This is how the European citizens are guaranteed that the community obligations imposed upon them conform to the rules and principles of the EHCR. It is useful to recall here that states, citizens and the institutions can appeal to the Court of Justice in order to control unilateral acts (regulations, directives). Among the means of lawfulness that could be invoked, an argument based on the unawareness of fundamental rights can be brought up by the appellants.

When the Lisbon treaty will enter into force in 2009, it is agreed that the Charter of fundamental Rights of the European Union adopted on 7 December 2000 which, enhanced with its 54 articles, updates and enriches its precursor (EHCR) and will be enforced in the legal order of the Union with the same value as the treaty. The citizens of the European Union will thus be subjected not only to their proper internal catalogue of fundamental rights but also to that of the Union (The Charter) and the ECHR. The European Union is expected to adhere to the European Convention on Human Rights.

In view of the above, it is difficult to question the democratic aspect of the European Union. Not only are the people represented and enabled to control the Union institutions, but also, fundamental rights are guaranteed by and in the Union. The notion of democracy hinges on these two pillars:

the representation and popular control on the one hand and the guarantee of fundamental rights on the other.

Powerful Legal Levers Ensure the Prevalence of Common Values

The law of the European Union is full-fledged as much from the point of view of its sources as from that of its enforcing principles. It is a law that has a specific reach and an original nature: it is the law of the common.

The sources of the European Union Law are mainly two: the treaties (substantive law) and unilateral acts which are mostly regulations and directives (procedural law). This law arises out of procedures that we think are not without direct link to democratic principles and values. The jurisdictional control exercised by the Court of Justice guarantees both the states and the citizens that their rights and liberties will not be called into question, altered by the institutions of the Union.

The prevalence of the values of the Union, the effectiveness of its principles and to put it concisely the very existence of this union and this common law are rendered possible by two legal principles well known to the federal systems: the principle of primacy and that of direct effect. The first principle was found by the Court of Justice in a 1964 case Costa v ENEL in which the court asserted that community law takes precedence over national law with preponderance on all the regulations, including constitutional ones. This makes it a system of protection of fundamental rights within the European Union all the more important. Concretely, the principle of primacy requires that some laws be not enforced and in some cases, administrative acts contrary to community law be annulled by member states and especially their courts. It is difficult to enforce this principle in the member states notably in France. As regards the principle of direct effect, it means that not only does the community law prevail over the national law which is contradictory, but it is also empowered to confer self-executing (directly applicable) rights in favour of those who invoke them. These two levers—primacy and direct effect-entirely developed by the Court of Justice thus offer the European Union and its law the possibility to exist.

Conclusion

What made Europe and what is continuing to build it are the aforementioned values, the determination to preserve them and the political will to enforce them which are but the consequence of the awareness that there exists no alternative to Europe for the Union's member states. We can conclude that the stake for us, Europeans in the 21st century, is to know how to organize this Union. Should it be endowed with a constitution? Should we build a federal state out of it? Should the governments of member states gradually disappear? My feeling is that the disappearance of member states is not on the agenda and was never on the agenda. We are inventing on a daily basis a unique and specific model which is legally an alloy, an alliance of governmental powers which are exercised on a revolutionary mode which is quite new and which consists in the common exercise of governmental powers detained by entities that are still sovereign. For the jurist, the European Union is a true legal laboratory that cannot be compared to other models of organization of societies. Peace was thus constructed in Europe around community law, free market economy and the political will of the social democrat elite to do away with the most abject forms of political and economic nationalism—wars.

Translated from French by
Geetha Ganapathy-Doré

NOTES AND REFERENCES

1. Only the European Community is an international organization in the legal sense of the term and has the capacity to sign economic agreements with the rest of the world.
   The European Union is a general term that refers to the system of collaboration set up by the 27 member states. This collaboration rests on three pillars: the European Community (the first pillar which has the form of the international organization), the Common Foreign and Security Policy (the second pillar which takes an intergovernmental form among the 27 member states) and Co-operation in the field of Justice and Home Affairs (which also functions according to an intergovernmental mode).
   Therefore the European Union is not an international organization legally speaking and does not have any competence to enter into agreements. If the Lisbon Treaty enters into force, the European Union will become an international organization and the European Community will vanish to pave the way for the new organization.

3

Policy of Access to European Union Documents: *The End of Opacity*

CLAUDINE MOUTARDIER

The citizens' right to access information held by public authorities is an essential element in any democratic society. It is a relatively ancient right that appeared in the Swedish Kingdom two hundred years ago[1]. At that time, Sweden became the first country to set up an open administration. In 1776, the Swedish Parliament included a law on the freedom of the press in its constitution which recognized the principle of transparency and the right of everyone to access public documents.

More than two hundred years after this revolution, the European Union, confronted with a legitimacy crisis regarding its institutions, is trying to find solutions. The concept of transparency got established as an element of response which might simultaneously counter the veering off of institutions and particularly improve their governance.

Generally, the concept of transparency corresponds to the opening up of an organization's internal processes and decisions to a third party. It is applicable in a number of areas (documentary transparency, organizational transparency, budgetary transparency and accounting transparency).

The basis of any law on access to information resides in the opportunity given to the citizen to ask, without having to justify such a request, a piece of information or a document issued by a public authority. These laws help give a more active role to citizens with regard to public administration, especially the implementation of public policies.

EU member states which practise transparency such as Denmark, Holland and Finland have sought to introduce a provision on the citizens' right to access documents on EU institutions. In spite of divergence of points of view among the member states, they have succeeded in doing so.

Up until then, the practice of secret in the European Union had never been called into question. The EU administration reflected what was practised in most of the continental countries (France, UK, Germany, Belgium, and Luxemburg) which formed the hard core of a closed administrative system[2]. But after Maastricht, the governments of EU member states found themselves confronted with the idea of transparency, an idea that was to enable European institutions to retrieve citizen's confidence and strengthen democracy.

For such an idea to be implemented, it was necessary to fix the terms and conditions by a regulatory provision. This was done in 2001. This regulation allowed the citizens of the European Union to have access to documents which remained inaccessible to them till then. Rules of access have been fixed in almost all the Community institutions, bodies and agencies.

In fifteen years, much has been done by the European Union to get rid of its image as an opaque and secret institution. At a time when the European Union is trying to further develop its transparency policy, it is interesting to see how it has moved from darkness to light in matters of access to documents (I). Then we shall see how far the revision of this legislation (II) has gone.

I. THE REGIME OF ACCESS TO DOCUMENTS: FROM DARKNESS TO LIGHT

In order to evaluate the implementation of principles of transparency, it is useful to recall the Community's legal framework for access to documents.

(A) The Premises of a Legal Framework

The Treaty of Maastricht: The Starting Point

The notion of right to access is enshrined in the Treaty on the European Union signed in Maastricht on 7 February 1992 or rather in one of the thirty one "Declarations" adopted by the Intergovernmental Conference. Declaration 17 deals with the "right of access to information". It states: transparency of the decision-making process strengthens the democratic nature of the institutions and the public's confidence in the administration. This declaration makes transparency appear as a condition for both the efficiency of Community action and the legitimacy of the Community. It constitutes a milestone in the development of the Community.

Indeed it must be noted that transparency in the European Union is not a thing to be taken for granted. The terms and conditions for implementing the principle of transparency are a matter of diverging opinion among member states about how to respect the balance between necessary confidentiality in certain areas and the need for transparency demanded by the citizens.

After the entry into force of the Treaty on the European Union, the striving towards information and openness was translated in terms of modification of certain rules of functioning. In accordance with the wishes expressed in the Maastricht summit, the European Council of Birmingham wanted to "open up the work of the Community's institutions, including the possibility of some open Council discussion"[3].

This appeal for increased transparency was again made in the conclusions of the European Council of Edinburgh of 12 December 1992 which specified that the "Council reaffirms its attachment to a more open community"[4].

In order to comply with Declaration No. 17, the Commission had to "submit to the Council no later than 1993 a report on measures designed to improve public access to the information available to the institutions". But such a text had no binding force as the declaration did not form part of the Treaty itself. But the impetus was given.

In 1993, the Commission published two papers on the topic of transparency[5]. The first is a comparative study of practices followed in the Community institutions, the member states and some third countries (Canada, Sweden, Norway, and the United States). The second is more technical and describes the terms and conditions of access to documents in view of a discussion with other institutions.

After the publication of these documents, the Commission, and then the Council adopted a common instrument called the Code of Conduct concerning public access to documents of the Council and the Commission[6].

This text establishes the principle of a wide access to unpublished documents held by the two institutions, refusal being made only in some exceptional cases where public or private interests need to be safeguarded or the proper functioning of the institutions. The code also determines the terms and conditions of processing the applications, the time limits and the appeal procedures. It is applicable only to the documents of the Commission and the Council. Documents issued by third persons and held by the institutions fell outside its purview.

The code was completed by two Commission decisions, the first amending its internal rules[7] and the second dealing with public access to Council documents[8].

A little later, the Commission also adopted a decision relating to public access to its own documents[9]. On 10 July 1997, the European Parliament in turn adopted rules similar to the Council and the Commission's Code of Conduct.

The Treaty of Amsterdam: Article 255 EC

On the regulatory level, it is the Treaty of Amsterdam which gives a formal legal basis to the principle by introducing a new article 191a, which has now become Article 255. This article "enshrines transparency in the treaties"[10].

Article 255 of the treaty lays down "a true subjective, fundamental right granted to the individual[11]" which can be demanded from the institutions and is a guaranteed right. The first paragraph of this article grants to any citizen of the Union, and any natural or legal person residing or having his/its registered office in a member state, right of access to European Parliament, Council and Commission documents. This inclusive wording excludes only nationals of countries who do not reside in the Union. Similarly, the paragraph does not lay down any condition regarding the applicant's ground for action. Even if Article 255 focuses only on Parliament, Council and Commission documents, these institutions have underscored in a common declaration that "similar agencies and bodies set up by the European lawmaker" have to comply with the provisions of this text.

A question still remains unanswered. Could the right of access referred to in Article 255 be extended to documents held by Parliament, Council and Commission but issued by the member states? At the time of drafting the Code of Conduct in 1993, such a possibility was ruled out. However, this standpoint does not seem to be valid in so far as Declaration No. 35 annexed to the Treaty of Amsterdam makes us suppose that the right of access to national documents held by community institutions is applicable except in cases where the member state requires that the documents be not available for consultation[12].

The second paragraph asks the Council to adopt, within two years from the entry into force of the Treaty, an act of secondary legislation fixing the general principles of and the limits on the exercise of this right, through the co-decision procedure. It also justifies the limits on the right of access on grounds of protection of public or private interests. Public interest pertains to public security, defence, military matters, international relations as well as the monetary policy of the Community. Protcction of private life has also been included (protection of personal data). The reference to public interests and private life is a justification for the confidential nature of the document which obliges the institution to refuse access to it[13]. The expression "private interests" refers basically to protection of commercial interests and judicial procedures. These indications have a mandatory nature even if it is not expressly specified in the text itself of Article 255.

The third paragraph requires all the three institutions to take necessary measures to enable access to all their documents. These rules of primary legislation are strengthened by article 42 of the Charter of Fundamental Rights to which article 6§1 of the Treaty on the European Union gives the same legal value as the treaties. The rules concerning the right of public access to documents must also be interpreted and applied in accordance with this article which stipulates:

Any citizen of the Union, and any natural or legal person residing or having its registered office in a Member State, has a right of access to European Parliament, Council and Commission documents.

The legal basis having been fixed, it was then necessary to enforce it.

(B) Regulation (EC) 1049/2001 Concerning Public Access to Parliament, Council and Commission Documents

The new Commission set up in September 1999 was entrusted with the task of establishing the legislation applicable to the right of access to Community documents within the time limits set down by the Treaty of Amsterdam. The text was proposed to the Parliament and the Council on 26 January 2000[14]. A tug of war between member states which have a long history of openness (Sweden, Denmark, and Finland) and the other more suspicious states on the necessity for greater transparency ensued. After numerous compromises and amendments, the new regulation was adopted on 30 May 2001 by the Parliament and the Council.

The Characteristics of the Regime of Access to Documents

The regime of access to documents which was adopted by the European Union resembles that which already exists in a good number of member states which have legislated on the matter. The EC text is intended to accommodate the recommendations of the Council of Europe and the provisions of the Arhus Convention[15]. Basically it is a rehash of the rules adopted in the 1993 Code of Conduct. Nevertheless the text contains many major innovations.

(a) Scope of the Right of Access

The regulation sets down a general and not a conditional right of access. In accordance with Article 225 of the EC Treaty, the regulation guarantees a right of access to citizens and residents of the Union as well as to any moral person having its registered office in one of the member states. The regulation also gives the institutions the option to extend the scope to other categories of people. This option was widely used by the Council and the Commission which have extended the right of access to any natural or moral person within the regulation's implementation framework[16]. The European Parliament has also modified its internal rules in order to extend its right of access to all the citizens of third countries[17]. The three institutions thus apply the regulation indiscriminately to citizens of third countries not residing in one of the Union's member states or moral persons not established in the Union's territory.

These extensions of right of access are all the more necessary because they are also imposed by the Arhus Convention which does not allow the right of access to be limited only to citizens and residents of the European Union[18]. It must be remembered that this right of access is unconditional. It is indeed not necessary for the applicants to specify why they want to have access to documents. It is for the regulation to indicate the nature of documents that can be consulted.

(b) Nature of Documents

Materially speaking the regulation covers the vastest scope. Its article 2§3 indicates that it is applicable to "all documents held by an institution, that is to say, documents drawn up or received by it and in its possession, in all areas of activity of the European Union". The text put an end to the "author's rule" which was in force till then. In fact, on the basis of the Code of Conduct, the right of access concerned only the documents held by the institutions and issued by them. If the document came from a third person, the author's rule was applied. When such a document was to be dealt with, the institution was not authorized to disclose the document asked for without the author's authorization. EC Regulation 1049/2001 abandons the author's rule as accessibility is henceforth a right, once a document has been issued and is in possession of an institution, including those issued by third parties, subject to some reservations which we shall examine later.

The regulation gives to Article 3, paragraph (a), a very large definition of the notion of "document". Owing to this, any information kept in any form whatsoever constitutes a document according to the regulation. This refers to documents written on paper, stored in electronic form, audio, video or audio-visual recordings. The regulation is nevertheless silent as to the conditions in which a document can be said to be "held" by an institution. This question is not an ordinary one in the sense that it is raised in every institution in different terms, as the said institutions are not composed of the same categories of persons (elected representatives, civil servants, delegations…). It is therefore in the internal rules of each of them that we ought to search for the nature of "documents".

As regards Parliament, this notion covers those documents that are issued or received by the members holding an elected office and by its bodies, commissions and delegations as well as its general secretariat. For the Council, there is no definition. It is the same for the Commission but it is believed that any document held by the President, Vice-President or a member of the Commission is considered to be the "Commission's document", just as all documents held by one of its services become Commission documents. Another element is also not very clear. In fact, the drafting of the regulatory text does not lay down any formal criteria with respect to the document itself.

The text does not contain any indication as to the more or less official nature of a document. It is obvious that the value of the document's content and the prejudice caused by its disclosure can vary according to the degree of completion, the presence of signatures etc.

By virtue of the application of case law of the Court of First Instance and the Court of Justice of the European Communities[19], the regulation stipulates that when only part of a document is concerned by one of the exceptions to the right of access, the other parts can be made available (Article 4§6). The practice of partial access allows for a great transparency vis-à-vis of the public, while protecting some interests that may be compromised by a total disclosure. It is clear that the combination of a very large definition of "document" with a partial right of access to documents reduces the gap that exists between "document" and "data"[20].

(c) Limits to Right of Access

The text explicitly recognizes limits on rights of access. These limits may be absolute, and in this case, the institution appealed to is supposed to refuse access to the documents asked for. Limits may be quite relative, on the other hand. In this case, access to documents is possible. But then a balance has to be found between interests to be protected and the rights of the applicant.

(i) Absolute Limits

There are two absolute limits on the right of access. The first concerns the protection of public interests and the second protection of private life. They are based on Article 4§1 a) and b) of Regulation No. 1049/2001 and forbid disclosure of documents. The judges interpret it strictly: "The exceptions set out in Article 4(1) of Regulation No. 1049/2001 are framed in mandatory terms and it follows that the institutions are obliged to refuse access to documents falling under any one of those mandatory exceptions once the relevant circumstances are shown to exist"[21].

The limits prevail over the right of access because the overriding interests they protect cannot be cancelled by another law. These restrictions concern many domains. The protection of public security covers at the same time internal and external security, situations involving fight against criminal activities and the protection of defence and military affairs. The protection of international relations is also covered by the provision of the regulation. Nevertheless the documents concerned by this exception are not all affected in the same manner. In the case of the Council, refusal concerns exchanges with third countries or international organizations in the field of external policy and security. In the case of the Commission, it is necessary to protect negotiations with third countries within the framework of the World Trade Organization. This exception is often nuanced by the possibility of partial access to information contained in the documents.

The second absolute limit is contained in Article 4§1 b) which stipulates that "The institutions shall refuse access to a document where disclosure would undermine the protection of privacy and the integrity of the individual, in particular in accordance with Community legislation regarding the protection of personal data". The regulation refers to Community legislation in the matter[22]. Generally, every request for access to documents relating to personal data is countered with the exception laid down in regulation 1049/2001 and the reference to Regulation 45/2001. For documents or for parts of the documents to be made available, it is necessary that the conditions foreseen in Regulation (EC) 45/2001 be met. However the regulation brings a nuance to these exceptions by introducing the notion of public interest, which is difficult to reconcile with the interests to be protected.

This "exception to exceptions" is applicable only when two conditions are met: There is a public interest in disclosing the information contained in the document and this interest prevails over the interest to be protected. There is no precise definition of public interest and it is difficult to fix the criteria enabling us to ascertain it. "The real problem is to determine whether the interest in disclosure is such that it justifies disregarding the harm that would thus be caused to interests protected by the Regulation"[23]. There are no established rules in the matter. Each case is specific and it is up to each institution to evaluate the prejudice and assess the interest in disclosure.

(ii) Relative Limits

Other restrictions can interfere in the access to documents but their scope is not so significant. The refusal of access can be surmounted by invoking an "overriding public interest" which justifies the disclosure. The regulatory text abandons the mandatory nature of exceptions fixed by the Code of Conduct and weighs the interests at stake before refusing access. Many cases can thus be envisaged.

Article 4§2, paragraph 1 of the regulation lays down: "The institutions shall refuse access to a document where disclosure would undermine the protection of the commercial interests of a natural or legal person". This exception can, however, be overridden, if an overriding public interest justifies it. Such documents may contain confidential information about the companies concerned with regard to their business relations. But it is possible to envisage that a part of the documents might be disclosed in so far as public interest requires it.

The regulation also protects judicial procedures and legal opinions. Legal opinions enjoy a particular status in the Community order. Case law has made the exception to right of access an absolute exception as regards legal opinions. It endorsed the stand according to which such documents constitute legal opinions coming from the Community's legal services whose disclosure might harm public interest. But the regulation's text invokes an "overriding public interest" which can hereafter justify the disclosure of this opinion. The Community's lawmaker has thus set aside the reasoning which prevailed till then. In order to ensure transparency and guarantee citizens' real access to documents, the institutions, having regard to particular circumstances, must weigh the interests at stake even in cases where the documents are confidential.

Implementation of the Regulation

The Commission published on 30 January 2004 a report on the implementation of the Regulation as laid down in Article 17 of Regulation 1049/2001. This report shows that this text represents a considerable advance in matters of transparency and constitutes a major document in the policy of information to the public. Besides, the regulation has introduced a certain number of innovations which have enlarged the right of access. Thus, the text contains provisions relating to "active" information, availability of public registers and direct access to documents via electronic media. The regulation also foresees a form of interaction with the legislation of member states on access to information.

(a) Direct Access to Documents: An Innovation

Article 11 of the regulation stipulates: "To make citizens' rights under this Regulation effective each institution shall provide public access to a register of documents. Access to the register should be provided in electronic form."[24]. These registers are meant to allow citizens to identity documents likely to interest them. The fact that they are mentioned in the register does not render them automatically available for the public. The regulation does not specify the type of documents which ought to be contained in the register. There is no obligation for the institutions to make their register cover the whole set of documents available with them. Given the large definition accorded to the notion of document, it would be impossible for the registers to list all the documents produced or received by the institutions. Each document is referenced and the documents directly accessible can be displayed by a hypertextual link. The regime of exceptions also affects the registers. No "sensitive" document in the sense of Article 9 of the regulation shall be recorded in the register.

Each institution has defined the documentary purview of its register. The coverage of Parliament's register is quite large. Parliamentary works are found there as well as letters received by Parliament. This body is getting larger and larger. The Council has planned to extend access to documents connected with the Council's work and submitted to one of its bodies. The Commission has in its possession a large collection of documents. It has had to make a choice about the documents to be covered by the register. It has chosen to record documents connected with the legislative and regulatory activity of the institution. Thus, we can find minutes of the Commission meetings, documents belonging to the COM, S and SEC series[25]. The register has been completed by documents relating to committees helping the Commission in the exercise of its executive powers (comitology register). For an improved readability, all the instruments are gathered under one gateway.

In order to guarantee the largest dissemination of information, the documents contained in the register must be made available to the public. Besides, Article 12 of the regulation specifies that the documents must be made available for "direct access" in electronic or other forms. Today a significant portion of the documents of the three institutions recorded in the registers is accessible in full text form. In 2004, more than half of the documents appearing in the Parliament and Council's registers were directly accessible. The Commission for its part uses links towards the EUR LEX and Publications Office sites. Other data are also made available for citizens in the specific sites of each of these institutions.

(b) The Regulation and National Legislations

Regulation 1049/2001 deals only with public access to the documents of these three institutions. Its purpose is not to modify member states' national legislation on access to documents and information[26]. A legal basis in view of harmonizing national legislations in this area does not yet exist. Nevertheless, connections and interactions exist between the regulation and national legislations.

Article 4§5 foresees a particular regime for documents issued by member states. By virtue of this provision which transposes Declaration No. 35 of the Treaty of Amsterdam, a member state can demand an institution not to disclose a document issued by it without its prior consent. The wording of this article of the regulation does not specify in what way the institutions are supposed to abide by the negative opinion that would have been expressed by a member state with regard to the disclosure of a document issued by it. The member states have, with regard to third parties, a rather privileged position which is due to the fact that the regulation does not affect national legislation in matters of access to documents. EU institutions cannot afford to take a decision against a decision made by a member state in compliance with its national legislation.

The connection with the legislation of member states arises also in cases where it is the member state which is presented with a request for access to a Community document. In this case, the member state can disclose the documents by virtue of the provisions of its own legislation. However, Article 5 of the regulation lays down for the sake of coherence, that the original institution be consulted. The refusal by the institution must be based not on the regulation but on the concerned national legislation.

The purpose of Regulation 1049/2001 is to render the workings of the institutions more transparent and thus bring the institutions closer to the citizens. Transparency is not an objective in itself but an important element in the democratic process. The implementation of the regulation was a milestone in the development of a policy of transparency at the level of the European Union. Experience tends to confirm that the regulation does not bring an answer to all the needs and that certain grey areas do subsist. That is the reason why it appeared necessary and opportune to review and extend the right of access to information within the framework of EU's policy of openness and transparency.

II. EUROPEAN TRANSPARENCY INITIATIVE: TOWARDS THE REVISION OF EC REGULATION 1049/2001

In the course of the past fifteen years, the institutions of the European Union have gradually opened up to the public. The regulation applicable since 3 December 2001 has enabled the EU to open a large number of documents held by its institutions to the public. In January 2004, the Commission, in a report on the implementation of the regulation came up with the first evaluation of the practical functioning of the regime of public access to documents made possible by the European Union[27]. It concluded that the regulation had worked remarkably well and allowed the public to consult a considerable volume of documents not published till then. The Commission had then thought of bringing some improvements without amending the legislation as such.

Three years have elapsed since this evaluation. The lessons to be learnt from the experience acquired by the institutions in the implementation of the regulation are rich. It now seems necessary to integrate these contributions in a new text in order to guarantee the citizens of the European Union as well as its economic players the legal security to which they are entitled and provide the institutions specific indications which will be useful in processing the requests for access. It is in this context that the Commission launched in November 2005 the "European Transparency Initiative" [28] which led to the publication in May 2006 of a Green Paper[29]. It is part of a series of measures intended to promote "better governance" of the European institutions. The Commission has made transparency one of the priorities of its political strategy. The revision of EC Regulation 1049/2001 is one of these objectives. The European Parliament continued the trend by adopting on 4 April 2006 a resolution in which it asked the Commission to present proposals for amending the regulation[30].

Finally, with a view to complying with the requirements of a modern society, the European Commission adopted on 18 April 2007, a Green Paper on public access to information[31]. This adoption marked the beginning of a large public consultation that everybody was waiting for and which aimed at evaluating possible modifications to be brought to Regulation No. 1049/2001 on public access to documents.

(A) Commission Green Paper: Act I of Revision

The Green Paper comprises two parts which formed the basis of public debate.

(a) Review

The Green Paper shows that the evaluation is positive. The successive reports published by the Commission throw light on the fact that there is a constant increase in the requests for access as well as a satisfactory functioning of the provisions of the regulation. Experience seems to confirm that documents of institutions are more and more open to the public. It is to be observed that most of the requests come from specialists in European business such as economic players, law firms, NGOs and the academic world.

The Green Paper highlights two major legal problems. The first is the difficult compromise to be made between public access to documents and protection of personal data. Secondly, the combined application of the regulation and the Arhus Convention on access to information, public participation in decision-making and access to justice in matters of environment and Regulation 1049/2001. With reference to reconciling the right of access with the right to protection of personal data, the Green Paper notes that both the rights are enshrined in the EC Treaty (Articles 255 and 286) and that their implementation has been made possible by two regulations—EC Regulation 45/2001 and EC Regulation 1049/2001. It is obvious that these rights overlap because the request for information pertains to the data of a natural person. The European Data Protection Supervisor has dealt with this question and provided practical information on this point. According to him a proper processing of requests for documents on personal data is an important aspect of "good governance". It falls to the European Union institutions to proceed with a concrete and individual scrutiny in each case, by correlating the principles of right to information and proportionality[32].

Moreover, the question of implementing EC Regulation 1367/2006 on the enforcement of the Arhus Convention (establishing a citizen's right to information within the framework of Europe's environmental policy)[33] in Community institutions and bodies, and its reconciliation with EC Regulation 1049/2001 generated some difficulties in so far as the respective scopes of these texts are different. Indeed EC regulation 1049/2001 fixes a general regime for access to documents and is based on Article 255 of the EC Treaty and is applicable only to Parliament, Council and Commission and by extension to Community agencies. EC Regulation 1367/2006 is applicable to all the institutions and all the bodies of the Community. Similarly, the exceptions made to right of access in the two texts are not identical. Concrete solutions must be quickly found to fix these problems.

(b) Perspectives for Improvement

The second part of the Green Paper enumerates possible options for improving the transparency of rules of access. Recent experience acquired during the implementation of the regulation as well as recent developments have helped identify ways to modify rules of public access to documents.

Active Dissemination Policy

In this regard, the Commission wants to promote a more active dissemination of documents, especially public registers. The registers of the three institutions contain numerous documents drafted or exchanged within the framework of the legislative process, a good number of which are available in their full text form. The Commission wants to revise the definition of "legislative documents" mentioned in the regulation's Article 12 which does not seem to be sufficiently specific. The purpose is double, to simultaneously extend the number of documents directly and fully available for the public, but also facilitate their identification in the institutional websites[34].

Indeed, the institutions disseminate a large quantity of data via these websites but the Commission would like the institutions to develop a more systematic policy of direct access by using more user-friendly means. The Commission also wants to improve the integration of rules of access to environmental data in the general framework of access rules. We have seen how these two regimes differ with respect to certain points. In order to set up a unique regime, the EC regulation 1049/2001 has to be reviewed by modifying certain elements (taking into consideration of general interest while enforcing rules of exception, disclosure of environmental data even when the documents are covered by the exception foreseen in Article 4, paragraph 1).

Weighing of Interests

Among the improvements to be brought to the regulation, the Commission is faced with the difficulty of finding a balance between the public's right to be informed and the safeguarding of public or private interests protected by the regulation. Everything resides in finding a good compromise. The problem arises with regard not only to processing requests for access to documents containing personal data as pointed out earlier, but also to commercial or economic interests. Indeed, the EC treaty establishes a balance between the principle of transparency set forth in Article 255 and the obligation for professional secrecy imposed by Article 287 which concerns data relating to companies and their business relations. For the Commission which holds data provided or obtained from private parties within the framework of investigations on understandings, concentrations etc., such a balance is essential. The protection of this information is crucial within the framework of investigation procedures.

As it is, the regulation does not guarantee this legal security either to the private players or the institutions. Relying on a judicial decision rendered on 30 May 2006[35] which enumerated a certain number of criteria that help define the type of data falling within the purview of professional secrecy, the Commission would like to lay down that "no access can be granted to documents containing information, known to a limited number of persons, the disclosure of which is liable to cause serious harm to legitimate interests of the person who has provided it or to third parties"[36]. These criteria have to be nevertheless clarified in order to take into account different limits which weigh on this type of information.

The Notion of Document

The current definition of document as a "document held by the institution" derives from the combination of the notion of document that figures in Article 3(a) of the regulation:

> 'document' shall mean any content whatever its medium (written on paper or stored in electronic form or as a sound, visual or audiovisual recording) concerning a matter relating to the policies, activities and decisions falling within the institution's sphere of responsibility.

The scope is defined in Article 1, Paragraph 3.

> This Regulation shall apply to all documents held by an institution, that is to say, documents drawn up or received by it and in its possession, in all areas of activity of the European Union.

This definition is not satisfactory in the sense that certain aspects need to be clarified. The Commission has referred to the connection between the definition of "document held by an institution" and the institution's rules of data management, especially of data recording. The other objection concerns the data bases which handle an important in and outflow of documents. The Commission would like to include the content of the data bases in the notion of document, considering the data bases as an electronic library and providing for some specific and restricted data to be extracted from the data bases and considered as "documents" as defined in the regulation. All these improvements had been proposed for discussion on a website on transparency[37] that was opened by the Commission on the internet. The public was invited to comment on the regime of access to documents and react to proposed options.

(B) Act II: Outcome of the Public Consultation, Case Law and Proposal for a New Regulation

Pursuing its policy of transparency, the Commission submitted to the citizens of the European Union, its proposals to improve access to documents and thus guarantee a better governance of its institutions. The Commission sought the opinion of EU citizens, notably organizations belonging to the civil society, economic players, public authorities and all organizations interested in European affairs. It is on the basis of these responses that the Commission established the proposal for redrafting EC Regulation 1049/2001.

Outcome of the Public Consultation

On 16 January 2008, the Commission published the outcome of the public consultation[38] that was launched after the publication of the Green Paper. The Commission received a total of eighty-one responses to its Green paper; thirty came from the civil society, twenty-five from public authorities, fourteen from the world of economics and twelve from the citizens of the European Union. The responses helped identify the elements for revision.

Concerning the Active Dissemination Policy

A vast majority of responses from the civil society were in favour of a more active policy with regard to the disclosure of information. The public authorities were also unanimous in this regard. According to them, direct access to documents could have an impact on the legislative process. Citizens, for their part, were more nuanced; some of them were happy with the increased access to information, while some had expressed doubts about the effects of such a policy.

On the contrary, all the responses were unanimous with regard to the difficulty in finding information on the registers or institutional websites. For half of the respondents, the coverage of these registers and data bases is insufficient. In all the cases, the responses insisted on the necessity to set up one single gateway for access to documents in order to direct the search for information more easily. The registers and sites ought to also contain more documents that could be directly accessed and in many languages.

With reference to access to environmental data, the representatives of civil society and two thirds of public authorities were in favour of aligning EC Regulation 1049/2001 with the provisions contained in the Arhus Convention on access to information. However, some representatives of the economic world and some States (Czech Republic, Denmark, and France) were not favourable towards a common regime of access. For some, the provisions of the Arhus Convention ought to be considered as "*lex specialis*" with respect to the general regime[39].

Weighing of Interests

The responses have put forward the idea that data protection should not withhold the name of individuals acting within an official framework or for a European organization. The refusal to disclose personal data should be weighed against the material consequence for the concerned individual. However, economic players asked for an adequate protection of personal data to be provided in certain areas because employees who have access to sensitive information may fall a prey to criminal acts, if their name is revealed.

It is also necessary to protect commercial interests and professional secrecy. Economic actors are asking for an improved protection of confidentiality in business dealings especially with regard to intellectual property and competition. Representatives of civil society would like to see more information disclosed about companies which could help limit cases of bad corporate governance (corruption, insider dealings). For many, public interest must prevail over private interests (companies and others).

The Notion of Documents

This issue was raised essentially with regard to information included in the electronic data bases. The idea was to be able to retrieve some elements from them. The representatives of the civil society (NGOs, journalists) as well as public authorities clearly think that the content of the data bases must fall within the purview of the regulation's scope. Certain organizations were keen on getting the right of access to data rather than the documents themselves, whatever may be the method or place where such data are stored. Public authorities suggested the establishment of a general obligation to take the notion of transparency into account while designing and managing data bases. Indeed, the current standards used for retrieving information from the data bases are not suitable and this can create restriction for access to documents.

In most of the responses coming from NGOs and some public authorities, there was a question of extending the regulation to documents held by all the institutions and bodies of the European Union. But they observed that there is currently no legal basis in the Treaty for this extension. The Treaty of Lisbon contains some provisions to solve this problem but one needs to wait for its ratification. The general tendency on this issue is to maintain the notion of "document" as it is. But clarification has to be made regarding data bases. At the end of this public consultation, the Commission had some concrete elements to take into account in order to envisage a profound revision of EC regulation 1049/2001 to which the input of case law must be added.

Input of Case Law

In a series of rulings, the Court of First Instance and the Court of Justice determined some issues relating to the enforcement of EC regulation 1049/2001. In a decision given on 8 November 2007[40], the Court of First Instance examined the connection between EC Regulation 1049/2001 and EC regulation 45/2001 on the protection of personal data. The judge emphasized the necessity to clarify the articulation between EC Regulation 1049/2001 and the protection of personal data by balancing the two texts. One has to bear in mind that "they have different objectives"[41]. The Court held that "the right to the protection of personal data may constitute one of the aspects of the right to respect for private life [...] does not mean that all personal data necessarily fall within the concept of 'private life' [...] A fortiori, not all personal data are by their nature capable of undermining the private life of the person concerned"[42]. The legal principle found in this case favours the obligation for transparency. In order to avail the legal exception to the right to information, it is necessary to ensure that the disclosure of information will seriously undermine the private life of the person concerned. The sole invocation of this private life is not enough to curtail the right to access documents[43].

On 18 December 2007[44], the Court of Justice annulled a ruling of the Court of First Instance dated 30 November 2004 in a case dealing with the rights of member states to refuse disclosure of documents issued by them by

Community institutions. The Court confirmed that the requests for access to documents held by national authorities are governed by national rules applicable to these authorities. The judge held that Regulation 1049/2001 "did not aim to establish a division between two powers, one national and the other of the Community, with different purposes" [...] and that it "creates a decision-making procedure the sole object of which is to determine whether access to a document should be refused under one of the substantive exceptions listed in Article 4(1) to (3) of the regulation, a decision-making procedure in which both the Community institution and the Member State concerned play a part" [45]. This legal decision finds the principle that the regime of access to documents cannot vary according to circumstances and that the member states should not undermine its proper enforcement. The revision of the regulation might offer the occasion to clarify this point.

In a recent ruling, the Court of First Instance considered that the pleadings presented before the Community's courts were covered by the exception intended to protect legal proceedings[46]. However, it established a fundamental distinction by weighing the consequences that the disclosure might entail. It reasons differently depending upon whether the litigation is pending or the case is under consideration: "since pleadings to which access has been requested relate have not yet reached the hearing stage, the refusal to disclose those pleadings must be considered to cover all aspects of the information contained therein. On the other hand, after the hearing has been held, the Commission is under an obligation to carry out a concrete assessment of each document requested in order to ascertain, having regard to the specific content of that document, whether it may be disclosed or whether its disclosure would undermine the court proceedings to which it relates"[47].

The challenges posed by transparency are considerable. The development of case law has played and will continue to play an important role in guaranteeing the right to access. Recent legal decisions show that even if Regulation 1049/2001 has more or less worked in a satisfying manner, it needs to be revised in order to make the citizens benefit from it and ensure a better administration of the Union.

Proposal for Redrafting the Regulation

Relying on the outcome of the public consultation and the proposals put forward by Parliament in its resolution of 4 April 2006, the Commission proposed modifications concerning several points[48].

Purpose and Beneficiaries

The drafting of Article 1(a) has been modified in such a way as to specify that the purpose of the regulation is to grant public access to documents. This wording is thus consistent with the legal base and the case law established by the Court of First Instance[49]. The beneficiaries of the regulation have also been modified. Reference is no longer made to the applicant's nationality or country of residence. The text has thus become compatible with EC Regulation 1367/2006.

Scope and the Notion of Document

The scope remains unchanged. It applies to "all documents held by an institution concerning a matter relating to the policies, activities and decisions falling within its sphere of responsibility". This element has, more over, been withdrawn from the definition of the notion of "document" for it relates more to the scope than to the definition of document.

A new paragraph has been added to Article 2, which clarifies the fact that documents presented before the Courts by other parties than the institutions do not fall within the scope of the Regulation. The Court of Justice is not affected by the right of access to documents referred to in Article 255. The Lisbon Treaty is expected to extend the right of access to the Court but only with regard to documents relating to its administrative activities. This new paragraph also contains provisions concerning the right of access to documents relating to investigations. It is specified that "documents forming part of the administrative file of an investigation or of proceedings concerning an act of individual scope shall not be accessible to the public until the investigation has been closed or the act has become definitive". During this investigation phase, only the specific rules in this field will apply. In fact, rules governing procedures in matters of competition and trade barriers etc contain provisions on the right of specific access granted to the interested parties. If the right of access was to be enlarged to cover this type of procedures, one would be compromising the rules.

The draft proposal for a new regulation has not modified the notion of "document" which has been deliberately left large. Nevertheless, the draft proposal stipulates that a "document" only exists "if it has been transmitted to its recipients or circulated within the institution or has been otherwise registered". Besides, as it had been mentioned during the public consultation, the definition of document must also cover data contained in the data bases if they could be extracted in readable form.

Exceptions

The exception aimed at protecting environment included in Article 6, paragraph 2 of EC Regulation 1367/2006 has been added to Article 4§1 of EC Regulation 1049/2001 to align it with the provisions of the Arhus

Convention. Similarly, paragraph 4 states that "an overriding public interest in disclosure shall be deemed to exist where the information requested relates to emissions into the environment".

The protection of intellectual property rights appears as a clear exception. The draft proposal also adds arbitration procedures and dispute settlement to the notion of "legal protection". Another new exception has been added to the text. It aims at protecting procedures for selecting the staff and contracting parties. The proper functioning of boards of examiners for competitive examinations and evaluation committees should thus be protected. Paragraph 3 of Article 4 has been reorganized without modifying its ultimate content.

With reference to personal data, the proposal contained in Article 4, paragraph 1 b) of EC Regulation 1049/2001 has been shifted, in the new text, to the new Article 4, redrafted paragraph 5 with a view to clarifying the connection between EC Regulation 1049/2001 and EC Regulation 45/2001.

"Names, titles and functions of public office holders, civil servants and interest representatives in relation with their professional activities shall be disclosed unless, given the particular circumstances, disclosure would adversely affect the persons concerned. Other personal data shall be disclosed in accordance with the conditions regarding lawful processing of such data laid down in EC legislation on the protection of individuals with regard to the processing of personal data"[50].

Documents Issued by a Member State

The new Article 5§2 establishes the procedures to be followed in case of requests for access to documents issued by a member state. The regulation stipulates that the member state must be consulted. "The institution holding the document shall disclose it unless the Member State gives reasons for withholding it, based on the exceptions referred to in Article 4 or on specific provisions in its own legislation preventing disclosure of the document concerned". This new provision thus takes into account the ruling given by the Court of Justice on 18 November 2007[51].

Active Dissemination

This is an important element in the transparency policy we have previously referred to. The new text does not modify the provision contained in the regulation. It has simply been reformulated to authorize direct access to documents which form part of the procedures intended to adopt legislative acts of the European Union or generally enforceable non-legislative acts.

These documents must be rendered public by the institutions from the very beginning. The text, however, specifies that this disclosure will not be possible, if an exception to the right of access is applicable. It falls to the institutions to define in their internal rules the other categories of documents directly accessible to the public.

Conclusion

Within the framework of the co-decision procedure, this new draft proposal will be jointly examined by the European Parliament and Council. The Parliament has already got hold of the file and started hearings on 2 June 2008[52]. These hearings constitute an ideal opportunity for assessing the positive and negative aspects of the legal framework of EC Regulation 1049/2001 in the light of the Commission's newly revised draft. In this perspective, particular attention has to be paid to provisions on transparency laid down by the Lisbon Treaty.

The work headed by the EU ombudsman and the European Data Protection Supervisor as well as exchange of ideas with NGOs, lawyers and academics will provide precious expert opinions on the way in which the regime of access to documents can be improved. In the course of these discussions, Parliament hopes find the necessary inspiration for the revision of this legislation.

The transparency policy preoccupies European Union institutions more than ever. In her Press Release dated 30 April 2008, the Vice-president of the European Commission and the Commissioner for Communication Strategy, Mrs Wallström, had this to say about the publication of the new text:

> "Our objective is increased transparency, increased access and increased outreach and understanding. This is fundamental in any democratic system: the citizen's right to know. Access to documents is an essential tool for democracy and now we want to improve it".

More than ever, these words take on a real significance in the European society. It is a big opportunity for the European Union institutions to reconstruct the bond with the citizens that legitimizes the policies and legislation which affect their daily life but which appear to be very often opaque from their point of view. The redrafting of EC Regulation 1049/2001 for the sake of enhanced transparency in the EU institutions will help perhaps eradicate the growing tendency for Euroscepticism.

APPENDIX
WEBSITES OF EU INSTITUTIONS

The Institutions' Internal Documents

***Registers of documents* proposed by European institutions:**
Designed as instruments of assistance for research, they itemise different categories of documents issued or conceived by European institutions

European Parliament Register

- http://www.europarl.europa.eu/RegWeb/application/registre/guideAccessDoc.faces

Council of the European Union Register

- http://www.consilium.europa.eu/cms3_applications/showPage.asp?lang=en&id=549&mode=g&name=

European Commission Register

- http://ec.europa.eu/transparency/regdoc/registre.cfm?CL=en

Register of comitology

- http://ec.europa.eu/transparency/regcomitology/registre.cfm?CL=en

Register of Experts

- http://ec.europa.eu/transparency/regexpert/index.cfm
  Information on lobbies (under construction)

Codecision Procedure

Information on the legistative process of codecision (article 251 EC Treaty) as well as the respective role of and interaction among the three institutions (Council, European Parliament and Commission) http://ec.europa.eu/codecision/index_en.htm

EU Bulletins

Mainly a chronicle of the activities of the Commission as well as other Community institutions and bodies—http://europa.eu/bulletin/en/welcome.htm

Historical Archives

Archives of the European Union: They are managed by the European

University Institute of Florence—http://www.iue.it/ECArchives/EN/Index.shtml

Archives of the European Commission—http://ec.europa.eu/historical_archives/index_en.htm

Data base on Law and Legislative Process

EUR-Lex: Gateway to the European Union—http://eur-lex.europa.eu/en/index.htm

Accessible Areas

- Treaties
- International conventions
- Legislation in force
- Jurisprudence
- Parliamentary issues
- Preparatory work

Pre-Lex: data base on inter-institutional processes which enables us to follow the several stages of the decision making process between the Commission and other institutions. http://ec.europa.eu/prelex/apcnet.cfm?CL=en

Gives Information on

- The stages of the adoption process of a legislative act
- Decisions taken in this framework by each institution
- Names of persons concerned (Commissioners, rapporteurs…)
- Reference documents

ŒIL: Legislative observatory of the European Parliament. This base analyses and follows the interinstitutional decision making process of the European Union, the role of the Parliament in the elaboration of the European legislation and the activities of the institutions invovled in the legislative process. http://www.europarl.europa.eu/oeil/index.jsp?language=en

- Allows you to follow the evolution and progress of a process
- Follow up and be aware of the stage of advancement
- Work on forecast

CURIA: Data base on the Court of Justice of the European Communities. http://curia.europa.eu/en/transitpage.htm

- Allows you to search for court rulings, rulings of the Court of First instance and the civil service tribunal

- Allows you to access the Court's reports and statistics

DEC.NAT: Data Base of the jurisdictions of member states in the field of community law—http://www.juradmin.eu/fr/jurisprudence/jurisprudence_fr.lasso

N-Lex: Experminental site giving access to the sources of domestic law of the member states of the European Union. http://eur-lex.europa.eu/n-lex//pays.html?lang=en

SCADPLUS: Website that compiles the digests of European legislation on community policies. http://europa.eu/scadplus/

TED (Tender Electronic Daily): Supplement of the Official Journal of the European Union devoted to public procurement.http://ted.europa.eu/

SIMAP: Gateway to public procurement in the European Union—http://simap.europa.eu/index_en.html

Civil Society (Lobbies): Relations between Civil Society, lobbies and European Union

The European Commission

http://ec.europa.eu/civil_society/apgen_en.htm

The European Parliament

http://www.europarl.europa.eu/parliament/expert/lobbyAlphaOrderByOrg.do?language=EN

Others Documents

EU BOOKSHOP: EU Bookshop is an online service giving access to publications from the EU institutions, agencies and other bodies. In addition to the online bookshop, this service offers an online catalogue and archive of all EU publications—http://bookshop.europa.eu/eGetRecords?Template=en_index&indLang=EN

Office for Official Publications of the European Communities

European Union's official publishing house (publication of the official journal and various other titles related to EU activities and policies)—http://publications.europa.eu/index_en.htm

Catalogue of the Commission's main library (ECLAS)—http://ec.europa.eu/eclas/F

Translated from French by
Geetha Ganapathy-Doré

NOTES AND REFERENCES

1. Sweden was then witnessing a serious crisis of confidence among the population with regard to its leaders. The crisis worsened and ended with the victory of the Party of Bonnets (champions of transparency) over the Party of Hats in Parliament.
2. I. Calberg, «L'opaque transparence de l'Union européenne», *Le Monde diplomatique*, June 1997, p.32.
3. DOC/92/6 dated 6th October 1992. These elements are recorded in Appendix I: «A Community close to its citizens».
4. Edinburgh Council, 12 December 1992, Appendix 3.
5. COM (1993) 1991 final version dated 5th May 1993, *OJEU*, C 156, p. 5 et COM (1993) 258 final version dated 2nd June 1993, *OJEU*, 1993 C 166, p. 4.
6. Code of Conduct 93/730/EC dated 6th December 1993 *OJEU*, L 340 dated 31st December 1993, p. 43.
7. Decision 93/662/EC dated 6th December 1993, *OJEU*, L 340 dated 31st December 1993.
8. Decision 93/731/EC dated 20th December 1993, *OJEU*, L 340 dated 31st December 1993.
9. Decision 94/90/ESCC, Euratom, *OJEU*, L 46 dated 18th February 1994, p.58.
10. Th. Blanchet, «Transparence et qualité de législation», RTDE, 1997, No. 4, pp. 207-220.
11. CJEC, 18th December 2007, Sweden v Commission, C-64/05, Maduro's conclusions, para 40.
12. J.P. de la Rica, «Commentaire de l'article 255 du Traité d'Amsterdam» in Constantinesco (V.), Gautier (Y.), SIMON (D.), *Traité d'Amsterdam et de Nice. Commentaire article par article*, Economica, 2007. For a quite different point of view see P. Leger, *Union européenne, commentaire article par article,* Dalloz/ Bruylant, 2000.
13. G. Druesne, «Le régime communautaire d'accès aux documents», in *Transparence et secret*, Colloquium for the 25th anniversary of the Law of 17th July 1978 on Access to Administrative Documents, La documentation française, 2004, pp.175-181.
14. COM (2000) 30, *OJEU*, C 177 E, p. 70.
15. The Århus Convention deals with access to information, public participation and access to justice in the field of environment. It was signed on 25th June 1998.
16. Council Decision dated 29th November 2001 (2001/840) modifying internal rules; Appendix III of internal regulations, Article 1; Commission Decision dated 5th December 2001 (2001/937); Appendix II of internal rules, Article 1, Paragraph 2.
17. Internal rules of the European Parliament, Title III, Article 97.
18. Council Decision 2005/370 EC dated 17th February 2005 finally approved this

Convention. Its implementation in all the institutions of the Union was done thanks to Parliament's and Council's EC regulation no. 1367/2006 dated 6th September 2006, concerning the applicability to European Union institutions and bodies of the provisions of the Arhus Convention on access to information, public participation and access to justice in the field of environment *OJEU*, L 264 dated 25th September 2006, pp. 13-19.

19. T-14/98 *Hautala v Council*, Rec. 1999, II-02489 et C-353/99 *Council v Hautala*, Rec. 2001, I-09565.
20. M. Maes, «L'accès public aux documents des institutions de la Communauté européenne: vers une révision du règlement (CE) 1049/2001», *Revue du Droit de l'Union européenne*, no. 2, 2007, p. 417.
21. Judgement of the Court of First Instance (Fourth Chamber), 25 April 2007, WWF European Policy Programme v Council of the European Union, T-264/04, para 44.
22. Regulation (EC) No. 45/2001 of the European Parliament and Council of 18 December 2000 on the protection of individuals with regard to the processing of personal data by Community institutions and bodies and on the free transmission of such data, *OJEU*, L8/1, 12 January 2001.
23. Report from the Commission on the implementation of the principles in EC Regulation No. 1049/2001 regarding public access to European Parliament, Council and Commission documents, COM (2004) dated 30th January 2004, p. 24.
24. Only the Council had a register on the internet before the entry into force of Regulation 1049/2001. Parliament and the Commission later made available their own registers.
25. http//europa.eu/documents/comm/index_en.htm

    COM documents: proposed legislation and other Commission communications to the Council and/or the other institutions, and their preparatory papers.

    C documents: legal acts adopted by the Commission in the exercise of its own or delegated powers.

    SEC documents: internal documents associated with the decision-making process and the general operation of Commission departments.
26. EC Regulation 1049/2001, Consideration 15.
27. Report from the Commission on the implementation of the principles in EC Regulation No. 1049/2001 regarding public access to European Parliament, Council and Commission documents, COM (2004) 45 dated 30th January 2004.
28. SEC (2005) 1300 et SEC (2005) 1301.
29. COM (2006) 194 final dated 3d May 2006, Green Paper "European Transparency Initiative".
30. P. 6_A (2006) 052.
31. Public Access to Documents held by institutions of the European Community. A Review, COM (2007) 185 final dated 18th April 2007, p. 22.

32. EDPS. *European Data Protection Supervisor*, « Public Access to Documents and Data Protection", Paper Series, July 2005.
33. EC Regulation 1367/2006 dated 6th September 2006, *OJEU*, L 264 dated 25th September 2006, p. 13.
34. See the list of websites attached.
35. Case T-198/03, *Bank Austria Creditanstalt v Commission*, especially para 71.
36. Green Paper, p.16.
37. http:/ec.europa.eu/transparency/revision/index_en.htm
38. Report on the Outcome of the Public Consultation on the Review of Regulation (EC) n°1049/2001 regarding public access to European Parliament, Council and Commission documents, SEC(2008) 29/2 dated 16 January 2008. Document available only in English.
39. SEC (2008) 29/2 dated 16th January 2008, p. 4.
40. Case T-194/04, *The Bavarian Lager Co. Ltd v Commission*
41. Court of First Instance, 8 November 2007, *The Bavarian Lager Co. Ltd v Commission*, T-194/04, point 98.
42. *Op. cit.*, points 118 & 119.
43. H. Labayle, *L'accès du public aux documents de l'Union européenne. Etat du droit à l'instant de la révision du règlement 1049/2001*, Working Paper, European Parliament, Hearings of 2nd June 2008. This document could be retrieved at: http://www.europarl.europa.eu/document/activities/cont/200805/20080530ATT30435/20080530ATT30435EN.pdf
44. CJEC, 18 December 2007, *Sweden v Commission*, C-64/05.
45. CJEC, 18 December 2007, *Sweden v Commission*, C-64/05, para 93.
46. Case T-36/04, *Association de la presse internationale ASBL v Commission.*
47. *Op. cit.*, para 82.
48. COM (2008) 229 dated 30th April 2008, Draft Resolution of the Parliament and Council on public access to documents of European Parliament, Council and Commission (presented by the Commission).
49. Ruling of 6th July 2006, T–391/03 et T–70-/04, *Franchet & Byk v Commission*, Law Reports 2006, p. II-2023.
50. COM (2008) 229 dated 30th April 2008, p. 20.
51. Case C-64/05 Sweden v Commission and others. This decision annulled a ruling by the Court of First Instance dated 30th November 2004 in a case concerning the right of member states to oppose disclosure by Community institutions of documents issued by them.
52. For further information on the hearings and working papers, browse the European Parliament website. Commission for Civil Liberties, Justice and Home Affairs. http://www.europarl.europa.eu/activities/committees/hearingsCom.do;jsessionid=A8EC3715AEAC63F39DC3506D16A6580F.node1?body=LIBE&language=EN

BIBLIOGRAPHY

Banisar, D. "Overview of Access to Information. Legislations and Trends in EU Members States" Working paper, European Parliament Hearings, Commission for Civil Liberties, Justice and Home Affairs, 2 June 2008. Text retrievable at:
http://www.europarl.europa.eu/document/activities/cont/200805/20080529ATT30376/20080529ATT30376EN.pdf

Druesne. G. « Le régime communautaire d'accès aux documents » in *Transparence et secret »*, Colloquium for the 25th anniversary of the law of 17 July 1978 on access to documents, La documentation française, 2004, pp. 175-181.

De Leeuw, M. « Openness in the Legislative Process in the European Union », *European Law Review*, no 2, 2007, pp. 295-318.

Driessen, B. « The Council of the European Union and Access to Documents », *European Law Review*, no 5, 2005, pp. 675-696.

European Parliament, *Transparence et accès du public aux documents: quelques aspects relatives à l'e-transparence dans les institutions européennes et les Etats membres*, Direction générale politiques internes de l'Union, March 2008, EP 393.285.

Heloski, J. & Leino, P. « Darkness at the Break of Noon : The Case Law on Regulation n°1049/2001 on Access to Documents », *Common Market Law Review*, Volume 43, 2006, pp. 735-781.

Labayle, H. *L'accès du public aux documents de l'Union européenne. Etat du droit à l'instant de la révision du Règlement (CE) 1049/2001*, Working paper, European Parliament Hearings, Commission for Civil Liberties, Jusice and Home Affairs, Text retrievable at
http://www.europarl.europa.eu/document/activities/cont/200805/20080530ATT30435/20080530ATT30435EN.pdf

Maes, M. « L'accès du public aux documents des Institutions de la Communauté européenne: vers une revision du réglement (CE) 1049/2001. », *Revue du Droit de l'Union européenne*, no 2, 2007, pp. 411-431.

Meisse, E. « Modalités d'accès aux documents des institutions », *Europe*, no 10, 2006, pp. 15-16.

Pasquier, M. & Villeneuve, J-P. *Transparence et accès à l'information*, IHEAP, Working Paper, no 2, 2005.

4

It's Fun to Comply with the Foreign Corrupt Practices Act

CHARLES REIPLINGER

In the past thirty years, fight against bribery in international trade has become a unanimously accepted international value, legally transposed and implemented by a constantly increasing majority of states. It has caused major legal changes around the world in a short time, and such a movement deserves to be particularly focused upon, in order to show how quickly and significantly evolutions of the law can occur sometimes. Recent international anti-corruption rules cannot be properly understood without considering other political issues.

There is no doubt that corrupting public officials is unethical and bad. The very idea and its consequences go against our societies' fundamental values. Forbidding it effectively is obviously necessary. We can rejoice in the fact that corruption is being actively fought today, but also hope that it will be fought fairly, and regret the way this fight was first conceived by a single state, which managed to impose its vision and methods upon its partners. At the beginning only American companies involved in corruption scandals were concerned, following the Watergate scandal, enough to push Congress to pass, in December 1977, the Foreign Corrupt Practices Act ((FCPA).[1] One of its main provisions, making corruption of a foreign public official a crime, was to become and became an international rule, transposed in their own legal systems by many states today. In North and South America, in Europe, and soon in Asia and Africa, corrupting foreign public officials is and will have become a crime twice punishable, as "normal" bribery in the national space, in the country where it took place, but also as active foreign corruption in the country where the suspected company is registered. This goal which is in conformity with fundamental liberal values has been pursued, while economic competition has been getting ever stronger. The battle is not over, as there is still time for transition, during which international commitment to fight against bribery is being implemented with marked differences in practice.

Punishing Bribery of Foreign Public Officials, A National Concern

As a prelude, first a rumour spread in July 1970, according to which the American company ITT had offered the CIA one million dollars to put down a candidate for the Chilean presidency, Salvador Allende, who intended to nationalize the Chilean national phone company, partially owned by ITT[2]. The Senate Committee on Foreign Affairs heard about it and set up a Sub-Committee to investigate the rumor. It finally concluded that according to American laws, nothing could be held against ITT. But for the first time, public opinion and Congress became aware of the fact that respectable international companies, or so they seemed, could have unethical behaviour for achieving economic and political objectives abroad. Then and mostly due to the Watergate scandal, American federal authorities were able to find out that some U.S companies had not only illegally given money to the famous Committee for the Reelection of President Nixon, but also regularly paid bribes to foreign public officials, in South America, as well as in Europe and Asia, for business and/or political purposes. To such an extent that there was a "Business Watergate" so to speak, a series of scandals that constituted the prelude to the drawing up of the FCPA. More than a hundred companies decided to collaborate with the federal administration, confessing that they had, in the past, used bribery abroad; they, of course promised, to cease, but also to conform, in partnership with the federal authorities, to surveillance programmes, meant to prevent such behaviour[3]. Thus, the Securities and Exchange Commission (SEC) took stock of international bribery and the several forms in which it was practiced so as to conceive an efficient mechanism against it. On 12 May 1976, the Commission handed in a report[4] to the Senate Committee on Banking, Housing and Urban Affairs, which began the process leading to the adoption of the FCPA[5] in December 1977. The Commission told the Senate what it had discovered about illegal corporate payments, and requested the Senate to enact suitable legislation to prevent and punish those who involve in this illegality. In the late 1970's, Congress as well as the SEC had come to the same conclusion, it was necessary to pass new laws, specifically designed to fight international bribery. Considering the obvious fact that corruption is unethical, the US companies could not go against such legislation. On the contrary, during the Senate hearings, businessmen even came forward to say they wanted such a regulation to be passed, as it would allow them to efficiently resist corruption requests made by foreign officials themselves. According to former Gulf Oil Co., Chairman

Bob Dorsey, "If we could cite our law which says we just may not do it, we would be in a better position to resist these pressures and refuse those requests[6]».

The FCPA was finally adopted in late December 1977, as a complement to the Securities Exchange Act of 1934. It has since been modified by the International Anti-Bribery Act, conceived to adapt it to suit the needs of the OECD Convention of 1998. In between, Congress had not ceased to take care of both business ethics and competitiveness of the US companies. It passed the *Omnibus Trade and Competitiveness Act* in 1988, explicitly for that purpose, as competition in international trade was growing stronger. "Super 301", one of the main provisions of the bill, was intended to identify and eradicate all illegitimate obstacles to a free and fair market that US companies could encounter in their way abroad (This is how India, notably, next to Brazil, got to be blacklisted as a country where doing fair business was hardly possible, because of corruption. The purpose of such a ranking was not to ban countries from international trade—as was the case for Cuba or the former Communist countries, and Iran nowadays—but to negotiate in order to suppress the aforementioned obstacles, and make sure that these countries conform to international business standards). In the meantime, it also had appeared that other countries did not have such laws as the FCPA and that the US companies' international rivals found it to be an advantage, certainly not an inconvenience. This was what the US companies[7] believed, and it was not totally false.

The FCPA Goes International

At the start, the Carter administration informed US companies it would enforce the FCPA with indulgence[8], but such a policy certainly had its limits. Corrupting foreign public officials was now a criminal offence, and US companies could not be satisfied with a promise, as they now had to be very careful when doing business in foreign countries, where sometimes it was hard not to bribe, especially when foreign rivals were still more or less allowed to do so. It is one of the reasons why, in the late 1980's, the federal administration started to incite its international partners, that is to say, the rest of the world, to pass rules equivalent to the FCPA. It appeared to be an explicit answer to the complaints of International American companies, during the debates that led in 1988 to the *Omnibus Trade and Competitiveness Act*, designed to improve the competitiveness of American companies abroad: « "*Anti-bribery Provision—Negotiation of International Agreement House bill*". The House bill included the Congress guideline that the President should pursue the negotiation of an international agreement, "among the largest possible number of countries," to govern acts now prohibited under FCPA. Within one year of enactment of the trade bill, the President must submit to the Congress a report on the progress of the negotiations and those steps which should be taken in the event that the negotiations fail[9]».

Beyond US companies' competitiveness, we must remember that the United States is not a former colonial power, and that initially, illegal corporate payments denounced by the US companies were mostly imputed to European companies, using their old and privileged relations with some Asian and African countries to do business. Such a complaint is obviously fair, in the name of ethics as of interest, and can also be linked to remains of the Monroe doctrine, where the moral struggle against corruption joins the struggle against colonialism and the drive towards a free market, all of this in a truly liberal perspective. And at the same time, since the late 1960's, the United States has become the world's leading economy, now plainly globalized. It is reasonable to believe that effectively US companies did face unfair competition, in Asia and Africa, from corrupting European companies. France for example has kept strong bonds, economic and political, with its former colonies, especially in Africa[10]. This does not mean the French companies were the only ones suspected and targeted, but certainly they were and still are, not less than others, on fair grounds, as several judicial cases have shown[11]. Yet in October 2006, according to Transparency International, French companies (as also some Italian ones) were considered to be the most susceptible Western companies to commit the offence of bribery in international trade, such a suspicion being grounded on the significant French presence in Africa[12].

European companies, then the main rivals of American companies, were secondly targeted to make them comply with the FCPA. Not directly as a federal law, as the act itself was not meant to apply to foreign companies[13]. The Organization for Economic Cooperation and Development (OECD) appeared to be the best structure to take up the matter, as in the late 1980's twenty-four states, mostly European countries, were its members, besides the United States and Japan. Drawn within the Marshall Plan, built for the Cold War, OECD happened to be the international organization which could better affect the principal rivals of the US companies. Let us add that it is more likely to be open to a strong US influence than WTO or the UN. So in 1990, after a proposal made by the American delegation, the OECD's Committee on International Investments and Multilateral Companies started to think about coordinating the fight against bribery in international trade. This led in 1994 to a first recommendation, then to a second, passed on 23 May 1997, announcing the drawing up of an international agreement. The final negotiation ended on 21 November 1997, and the text (The OECD Convention on Combating Bribery of Foreign Public Officials in International Business Transactions) was signed on 17 December by the twenty-eight OECD members, after a remarkable seven year itch, and entered into force on 15 February 1999. It is not certain that the United States wanted the OECD to draw up an international agreement. It did want their partners to fight international bribery effectively, but in general the US was reluctant to signing binding international conventions; it could have gone along with recommendations and serious promises from their partners. Curiously, the French were pushing for a treaty to be signed, as a way to make sure every state that was party to the convention would have equal and precise duties in the fight against corruption[14].

The OECD members were a priority target, but the US had a bigger—and comprehensible—ambition, consisting in having the entire world pass laws equivalent to the FCPA. To do so, the United Nations appeared to be a good place, and so the organization started to build up a common initiative against corruption in 1990s[15]. But such a worldwide initiative takes time, and the General Assembly of the United Nations only came to a final international agreement in October 2003. The text was open for signature on 9 December 2003 in the margins of the Merida (Mexico) summit[16], and is now known as the Merida Convention. Regional organizations also adopted their own instruments: the Organization of American States adopted the Inter-American Convention against Corruption on 29 March 1996[17], as a matter of fact, the first one ever. The African Union also established a Convention on Preventing and Combating Corruption on 12 July 2003[18].

In a short period of time (1996 to 2003), four major international conventions had been signed, for the same purpose. Bribing foreign public officials is now a punished and actively prevented criminal offence, in all American[19] and European countries. Around the world, the process is an ongoing one. Next to the OECD Convention, signed by the thirty current members (and seven more countries, South Africa, Argentina, Brazil, Bulgaria, Chili, Estonia and Slovenia), the Merida Convention has now become a major anti-corruption instrument worldwide. Russia, which is not (yet) an OECD member and has not signed the OECD Convention, was one of the first countries to sign the Merida Convention in December 2003, and ratified it on 9 May 2006. China signed the treaty in December 2003, and ratified it on 13 January 2006. Iran signed it in December 2003, and India two years later, but both these countries have still not ratified it. Also in Africa, especially in petroleum exporting countries, ratifying international agreements sometimes seems to take long.

Anti-corruption rules are being adapted, extended, to a globalized economy, as Brazilian, Russian, Indian and Chinese companies (among others) have now become serious rivals, even outside their own country, to American and European companies. And as Europeans had to submit themselves to the anti-corruption movement, they now also would expect the Russians, Africans and Asians to do the same. More or less, European companies are now in the same position as the American Companies in the 80's, still suspected of unethical behaviour, but also victims of a sometimes unfair competition.

The Fight against Corruption is Still Precarious

Just considering the number of countries that signed the Merida Convention, it is certain that a war against corruption in international business has now been declared in the whole world. Therefore, the problems are not the same anymore. After making sure that every state fairly applies its binding international duties—it is not yet fully the case, but it is happening: first America, then Europe, today Asia, tomorrow Africa—what matters now is to avoid too big differences in implementing these anti-corruption rules, and seeing to it that they are not diverted from their legitimate ethical purpose to serve economic ones.

When ratifying the OECD Convention, some French senators still had a few doubts, «legitimate worries», about the agreement's possible consequences. They were voiced in a Senate report, according to which « the bill proposed to the commission of laws, if it deserves approval of its principles, generates legitimate worries. These worries can be summed up in the fact that the Convention on Combating Bribery of Officials in International Business Transactions, if it is not implemented by all the states the same way, might lead to distortions of competition multiplying rather than a moralisation of international trade[20]». One of the worries was that the United States itself did not appear to be wild prosecutors on its own soil, notably as a consequence of plea bargaining which consists in allowing suspects to make a deal with the prosecution, and thus avoid trial. Far and above the debate on prosecution's intensity[21], and leaving the United States aside, the significant differences likely to arise in the implementation of the convention in each country was considered to be the main danger: «the principle of a functional equivalence declared by the OECD Convention is very difficult to appreciate, and the high risk is that the violation of this principle will lead us to a twisted competition. (…) The French members of the OECD working group ought to be very careful in examining the national laws transposing the Convention[22]".

To avoid such problems, the OECD and the OAS[23] have set up « working groups », comprising representatives of states, in charge of a permanent evaluation. The Merida Convention does not contain any provision for such a surveillance programme, and it is a pity, as it seems to work quite efficiently. For example, recently, Luxembourg has been clearly asked by the OECD working group to make a substantial effort in implementing the OECD Convention, implying important changes in Luxembourgian law[24]. And Mark Pieth, Chairman of the OECD working group, seemed to be quite satisfied about its efficiency in Spring 2007: "Don't underestimate peer pressure. People believe it is important. Recommendations issued by the working group on corruption as also our investigations of each country are a powerful engine for change. A lot of countries have modified their laws and there are every day more investigations and prosecutions in the OECD zone. It's a proof that the convention against corruption is working. Countries trying to justify corruption might find themselves a minority, even alone. Such an attitude certainly does not generate trust from international partners, and it may even concern different economic interests. This is how peer pressure operates[25]". He can sure be trusted, considering his experience[26], and the fact is one must not underestimate the kind of international pressure he is talking about.

American federal authorities, who started this wide movement, do take enforcing anti-corruption regulations seriously, and will not hesitate to step in to help their partners, when they feel it is needed. The FCPA appears to be a good example of what might be called legal imperialism: every single state had, has or will have to change its domestic rules to conform with these new anti-corruption standards; worldwide companies now have to conceive and implement "FCPA compliance programmes", and states suspected to be too lax in the fight against bribery severely risk exclusion from the international trade community. In Europe already, major companies have adapted themselves to these new rules, naming internal authorities to monitor ethical issues, especially to prevent and detect corruption. These precautionary steps are made even more necessary by the fact that international judicial cooperation is facilitated by this international movement[27], as the above mentioned conventions explicitly provide for it. And even if they did not, as most states have now officially erected, politically and legally, bribery of foreign public officials as a crime and ethical tort, they will be more likely to cooperate with respect to a judicial request on such a ground. And as long as a state has enacted anti-corruption rules and made corrupting foreign public officials a crime, even if it is reluctant to prosecute its national companies, it could be forced to judicial cooperation with the state where the corruption took place or at least strongly incited to prosecute, after having received information on questionable corporate payments officially transmitted by another country's judicial and/or executive institution. It would be hard not to investigate such a crime, at least in a democratic country. The best informed states will then not hesitate to use their information capabilities to track down illegal international corporate payments, and do what is possible to have them effectively punished by their own country.

Now a practical case study, with the example of a natural gas field, in Iran, called South Pars. Iran, more than ever, is considered by the United States as a "rogue state", and as a result has been blacklisted by Congress, forbidding all companies to do business in Iran (first under the D'Amato-Kennedy Act of 8 August 1996[28], now under the Iran Sanctions Act, the implementation of which has been extended on 30 September 2006 to the end of 2011). Iran also faces an embargo declared by the UN Security Council, limited to nuclear energy; but there is for the moment no international rule forbidding a country to do business, other than in the nuclear industry, with Iran. So what was to happen, happened. European companies, as also Russian and Indian companies, do not feel bound by Congress's decision, and fill in the gaps left by American companies in Iran. Among others in the petrol industry, the French company Total and the Royal Dutch Shell kept on working with the National Iranian Oil Company (NIOC) on the *South Pars* field. In early May 2008, the Royal Dutch Shell publicly stated that it had decided to stop exploiting the South Pars field, giving no precise reason[29]. Everybody understood nevertheless that among other reasons, the company had decided to comply with American demands, as it is a public fact that the United States would like European companies to cease trade with Iran[30]. Unlike the FCPA, Congress's decision to boycott Iran appears to be, from the US companies' point of view, an inconvenience, when all other countries don't recognize nor apply such an embargo on their national companies. In 2003, in a report on Iran, French Senators themselves underlined that « on an industrial level, French companies, mostly in the energy sector, are being favoured by the absence of American competition, and take benefit, on a political level, of the favourable context created by France's position, which clearly disagreed with the United States in two matters: the D'Amato Act, which has been firmly and repeatedly condemned; the evacuation of oil and gas from the Caspian Sea, on the question of which France has always been open minded, excluding no possible track, including the Iranian one[31]».

The case of the French company Total directly involves the new anti-corruption rules. Here is how the company itself, in its public report for the year 2007, tells one of its recent judicial troubles: « in 2003, SEC launched a private investigation concerning several petrol companies, including Total, in relation to the search for business in Iran. In 2006, an investigation involving Total was started in France and the company's CEO indicted on the account of his previous office of director for the Middle-East. This investigation mentions an agreement concluded by the company about the South Pars gas field and allegations according to which payments, consecutive to the agreement, had been made to Iranian officials in relation to the contracts between the company and the National Iranian Oil Company[32]». My point is certainly not to judge whether these accusations are or not reasonable, but only to notice that they exist, and that they are grounded upon the new French criminal offence making bribing foreign public officials punishable which was enacted by the French Parliament to comply with the OECD Convention. It should also be noticed that Total believes the SEC initiated the case, by a "private investigation concerning oil companies…in relation to the search for business in Iran". Yet the French judicial inquiry began by a Swiss request, as Swiss judges were first investigating financial transactions involving persons linked to Total and Iranian public officials[33]. The thing is some French papers[34] mentioned that the American authorities had used their influence to make sure that the involved Swiss banks would actively cooperate with the Swiss judges, who then transmitted their information to the French judges, who, in turn, opened an investigation grounded upon French law derived from the OECD Convention, which itself was born out of the FCPA.

This recent international anti-corruption movement is in many ways interesting. Such a legal profusion, domestic and international, has rarely been seen in so little a time, and it is good to study these cases in business and international law. Starting from a domestic initiative, anti-corruption rules have been extended to America, then to Europe, and then, as the federal administration undertook to eradicate all obstacles to international trade and fair competition, to ban a few rogue countries from it, and as new countries were emerging, it became necessary to extend anti-corruption rules to the rest of the world, which has mostly been accomplished already.

Sometimes the following three different problems can boil down to a single one, the fight against corruption, for competitiveness, against rogue states. And it is consistent, as the background to all of it is formed by liberal economic and political values. Still, a real multilateralism has been missing, being but an appearance in such matters. There have been disagreements between Americans and Europeans, about international corruption as about Iran, and these disagreements concern today new economic powers: Russia, India and China. These countries have signed the Merida Convention, and will shortly have to comply with new international anti-corruption standards. Full consent might make it less painful.

NOTES AND REFERENCES

1. United States Code, Title 15, *Commerce and Trade*, Chapter 2B, §§ 78m(b), 78dd-1, 78dd-2, 78ff (n° 95-213, 91 Stat. 1494, 1977).
2. Cf. Paul E. Sigmund, "The "Invisible Blockade" and the Overthrow of Allende", *Foreign Affairs*, 52, no. 2 (*January 1974*), pp. 322-340.
3. Cf. Wesley A. Cragg and William Woof, in *The Political Economy of Corruption*, edited by Arvind K. Jain, London: Routledge, 2001.
4. Committee on Banking and Urban Affairs (1976), *Report of the Securities and Exchange Commission on Questionable and Illegal Corporate Payments and Practices*, p.30 and the following.
5. Cf. Bathen, T.E, "A Congressional response to the problem of questionable corporate payments abroad: The Foreign Corrupt Practices Act of 1977", *Law and Policy in International Business*, 1978, Vol. 10, p.1253 and the following.
6. In *House Report*, n°95-640, 1977.
7. Cf. Diane P. Caggiano, "The Foreign Corrupt Practices Act: the case for multilateral cooperation", in *New England International and Comparative Law Annual*, vol. 5, 1999. Can be retrieved at http://www.nesl.edu/intljournal/vol5/caggiano.htm
8. Cf. Philip Mattera, "The New Business Watergate: Prosecution of International Bribery is on the Rise", in *Corporate Research E-Letter*, n°68, Nov.—Dec. 2007.
9. Cf. *House Conference Report*, n°100-576, 1988.
10. As a late witness and victim of these relations, Mr. Jean-Marie Bockel, former French Secretary of foreign cooperation, was replaced in April 2008 because he had publicly denounced the « Françafrique », neologism sometimes used to describe the links between France and its former African dependencies.
11. The « ELF case », in the late 1990's, could be a good example. Elf was a French petrol company notably involved in Africa. An important trial in France has shown that in some countries it had in the past used corruption as a regular practice.
12. France was ranked fifteenth out of the thirty biggest economies (and India last). Cf. www.transparency.org/news_room/latest_news/press_releases/2006/fr_2006_10_04_bpi_2006.
13. Of course, it is not that easy. Major European companies all have clients, subsidiary companies, joint ventures in America. If American authorities do not have jurisdiction over foreign actions done by foreign companies, a single action linked to the American soil can be sufficient to justify American jurisdiction. Mr. Victor Kozeny's case, often cited on this matter, is a good example: he was charged in October 2006 by the Department of Justice for alleged violations of the FCPA, and arrested in the Bahamas, even though he is a Czech citizen, suspected of corruption in Azerbaijan, upon information obtained in the Netherlands and Switzerland. As it is possible that he acted for American investors, or tried to do so, since he had a few business meetings on the American soil, the American authorities believe they have jurisdiction over the case. Apart

from that, all companies operating in the American markets have to hand in annual written declarations about their activities, including foreign activities, to the Securities and Exchange Commission (« form 20-f »).

14. Cf. Philippe Montigny, *L'entreprise face à la corruption internationale*, Paris: Ellipses, 2006, p.54 and the following.
15. After the first Gulf war, during the 1990's the UN had to face a corruption scandal linked to the Oil-for-Food programme in Iraq. Corruption of foreign public officials has also been extended to international organizations. It is a crime in the EU since May 1997, and the Merida Convention makes provision for it.
16. Cf. http://untreaty.un.org/FRENCH/bible/frenchinternetbible/partI/chapterXVIII/treaty18.asp, for the text of the convention and a list of the signatory states.
17. Cf. www.oas.org/juridico/english/treaties/b-58.html.
18. It was signed, in January 2008, by 41 countries, among which 26 have ratified it. Cf. www.africa-union.org/root/au/Documents/Treaties/List/African%20Convention%20on%20Combating%20 Corruption.pdf
19. The list of the parties can be found on www.oas.org/juridico/english/Sigs/b-58.html.
20. Rapport n°42 de la Commission des lois du Sénat (1999-2000): *« le projet de loi soumis à l'examen de [la] commission des lois, s'il mérite d'être approuvé dans ses principes, suscite des inquiétudes légitimes. Ces inquiétudes se résument au fait que la convention sur la lutte contre la corruption d'agents publics étrangers dans les transactions commerciales internationales, si elle n'est pas appliquée de la même manière par tous les Etats parties, pourrait entraîner davantage une multiplication des distorsions de concurrence qu'une moralisation du commerce international*".
21. Curiously the report is not very precise on this matter, it must be noticed; its author writes summarily that « according to the information [he] could gather, the number of pronounced sentences for violations of the FCPA since it came into effect 22 years ago is very low, and the heaviest punishment was one year of imprisonment ». In *Ibid.*
22. *Ibid.*: « *le principe d'équivalence fonctionnelle posé par la convention de l'O.C.D.E est particulièrement difficile à apprécier et [il] existe un risque important que le non-respect de ce principe conduise à des distorsions de concurrence. (...) Il est indispensable que les représentants de la France au sein du comité de suivi de l'O.C.D.E soient particulièrement vigilants en ce qui concerne l'examen des législations de transposition de la convention* ».
23. Cf. The Washington File (an official US federal service), 08 March 2005, "Inter-American Group Wants Anti-corruption Treaty Strengthened".
24. Cf. *Luxembourg: Phase 2bis, Report on the application of the convention on combating bribery of foreign public officials in international business transactions*, OECD Working Group, 20 March 2008, www.oecd.org/dataoecd/4/21/40322335.pdf.
25. In *L'observateur de l'OCDE*, n°260, March 2007: *"Ne sous-estimez pas le pouvoir de la pression par les pairs. Les gens y attachent de l'importance. Les*

recommandations du Groupe de travail sur la corruption et nos examens par pays constituent un puissant moteur de changement. De nombreux pays ont modifié leur législation et il y a chaque jour davantage d'enquêtes et de poursuites dans la zone OCDE. C'est la preuve que la Convention sur la lutte contre la corruption fonctionne. Les pays qui tentent de justifier la corruption risquent de se retrouver en minorité, voire complètement isolés. Une telle attitude ne contribue certainement pas à susciter la confiance des partenaires internationaux, et cela risque même de se retourner contre d'autres intérêts économiques. Voilà comment opère la pression par les pairs".

26. Mark Pieth teaches criminal law at Basel University, and has worked for the Swiss federal state and the United Nations as a specialist of organized crime and corruption issues.
27. Cf. « Commentaries on the Convention on Combating Bribery of Officials in International Business Transactions », adopted by the Negotiating Conference on 21 November 1997 (www.oecd.org/dataoecd/4/19/38028103.pdf): 31 «Within the framework of paragraph 1 of Article 9, Parties should, upon request, facilitate or encourage the presence or availability of persons, including persons in custody, who consent to assist in investigations or participate in proceedings. Parties should take measures to be able, in appropriate cases, to transfer temporarily such a person in custody to a Party requesting it and to credit time in custody in the requesting Party to the transferred person's sentence in the requested Party. The Parties wishing to use this mechanism should also take measures to be able, as a requesting Party, to keep a transferred person in custody and return this person without necessity of extradition proceedings ».
28. This law, as the Helms-Burton Act, has been and remains a bone of contention between the European Union and the United States. Europeans have always said they do not feel bound by such a decision. The European Union reacted in 1996 by a resolution of the European Parliament, followed by a European regulation. Cf. also the public words of Jacques Chirac, the then President of the French Republic, on 17 May 1998: « *Pour ce qui concerne la loi d'Amato et la loi Helms Burton, comme vous le savez, il y a la position de la France, qui n'accepte pas le principe même des lois extra territoriales. Il y a la position de l'Europe, qui est exactement la même, c'est-à-dire le refus sans réserve ni concession du principe même des lois extra-territoriales, donc, nous ne nous sentons pas concernés. Néanmoins, nous souhaitons que les choses puissent s'arranger, sans que les principes que je viens de rappeler soient mis en cause* ». In English: « As regards Amato Law and Helms Burton Law, as you know, there is the stand of France which does not accept the principle itself of extra-territorial laws. There is the stand of Europe, which is exactly the same, that is to say, the refusal without any reservations or concession of the very principle of extra-territorial laws. We do not therefore feel involved. We nevertheless wish things to be sorted out without calling into question the principles that I just recalled".
29. Cf. *Le Monde* dated 14 May 2008, « *Le retrait de Shell d'Iran ne peut que favoriser la Russie* ».

30. Cf. « Washington tells EU firms: quit Iran now", *The Guardian*, November 9 2007.
31. In « *Rapport de la Mission effectuée en Iran du 15 au 18 avril 2003 par une délégation de la commission des Affaires économiques et du Plan », Sénat, n°385, July 7, 2003: « sur le plan industriel, les entreprises françaises, notamment dans le secteur énergétique, sont favorisées par l'absence de concurrence américaine, et bénéficient sur le plan politique du contexte très favorable créé par les positions de la France, qui s'est nettement démarquée des Etats-Unis sur deux sujets importants: la loi d'Amato, qui a fait l'objet d'une condamnation ferme et répétée; l'évacuation des hydrocarbures de la Caspienne, sujet sur lequel la France s'est montrée systématiquement ouverte en n'excluant a priori aucun tracé, y compris iranien*". Building a pipeline between Iran and India (maybe later China), via Pakistan, is today a serious project. India is Iran's neighbour, and has increasing needs in fossil energy when the latter has a lot of natural gas to sell. But India will put itself in a difficult position, along with Russia, Pakistan, China, and perhaps France and a few European countries, by refusing to comply with the American boycott wishes. Moreover, India has not yet ratified the Merida convention, has already been blacklisted in the 1980's, and is a country where corruption remains strong, even if things are getting better (Transparency International has its annual corruption rating, and gave India for the year 2006 3.3 out of 10, 10 being the best grade. India's grade is in constant progress, yet in October 2006 the same association believed the Indian companies were, among all major exporting countries, the more likely to commit foreign bribery).
32. Cf. « *Document de référence 2007* », available in the company's website, www.total.com: « *la SEC a lancé une enquête privée concernant plusieurs compagnies pétrolières, dont TOTAL, en liaison avec la recherche d'affaires en Iran. En 2006, une enquête visant TOTAL a été lancée en France, et le Directeur Général de la Société a été mis en examen en 2007 au titre de ses précédentes fonctions de directeur Moyen-Orient. Cette enquête se réfère à un accord conclu par la Société au sujet du champ gazier de South Pars et à des allégations selon lesquelles des paiements, effectués en vertu de cet accord, auraient été versés à des officiels iraniens en relation avec des contrats passés entre la Société et la National Iranian Oil Company* (NIOC)".
33. Officially the French inquiry was launched by a 5 pages report, sent to the French justice in December 2006 by the Federal Prosecutor of Lausanne, who considered that Total could eventually be indicted in Switzerland on the ground of bribing foreign public officials.
34. Cf. *Le Canard Enchaîné* of 28 March 2007.

5

The European Union in Poland

HUGO-BERNARD POUILLAUDE

It would perhaps be more obvious to talk about Poland in the European Union and explore the issue of the integration of Poland in the European Union on 1 May 2004 or the reintegration of Poland in the Western world. Such an approach would rely on an analysis based on a logic that is external to Poland's. Such an analysis would deal more with Polish "receptivity" to the European Union whereas, on the contrary, the purpose of my paper, is to come up with a complementary study and focus on the "perception" of the European Union in Poland[1] and try to understand it.

Far and above the fact that it is impossible to be exhaustive on such a vast topic, two pitfalls, which I do not pretend to avoid, emerge immediately. The difficulty is due partly to the task of engaging in a study of "perception" on the part of someone who is but a jurist and partly to the fact that it speaks about Poland which, like any other country, is rich in its diversity. However, from the political and legal choices and the debates that have given rise to such choices, a salient aspect, that of a rational nation in the Community space, stands out. A sort of "*natio oeconomicus*" borrowing the traits from the "*homo oeconomicus*"—contested for the sublimed rationality that it endows the individual with, Poland is making reasoned choices, which are its own in a European Union which might be tempted to reject this "individualism". Transformed, indeed even determined to a certain extent, by its history, Poland has succeeded more than ever in making the voice of its national sovereignty heard by joining the European Union. Institutional stability, economic prosperity, and military security are the many issues defended jealously by Poland.

Could anyone hold grudges against Poland for that? Could anyone rebuke Poland, as it was done in Ireland after Poland had said "No" to the Lisbon Treaty, for its lack of gratitude towards the European Union? Such a point of view cannot be sustained in Poland. Not only for obvious diplomatic reasons, but having regard to the place that a part of the Polish public opinion accords to its country in Europe.

As the eminent and recently defunct Polish thinker Bronislaw Geremek puts it, since 1989, Poland has not been winning its place in Europe but has been "winning it back"[2], thus giving vent to the idea that Poland had its historical place among Western democracies and that it had only "rejoined" Europe in 2004.

In this context, the beautiful description of Poland made by Professor Beauvois might be recalled: "A State subject to eclipses and whose borders have a variable geometry, a nowhere country in the 19th Century whose people are a people who belong everywhere because of their tendency to migrate all over the world, a European exception in the 16th century when a unique political system emerged there and when Poland covered the vastest European territory after Russia, a mere piece of confetti in the Duchy of Warsaw under Napoleon, a phoenix flapping its wings and paws again under Pilsudski after 1918, the phantom Poland of the Communist decades after 1945, David of 1980 who slew the Soviet Goliath, Poland rejoined the European Union in 2004, rich with the thousand facets that history had bestowed upon it and the energy that its many trials had conferred on its people"[3]. From this tormented history has arisen a haughty Poland that is attached to certain values and which appears ambitious, indeed even capricious, from the point of view of some.

The defence and intense promotion of Christian values, ostentatious military collaboration with the United States, parliamentary debates relating to the revival of the death penalty and the determination to hold on to the Treaty of Nice because it gave Poland more weight in terms of number of votes are the points raised as being conflictual. All these contrast with the rapid transformation of Polish institutions and Polish law under the influence of Community and European Union Law[4] as well as with the strong Polish adherence to the Union[5], or else with the presence of the Natolin College of Europe in Warsaw. This is nothing but a very normal state of affairs. Poland is torn between adherence to certain values that the Union is promoting and hostility towards others. The political parties themselves—and this seems quite lucky—differ on these issues. Besides, the goals assigned to the Community do not form part of any consensus. Is it simple union for economic interest or Community of values? This dichotomy is simplistic as the subject is so complex. The choices made by Poland are nevertheless significant. Not only in their consistency obviously, but also in their ways of reasoning. Being a clever bat as in La Fontaine's fable entitled « The Bat and the Two Weasels »[6], Poland knows how to defend its interests and values like any sovereign State—or should we say nation?—in a European Union which is struggling to overcome this common defect.

In order to better understand this behaviour, we shall first analyse how the European Union has a strong presence in Poland because it is a vector of democracy and economic prosperity (I), then see why the EU does not join Poland, speaking from the point of view of defence and values, because it is not found to be convincing (II).

I. DEMOCRACY AND ECONOMIC PROSPERITY: CHOICE IN FAVOUR OF THE EUROPEAN UNION

The democratization of institutions and law as a rule (1) and economic prosperity (2) are linked, of course.

It is not necessary to recall here the state of economic decline in which Poland found itself in 1980s when the then Chief of State, General Wojciech Jaruzelski[7], declared the state of siege[8]. It was a case of concordance between the arbitrary nature of the Communist power and the decadence of the economy, which constituted the anti-thesis of the parallel that I would like to draw between the democratization of the Polish legal system and the advance of its economy.

Democratization of Institutions

In order to join the European Union in 2004, Poland had to adapt to mandatory legal requirements[9]. The principal requirement was naturally the incorporation into Polish domestic law of Community law, in other words, the integration of all EU law[10] in Polish legislation. Poland, as Jan Kulakowski[11], Secretary of State, principal negotiator for the accession of Poland in the European Union pointed out in 2001, "had confirmed its determination to enforce Community *acquis* and not apply for long and numerous transitory periods". This eagerness and this goodwill with respect to Community *acquis* fit in line with the Polish drive towards the democratization of its domestic law. For this reason, Poland did not disappoint the European Union. The European Council of Copenhagen of the 21-22 June 1993 accepted the principle of enlargement, but demanded from future members as prerequisites for accession that they have "stable institutions to guarantee democracy, the rule of law, human rights and respect for and protection of minorities".

But already, at the end of 1989, Article 1 of the Polish Constitution had been amended to substitute the notion of the "Socialist State" with a "democractically constituted State" prefiguring the emergence of the rule of law[12]. The notion of rule of law was taken to mean not simply a State that acts by means of law which the Poland had already been doing just like the URSS, but as a will to submit State action to law as opposed to the arbitrary nature of power that prevailed before 1989. This will is more significant politically than legally. Indeed, the idea of the rule of law is, if we go by a standard legal analysis, not substantial[13]. It is an empty shell in which one can lodge either a law qualified as authoritarian or a democratic law called as such. In 1989, this designation illustrated an important political will which later gave rise to substantially democratic rights.

From then on, the principle guiding the democratic transition of Poland was at loggerheads with the Communist system. Thus, principles which were previously regarded as "bourgeois" such as the separation of powers or the mechanisms implementing the responsibility of public power—each of them undermining the efficiency of Party decisions—constituted the basis for building the modern Polish system, modelled on Western democracies. It was the same for the protection of individual liberties and private property, or the moderation of state intervention in the social sphere.

These principles were enforced thanks to the Constitutional Court of Poland[14] which was set up in 1985 and had acted but as a puppet before 1989 under the 1952 Constitution[15], but which had been able to assert the overriding nature of these principles—and incidentally its own overriding power—by releasing them from the notion of "democratically constituted State"[16]. In a very subtle way, it is the constitutional court which paved the way for a smooth transition from the law of the ancient regime to modern law[17] which, in reality, constituted a truly axiomatic break. Founded on constitutional principles common to democratic States and the conditions for accession of Poland to the Union, the Constitutional Court had, as its then President put it in 1997, contributed to the strengthening of the rule of law and applied a break on trends which, particularly during the years 1991 and 1992, tried to accelerate the process of transformation of the regime. Pr. Zoll followed up these comments more explicitly by saying "I am particularly satisfied when, in the course of the parliamentary session, I hear, among the ranks of Parliament, that such and such solution could be unconstitutional or form the object of a court enquiry[18].

It is in this transitional context, very briefly and partially sketched in this article that the incorporation of Community law in Polish domestic law occurred. The Constitution of the Third Republic of 1997 specifies in this regard and for the first time, the relationship between international law and Polish domestic law[19] and more particularly (but in an implicit manner) the relationship between Poland and the European Union. It expressly lays down in its Article 91 the principle of direct applicability of international law[20] in domestic law, the superiority of international law over domestic law and extends these criteria, in Paragraph 3 of this Article, to secondary legislation coming from an international organization, thus attributing EU law a force superior to that of domestic law[21].

This modification of the Polish legal system facilitated the transition from a planned economy to a liberal economy. It was a mandatory prerequisite.

Economic Prosperity

By joining the European Union on 1 May 2004, Poland strengthened and accelerated the economic change that it had been implementing since the 1990s. Under the influence of this new law and the subsidies given by the Community as early as 1989[22], Poland carried out several important deregulation measures which were translated by "the multiplication of contracts under private law, flexibility of employment, the decline of trade unions, weakness of collective labour agreements" as François Bafoil notes[23].

This economic transition was perceived with more reservations than the democratic transition talked about here above. Qualified as a "shock therapy"[24] as early as 1989, this economic revolution entailed varied consequences. In the first quarter of 2004, Poland had known the highest unemployment rate, i.e., 20.7 per cent of its active population, among the twenty-five member states of the Union. This high rate of unemployment was mainly attributed to the deregulation of the market in the 1990s. It was, however, reduced to half in a period of three years. Parallely and correlatively, from 1 May 2004, Poland was able to obtain a sustained growth of its GDP (6.9 per cent year-on-year, in the second quarter of 2007)[25]. The gradual opening of the European market—opening of the labour market as early as 2004 in Great Britain, Ireland and Sweden to the workers of the new EU member states, enlargement of the Schengen area of free movement on 21 December 2007, effect of factory relocations etc—contributed to this growth. For this reason, the Polish accord the European Union a massive satisfaction[26].

Some tempering elements have to be, nevertheless, signalled. In the first place, the issue of emigration poses problems. Indeed two million Polish migrated abroad to work, that is to say, 12 per cent of Poland's active population. As Philippe Rusin remarks, "given the amplitude of the migratory phenomenon, it has become today a source of worry for the country's future".[27]

Secondly, the gap in salary between urban and rural territories got widened as well[28]. Similarly, precarious employment—we find here the eternal debate between the trap of unemployment and of precariousness. Contracts for precarious employment concerned 4.5 per cent of the active population in 1985 compared to 24 per cent in 2004[29].

Finally, this high growth brought inflationist tendencies and budgetary drifts that the European authorities did not fail to point out. As Edith Lhomel aptly remarks, "irritated by the warning of the Commission on the rate of inflation and the level of their budgetary deficit, the new member states felt constricted in their adjustment efforts by certain member states who blamed their faith in liberalism which was found synonymous with less social welfare. In this debate opposing those who want to see the European Union only as a free trade area and those for whom the construction of the European Union is a guarantee of a certain social progress, the new member states found themselves in the camp of the most liberal-minded with regard to controversial issues such as the liberalization of services (Bolkestein directive) or the opening of the European market"[30].

Apart from agriculture—issue of considerable importance in Poland and which I shall deal with more amply later on—the Union represents a formidable tool of economic prosperity in Poland[31].

This European efficiency, which is radically opposed to the Soviet economic policy, naturally explains Polish adherence to the Union. In contrast, the real or supposed inefficiency of the European Union in matters of defence tilts Poland towards the United States. This choice which is considered the most reasonable by and for Poland is not meant to disappoint the Union. It seems that EU's "offer" in certain areas is not simply attractive for the Polish.

II. DEFENCE AND CERTAIN VALUES, EUROPEAN OFFERS FOUND UNSATISFACTORY BY POLAND

Compared to the US, Europe does not appear reassuring to Poland in matters of defence (1). The Union is far from being a federal State with unified values. Poland itself is a leading example for this in so far as it leans heavily on its own values (2).

Defence: The Choice of America

The integration of Poland in Europe is a guarantee for Poland's security. This security is henceforth connected with that of all the EU countries[32]. However, Western countries remain those which, when faced with the Soviet threat, have not been able to or not managed to help Poland free itself[33]. In Polish public opinion, only the United States played and could play an efficient role, an efficient role in 1918 for the renaissance of Poland, in the 1980s for their intransigence towards the USSR or else the Marshall Plan which Jan

Kulakowski recalls "was initially intended to help the whole of Europe reconstruct itself"; it was but "under the pressure of the Soviet Union that the countries of Central Europe had to reject it"[34].

Whereas the European Union has been struggling since the days of its creation to define a common and efficient defence policy (regarding the conflict in ex-Yugoslavia at the beginning of the 1990s for instance), Poland joined NATO right in1999 and fit in line with American foreign policy. As Professor Jacques Rupnik explains, "Poland had always managed to find a consensus among its elite in order to remain an exemplary ally of the United States"[35], thus strengthening the uncontested American leadership. Considering the hesitations of the European countries with regard to the United States, "either as a pipe dream or as an unacceptable menace for the cohesion of NATO"[36], Poland has incited stringent criticism owing to its strategic choices, the very choices that allowed it to assert itself within the European Union. Two significant events have to be underscored. First, the active support given to the Americans by the Polish government at the time of launching the war in Iraq and the involvement of Polish troops on the field a few months before Poland's integration in the European Union[37]. The other is the purchase of military equipment from the United States which is preferred to the EU's.

The then Minister of Foreign Affairs, Adam Rotfeld quoted by Jacques Rupnik does not mince words: "Americans awaited European solidarity and Poland reacted consequently. Our involvement in Iraq reinforces our close relationship with the United States far above what was anticipated. Poland's prestige in Washington is at its zenith and this has a great value for us, because it is the only country capable of guaranteeing Polish security"[38]. On 30 January 2003, together with seven other European countries Poland signed the "Letter from Eight European Countries for a United Front against Iraq"[39] which was to entail discord with the Paris-Brussels-Berlin axis, discredit the idea of a common external and defence policy and throw light on a hell broke loose.

Already in the year 2002, Poland had taken everyone by surprise owing to its choice of purchasing military equipment from America in order modernize its army. Indeed, Europeans were expecting Poland, a candidate country for accession[40], to buy their fighter jets[41], while Poland preferred American ones[42], with appreciable consideration[43] granted for a market of 3.8 billion euros. Poland was bound by no legal obligation, but the political expectations were strong, and were perhaps legitimate.

Once again we find the Polish will to collaborate with the United States in matters of defence, but it is important to consider the fact that this cooperation has been established and imposed on Poland for a long time in NATO.[41]

This Polish inclination can also be explained by common values shared with the United States and a common way of proclaiming them, in contrast to the European Union. Far and above their shared anti-Communism, it is the foregrounding of their Christian faith that contrasts with European nervousness regarding this subject.

Values: Not a Question of Choice, but an Obvious Fact

The debates on the reference to Christian values in Europe in the Treaty establishing a Constitution for Europe highlighted the idea that Poland has of the European Union. Very strong in its determination to mention the Christian heritage of Europe in the preamble to the treaty, Poland set forth its arguments explaining its intransigence[45].

It is first important to recall here the very strong idea that prevails in Poland and according to which the integration of the so-called East bloc countries amounts to, in reality, a reunification of Western Europe. From a purely rhetorical point of view, Poland is considered more a Central European country than an Eastern European country, placing it thus at the heart of Europe and people talk more willingly about reintegration rather than integration. From this vantage position, Poland does not in any way want to deny its values for the real or supposed values of the European Union.

The preponderance of Catholicism in Poland is well known to everyone. 90 per cent of the Polish people are baptized and more than 80 per cent seriously practise Catholicism galvanized by the stature of the former Polish Pope Wojtyla and highlighted by a whole political class. Christian values are not objects for debate in Poland just like societal values such as abortion or rights of the homosexual which are nevertheless fundamental. The wounded history of the nation has even prompted some political leaders to speak about Poland as a nation tortured like Christ. In this sense, Poland could be viewed as anti-European and take on the role of a preacher with obviously opinions varying according to the political parties and leaders in power. As Laure Neumayer points out in her thesis, "some affirm that the Central European peoples form fully part of Europe and adopt a stand of intellectual and spiritual superiority. Even though these populations are less well-to-do, they have preserved traditional values which were fumbling in Western societies"[46]. Thus, according to Adam Michnik, Chief Editor of the daily, *Gazeta Wyborcza*, "Europe is gradually ceasing to be the symbol of parliamentary democracy, free market economy, welfare state, a system based on tolerance and a culturally open society. Europe is becoming the symbol of abortion and pornography, drug and divorce, decadence and the separation of the Church from the State".

This vision colours the discourse of conservative parties and the extreme right wing parties. Ever since (2001) the right wing party AWS split into the Conservative PiS (Law and Justice)[47] whose leaders are the Kaczynski twins (Lech, current President of the Republic and Jaroslaw, former Prime Minister) and the liberal PO[48] (Civic Platform) whose leader is the current Prime Minister Donald Tusk, a very clear camp has taken shape around the radical defence of Christian values. Supported by two extreme right wing parties[49], the *Samoobrona* (Self-Defence) party of the very turbulent Andrej Lepper and the *Ligue* of Polish Families[50], but also by the media such as the ultra-reactionary Radio Maryja, President Kaczynski who was in the opposition in 2001 and then in the ruling party fought tooth and nail the Treaty establishing the Constitution for Europe which was rejected by the French and Dutch people as well as the Lisbon Treaty which is intended to bypass these rejections.

There were three major reasons for his stand. First, the fear of seeing the subsidies granted to Polish agriculture gradually dry up while this area, culturally and economically speaking, enjoys considerable importance in Poland. The negotiations for accessions dealt extensively on this issue[51]. Secondly, the determination—more or less assumed—to hold on to the Nice Treaty of 2001 which was denounced for its minimalism and its faulty functioning but which gave Poland considerable advantage in terms of number of votes in the Council. Thirdly, for the reference to the Christian heritage dealt with hereabove.

In 2005, the French and Dutch 'No' put an end to the process which suited the Polish President. In 2008, the Irish 'No' to the Treaty of Lisbon was invoked by the President in order not to ratify it, but this was done in a complex situation. In fact, Poland is currently witnessing a situation that could be called as one of cohabitation as France had known earlier where the President of the Republic does not have a majority in Parliament and has to consequently designate a Council of Ministers that is not favourable towards him. Poland has a Parliamentary regime[52], but it nevertheless elects its President by means of direct universal suffrage as France has been doing since 1962. More legitimate after such a consecration as Tocqueville would have said, the President, though he has only limited constitutional prerogatives, takes fully part in the political debate. Moreover, the President has, by virtue of Articles 89 and 133 of the 1997 Constitution, the power to ratify international treaties after Parliament's vote. This is how the Polish Parliament under the influence of a Council of Ministers, which has a liberal and Pro-European majority, voted the law authorizing the ratification of the Lisbon Treaty, but the President refuses to do so.

Drawing on the Irish 'No', Lech Kaczynski considers that the ratification is no longer relevant. But what is behind this specious argument is the determination to go no further than the Treaty of Nice and assert the values that Poland wants to safeguard, indeed even proclaim.

Conclusion

The several traits of Poland examined do not allow us to say either that Poland is unashamedly making use of the European Union or that it is espousing the construction of a political Europe in the current state of affairs. We cannot but notice a State whose choices tend to rationally maximize its benefits and which, obviously, stem from its history. These choices are made in terms of what the European Union has to offer and in this sense the example of Poland could be significant to draw lessons on how Europe is being built and to objectively distinguish where the construction of Europe stands. Like NATO, the European Union confers some advantages on Poland directly or indirectly. This behaviour of Poland is not unusual[53]. On the other hand, Poland's accession to the European Union helps it assert its national sovereignty more than ever. This is indeed a paradox that deserves to be underscored. The idea of harmony as a science of sequencing chords was differently apprehended by Fryderyk Chopin…

Translated from French by
Geetha Ganapathy-Doré

NOTES AND REFERENCES

1. For this approach Laure Neumayer, *L'enjeu européen dans les transformations postcommunistes. Hongrie, Pologne, République Tchèque, 1989-2004,* Belin, 2006.
2. Bronislaw Geremek, *La Pologne au XXe siècle,* Teresa Wysokinska & Alain van Crugten eds, Brussels: Editions Complexe, 2001, p. 15.
3. Daniel Beauvois, «Le retour de la Pologne comme acteur européen», *Pouvoirs*, no. 118, 2006, p. 5.
4. Poland became a member of the Council of Europe on 26 November 1991; ratified the European Convention on Human Rights on 19 January 1993 and accepted individual proceedings before the Court on 1 May 1993. cf. Pierre Lambert, «La transition démocratique de la Pologne au regard de la jurisprudence de la Cour Européenne des Droits de l'Homme» in *Revue Trimestrielle des droits de l'Homme*, n°65-66, 2006, p. 151.
5. Around 78% of the Polish voted «Yes» to the referendum on accession to the European Union. A very large majority of the Polish are always very favourable towards the Union.
6. English translation retrievable at http://oaks.nvg.org/fonta2.html#batwea

7. In fact, General Jaruzelski simultaneously held the offices of the First Secretary of the Party, Prime Minister and Minister of Defence.
8. The state of siege (*stan wojenny*—literally the state of war) was declared on 13 December 1981.
9. The first document signed between the European Community and Poland in view of its accession was an association agreement dated 16 December 1991. As Jan W. Piekarski recalls (Jan W. Piekarski is Ambassador of the Republic of Poland in Belgium, «Discours introductif» in *La Pologne et l'intégration européenne,* Editions de l'Université de Bruxelles, 2003, p. 13.) « in its preamble, after tedious negotiations, it was set down that the purpose of this agreement was the future accession of Poland to the European Community. The agreement entered into force in February 1994. Two months later, Poland officially submitted an application for accession to the Union on 5th April 1994". Official negotiations started on 31 March 1998.
10. Treaties, Secondary legislation or case law of the Court of Justice of European Communities.
11. Jan Kulakowski, «Vers l'Union européenne» in *La Pologne au XXe siècle*, p. 152.
12. On the notion of the rule of law, consult Maria Kruk, « Progrès et limites de l'Etat de droit» in *Revue Pouvoirs*, *op. cit.*, p. 73 & the following pages.
13. For Hans Kelsen, it is a pleonasm.
14. Trybuna³ konstytucyjny w Rzeczypospolitej Polskiej in Polish. It has a good website and the pages are available in French as well as English translation.
15. After the «Little Constitution » of 1992, Poland adopted a new constitution on 25 May 1997 which was promulgated by the President on the 15 July and entered into force on 16 October 1997 which completely revised the 1952 constitution, thus giving birth to the 3d Republic in Poland. See Jean-Jacques Urvoas, «Evolution constitutionnelle de la Pologne: la refondation du parlementarisme» in *Revue française de droit constitutionnel*, no. 40, 1999, p. 895.
16. On Polish constitutional case law of this era, consult: Piotr Tuleja et Krzystof Wojtyczek, «La protection des droits acquis élément constitutif de l'Etat de droit? Remarques sur la jurisprudence constitutionnelle polonaise», in *Revue Internationale de Droit Comparé*, no. 3, 1995, p. 737.
17. Decommunization and the effort to eliminate the avatars of the law of the earlier regime from the new legislation had been tempered by constitutional judges who established a balance between acquired rights (legal security) and change in the system. See the note cited above.
18. On Polish constitutional case law of this era, consult: Piotr Tuleja et Krzystof Wojtyczek, «La protection des droits acquis élément constitutif de l'Etat de droit? Remarques sur la jurisprudence constitutionnelle polonaise» *in Revue Internationale de Droit Comparé,* no. 3, 1995, p. 737.
19. Title III of the 1997 Constitution, Art. 87 and the following.
20. Article 91:
    1. After promulgation thereof in the Journal of Laws of the Republic of Poland (*Dziennik Ustaw*), a ratified international agreement shall constitute part of the domestic legal order and shall be applied directly, unless its application depends on the enactment of a statute.

2. An international agreement ratified upon prior consent granted by statute shall have precedence over statutes if such an agreement cannot be reconciled with the provisions of such statutes.
3. If an agreement, ratified by the Republic of Poland, establishing an international organization so provides, the laws established by it shall be applied directly and have precedence in the event of a conflict of laws.

21. See Wladyslaw Czaplinski, «L'intégration européenne dans la constitution polonaise de 1997» in *Revue du Marché commun et de l'Union européenne*, no. 436, mars 2000, p. 168.
22. For instance, the PHARE (Poland and Hungary: Assistance for Restructuring their Economies) programme of December 1989.
23. François Bafoil, «L'adaptation de la société polonaise à l'Europe» in *Revue Pouvoirs*, *op. cit.*, p. 21 and the following.
24. The « Balcerowicz plan», after the name of the Finance Minister of the first non-Communist government of Poland in 1989 tried to implement a quick, indeed even an abrupt transition towards free market economy. This plan was qualified as a shock therapy.
25. Philippe Rusin, «Elargissement et flux migratoires, L'expérience de la Pologne en perspective» in *Le courrier des pays de l'Est, Nouveaux Etats membres de l'UE, une intégration réussie?*, La Documentation Française, no. 1063, September-October 2007, p. 22.
26. In 2007, 78 per cent of the Polish considered that their accession to the European Union was beneficial to their country. *Le courrier des pays de l'Est*, *op. cit.*, p. 5. European Commission Sources.
27. *Op. cit.*
28. On this point, see François Bafoil op. cit., p. 22 and the following.
29. Idem, p. 25.
30. Edith Lhomel, «De Quinze à Vingt-Sept. Les nouveaux Etats membres face à la construction européenne» in *Le Courrier des pays de l'Est*, *op. cit.*, p. 7.
31. Volume of European investments, commercial partnerships, funds devoted to the modernization of Polish infrastructure (structural funds) etc.
32. See Pawel Swieboda, "Po Gruzji gra o Ukraine" (After Georgia, Ukraine?), *Gazeta Wyborcza*, 19 August 2008, p. 18 in which the author pleads for the integration of Ukraine in the European Union «*ziemi obiecanej*» (a promised land) against the Russian threat.
33. Please read Piotr Stanczak, "Les Polonais s'identifient aux Géorgiens et s'inquiètent des visées russes" in *Le Monde* of Friday 15th August 2008, p. 4, on the conflict between Georgia and Russia for South Ossetia.
34 Jan Kulakowski, op. cit., p. 154.
35. Jacques Rupnik, «La Pologne à l'Heure américaine, entre l'Europe et les Etats-Unis» in *Revue Pouvoirs*, *op. cit.*, p. 137.
36. Idem, p. 141, citing Jan Nowak-Jezioranski, "Czy NATO jest zagrozone?" (Is NATO under threat?), *Gazeta Wyborcza*, 15th May 2001.
37. The government at that time was opposed to the population on this specific

point. The population was, without in any way denying its love of America, for the major part opposed to the war in Iraq.

38. *Idem.*
39. Denmark, Spain, UK, Hungary, Italy, Portugal and the Czech Republic.
40. This announcement was made one week after the Copenhagen Summit on European Union Enlargement to the countries of Central Europe.
41. The French Mirages and the British and Swedish Grippen.
42. F-16.
43. The absence of necessity for visa for the Polish wanting to travel to the United States or especially the implantation of American bases on the Polish soil or the very controversial anti-missile shield.
44. Cf *Polish Defence YearBook 2008, Industry, Armed Forces and Security Services*, vol. III, 2008 (2), with a note by the current Under-secretary of State for Armament and Modernization of National Armament, Zenon Kosiniak-Kamysz, p. 5.
45. On this point, see Jean-Paul Jacqué et Catherine Prieto, «L'Union, une communauté de valeurs?» in *Revue trimestrielle de droit européen*, n°44 (1), January-March 2008, p. 1.
46. Laure Neumayer, *op. cit.*, p. 24.
47. Pravo i Sprawiedliwosc in Polish.
48. Platforma Obywatelska in Polish.
49. On this point see Hieronim Kubiak, « La rhétorique anti-européenne des partis politiques polonais. Le cas de Samoobrona (Autodéfense) et de la Ligue des familles polonaises (LPR)» in *La Pologne et l'intégration européenne*, *op. cit.*, p. 43.
50. Liga Polskich Rodzin in Polish.
51. In this short article, I cannot dwell on this issue which had been extensively dealt with by scholars. See Wojciech Prazuch, «La situation de l'agriculture polonaise et ses perspectives dans l'UE», Hanna Podedworna, «L'environnement institutionnel de l'agriculture en Pologne», Krzysztof Gorlach, «La disparition des derniers pays d'Europe», Hanna Podedworna, «L'intégration de la Pologne à l'Union européenne dans la conscience des fermiers polonais» in *La Pologne et l'intégration européenne* cited herein, p. 133 and the following.
52. See Jean-Jacques Urvoas, «Evolution constitutionnelle de la Pologne, la refondation du parlementarisme», cited herein.
53. The UK (see, Jean-Paul Jacqué, Catherine Prieto, «L'Union, une communauté de valaurs?» *op. cit.*) or France (case of negotiations dealing with the Common Agricultural Policy).

6

Implementation of EU Policies:

Remarks on the Exercise of Economic Competences by the Union

PIERRE-YVES MONJAL

The European Union is one of the major economic actors at the global level. It rivals the United States in a certain number of fields: services, agro-food, electronics... It represents more than 20 per cent of world trade. Trade among member states accounts for 75 per cent of their exports. Nevertheless EU cannot be merely regarded as an economic area for free trade. It is true that the European Union ensures the free movement of goods and in order to do so, it has done away with physical barriers and abolished customs duties. But what remains unique is the fact that the Union also holds a set of competences that it can implement. These are called European Public Policies. This article looks at these competences, determines their nature and rules of attribution and presents the terms and conditions of their institutional and juridical implementation.

Competences of the European Union

The term competence corresponds more to legal terminology derived from the law of international organizations. As mentioned in the earlier chapter (pp. 33, 43) the European Union is not an international organization but an intergovernmental and supranational one without a legal personality until the Lisbon treaty is ratified. Union is the name given by the members states in 1992 (Maastricht Treaty—Holland) to the system of political, economic and institutional cooperation they had established. This system comprises three pillars or components: The first is mainly economic and rests upon the European Community instituted on 25 March 1957 by the Treaty of Rome. The European Community is indeed an international organization in so far as the treaty set up an international organization with a distinct legal personality.

The second pillar, which is intergovernmental, enables member states to put into place a common foreign and security policy. The last, also intergovernmental, aims at ensuring police and judicial co-operation in criminal matters among member states.

The Economic Competences of the First Pillar

To cut a long story short, it is sufficient to refer to the third part of the EC Treaty to note a list of twenty-two actions or policies that are listed therein. Much easier to access is the list of Union activities summed up in the EU Gateway (http://europa.eu): Customs Union and Free Movement of Goods, Agriculture and Fisheries, Free Movement of Workers, Social policy, Right of Establishment, Transport Policy, Competition policy, Fiscal policy, Economic and Monetary Policy (€), Energy (former ECSC Treaty and Euratom Treaty), Industrial Policy and Internal Market, Regional Policy and Coordination of Structural Instruments, Environment, Consumers, Public Health, Science, Information, Education, Culture, Company Law and Europe of Citizens (free movement of persons and citizenship). Each of these sections is further divided into as many subsections as there are community action plans. It is by reading them that one gets a full and precise picture of the extent of internal competences. Just to give you an example, agriculture is organized into fifty-one subsections: agricultural subsidy, forests, cereals, sugar, silk ....

These competences are deployed in the European Union. They are called internal because they concern only the twenty-seven member states among themselves. But it is necessary to remember that the European Community, like any other international organization, is endowed with a legal personality and the capacity to sign conventions and that it has the competence to sign agreements with third parties or other international organizations. The areas coming under the purview of external competences include the above mentioned competences. From a legal point of view, the technical terms and conditions regarding the signing of agreements form part of the most complex questions of the Union[1].

Competences in Foreign Policy and Security Matters

The objective is two fold: to put into place a distinct European Diplomacy; organize security, including military security, of the Union. Owing to the peculiar nature of this area of competences, the member states of the Union work by consulting each other and by adopting action plans unanimously.

Competences in the Area of Police and Judicial Co-operation in Criminal Matters

The free movement of persons in the European Union is ensured by this plan. This involves the disappearance of border control among member states (Schengen Area) and a simultaneous reinforcement of police co-operation. Once the people have been arrested, they have to be judged in more or less similar conditions. This is the cooperation in criminal matters aspect of the intergovernmental action. Co-operation in police and criminal matters is going to fall within the scope of community policies in the new Lisbon Treaty framework.

Mode of Attribution of Union Competences

This is a fundamental question. It is in the interests of the twenty-seven member states to know what they would like to wield in common. Once this problem has been solved, the terms and conditions of implementing these competences might be defined.

Competences Attributed by the Treaty

One of the frequent errors of analysis is to sustain that the member states are victims of the Union, that they suffer it. The Eurosceptics very often use this argument. It is true that they have a convenient and verifiable legal argument: the legal personality of the Community (and soon, of the Union). Indeed, all the regulations and directives that implement community competences are legally attributable to the Community and are decided in its name. But if the Community acts in such and such area, it is obviously on the basis of the Treaty. If we have lately witnessed a liberalization of postal services or railway transport, it is only by virtue of the Treaty (principle of competition). Let us remember that the Treaty has been drafted by the member states. It is the outcome of their political agreement, their negotiation and their unanimous ratification. The member states, true masters of the treaties, cannot legitimately pretend to be surprised, when the Community activates a competence, as it was they who had attributed this power to it. The Community and in a more general manner, the Union act according to the foundation laid by the exclusive will of its creators: the member states. The Union is nothing but the organized form of collective action of member states at the European level.

Governmental Competences

One of the essential features of the Community and the Union (especially within the framework of the future Lisbon Treaty which will confer a legal personality on the latter) is to hold powers that once fell under the scope of the governments of member states. In its ruling of 1964, *Costa v ENEL*, the Court of Justice particularly insisted on this point and brought out the fact that contrary to ordinary treaties, the Treaty establishing the European Community is the outcome of the transfer of state sovereignty. What one should be aware is that on the international scene any organization is obliged in a way to invent its role. The WTO, for instance, as a body for regulating international trade, exercises this role of international regulation. Its mission and its competences are by nature international. There does not exist in the internal competences of governments the role of "regulation of world trade". Of course the need for international trade was felt before the setting up of the WTO in 1994. It is this need and the need to regulate it which led to the creation of the body. Whatever the case, it is difficult to deny that WTO's competences are intergovernmental in nature.

In contrast, the purpose of the Community is something else. The competences attributed to it allow it to act in the "internal" market with reference to fields where traditionally intervention was governmental: agriculture, fisheries, steel industry, transport, competition. In the treaties they have adopted, the member states have conferred some of their competences on the EC in order for it to act in their name and place. Of course, the governments represented in the Council of Ministers exercise, in common, their competences which have been transferred to the Community. The deeply governmental nature of competences exercised by the Community remains nevertheless undebatable. It is the reason why Community law is first and foremost intended for physical and moral persons. It is one of the main features of the Community and bears evidence to the fact that the regulatory competences exercised, which are but levers for the implementation of material competences attributed, are of a peculiar nature, governmental to put it in one word. The European citizens are regularly subjected to the law of their State, but also to Community Law. As regards the second (CFSP) and third (PJC) pillars, the logic is different. In this case, it is the states which constitute the agents and objects at the same time. Individuals are not directly concerned by this intergovernmental law, which is nothing but a reflection of the implementation of international competences. The community competences are, therefore, of a very singular nature which gives the Community its specific and original character.

Withheld Competences

These refer to competences which the states did not want to confer on the Community. These are areas which are more or less closely linked to the sovereignty of states: police, army, justice, criminal law in particular. This does not prevent the member states from implementing an intergovernmental collaboration in these areas as the second and third pillars amply demonstrate. From the legal point of view, it is important to note, competence in these areas is not attributed to the Union, as it is not an international organization.

Exclusive Competences

As opposed to the foregoing situation, exclusive competences are those that are retained by the European Community so to speak. In this case, the EC Treaty, which, we know, has been drafted by the member states and approved by them, grants the Community the competence to act alone by excluding the member states in this or that particular area. In other words, the states have voluntarily given up their political and juridical competences in those sectors which they have confided to the European Community. This renunciation from acting individually at the governmental level does not signify that, in terms of exercise of political power and not in terms of law, it is true, the states have no longer control over the competences they have transferred to the Community. Indeed at the level of the Council of Ministers, it is the member states that make decisions.

The areas in which the Community acts exclusively are very few from the legal point of view. Three very significant ones might be cited: Common Agricultural Policy, Common Trade Policy and Single Currency (€). In these three areas, the states can no longer act alone. They have entrusted this power to the Community to act on their behalf owing to the economic and political stakes at play on a European level.

Shared or Mixed or Concurrent Competences

Quantitatively and qualitatively speaking, this set of competences is the most significant. In all other areas that were mentioned above (transport, environment, culture, competition...), the Community and States have the right to act. It means that for the same area of political or legal action, there are two levels of action: the member states and the Community. But as soon as the Community acts, as soon as it has regulated, the States lose their power to intervene in the area covered by the EC (spill-over principle).

Implementation of Competences

The implementation of the European Union competences is accomplished in two stages. In the first, it is the Union which decides to act and in the second, it is the States which enforce them. Contrary to widespread belief, the EU's political system is entirely decentralized. But in order for the policies to be properly implemented, technically efficient legal principles are needed.

The Principle of Subsidiarity

It is Article 5, Paragraph 2 of the EC Treaty that defines the principle in question: "In areas which do not fall within its exclusive competence the Union shall act only if and insofar as the objectives of the intended action cannot be sufficiently achieved by the Member States, either at central level or at regional and local level, but can rather, by reason of the scale or effects of the proposed action, be better achieved at Union level". Specific to the European legal order and a substitute for the "federalist vocation" of the Union, a formulation rejected by the British in 1992, the subsidiarity principle was enshrined in the Maastricht Treaty. This principle can only be understood in the light of the nature of competences attributed to the Community.

Indeed there are areas where the member states have deemed it legally relevant to designate the EC as the only holder of the power to act. These exclusive and original competences, i.e., defined in or inferred from the Treaty are in reality very few: economic and monetary union (article 111), common trade policy (article 133) and the conservation of fisheries resources (CJEC, 14.07.1976, Kramer). But there are cases where the Community has fully regulated an area. Besides, in a paper published in 1992, the Commission thought it useful to add to the existing original and exclusive competences, a list of derived but exclusive competences still called competences acquired through exercise: internal market, the crucial elements of CAP, fisheries, common transport policy and free competition. Apart from these eight areas in which the regulatory exclusivity of the EC is without doubt, for the remaining areas—the surplus—community competences are shared with member states.

It is precisely in this vast area of concurrent or shared competences that the principle of subsidiarity enters into play. As soon as two levels of power (Member States/Union) hold the power to regulate an area or a public policy, the question is to know who should intervene. Article 5 Paragraph 2 relies on an affirmation in principle: competence is inherently governmental. Government prevails over the Union, even if the EC has been granted some competences. But if it appears that the twenty-seven different national regulations are not in a position to efficiently reply to a Europewide objective, then the action to attain this objective can be undertaken only by the Community. In legal terms, subsidiarity is a determining principle, constituting the basis of and triggering community competence. Politically, it determines the common interests of states by answering the following question: what do the members of the EC want to do together in the community way?

No regulatory action of the Community can be carried out if it is not justified in the light of the subsidiarity principle. In practice, it is the Commission which, through its legislative initiatives (whose grounds for action are introduced by the term "Considering"), has to argue in favour of community competence, show that the appropriate level of action is EC's with the help of supporting studies. The Council and the Parliament will then be free to contest the relevance of community action.

Political by nature, the principle of subsidiarity is not easy to grasp legally. The issue of its legal force was therefore raised as well as the scope of the jurisdictional control. Initially the Court of Justice acknowledged its own competence to carry out its restrained control in Article 5 § 2 (CJEC, 12.11.1996) *United Kingdom v The Council*, Case C-84/94, Rec. I-5755). Then, the Court effectively proceeded with a true appraisal of community action with reference to the principle of subsidiarity (CJEC, 10.12.2002, British Action Tobacco, aff-C-491/01, Rec. I-11453).

The internal and external competences of the Community are obviously involved in this sharing, this concurrence between two levels of intervention (Member States/Community). As regards external competences, agreements which are concluded between the Community and third countries or international organizations are called mixed. The notion of concurrent or shared competences signifies that for one and the same policy to be implemented, one and the same sector to be regulated, the Community as well as the member states are empowered to act. However, this joint-action rules out any idea of superimposition of interventions. What depends on the Community does not obviously depend on the states and vice versa. Justification of the principle of primacy is thus found. Indeed, when a national regulation conflicts with a Community regulation, the question of competence of the agent of this act (national) is obviously raised. To put it simply, this means that the initiating authority had regulated an area that fell within the scope of community competence.

Besides, the implementation of shared community competences produces a spill-over effect whose outcome, in terms of either time or content, may result in the phasing out of national competence. Three degrees of exercise of concurrent powers could be observed: absence of exercise of community competence which leaves the floor free for the states; partial exercise of community competence which involves the principle of subsidiarity and a restrained and complementary national competence, and finally the full-fledged exercise of community competence which means that the states have no longer the power to act.

Lastly, the evaluation of the degree of community intervention in the areas of its competence cannot be measured by the yardstick of the Treaty alone. The Treaty fixes only the dynamic competences. It is the exercise of these competences, the institutional and regulatory dynamics which will then inform these areas. Five cumulative criteria enable us to assess the degree of intervention: a textual criterion (terms of the Treaty), a formal criterion (regulation or directive), a procedural criterion (procedure leading to the adoption of the act), a material criterion (content of the act) and a quantitative criterion (number of measures adopted for the same sector).

Internal Regulation

The Institutions have been given decision making or regulatory competences in order to implement actions, carry out missions or public policies attributed to Communities and the Union. In order to do that they adopt unilateral legislation according to the procedures predefined in the Treaty, which, if they are not complied with, entail the annulment of such legislation where necessary. In so far this decision making role results in legislation in the member states, it might be admitted that its sphere of intervention is internal, i.e., circumscribed within the member states of the Union alone.

The decision making process depends on a succession of phases some of which are practically unchangeable. It is the states which defined these phases at the time of drafting the treaties. A careful scrutiny of these decision making processes reveals each time the initial intention of states with regard to their wish to confide more or less regulatory competences to Union institutions. An interpretative grid that takes into consideration the participation or non-participation of Parliament, the nature of the vote in the Council (qualified majority or unanimity) and the consultation of different committees helps us discover who holds the power in the Union. This research is important, particularly because it can throw light on the sources of legitimacy of unilateral legislation. Indeed and in spite of the criticism that regularly crops up against the European Union underscoring its democratic deficit, when the decision making mechanisms are analysed, it is clear that such a criticism cannot be reasonably levelled against the Union, when, for example, the European Parliament was the initiator of the enacted legislation.

The Law Making Procedure

The expression law making procedure seems more neutral than legislative procedure. The latter which is widely used in the doctrine and institutions of the Union (internal regulations of the Council for instance) refers in fact to a specific governmental decision making diagram and a specific legal instrument, but which do not exist so to speak in EU law. However, customary language considers the following terms as synonyms—regulatory, legislative and law making. To have a look at the institutional triangle alone (Council, Commission and Parliament), decisions made with regard to general (or specific) legislation adopted on the grounds of the treaties (EU or EC) correspond to the implementation of this law making role. The participation of each of these institutions in the adoption of legislation depends on a combination of parameters some of which are unchangeable and some variable. The Council and the Parliament constitute the law making authority of the Union.

The Quasi Invariable Involvement of the Commission and the Council

According to a principle henceforth accepted: the Commission proposes and the Council disposes. From a legal point of view, this aphorism simply means that in most of the cases, the Commission takes the initiative of proposing drafts of unilateral legislation and the Council simply adopts them. This unavoidable step in the decision making process is true with regard to the first and third pillars, with some cases of shared competences between the member states and the Commission at the initiatory stage (Article 34 of the Treaty on the European Union). It does not operate in the second pillar, where, owing to the specific nature of the matter dealt with, it is the European Council and the Council of Ministers which detain the control of the decision making process. Similarly, there are cases where the Council does not have the power to make decisions, but the Commission. This is particularly the case in the area of competition and services of general economic interest, where, by virtue of Article 86 § 3 EC, the Commission addresses, where necessary, appropriate directives and decisions to member states in addition to checking that the provisions of articles relating to this subject are enforced with the result that the simplified decision making process boils down to a proposal made by the Commission and a decision taken by the Council. Three additional remarks have to be made.

In the first place, contrary to a tenacious idea, the Commission does not have the monopoly of the initiative. At least, this monopoly operates only in the area of law. In practice or politically speaking, the Commission draws inspiration from the conclusions of the European Council, the recommendations of the European Parliament, the questions from the Council (Article 208, EC) or, we have to admit, the requests from pressure groups. Of course, the Commission has a capacity of expertise and proposal which are specific to it. But the powerful relations existing among the institutions should not be underestimated.

Secondly, when the Council adopts unanimously or by a qualified majority draft regulations or directives proposed by the Commission, it will do so only at the end of a reviewing process involving national governments acting through their permanent representatives, the COREPER and at the end of a series of amendments. It is this faculty to modify the legislation proposed by the Commission that is legally and politically decisive. It is what allows us to finally and precisely identify what was decided, how and when. All the decisions taken by the Council (regulations, directives, decisions, draft decisions...) are recorded in a register accessible to the public and containing all this information.

Finally, it is not the Council or the Commission which decides the order of implementing the process. If it corresponds to an administratively logical or functional measure, it is wholly determined by Treaty stipulations (EU or EC). The institutions, except when acting unlawfully, do not have any power to alter this order of things.

The Variable Participation of European Parliament

This is the most interesting element to explore in so far as the participation of the European Parliament in the decision making process is what confers on the legislation all its legitimacy. Moreover, and this is the salient point in the institutional history of the Union, the involvement of the European Parliament grew as the number of cases by qualified majority vote in the Council diminished. It is possible to draw up a spectrum of the participation of the European Parliament according to whether this participation, between the stage of proposal by the Commission and the stage of decision by the Council, was restrictive or had a decisive impact on the content of the proposed legislation (amending capacity). It must be noted that the participation of the committee of regions and the social and economic committee comes in between these two phases. Except for the assent procedure, the procedural diagrams which follow occur only in the European legal order (EC).

Consultation Procedure

The consultation procedure (Article 192 EC) enables the European Parliament to give its opinion on a Commission proposal in the cases laid down by the treaty. In this case, the Council consults the Parliament before ruling on the Commission proposal. After a state of flux in practice, the Court has demanded that the Council take into account the opinions given by Parliament which, at a closer look, could be analysed as amendments. The Council, however, is not bound by these opinions. The power of Parliament remains fairly limited in this procedure in so far as it is the Commission, which, once the opinion has been given, will be entrusted with reworking it or not. Moreover, the Council can reject the amendments proposed by the Commission. But Parliament has to be consulted again if the Council deviates too far from the original proposal. Except in the cases laid down by the treaty, the Council is obliged to consult the Parliament on most of the important issues. This consultation is facultative. Besides, the consultation procedure is used for non-mandatory instruments, notably recommendations and opinions of the Council and the Commission.

Conciliation Procedure

The procedure of conciliation between the Parliament and the Council, with active help from the Commission, was initiated by the Common Declaration of 4 March 1975 "for Community Legislation of general interest and which has notable financial implications and whose adoption has not been made mandatory by pre-existing legislation". The conciliation procedure the purpose of which is to reach an agreement between Parliament and the Council takes place in the form of a conciliation committee. The Parliament by giving its opinion and the Council, when it wants to depart from the opinion of the Parliament, could ask this procedure to be launched. The Council gives a definite ruling after the new opinion that Parliament might give, when the respective stands of both the institutions are sufficiently close.

Co-operation Procedure

The co-operation procedure (Article 252 EC) was introduced by the Single European Act. It gave the European Parliament a greater possibility of influencing the legislative process through a system of two readings or shuttling. The co-operation procedure is applicable only to the field of Economic and Monetary Union (Title VII, EC). Under this procedure, the Council can exercise a veto by refusing to rule on the proposals for amendments made by the European Parliament or the modified proposal of the Commission and thus block the legislative process.

The co-operation procedure is launched by a proposal initiated by the Commission and forwarded to the Council and the European Parliament. The Council, acting by a qualified majority, draws up a common position which is forwarded to Parliament together with all the necessary information and the reasons which led the Council to adopt this common position. Parliament examines this common position at second reading, and within three months may adopt, amend or reject the common position. In the latter two cases, it must do so by an absolute majority of its members. If it rejects the proposal, unanimity is required for the Council to act on a second reading. The Commission then re-examines, within one month, the proposal upon which the Council based its common position and forwards its proposal to the Council; at its discretion it can include or exclude the amendments proposed by Parliament. Within three months, the Council may adopt the re-examined proposal by qualified majority, amend it unanimously or adopt the amendments not taken into consideration by the Commission, also unanimously.

Co-decision Procedure

Introduced by the Maastricht treaty, the co-decision procedure (Article 251 EC) concerns thirty-three areas of the first pillar. Co-decision constitutes the central legislative procedure in community decision making. Looking complex at first sight when one reads the aforementioned article (see the diagram), it is founded on the principle of parity and sees to it that neither of the two institutions (European Parliament or the Council of Ministers) adopts basic legislation (general legislation such as regulations and directives activating community public policies defined in the EC Treaty) without the consent of the other. This procedure also confers on the adopted legislation all its legitimacy.

The capacity for action of the European Parliament is immense in so far as it can prevent the Council from deciding anything within a system of two successive readings, if the Council does not take into account its amendments. The Council can decide by qualified majority or on a unanimous basis according to the cases defined in the articles governing co-decision. A "rescuing" procedure ensured by a conciliation committee gathering equal number of representatives from both institutions (27 + 27) could be activated at the end of the procedure. During the past five years (legislative term 1999-04), four hundred and eighteen co-decision procedures were successfully concluded (with the exception of two cases). The average duration of the procedure is eighteen months. 70 per cent of joint legislation (regulations or directives) adopted thanks to the co-decision procedure are so made at the stage of the first reading itself. It is useful to recall here the areas concerned by co-decision as the legislative future of the Union is involved here and also that of its citizens.

Article 12: non-discrimination on grounds of nationality
Article 13-2: combat discrimination (incentive measures)
Article 18-2: freedom of movement and residence
Article 40: free movement of labour
Article 42: social security of migrant workers in the Community
Article 46-2: right of establishment: special regime for foreign nationals
Article 47: access to activity as self-employed persons; recognition of diplomas

Article 47-2: idem if there is modification of national legislation
Article 55: right of establishment, services
Article 62-1: the absence of any controls on persons when crossing internal borders;
Article 62-2 a: checks on persons at external borders
Article 62-3: freedom to travel of nationals of third countries under visa
Article 63-1: measures on asylum
Article 62-2 a: persons under temporary protection
Article 62-3: receiving refugees and displaced persons
Article 63-1: measures against illegal immigration
Article 65: judicial cooperation in civil matters (except family law)
Article 71-1: transport (rail, road, inland waterway)
Article 80-2: transport (extent: sea and air)
Article 95: internal market
Article 129: employment (incentive measures)
Article 135: customs co-operation
Article 137-1-2: social policy
Article 141: social policy; equal opportunities, equality between men and women
Article 148: European Social Fund (implementing decisions)
Article 149-4: education (incentive measures)
Article 150-4: professional training
Article 151-5: culture (incentive measures)
Article 152-4: public health (incentive measures and action)
Article 153-4: consumer protection
Article 156: trans-European network
Article 157-3: industry (specific measures in support)
Article 159-3: social and economic cohesion (specific actions outside the Funds)
Article 162: European Regional Development Fund (implementing decisions)
Article 172: research, implementation
Article 175-1.3: environment, art
Article 179: development co-operation
Article 191: political parties at the European level (statutes and regulations)
Article 255-2: right of access to European institution documents
Article 280-4: the prevention of and fight against fraud
Article 285-1: statistics
Article 286-2: independent supervisory body responsible for monitoring personal data

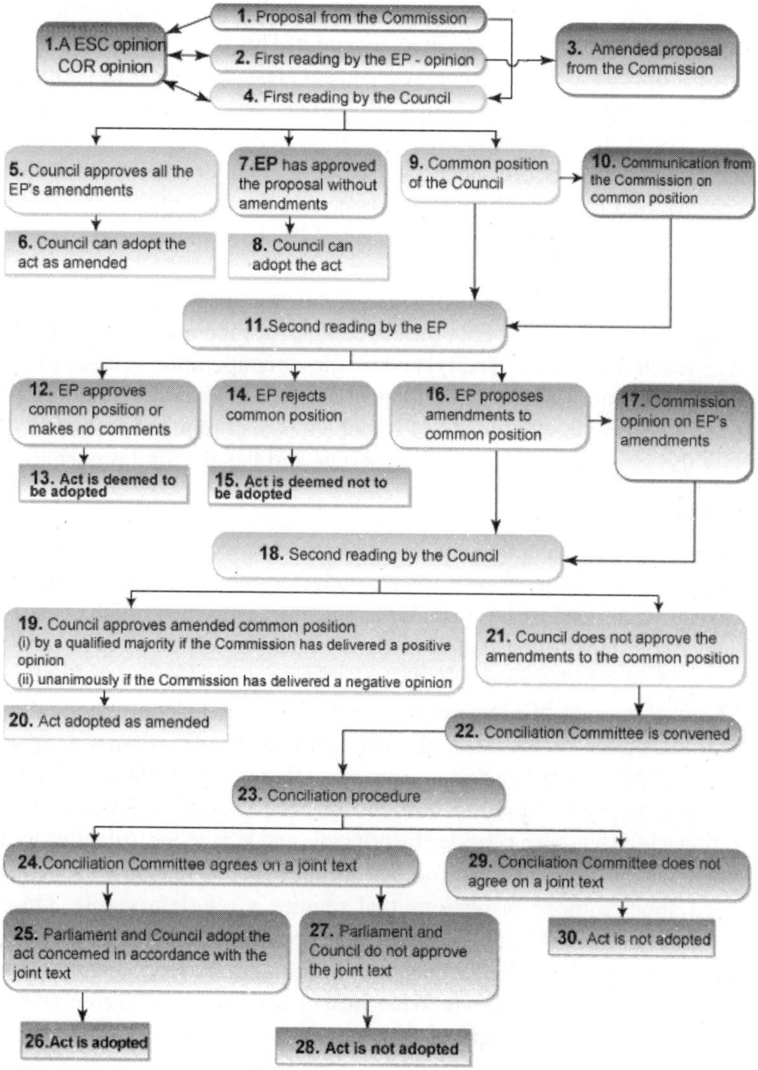

Source: Europa.

Assent Procedure

The assent procedure (Article 192 EC) was introduced by the Single European Act. It requires the Council to obtain the European Parliament's assent before certain politically and legally important decisions are taken.

The assent principle is based on a single reading in Parliament which may accept or reject a proposal but cannot amend it. This is a convenient position for the European Parliament because it can put pressure at the time of drafting the decisions which will be validated by it later on. If Parliament does not give its assent, the act in question cannot be adopted. The areas in which assent is needed concern: accession of new member states, association agreements and other binding agreements with third countries; citizenship, the specific mission of the European Central Bank, Structural and Cohesion Funds, and uniform procedure for elections to the European Parliament. Lastly, the European Parliament gives its assent for the application of sanctions imposed on a member state for a serious and persistent breach of fundamental rights (Article 7 of the EU Treaty) and for closer cooperation in areas subject to the co-decision procedure. Parliament's assent is given by a majority of votes cast. However, a majority of Members is also required in two cases, namely the accession of a new member state and the electoral procedure.

Executive Procedure

The notion of execution can be understood as referring to the material (carrying out of administrative tasks), budgetary and regulatory activities. The executive procedure has to do with regulatory activities which consist in implementing general legislation or those which, by virtue of their unified formulation require more details to be enforceable and make their effects felt. From this point of view, when the Council or the Commission adopts general legislation on the basis of a detailed and specific stipulation of the Treaty, they perform a role that is more executive than lawmaking so to say. But in customary community terminology, the executive function is an operation which has been confided by principle and in practice to the European Commission by the Council. The last articles of the fundamental Treaty adopted specify those provisions that require a regulatory role. On an instrumental level, the Commission will adopt executive regulations, directives and decisions whose legal grounding is to be found in the fundamental Treaty that the Commission implements. What must be understood is the empowering process which is at the origin of the execution as it has been organized in Articles 202 to 211 of the EC treaty.

Article 202 which defines the Council's powers specifies in its line 2 that it "confer on the Commission, in the acts which the Council adopts, powers for the implementation of the rules which the Council lays down". Article 211 of the EC treaty with reference to Commission's powers stipulates in its line 4 that it "exercises the powers conferred on it by the Council for the implementation of the rules laid down by the latter".

This mechanism, which is grounded in the attribution of powers delegated by the Council to the Commission, has many consequences. First of all, the Brussels executive has this regulatory power only exceptionally and upon initiation. It is not a power in principle that the Commission may exercise at its discretion. The Commission, once it has been empowered to act, executes only those articles of basic legislation specifically endorsed by the Council. It cannot obviously add to or modify the regulations contained in the basic legislation, if this modification or addition affects the very substance of the legislation. To put it simply, the Commission cannot alter the essential elements of the matter regulated by the Council without acting unlawfully. Lastly, Article 202-3 adds that "the Council may also reserve the right, in specific cases, to exercise directly implementing powers itself". The Council thus keeps the upper hand with regard to this role in so far as it can exhaust its power at the initial stage of the proposal, implements its own basic proposals at a later stage in a dissociated executive act (Koester case) and recovers the executive power in case the Commission has been declined jurisdiction (herein). In all these cases, the execution activated by the Commission remains exceptional and may, when it keeps this role to itself, only concern topics that are politically sensitive and therefore indefinable.

At the end of the 1970s, the Court of Justice ratified the practice of the Council consisting of setting up according to areas (foreign trade for instance) adhoc or standing committees comprising civil servants and national experts responsible for representing the member states when the Commission implements its executive duties. The functional justification for these committees arises out of necessity to maintain good coordination between the community level and the national level, for in any event it is up to the member states to finally implement this regulation. The political justification resides in the will of the states to supervise the Commission's regulatory role.

In practice, and in substance, four types of committees, corresponding to four procedures or controls, exist by virtue of the decision of the Council dated 28 June 1999 (1999/468/EC) modified by that of 17 July 2006 (2006/52). Each time it is the Council which defines the terms and conditions of the general legislation it adopts and which requires implementation measures by relying on article 202 § 3 which defines the terms and conditions. The procedure of advisory committees can thus be distinguished. It is not frankly restrictive (nor supervisory with reference to the Commission). The procedure of management committees involves the return of the executive power to the Council in case of negative opinion by the committees, but it nevertheless allows the Commission to adopt provisional execution of general legislation. The procedure of regulatory committees, which, as in the previous case, not only deprives the Commission of its executive role, but also prevents it from adopting provisional measures. As regards legislation that has been adopted by virtue of the co-decision procedure (Art 251 EC), the comitologists ruling of 17 July 2006 enables greater involvement of Parliament at the execution stage thanks to the implementation of the "regulatory committees with scrutiny" procedure for general measures whose objective is to modify, suppress or complete the non-essential elements of a joint legislation.

Budgetary Procedure

The budget is a politically decisive document for any local government retracing all the revenues and planned expenditure during the course of a civil year. The general budget may be completed by complementary or corrective budgets if they are justified by unavoidable, exceptional or unforeseen circumstances. The Union's budget (126.5 million € for 2007) abides by the principles of unity, yearly recurrence, speciality, balance, universality and transparency. The budget occupies an important place in the functioning of the institutions, ever since the EU has had its own financial resources.

The vote for the Union budget gives the opportunity for the institutions to collaborate more closely (Articles, 268-280 EC). The European Parliament and the Council together form the budgetary authority. The procedure unfolds as follows: The Commission submits a draft budget containing all the forecasts regarding the European Parliament, the Council, the Commission, Court of Justice, Court of Auditors to the Council and Parliament. The Council establishes a draft budget on the basis of these documents which it forwards to Parliament. Parliament in cases of compulsory expenditure (CE) can propose amendments to the Council which has the final word. As regards non-compulsory expenditure (NCE), Parliament has the possibility of amending the budget established by the Council within the margin calculated by the Commission. The Council then adopts a modified project by taking into consideration Parliament's amendments (CE) and the proposals (NCE). In the conciliation procedure, the Council and Parliament try to reduce the gap in their respective positions. During the second reading, Parliament fixes the final form of the budget. It is then published in the Official Journal of the European Union. Parliament can, for important reasons, reject the budget as a whole and ask the Council to submit a new draft. In this case and if the budget had not been adopted at the beginning of the fiscal year (1 January), the Treaty foresees the implementation of transitory measures that draw inspiration from the previous year's budget.

Jurisdictional Control

According to the provisions of the Treaty of Rome regarding its statutes and procedural rules, the Court of Justice exercises six big functions that could be analysed in terms of checking and control.

Action for Failure to Fulfil Obligations

The Commission can start this procedure if it has reasons to believe that a member state does not fulfil the obligations imposed on it by Community law (Article 226 EC). This procedure could also be initiated by a member state against another. In either case, the Court examines the means and arguments put forward and gives a ruling. If it is found that a member state is at fault, the incriminated member state must terminate the breach without delay. If the Court finds that the member state does not fulfil the obligations of the decision, it can slap a fine on the country (Article 228 § 2 EC).

Action for Annulment

If a member state, the Council, the Commission or, under certain circumstances, the European Parliament think that a European legislation is unlawful they can ask the Court to annul it (Article 230 EC). This "action for annulment" could also be initiated by a physical person who could seek the Court's help to annul a specific provision because the said person is affected and harmed by it directly and individually. If the Court notices that the litigious act was not correctly adopted or was not correctly based on the treaties, it can declare it null and void. Article 241 of the EC Treaty has foreseen the procedure known as plea of illegality which allows the applicant to contest, after the expiry of the time limit for action for annulment which is two months, any general legislation at the time of an action for annulment directed against its implementation measures.

The means invocable in the name of the internal or external legality of legislation constitute the surest means of monitoring the regulatory activity of the institutions. The Court effectively implements the provisions of the European Convention for the Protection of Human Rights and Fundamental Freedoms.

Action for Failure to Act

The treaty makes it obligatory for the European Parliament, the Council and the Commission to make certain decisions in certain circumstances. If the institutions do not comply with this obligation, the member states, the other EU institutions, and under certain circumstances, physical persons or companies can take the matter to the Court in order for this failure to be officially identified.

Application for Compensation Based on Liability

The contractual liability of the Community is governed by the law applicable to the disputed contract. Incidentally, it must be noted that by virtue of Article 288 EC, the Court of Justice is competent to sit in judgement over an arbitration clause contained in a contract under public or private law signed by the Community or on its behalf. In matters of non-contractual liability, the Community has to repair, in accordance with general principles common to the law of different member states, the damages caused by its institutions or its agents in the exercise of their duties. This principle is enforced according to the same conditions in the case of damages caused by the ECB and its agents in the exercise of their duties. The personal liability of the agents with respect to the Community is regulated in the provisions specifying their status and the regime which is applicable to them.

Appeals on Points of Law

If the conclusion of an external agreement might affect the Treaty of Rome, in other words, if the agreement contains clauses that are contrary to the said treaty, the Court referred to by the member states or the institutions can be asked to give an opinion on this subject. If it notices a contradiction, its opinion will be negative (Article 300 § 6 EC). The conclusion of the agreement will be possible only if the Treaty of Rome (Article 48, EC) or if the agreement in question may be revised. If the opinion is positive, the conclusion of the agreement meets with no legal impediments.

Preliminary Reference

The courts of member states should ensure the correct application of EU law in their country. The risk of the courts of different member states coming up with a different interpretation of community law exists. A referral procedure has thus been foreseen to avoid this problem. If a national court has a doubt as to the interpretation or validity of an EU law, it may, indeed even must, in certain contexts, ask for the opinion of the Court of Justice (preliminary reference). This opinion is given in the form of a preliminary ruling (Article 234 EC).

Political Control

The European Parliament whose members have an unquestionable democratic legitimacy has been invested with significant controlling powers comparable to those in effect in the member states. These controls concern the European Commission. Therefore the view that the Commission has no legitimacy and that its statutory independence corresponds to an arbitrary and untouchable power needs to be highly nuanced. Apart from parliamentary procedures and the oral or written questions addressed to Commissioners, the Parliament exercises three forms of control with regard to the Commission.

The first could be qualified as initial or constitutive. Indeed Article 214 § 2 lays down that "The President and the other Members of the Commission thus nominated shall be subject as a body to a vote of approval by the European Parliament". This is known as the Parliamentary investiture. At this stage, the Parliament exercises a true control over the members of the future Commission. It may thus, thanks to this influence, refuse one or more Commissioners selected by the Heads of States and Governments. The power balance between the representatives of peoples (EP) and those of the states, the two pillars of legitimacy in the union, is in favour of the former.

The second control, which could be qualified as accidental or destructive is based on the well known parliamentary mechanism of motion of censure. Article 201 EC stipulates in this regard: "If a motion of censure on the activities of the Commission is tabled before it, the European Parliament shall not vote thereon until at least three days after the motion has been tabled and only by open vote. If the motion of censure is carried by a two-thirds majority of the votes cast, representing a majority of the Members of the European Parliament, the Members of the Commission shall resign as a body. They shall continue to deal with current business until they are replaced in accordance with Article 214. In this case, the term of office of the Members of the Commission appointed to replace them shall expire on the date on which the term of office of the Members of the Commission obliged to resign as a body would have expired". Finally, Article 200 EC lays down in a more pacific manner that "the European Parliament shall discuss in open session the annual general report submitted to it by the Commission".

These control mechanisms must be put into perspective with those existing in member states. If the European Parliament exercises a political influence on the executive branch which is the Commission, the national parliaments are perfectly capable of implementing motions of censure against governments acting within the framework of the Council and therefore against their European policy.

Conclusion

The European Union remains today and will remain for a long time to come, the outcome of the political will of the member states to put in common their legal, economic, industrial and particularly political competences. The discourse according to which politically unified Europe has not yet been made and/or will not be made does not mean anything to those who know the functioning of the European Union and its institutions. Europe is but political and this has been the case right from its birth on 9 May 1950 (Schuman Declaration). No action may be undertaken, no legislation adopted unless there is prior political agreement among member states. But with only one per cent of the annual wealth produced in the Union is earmarked for the Union's budget, nothing very concrete can be achieved. It is again the political agreement between member states that defines the budget and resources that the member states hope to mobilize.

The Union has reached a stage of its development today in which two ways of reasoning clash: (1) Enlargement to thirty, thirty-two, thirty-five member states in order to arrive at an economic market that is the vastest and most pacified in the world (Anglo-Saxon vision). (2) Giving more depth which consists in making the Union a territory of projects in which notions such public policy, democracy, liberty have real meaning and correspond to a true ambition for the years to come (Franco-German vision). The new treaty contributes to this depth by foreseeing a President for the Union, by setting up a new institution (European Council) and by restricting the political impact of the Commission by considerably reinforcing the powers of the Parliament.

One might deplore the fact that the centre of gravity, i.e., institutional balance, is not in favour of the member states. The risk is fragmentation of national interests at the expense of a Community project. Besides, the word, 'Community' is going to disappear from the European vocabulary, as the new treaty is going to replace it by the term Union. According to me the Union is a vector and an aggregative engine that is less powerful than that of the European Community.

SINGLE MARKET FOR SERVICES

General Policies

Services Directive

- Posting of workers in the framework of the provision of services
- Equal treatment of men and women outside the labour market
- Competitiveness of services related to businesses
- Recognition of qualifications

Sectoral Provisions

Liberal Professions

- Competition in professional services

Services of General Interest

- White Paper on services of general interest
- Social services of general interest

Road Transport

- Carriage of passengers: international carriage by coach and bus

- Goods: non-resident carriers in the national market

Marine Transport

- Freedom to supply services, competition, unfair pricing practices and free access to ocean trade
- Freedom to provide services within the Member States (ocean trade)
- Inland navigation: non-resident carriers
- Inland navigation: transport of goods or passengers by inland waterway between Member States

Air Transport

- Access for air carriers to intra-Community air routes (third phase)
- Air service agreements between Member States and third countries

Information Society

- Information procedures: technical standards and regulations and regulations on information society services
- Electronic communication services
- Regulatory framework for electronic communications
- Authorisation of electronic communications networks and services
- Universal service and users' rights
- Access to electronic communications networks
- Competition in the markets for electronic communications networks and services
- Competition in the markets in telecommunications terminal equipment

Postal Services

- The development and improvement of the quality of Community postal services
- Completing the postal services market

Translated from French by
Geetha Ganapathy-Doré

NOTES AND REFERENCES

1. See for instance the agreement between the European Community and India. Memorandum of understanding between the European Community and the Republic of India on arrangements in the area of market access for textile products, *Official Journal L 153, 27/06/1996* p. 0047-0068.

7

The Referendum on the Treaty Establishing a Constitution for Europe:

The Constitutionalisation of Europe despite the "Non" to a Treaty

JULIEN STERCK

For many, France staged the final scene of a legal and political tragedy on the 29 May 2005. With 54.56 per cent of voters saying «No» to the Treaty establishing a Constitution for Europe (TCE), there was no doubt left as to the future of European Union. The French people had stabbed the idea of a political Europe, which collapsed, fatally wounded.

For some, the TCE was the condition of a Copernican revolution in Europe. After a successful economic communitarisation, it was supposed to secure the future of Europe by qualitatively enhancing its political integration and bringing a real newness to European law[1]. According to the ideas of the founding fathers who saw in the economic cooperation the basis for a political union, the TCE was perceived as the symbol that Europe needed to fulfil its original purpose. Merging the different European institutions into a unique new European Union, it aimed to introduce Europe to the ideological framework that is characteristic of its Member States, i.e. constitutionalism. In this respect the codification and clarification of the relationships between the different European institutions, as well as the adjunction of the Charter of Fundamental Rights of the Union, fitted in with the constitutionalist motto that can be read in Art. XVI of the French Declaration of the Rights of Man and of the Citizen which states: «Any society in which the guarantee of rights is not assured, nor the separation of powers determined, has no constitution at all»[2].

This symbolic step further can be already noticed in the specific procedure used to draft the TCE with the significant participation of the national Parliaments in an attempt to compensate for the democratic deficit of Europe[3].

Initially entrusted to a European Convention, the project was subsequently negotiated and modified during an Intergovernmental Conference and the Treaty establishing a Constitution for Europe was signed on 29 October 2004 by the then 25 Member States of the European Union. At this stage, the process entered a national phase, as the different States had to ratify the Treaty in accordance with their national laws.

From this moment, the narrative leading to the popular vote against the statute enabling France to ratify the TCE sounded like the chronicle of a death foretold. It is certain that the European text, with its incredible length and to some extent its lack of legal strictness[4], did not help foster a sound debate. This partly explains the erratic quality of the political debate relating to the TCE in the course of which the most contrary opinions were expressed. At the end of the day, it is difficult to state what the French refused on 29 May 2005, and even whether it was in fact the TCE they refused. When one looks at the reasons of the "No", one can be struck by the fact that some of the main justifications are disconnected from the content at heart[5].

However, from a constitutional point of view, it has to be considered that it is the French sovereign as a whole that put an end to the European constitutional hope. And yet, could it be said that, even though the constitutional ambitions of Europe have been thwarted, a constitutionalisation of Europe is still occurring from the point of view of the French law? To put it in Lincoln's words: "15 million *nays*, one *aye*, the *ayes* have it?"

Indeed, 29 May 2005, from the European law's point of view, maintained a legal pluralism. However, the referendum cannot sum up the plurality of encounters between the French legal system and the TCE, which have not, from a constitutional point of view, left the relationship between them unchanged. First of all, the French President decided, in accordance with Art. 54 of the Constitution, to submit the TCE to the *Conseil constitutionnel* (Constitutional Council), the French jurisdiction entrusted with the protection of the Constitution. The *Conseil constitutionnel* stressed that some elements of the Treaty were contrary to the French supreme norm and therefore required a constitutional revision while assuring that some other major issues of the TCE, in particular the primacy of Union law, did not contravene the French Constitution. These points were therefore left silent in the People's vote.

A two-step revision was thereupon decided on 1 March 2005. Firstly, a transitory phase, consisting in the revision of Art. 88-1, enabled France to ratify the TCE by stating: "It (*the Republic*) shall participate in the European Union in the conditions provided for by the Treaty establishing a Constitution for Europe signed on 29 October 2005"[6]. The second step consisted in revising other articles and was supposed to be implemented at the time of the TCE's entry into force in order to ensure the conformity of terms between the two norms.

If, due to the referendum, the second revision never took place, some modifications can be found in the partial decision of conformity made by the French jurisdiction. If the *Conseil constitutionnel* played "mirror games" with the provisions of the TCE[7], one can argue that it reflected a distorted image of European law. Therefore, if the "No" prevented a European constitutional revolution, it did not prevent a constitutional dynamic to go on through what was left unsaid, i.e. the interpretive discrepancies between the two legal systems.

From this perspective, the "No" to the referendum underlined above all what was lacking in order for the TCE to be a constitution. As a consequence, the renewed relationship between the two legal orders in a persisting pluralism has to be assessed. A constitutionalisation of Europe seems to be noticeable within this framework. In this respect, rather than the parliamentary solution proposed by the TCE, it is the dialogue between the French and European jurisdictions that is the driving force behind this dynamics.

I. A NEW INTEGRATIVE DYNAMICS IN SPITE OF THE "NO" TO THE REFERENDUM

The frustrated attempt to give a constitution to Europe requires a closer look at the object of the referendum itself. From this point of view, one can doubt the ability of the TCE to be qualified as a constitution. Without this fully integrative instrument, it is in the renewed relationship between a sovereign domestic law and a specific international law that more fruitful consequences can be observed.

A. The Object of the Referendum: the TCE as a Treaty

Many have argued that the TCE was actually a constitution. If the text did not perfectly fit with its traditional definition, this was justified by the fact that the new European Union had been created in a post-national environment[8]. And yet, a closer analysis of the legal provisions leads to a different conclusion and, behind these, lies something more fundamental, the lack of a European sovereign.

The Normative Qualification of the TCE as a Treaty

The Court of Justice of the European Communities (CJEC) had already qualified the Treaty establishing the European Community as a "basic constitutional charter"[9]. However, the fact that the expression "constitution" was not used hinted at some difficulties that the TCE did not resolve. To be considered as a constitution, under a normative analysis, a norm needs to fulfil certain criteria. In this respect, two different approaches characterise a constitution.

From a material point of view, the constitution is considered as the norm governing the essential features of the State. Following the guidelines of Art. XVI of the French Declaration of the Rights of Man and of the Citizen stated above, it mainly comprises the separation of powers and the protection of fundamental rights. From this material point of view, the TCE could be a constitution as it recognises fundamental rights (Part I, Title II, Fundamental Rights and Citizenship of the Union; Part II The Charter of Fundamental Rights of the Union) and determines the competences within the European legal framework (Part I, Title III, Union Competences; Part I, Title IV, The Union's Institutions and Bodies; Part I, Title V, Exercise of Union Competence)[10].

From a formal point of view, which is the prevailing one from the preponderant positivist standing, the constitutional norms are distinguished by a specific procedure for their adoption and modification. This rigidity is the guarantee of its supremacy as it would be impossible for another norm, for instance a statute, to modify it. Once again, the TCE seems to fulfil this criterion as, through different modalities, unanimity governs the procedure for its revision[11].

Therefore, under these two criteria, the TCE could apparently claim to be a constitution. However, one can be disturbed by the fact that it is precisely on the basis of this specific procedure that the *Conseil constitutionnel* concluded somewhat differently on the nature of the TCE: "the provisions of the «Treaty establishing a Constitution for Europe», and in particular those pertaining to the entry into force and revision thereof and the possibility for signatories to withdraw there from, show that said instrument retains the nature of an international treaty entered into by the States signatory" (cons. 9)[12]. Indeed, unanimity is rather the sign that the European Union, finding its origins in international law, cannot determine its own competences. On the contrary, it depends on the sovereignty of the Member States, which still hold what was described by the German doctrine as the *Kompetenz-kompetenz*[13].

As a result, the TCE is deprived of an essential normative characteristic of the constitution. To be so-called, from a Kelsenian perspective, a norm has to be the condition of validity of the other norms within the legal system[14]. However, the TCE, according to the element stated above and as emphasized by its Art. I-5 does not constitute the condition of validity of the domestic legal systems. The *Conseil constitutionnel* reached therefore the conclusion that "The name given to this new Treaty does not require as such any ruling as to its constitutionality; Article I-5 thereof, pertaining to the relations between the European Union and the Member States thereof, shows that the title of said treaty has no effect upon the existence of the French Constitution and the place of the latter at the summit of the domestic legal order" (cons. 10).

The Impossible Constitution: the Absence of a European Sovereign

Grasping the notion of constitution from a strict legal point of view could lead to an important part of its significance being left in the shadows. A constitution also represents the legal translation of political elements. If, from a normative point of view, the constitution is the norm that founds the whole legal system without being founded by any other norm, it follows that, from a political point of view, it can only stem from a sovereign power[15].

When considered from the formal point of view, the constitution is the supreme norm of the legal system of the *state*. Again, from a material point of view, the constitution deals with the organization of the state[16]. Of course, it can be argued that the idea of the constitution can be constructed outside of it[17]. However, it could not free itself from an essential condition that exists within the state, i.e. sovereignty and in particular its democratic form. In this respect, the constitution, the state and sovereignty are the three parts of the same triptych[18].

This is the consequence of the development of this notion within the constitutionalist framework. This ideology appeared with the rising of the People as sovereign and the specific organization of political power, when this sovereign is practicably unable to express its will. The legal resolution of this issue relies on the establishment of a constitution of which the People is the putative author. Exercising thereby its constituent power, it set the rules conditioning its legitimate representation by those exercising its sovereignty[19].

On the contrary, Europe is characterized by the absence of a sovereign[20]. It is certainly due to the nature of the Union itself. Built on "factual solidarities" according to Schuman, the Union never really tackled the question of its constituent power. Moreover, it is unclear if the reasons leading to the TCE were either the application of constitutionalism to the European institutions or the adaptation of a system maladjusted to future enlargements[21]. One thing is certain though, the drafting of the TCE did not bridge this gap.

Different theories explain the relationship between the democratic sovereign and the constitution. To avoid the natural law explanation and the difficulty in ascertaining the factual existence of *demos* prior to the constitution[22], a positivist stance provides a more reliable criterion where it is the constitution itself that creates the *demos* by naming it. Even if connected to the social reality, it is thus created as a legal entity[23].

From this point of view, we must conclude that the Union did not undertake this qualitative step with the TCE. "We, the People of... "is a formula that one can expect in the first few lines of a constitution. Even when taking into account the constraint of the opposition to a federalist orientation, it is possible to argue that the TCE did not recall such affiliation. On the contrary, the preamble only declares that the TCE is adopted on behalf of the European citizens and the Member States[24]. The European Union does not possess the *Kompetenz-kompetenz* because it is deprived of constituent power on its own and because, *in fine*, it is a political community deprived of a proper sovereign. Therefore, as it relies on the will of the sovereign Member States, the TCE cannot possibly be a constitution from a legal point of view. Even though the term "constitution" is symbolically and politically significant[25], dissociated from the concept of statehood and its inherent sovereignty, the TCE falls in a broader definition where the constitution is merely synonymous with institution[26].

The TCE coined a new legal expression but failed to create a new legal entity. Its nature could hardly support the constitutional claim of the Union. This lessens the meaning and consequences of the "No" to the referendum for the future of Europe. Nonetheless, in the silence of the French sovereign, it is possible to notice the development of an integrative dynamics between the domestic and European legal orders.

B. The Limited Recognition of a Specific European Competence

The question of the formal recognition by the TCE of the primacy of Union law bore a meaning close to constitutional issues, in particular the notion of a normative hierarchy. The decision of the *Conseil constitutionnel* left this issue of the primacy of Union law outside the vote, by recognizing it as being in conformity with the French Constitution. However, it is not without distorting the European provisions through its interpretation that it agreed to approve them. These discrepancies entailed an integrative tension in terms of competence between the legal orders.

The Primacy of Union Law Constitutionally Limited

Art. I-6 of the TCE formally recognized the primacy of Union law over domestic laws established by case-law starting from the *Costa v. ENEL*[27] decision, linking this primacy with the specificity of European law compared to ordinary international law.

The decision of conformity made by the *Conseil constitutionnel*[28] is of great importance to the way French constitutional law sees the primacy principle. Until 2004, the conflicts between the two sets of law had been settled by the *Conseil d'État*, the French Administrative Supreme Court, on the basis of Art. 55 of the Constitution, dedicated to ordinary international law. The constitutional jurisdiction deduced differently from Art. 88-1 of the Constitution that: "the drafters of this provision thus formally acknowledged the existence of a Community legal order integrated into the domestic legal order and distinct from the international legal order"[29]. On this basis, the specificity of the European law was acknowledged by French constitutional law.

In the same way, this decision is also the logical conclusion of a development that took place during the summer of 2004 as to the transposition of directives, these former decisions being referred to in the decision on the TCE[30]. It thereby confirmed that Art. 88-1 creates a constitutional obligation to integrate and give primacy to European norms within the French legal system.

However, this apparent agreement cannot hide a small but essential difference between the French and European perspectives[31]. For the European jurisdictions this primacy is linked to the inherent specificities of the European treaties. Under a French constitutional perspective, if the wording is almost the same, this specificity and the consequent primacy result from the Constitution as expressing the will of the French constituent power.

In this respect the affirmation that Art. I-6 is a mere codification of European case-law, as stated in one of the declarations annexed to the treaty, could have borne some harmful consequences for the *Conseil*'s position. Indeed, according to European case-law, this primacy also concerns the national constitutional norms[32]. On the contrary, for the *Conseil constitutionnel*, the primacy of Union law finds its origins but also its limits within the Constitution[33]. Indeed, to rule out the non-conformity of Art. I-6 to the Constitution, it needed to modify the interpretation of primacy offered by the European jurisdictions. By means of a systemic interpretation[34], relying on "the close proximity of Articles 1-5 and 1-6" (cons. 13), the former protecting the political and constitutional structures of the Member States, it actually neutralized the supposed codification[35].

Therefore, as stated in its previous decisions, the constitutional immunity[36] of European law stops where it contravenes an "express constitutional provision"[37]. Many questions have been raised by the nature of this limit.

The *Conseil* clarified its position in 2006 and substituted this expression for "a rule or principle inherent to the constitutional identity of France"[38]. This implicit reference to Art. I-5 shows that, even though the French constitutional law is a discordant resonance of the European voice, the dynamics stemming from a different interpretation of the primacy principle made by the *Conseil constitutionnel* continues on the material basis of the TCE, in spite of the "No" to the referendum.

The Conflict between the European and French Legal Systems: A Matter of Competence

The recognition of the primacy of Union in the limit of the sovereign supremacy tends to orientate the analysis of the relations between the domestic and European law in terms of a Kelsenian pyramidal hierarchy.

Indeed, as mentioned earlier, until the decisions of the *Conseil constitutionnel* of 2004, the question of the conflicts between the French and European norms was resolved by the *Conseil d'État*, the Supreme Administrative Jurisdiction, on the basis of Art. 55 of the Constitution dedicated to the ordinary international law, in terms of an objective hierarchy in favour of the national Constitution[39].

However, the European jurisdictions could not and did not define the primacy principle in terms of a hierarchy. From their point of view, this principle rather requires members to put aside the contrary domestic norms. Their agenda as to the primacy principle is not concerned with issues of validity but rather aims to ensure the effectiveness of European law[40]. Even if this point is ambiguous, it seems that the *Conseil constitutionnel* reoriented the constitutional understanding of primacy in a sense more compatible with the European point of view, by analyzing the conflicts in terms of a subjective competence[41]. In its decisions of 2004, its interpretation entails two consequences.

Firstly, Art. 88-1 of the Constitution demands to integrate and give a full effectiveness in the French legal order to provisions adopted by the European institutions, recognizing thereby their own competence. This recognition of the European competence extends to one of its jurisdictions and explains its refusal to control the statute transposing a directive with regard to the Constitution. That would be tantamount to controlling of the latter by the French Constitution[42]. By refraining from doing so, the French constitutional jurisdiction confirms the concomitant monopoly of competence of the European jurisdictions with regard to the validity of Union law.

Secondly and according to the first point, the limit in the scope of the primacy of Union law can also be analyzed in terms of competence. According to Art. I-I and I-6 of the TCE, the primacy of Union law is only relevant in the field of competences conferred by the Member States on the European institutions. However, had the issue of the possible conflicts between the two legal orders been defined in hierarchical terms, the *Conseil constitutionnel* would have taken into account all the constitutional norms[43]. On the contrary, the fact that this limit is restricted to provisions contravening the French constitutional identity allows another interpretation. In this respect, the competence of the Union would not be affected by an action taking place in a constitutional matter as long as it presents, on the European level, the same substantial guarantee[44]. The specificity of the limit can thus be explained as the interpretation by the *Conseil constitutionnel* according tō which, and in such a case, the European institutions would be regarded as having taken an action outside the competences conferred on them by the treaty[45]. This competence would therefore still belong to the domestic legal order and its judges.

Whereas the TCE could not succeed in creating a constitution enforcing a fully integrated legal system, the *Conseil constitutionnel* deliberating on the issue of the primacy of Union law, recognized a legal pluralism based on Art. 88-1 where the degree of integration depends on the convergence between the jurisdictional interpretations of their respective competences[46].

This analysis allows us to conclude that the TCE could not fulfil its constitutional claim. At the same time, however, what was left unsaid during the referendum bears significantly upon the integration of the two legal systems. We can thus notice a process of constitutionalisation, even though it would take a different way from the one proposed by the TCE.

II. THE EUROPEAN CONSTITUTIONALISATION: A JURISDICTIONAL OPPOSITION RATHER THAN A PARLIAMENTARY PARTICIPATION

Some have argued that inspired by constitutionalism, the TCE aimed to implement parliamentary principles within the Union[47]. However, despite the French refusal, and maybe clarified by it, this option presents some difficulties. On the contrary, the jurisdictions have to be considered as the main actors if one can speak of a constitution in Europe. That would nonetheless involve a new understanding of the idea of constitution.

A. The Referendum or the Difficulties of the Parliamentary Way

Facing a democratic deficit, the Union opted for an increase in the role of Parliaments, either European or domestic, in the European framework.

However one can doubt whether this solution would have been able to fulfil its constitutional objective, i.e. building a representative democracy[48], had the outcome of the referendum been different.

The European Parliament and the Lack of Representation

From a constitutional point of view, the competences transferred to the Union require a revision of the French Constitution; if this transfer affects the essential conditions of the exercise of national sovereignty[49]. Therefore, the *Conseil constitutionnel*, reiterating a long established reasoning, decided that such a revision was necessary, prior to the ratification of the TCE. However, if this question covers the transfer of new powers to the Union, it is the new manner of exercising competences already transferred that becomes more significant[50].

As to the new competences, the revision was mainly required by the unification of the previous organizations, the European Communities and the European Union, in a new European Union and the subsequent submission of the second (Common Foreign and Security Policy) and third pillars (Police and Judicial Co-operation in Criminal Matters) to the community procedure, where the "ordinary legislative procedure" prevails.

However, the TCE did not so much increase the new European competences as modify their manner of exercise. On the one hand, the *Conseil constitutionnel* criticized the provisions "depriving France of any power to oppose (...) a decision or by depriving France of any power to act on its own initiative" (cons. 27). The first hypothesis concerns the switch from an unanimous to a qualified majority whereas the second one deals with the replacement of "the individual power of initiative vested in each Member State under previous Treaties by a joint right of initiative of a quarter of Member States, allowing the latter to put forward a draft European act in matters concerning the area of freedom, security and justice" (cons. 32).

On the other hand, the essential conditions of the exercise of national sovereignty were also affected by the increased decision-making power of the European Parliament introduced by the TCE. We know that it represented an attempt to increase the legitimacy of the Union. And yet, the *Conseil constitutionnel*, as it did for the first time in 1976[51], confirmed that the European Parliament "is not an emanation of national sovereignty" whereas according to Art. 3 of the French Constitution: "National sovereignty shall belong to the people, who shall exercise it through their representatives and by means of referendum".

According to the theory of representation, only the organs participating in the formation of the sovereign's will, i.e. statutory law according to Art. VI of the Declaration of the Rights of Man and of the Citizen can be qualified as representatives, regardless of the way they are designated[52]. Therefore, for French constitutional law, even though Art. I-20 states that "the European Parliament shall be composed of representatives of the Union's citizens"[53], it is not representative of the French sovereign[54]. This confirms that there is discontinuity as to the sovereignty between the Members States and Europe. It is not the domestic sovereignties that are transferred but only their exercise, entailing a loss of legitimacy within the domestic systems without any gain at the supranational level[55].

The development of the European Parliament could only improve the representativity of the Union, if this notion is understood as the ability of an organ to mirror the sociological features of a group. The increasing status of the elected body can enhance the quality of European governance[56] but falls short of fulfilling the constitutional aim of making the Union evolve towards a democratic government.

The Weaknesses of the French Parliament's Participation in the Union

The constitutionalisation of the Union as development of a European constituent power could therefore only result from the participation of the domestic sovereigns through their representatives. To this purpose, an interweaving of domestic Parliaments and European institutions was done by the TCE. It resulted in a constitutional revision in order to inscribe such procedures in the French supreme norm.

The participation of the national Parliaments in the decision-making power of the Union could occur in two instances. They could veto a simplified revision of the TCE under a bridge provision (Art. IV-444)[57] and were involved in the application of the principle of subsidiarity (Art. I-11 § 3).

The latter concerns the competences shared by the Union and the Member States (Art. I-12 § 2). The Union can act only if the Member States cannot effectively achieve on their own the objectives defined. In this framework, the national Parliaments were entrusted with the protection of the competences of their legal orders. Firstly, they could forward to the European institutions an opinion stating why this action may not comply with the principle of subsidiarity[58]. Secondly, they could also submit this matter to the CJEC, through their Government, in order to see the principle of subsidiarity enforced[59].

By saying "No", the French people did not seize the opportunity to remedy one of the main criticisms against the Union, i.e. its growing undemocratic intrusion. However, a more detailed analysis shows that these provisions could hardly do so.

From a domestic point of view, the French constitutional system is usually characterized as a rationalized parliamentary regime. It corresponds to the modification of the balance between the Government (Council of Ministers) and the Parliament in favour of the former in order to avoid a drift towards an assembly regime. It involves an institutional balance focused on the solidarity between the Government and the parliamentary majority under the direction of the former[60]. Due to this national specificity, one can conclude that the participation of the legislative chambers in the Union would not dramatically change the course of action decided by the French Government and involve a major enhancement in its democratic nature[61].

However, it can also be explained at the European level. The power of the Parliaments for this limited intervention[62] is purely negative in the sense that they can only preclude the European normative action. Moreover, the consequences of this participation are minimal. The only obligation faced by European institutions is to take into account these opinions[63]. Even if the draft must be reviewed when it entails the opposition of at least one third of the votes allocated to the national Parliaments[64], the European institutions can still decide to maintain, modify or withdraw it. Finally, even though it cannot be affirmed, one can doubt the willingness of the CJEC to side with the national Parliaments and protect the exercise of national sovereignties by domestic institutions against the expansion of its own competence[65]. Thus, in this submission of the Parliaments to the European will, we are far from the intervention of the representative of a national sovereign, owner of the *Kompetenz-kompetenz*.

The provisions of the TCE cast doubt on the constitution of a deeper participation of the national *demoi* through a parliamentary way. However, considering the dynamic explained above, a closer look at the relationships between the jurisdictions, a major figure of the constitutionalism[66], could throw a new light on the constitutionalisation of Europe.

B. The Existence of a Jurisdictional Dialogue: Constitutionalisation Despite the "no" to the TCE

Defined in terms of competence rather than hierarchy, the relations between the two legal systems give a central role to judges and their interpretations. Within this jurisdictional dialogue, it seems possible to notice a further step in the establishment of the "basic constitutional charter" ascertained by the European judge long before the debate on the TCE.

Sharing of Competences as the Result of a Jurisdictional Dialogue

The decision of the *Conseil constitutionnel* underlined the importance of the jurisdictions in the development of the Union. In this Europe that is getting more and more shaped by the judges' activity, the notion of interpretation, which is essential to their activity, has to be clarified.

Interpretation is analyzed by two main theories[67]. Its traditional understanding relies on the presupposition of a textual uniqueness of meaning that the judge must only recall. Where the meaning is unclear, the interpretation, defined as an act of knowledge, aims to discover it by the use of strict methods. Otherwise interpretation is unnecessary (*in claris cessat interpretatio*).

On the other side, the realist theory of interpretation presents an opposite account of interpretation, pointing out that considering a provision as a clear one already requires an interpretation. Under a Kelsenian analysis, the normative phenomenon is a matter of signification. In this respect a distinction has to be made between the legal text and the norm, which is the meaning granted to this text. Still, due to the inescapable ambiguity of language, a legal provision gathers a multiplicity of potential meanings. Therefore, a norm as signification is never the result of an act of knowledge. It is the consequence of an act of will, i.e. the choice of a certain meaning. Different interpretations cannot be said to be right or wrong but are distinguished by their ability to produce effects within a legal system. The ones that are recognized as having unchallengeable consequence are said to be authentic. Therefore, the *Conseil constitutionnel* and the CJEC are both authentic interpreters in their respective legal systems.

As a consequence, the scope of national and European competences and their alleged conflicts do not depend on the discovery of a fixed meaning but are the products of a continuous interpretation[68], in particular as to the significance of Articles I-5 and I-6 of the TCE.

This was the basis for a jurisdictional dialogue that the *Conseil* expressly took into account when ascertaining the conformity of the Charter of Fundamental Rights of the Union to the Constitution[69]. For example, difficulties could have arisen when the freedom of religion set down by the TCE (Art. II-70) is confronted with the secularism inherent to the French constitutional identity (Art. 1 of the French Constitution). Relying on the reference made by the TCE to the European Convention for the Protection of Human Rights and Fundamental Freedoms[70], the *Conseil constitutionnel* quoted the *Leyla Sahin v. Turkey* decision of the European Court of Human Rights (ECHR)[71]. By means of this reference, it affirmed its conformity by bending the recognition of the "constitutional tradition common to the Member States" on these matters[72] into a nationalistic one: "in harmony with the constitutional traditions of each Member State" (cons. 18).

This reference to the ECHR's decision can be criticized, as the decision had been appealed to the Grand Chamber[73]. However, from the point of view of the realist theory of interpretation, it could be read as an invitation addressed to the CJEC to engage a dialogue and to take into account the reasoning of the French jurisdiction. The *Conseil* asked for the recognition of the conditions under which the French legal system can effectively integrate Union law[74]

A Constitutionalisation of Europe and the Notion of Constitution

This dialogue as to the determination of the respective competences, in which the formal and the material aspects of law merge within the jurisdictional interpretation[75], gets closer to the first condition set by Art. XVI of the Declaration of the Rights of Man and of the Citizen. One can therefore legitimately wonder if the French debate on the TCE did take a genuine constitutional dimension.

Firstly, the power of the interpreter has to be assessed. According to the realist theory of interpretation, if the norm is a signification, the body that decides the meaning of a text is, at least, vested with the same power as its author. As a consequence, the *Conseil constitutionnel* by interpreting the Constitution participates in the expression of will of the constituent power[76]. Thus, according to the definition stated above, it can be considered as the representative of the French sovereign. Therefore, its participation in the determination of the constitutionally acceptable competences of the Union and the effectiveness of its law within the French legal system can complete, even more influentially, the purpose assigned to national Parliaments by the TCE. The participation of national sovereigns in the functioning of the Union, through their judges[77], would therefore be an answer to the issue of sovereignty in a Europe described by Jacques Delors as a "Federation of States".

Secondly, the national judge being the ordinary judge of European law, they are bound with the European jurisdictions in an interpretative relationship pointing at the same legal texts. Moreover, in the absence of hierarchical links, both are thereby authentic interpreters caught in a battle of authentic will continuously repeated[78]. In this opposition, they both possess specific means to have their interpretative claims recognized. On the one hand, the European jurisdictions can gain the primacy of Union law by engaging the responsibility of the Member States with its financial consequences. On the other hand, the *Conseil* can condition the agreement of the French sovereign, and the subsequent enhancement of the European legitimacy, to the respect of its constitutional identity[79]. On this basis, a cooperative recognition of their respective interests has already taken place, allowing us, from a normative point of view, to interpret this integrative process as a constitutionalisation[80]. For instance, it seems that the CJEC, when interpreting the scope of the primacy of Union law, paid recently greater attention to the concerns raised by the different constitutional jurisdictions as to their constitutional identities[81].

This mechanism involving competitive powers over the attribution of meaning to the same legal texts[82] seems to get closer to the understanding of the notion of constitution in the birth of constitutionalism. In the 18th century, the constitution was not considered as a norm, i.e. as a set of prescriptions. Its description on the contrary owed a lot to mechanical metaphors. As stated by Montesquieu in the *The Spirit of the Laws*: "It has to be that, by the disposition of things, power stops power". The constitution was considered as a mechanism that should produce, and not command, liberty[83]. In this respect the notion of "checks and balances" is typical of a mechanical conception of the constitution.

Considering the relationship between the French and the European judges stated above, this different understanding of the notion seems promising if one wants to describe the normative situation within Europe in terms of constitution.

The referendum that took place on 29 May 2005 forbade a Copernican revolution in the European legal system according to which the French legal system would have been organized around the supremacy of Union law. However, one can wonder whether the TCE was a legal instrument likely to remedy the absence of a European *demos*. However, the "No" did not have the fateful consequences that were once feared on the issue of the European constitution. It seems that, according to a different understanding of this notion, one could still describe the mechanisms resulting from what was left silent in the referendum in terms of constitution. In this respect, the structure determining the respective competences of the different legal systems would consist in the interpretive relativity of the French and European jurisdictions.

NOTES AND REFERENCES

1. S. Pina, «La révision du titre XV de la constitution et le Traité établissant une constitution pour l'Europe», *Revue de la recherche juridique*, no. 4, 2006, pp. 2153-2178 especially pp. 2153-2155.
2. My translation here as well as hereafter unless stated otherwise.
3. For a more detailed account of the drafting of the TCE, see K. Lenaerts and P. van Nuffel, "La constitution pour l'Europe et l'Union comme entité politique et ordre juridique", *Cahiers de droit européen*, no. 1-2, 2005, pp. 16-125 especially pp. 17-23.

4. For an overall criticism of the TCE's drafting, see P.-Y. Monjal, "Le projet de traité établissant une Constitution pour l'Europe: quels fondements théoriques pour le droit constitutionnel de l'Union européenne", *Revue trimestrielle de droit européen*, vol. 40, 2004, pp. 442-475 especially pages 446-460.
5. É. Perraudeau, "Les Français dans le miroir européen. Le référendum du 29 mai 2005", *Pouvoirs*, no. 116, 2006, pp. 151-161.
6. Translation of the French Constitution and of the most recent decisions of the *Conseil constitutionnel* can be found on its website: http://www.conseil-constitutionnel.fr.
7. For this logic of "mirror games" and its consequences, see A. Levade, "Le Conseil constitutionnel aux prises avec la Constitution européenne", *Revue de droit public*, no. 1, 2005, pp. 19-50.
8. É. Maulin, "Le pouvoir constituant dans l'Union européenne", *Droits*, no. 45, 2007, pp. 73-88 especially p. 80.
9. CJEC, Parti écologiste "Les Verts" v European Parliament, 23 April 1986, [ECR] 1339.
10. See V. Champeil-Desplats, "Commentaire de la décision du Conseil constitutionnel no. 2004-505 DC du 19 novembre 2004 relative au Traité établissant une Constitution pour l'Europe", *Revue trimestrielle de droit* européen, vol. 41, 2005, pp. 557-580 especially p. 561.
11. A. Auer, "*E pur si muove*. Le caractère constitutionnel de la Constitution pour l'Europe", *Revue du droit de l'Union* européenne, no. 1, 2005, pp. 65-90 especially p. 74.
12. Decision no. 2004-505 DC dated 19 November 2004.
13. P.-Y. Monjal, *op. cit.*, p. 465.
14. J.-C. Piris, "L'Union européenne: vers une nouvelle forme de fédération", *Revue trimestrielle de droit européen*, vol. 41, 2005, pp. 243-260 especially p. 250.
15. M. Troper, "Le projet de Constitution européenne et la question du pouvoir constituant", *Cités*, n° 13, 2003, pp. 101-111 especially p. 108.
16. P.-Y. Monjal, *op. cit.*, p. 464.
17. A. Auer, *op. cit.*, p. 73.
18. D. Ritleng, "Le principe de primauté du droit de l'Union", *Revue trimestrielle de droit européen*, vol. 41, 2005, pp. 285-303 especially p. 291.
19. C. de Aranjo, "Sur le constitutionalisme européen", *Revue de droit public*, 2006, no. 6, pp. 1545-1568 especially pp. 1558-1553.
20. O. Jouanjan, "Ce que «donner une constitution à l'Europe» veut dire", *Cités*, no. 13, 2003, pp. 21-35 especially pages 24 and 28.
21. J.-P. Feldman, "Existe-il un constitutionalisme européen?", *Droits*, no. 43, 2007, pp. 163-175 especially p. 163.
22. J.-C. Piris, *op. cit.*, p. 249.
23. M. Troper, "Le projet de Constitution européenne et la question du pouvoir constituant", *op. cit.*, pp. 103-104.
24. If the people constitute a legal entity, a peculiar form of sovereign, it has to be distinguished from the population. In this respect, the notion of citizenship is closer to the latter.

25. P.-Y. Monjal, *op. cit.*, p. 466.
26. M. Troper, "Le projet de Constitution européenne et la question du pouvoir consitutant", *op. cit.*, p. 102.
27. *Flaminio Costa v. ENEL* [1964] ECR 585.
28. Decision no. 2004-505 DC dated 19th November 2004.
29. V. Champeil-Desplats, *op. cit.*, p. 562 and S. Pina, *op. cit.*, p. 2157.
30. Decisions no. 2004-496 DC dated10th June2004, 2004-497 DC dated Ist July 2004, 2004-498 DC and 2004-499 DC dated 29th July 2004.
31. A. Levade, *op. cit.*, p. 29.
32. For instance, Internationale Handelsgesellschaft mbH v Einfuhr—und Vorratsstelle für Getreide und Futtermitte [1970] ECR 1125.
33. H. Labayle and J.-L. Sauron, "La Constitution française à l'épreuve de la Constitution pour l'Europe", *Revue française de droit administrative*, 2005, pp. 1-29 especially p. 7.
34. V. Champeil-Desplats, *op. cit.*, p. 563.
35. Of course, the reasoning of the *Conseil constitutionnel* is not devoid of strategic considerations but it seems contradictory to deny to the French jurisdiction this creative power while recognizing it with respect to the European jurisdictions.
36. J.-P. Jacqué, "Droit constitutionnel national, Droit communautaire, CEDH, Charte des Nations Unies. L'instabilité des rapports de système entre ordres juridiques", *Revue française de droit constitutionnel*, vol. 69, 2007, pp. 3-37 especially p. 13.
37. Decision no. 2004-496 DC, cons. 7.
38. Decision no. 2006-540 DC, cons. 19.
39. B. Mathieu, "Les rapports normatifs entre le droit communautaire et le droit national. Bilan et incertitudes relatifs aux évolutions récentes de la jurisprudence des juges constitutionnel et administrative français", *Revue française de droit constitutionnel*, vol. 72, 2007, 675-693 especially p. 686 as well as CE, Ass., 30th October 1998, *Sarran, Levachet et autres*, no. 200286, 200287 and more explicitly, CE, 3d December 2001, *Syndicat national de l'industrie pharmaceutique*, no. 226514.
40. D. Alland, "À la recherché de la primauté du droit communautaire", *Droits*, no. 45, 2007, pp. 109-125 especially p. 120.
41. D. Chamussy, "Le Conseil constitutionnel face à la primauté du droit communautaire", *Actualité juridique—Droit administrative*, no. 4, 2005, pp. 219-223 especially p. 220. It seems that the *Conseil d'État* followed this shift in the analysis of the conflict between the two legal systems. See CE, Arcelor, 8 February 2007 and Mathieu, *op. cit.*, pp. 687-688.
42. B. Mathieu, *op. cit.*, p. 676.
43. Cassia, "Le juge administrative, la primauté du droit de l'Union européenne et la Constitution française", *Revue française de droit administratif*, 2005, pp. 465-472 especially p. 466.
44. See Decision no. 2004-498 DC of the *Conseil constitutionnel* when the freedom of speech was at stake.
45. J.-P. Jacqué, *op. cit.*, p. 19.

46. D. Ritleng, *op. cit.*, p. 298.
47. C. Hiscok-Lageot, "Le traité établissant une Constitution pour l'Europe: une occasion manqué d'instaurer un régime parlementaire", *Revue française de droit constitutionnel*, vol. 66, 2006, pp. 303-320.
48. K. Lenaerts and P. van Nuffel, *op. cit.*, p. 91.
49. The question of bridge provisions, which involves the same kind of reasoning, will not be dealt with here as they are more distant from the present topic.
50. For a more detailed analysis, see for instance D. Blanc, "Les affectations du «traité constitutionnel» européen sur la Constitution européenne: une affectation minimale", *Revue de la recherché* juridique, no. 4, 2005, pp. 2257-2276 especially pp. 2270-2276.
51. Decision no. 1976-71 DC dated 30th December 1976.
52. M. Troper and F. Hamon, *Droit constitutionnel*, LGDJ, 27° ed., 2001, p. 166.
53. This idea that the citizenship cannot replace a European *demos* would require a more detailed analysis of the distinction between citizenship and sovereignty, see, for instance, C. Blumann, "Les institutions de l'Union dans le cadre du Traité établissant une Consitution pour l'Europe", *Revue trimestrielle de droit européen*, 2005, vol. 41, pp. 347-374 especially p. 364 and P. Dollat, "La citoyenneté française: une superposition de citoyennetés", *Revue française de droit administrative*, 2005, pp. 69-87.
54. V. Champeil-Desplats, *op. cit.*, p. 575.
55. Maulin, *op. cit.*, p. 78.
56. B. Buguet, "Union européenne, projet de Traité constitutionnel: éléments d'analyses", *Revue de droit public*, no. 2, 2005, pp. 463-474 especially p. 474.
57. Once again and for the same reasons as above, the question of bridge provisions will not be tackled.
58 Art. 6 of the Protocol no. 2.
59. Art. 8 of the Protocol no. 2.
60 P. Avril, "Le parlementarisme rationalisé", *Revue de droit public*, 1998, pp. 1507-1515 especially p. 1515.
61. H. Labayle et J.-L. Sauron, *op. cit.*, pp. 22-23 and D. Blanc, "Contribution à l'étude du «traité-constitutionnel» européen vu par le constituent: les pouvoirs du Parlement français entre continuités et ruptures. Á propos de la loi constitutionnelle n° 2005-204 du 1er mars 2005", *Revue française de droit* constitutionnel, vol. 64, 2005, pp. 845-874 especially p. 860-862.
62. H. Labayle and J.-L. Sauron, *op. cit.*, p. 21.
63. Art. 7 of the Protocol no. 2 § 1.
64. Art. 7 of the Protocol no. 2 § 3.
65. D. Blanc, *op. cit.*, p. 868.
66. C. de Aranjo, *op. cit.*, pp. 1551-1553.
67. For a more detailed explanation of the subsequent elements of the realist theory of interpretation, see M. Troper, "Interprétation" in Dictionnaire de la culture juridique, D Alland and S. Rials (dir.), Paris, PUF, 2003, pp. 843-847.
68. D. Alland, *op. cit.*, p. 121.

69. For comprehensive analysis of the questions raised by the Charter see, for instance, J. Roux, "Le traité établissant une Constitution pour l'Europe à l'épreuve de la Constitution française", *Revue de droit public*, no. 1, 2005, pp. 58-102 especially pp. 74-87.
70. Preamble of Part II and art. II-112 of the TCE.
71. Case no. 4774/98, 29 June 2004.
72. Art. II-112 § 4.
73. See, for instance, F. Sudre, "Les approximations de la décision 2004-505 DC du Conseil constitutionnel sur «sur la Charte des droit fondamentaux de l'Union». Réflexions critiques", *Revue française de droit administrative*, 2005, pp. 34-39.
74. A. Levade, *op. cit.*, p. 42.
75. M. Troper, *Pour une théorie juridique de l'État*, Paris, PUF, 1994, p. 220
76. M. Troper in *Dictionnaire de la culture juridique*, *op. cit.*, p. 846.
77. The constitutional revision of July 2008, which enables the *Conseil constitutionnel* to intervene in ordinary litigations on questions relating to fundamental rights, would also increase its representativity. Moving away the risk of a government by judiciary it would, at the same time, intensify the dialogue with European jurisdictions.
78. D. Ritleng, *op. cit.*, p. 296.
79. J.-P Jacqué, *op. cit.*, p. 20.
80. J.-L. Quermonne, "L'émergence d'un droit constitutionnel européen", *Revue internationale de droit comparé*, no. 2, 2006, pp. 581-591 especially p. 585.
81. T. Georgopoulos, "La neutralisation de la justice constitutionnelle en matière de droit européen", *Revue européenne de droit public*, 2006, pp. 1481-1511 especially p. 1506-1510.
82. D. Rousseau, "Une résurrection la notion de constitution", *Revue de droit public*, 1990, pp. 5-20 especially p. 16.
83. M. Troper, *Pour une théorie juridique de l'État*, *op. cit.*, p. 212 and the following.

8

The European Union and its Issue with Democracy:

A Closer Look at the Irish Rejection of the Lisbon Treaty

PATRICK B. GRIFFIN

A. THE ROLE OF THE LISBON TREATY

To appreciate the significance of the Lisbon Treaty (2), it is perhaps interesting to first consider its place in the legal structure of the EU (1).

The Place of the Lisbon Treaty in the Legal Structure of the European Union—the Different Treaties Making-up the European Union

The European Union is a creation over time and does not result from any one agreement or treaty. Prior to its evolution into the EU structure, its activities were confined to cooperation between the six original founding member states in specific fields. From these modest beginnings it has grown in fits in starts, both as regards the scope of its activities but also as regards its membership[1]. In all, there are six treaties that have led to the creation of the European Union as we know it today. Three of these treaties pre-date the actual creation of the European Union and for the sake of simplicity are referred to here as the founding treaties (a); the remainder concern the creation of the actual European Union and the ever increasing scope and competence of its powers (b).

(a) The Founding Treaties

(i) The European Coal and Steel Treaty[2]

The inspiration for the creation of the European Union resulted from a plan devised by Robert Schuman, the then French Foreign Affairs Minister and Jean Monnet who was responsible for overseeing French economic recovery after the World War II. Seeking a means of preventing future internecine wars between Germany and her neighbours, it was decided to pool French, German, Italian and Benelux[3] production of coal and steel, the main industries of war. So as to avoid the mistakes of Versailles[4], the formulators of the plan sought to promote German economic recovery but at the same time bind her to her neighbors within an organization of member states. The result was the Treaty of Paris[5] creating the European Coal and Steel Community (ECSC). The objective of the Treaty was to create a common market in the production of coal and steel and the signatory member states passed sovereignty over the management of these industries to a set of three institutions created for this purpose[6]. The Community was created for a period of fifty years and thus came to an end in 2002. However, its importance had waned long before both as a result of the near disappearance of Europe's coal and steel industries and the creation of the more successful European Economic Community constructed on the foundations it laid.

(ii) The European Economic Community Treaty[7]

In 1957 the signatories of the Treaty of Paris created the European Economic Community (EC)[8] and the European Atomic Energy Community (Euratom), the latter modeled on the ECSC. Euratom was limited to a single industrial sector, namely nuclear energy and has had a limited impact on the process of European integration. However, the EC Treaty was a far more ambitious undertaking and was intended from the outset to create "ever closer union amongst the peoples of Europe"[9]. The EC Treaty established four main institutions[10]: the Council of the European Union[11], the European Commission[12], the European Parliament[13] and the European Court of Justice[14] to oversee the coordination of the economic development of its member states through the integration of their economies. This was achieved mainly through the creation of a common market (hereinafter the Single Market), whereby goods, workers, services and capital could circulate freely between and among member states[15]. More importantly, the EC required its member states to pool sovereignty in the above named institutions in the areas covered by the treaty and in this way the organization resembled the federalist vision of Europe outlined by Churchill in his famous United States of Europe speech[16]. Indeed, it is this surrender of sovereignty that distinguishes the European Union from the other more traditional post World War II organizations such as the European Free Trade Association (EFTA)[17]. Neither federation nor confederation, the European Union nonetheless remains more than a mere intergovernmental structure. It is often described as a hybrid organization, part-intergovernmental, part-federacy, sharing some of the characteristics of both.

(iii) The Single European Act

The Single European Act (SEA) was signed in 1986 and represented the first real revision of the EC Treaty since its adoption in 1957[18]. Such a revision was considered necessary in light of the increased size of the EC and problems linked to the adoption of legislation for the creation of the Single Market. Indeed, primarily aimed at facilitating the creation of the Single Market, the real importance of the SEA, is that it increased the federal character of the EC by introducing:

- Qualified Majority Voting (QMV)[19], and
- Enhancing the legislative role of the European Parliament.

By introducing the practice of QMV, the SEA effectively removed the right to veto of individual member state over EC legislative initiatives[20]. Although QMV was primarily limited to measures aimed at establishing the Single Market, its introduction was significant as member states when acting alone no longer enjoyed a power of veto. Moreover, the weighted distribution of voting power between member states under QMV prevented the larger member states, such as Germany and France from dominating excessively the process of European integration[21]. The SEA also reinforced the federal character of the EC by extending the importance of the role played by the European Parliament in the EC legislative process. Under the SEA, the Parliament, especially as regards legislative initiatives concerning the creation of the Single Market, was given limited co-legislative powers along with the Council of Ministers. Prior to the SEA, the Parliament had mainly played a consultative role.

Thus, the SEA marked an important beachhead in the development of the EU and was only accepted by the EC's more Eurosceptic members, for example the United Kingdom (UK), because it secured the attainment of an important UK economic goal, namely the creation of the Single Market. Indeed, by 1992, just six short years after the adoption of the SEA, the Single Market programme was largely completed. However, the price was increased federalism and the SEA can be likened to a bridge that facilitated the journey of European integration from one of economic union established by the Treaty of Rome to something that has come to be called the European Union.

(b) The Creation of the European Union

Leading member states such as Germany and France considered that a true single market required the creation of a single currency and accompanying monetary union. However, they also felt that such Economic and Monetary Union (EMU) would not be possible without accompanying European

Political Union (EPU). Thus, following two Intergovernmental Conferences (IGCs) on both of these questions in 1990, the Treaty on European Union (TEU) was signed in Maastricht in December 1991[22].

(i) The Treaty on European Union

As we have seen, the aim of the TEU was to provide for limited economic and political union between the member states of the EC. It did so by creating a new organization, the European Union (EU). The EU created three separate pillars of European integration:

- The first pillar, involving the already existing three communities, the ECSC, EURATOM and the EC. These areas continued to be governed by their respective treaties, as amended by the TEU;
- The second pillar, coordinating Common Foreign and Security Policy, administered by way of intergovernmentalism[23] as opposed to the semi-federal type structure governing the EC, discussed above;
- The third pillar, also coordinating member state policy in the area of Police and Judicial Cooperation in Criminal Matters and also initially administered by way of intergovernmentalism[24].

The importance of TEU lies not just with its expansion of the scope of European integration beyond the simple creation of a Single Market. In retrospect, it also represents the moment that the populations of the member states increasingly began to signal a falling out of love with the process of European integration. Such disenchantment was not limited to traditionally Eurosceptic nations such as the UK and Denmark[25]. The citizens of founding states such as France also seemed less inclined to embrace increased integration[26]. Despite a sometimes rocky passage, the TEU came into force on 1 November 1993, after its ratification by all member states.

(ii) Treaty of Amsterdam[27]

In 1996 another IGC was held to consider both the application of the Maastricht Treaty and the challenge posed by the proposed further enlargement of the EU[28]. The results of its conclusions were set out in a new Treaty, referred to as the Treaty of Amsterdam (TA). The TA conserved and built upon the three pillar approach established under the TEU and further developed the social character of the Union. Intergovernmental cooperation under the third pillar—police and criminal justice—was intensified so as to allow better coordination of member state policy in areas coming under this heading. Further, the establishment of the Schengen area was officially incorporated into the legal system of the Union, with Ireland, the United Kingdom and Denmark remaining outside. Under the heading of common foreign policy arrangements, the treaty created the post of High Representative for EU Foreign Policy, so as to allow a single face to be put on EU foreign policy as regards the outside world[29]. The TA did not specifically provide for a common defense policy but laid the seeds for closer cooperation in this field by increasing EU responsibility in the area of peacekeeping missions. Institutionally, the Parliament's role in the legislative process was reinforced[30]. However, on the more general question of institutional reform, deemed essential in the light of the future enlargement of the EU, the TA remained largely silent. In particular member states appeared unable to agree on the general extension of QMV to legislative initiatives and how votes should be weighted in this regard. Equally, the proposed reduction in the number of Commissioners heading the European Commission proved sensitive, especially to smaller member states. Thus, the question of the distribution of power in a newly enlarged Union was largely left to the future treaty.

(iii) The Nice Treaty

With the proposed enlargement of the EU to the countries of Central Europe[31], it became urgent to finish off the uncompleted work of the TA and the institutional reform considered necessary to allow a twenty-seven member state Union function efficiently. Thus, the Nice Treaty was signed at the Nice European Summit on 26 February 2001. It turned out to be a hurried and generally unsatisfactory exercise. The treaty sought to redistribute power in the context of a twenty-seven member Union but did so unsatisfactorily. In particular, Germany wanted better representation in the European Parliament and increased voting power at Council level. France, who had previously enjoyed parity with Germany, rejected this and the result was a flawed document which left many issues unresolved[32]. As with the Lisbon Treaty, only Ireland actually held a referendum on the adoption of the Nice Treaty and to the surprise of many, voters rejected its terms[33]. However, a second vote was organized later and this time, in response to a coordinated "Yes" campaign, the country by a large majority voted "Yes"[34]; mainly in response to assurances from the EU concerning respect for Irish neutrality[35].

As a result, the Nice Treaty entered into force in February 2003. However, its failure to satisfactorily reform the EU's institutional structure in a post-enlarged Europe meant that even prior to its adoption; plans were being drawn-up to introduce more sweeping reforms consolidating the different treaties in one single document, later referred to as the draft European Constitution[36]. The draft European Constitution[37], the forerunner of the Lisbon Treaty arose out of the Laeken Summit[38] and the "Declaration on the Future of the European Union" whereby a Convention was summoned made up of representatives from EU institutions, national governments, trade unionists etc. Their function was to deal with questions that had not been settled by the Nice Treaty. However, the Convention Chairman, Valéry Giscard d'Estaing probably exaggerated the extent of his remit and out of the Convention, came, not a simplified Europe, but instead further complication in the form of a new Philadelphia styled Constitution[39]. Although in reality only a consolidating treaty[40], its ambitious name raised the angst of national voters resulting in French and Dutch rejection at referendum. As a way out of this impasse, the draft Constitution was scaled down into a reform treaty, the Lisbon Treaty[41], which although largely similar to the draft constitution in content, took the simpler form of just another treaty and by this rather undemocratic slight of hand, with the exception of Ireland, was considered to avoid the need for national referenda, ratification occurring instead by way of the twenty-six national parliaments[42]. Thus, it was hoped to avoid the vagaries of an irksome European public[43]. However, the fly in the European ointment has been Ireland's 109,964 "No" voters.

The Place of the Lisbon Treaty

So the Lisbon Treaty is to all intents and purposes the draft Constitution, now correctly identified not as a constitution but as the treaty it always was[44]. Thus, in reality the voters of France, the Netherlands and Ireland have now rejected what is essentially the same proposal. Moreover, it is given that were the voters of the other member states allowed to vote on its provisions, some would also have rejected its adoption[45]. It is submitted that this reluctance on the part of some of Europe's citizenry is not linked directly to the Treaty's provisions or anti-EU sentiment, but rather to a deeper more general suspicion that the Union is growing out of control and that they are powerless to stop it[46].

As regards its actual content, the Lisbon Treaty seeks to amend the provisions of the EC Treaty and the TEU. Long and complicated, briefly the treaty proposes that:

- QMV with certain limited exceptions will become the normal way of voting at Council level with the removal of many national vetoes. This is a clear reinforcement of the EU's federal character. Moreover, QMV will now require fifty five per cent of the member state votes at Council, representing sixty five per cent of the EU's population (referred to as the double majority);
- The European Parliament's co-decision legislative power be extended;
- A new position of President of the European Council be created,
- The number of national Commissioners be reduced;

- National Parliaments be endowed with the right to raise objections to EU legislation at adoption stage where they can demonstrate that national or local action would be more effective. This, along with the increase in the Parliament's legislative powers is a clear attempt to shore up the Union's democratic credentials;
- The EU be given a separate legal personality;
- An exit clause be established to allow member states leave the Union should they so desire;
- Asylum, immigration, police and judicial cooperation will no longer have a separate status (i.e. separate pillar, Ireland and the UK have negotiated an opt-out of this area);
- Foreign and Security Policy be integrated into other areas of EU activity; but that decisions in this area would continue to be taken by way of unanimity;
- Member states be required to develop their military capability with a view to reinforcing the EU's Common Security and Defense Policy; however, the sanctity of Ireland's policy of neutrality is specifically recognized;
- The EU will have greater control over the member states in the area of macroeconomic policy so as to curb member state budget overruns;
- New powers allowing for simplified treaty revisions will be introduced; and
- Introduction of new legal basis for EU activity to areas such as energy security, sport, space policy and public health[47].

Some of these developments can be viewed as a coherent extension of EU powers in the context of an enlarged twenty-seven member Union. For example, it can be argued that the extension of QMV is necessary to allow for the continued adoption of legislative policy. After all, member states have varying short-term political and economic needs; were the adoption of EU legislation to be subject to individual member state veto, EU policy would probably slowly grind to a halt as member states used their power of veto as a bargaining tool to secure the adoption or non-adoption of policy suitable to their specific needs. In the same way, monetary union is not feasible without centralized control exercised by the European Central Bank (ECB)[48]. Moreover, some of the changes introduced by the treaty actually supplement the EU's alleged democratic deficit, for example the increase in the European Parliament's legislative powers[49] or the introduction of a role to be played by the national parliaments[50]. However, the creation of a separate legal personality for the Union, developments in the area of Common Security and Defense and the extension of EU competences or powers do signal an increase in the scope and power of the EU at the obvious expense of the member states. This is not necessarily a negative development, but it remains a significant development and explains why, when the treaty took the form of the draft Constitution document, member state governments considered it necessary to refer the matter for referendum[51]. However, it is contended that it was not the attempted extension of the EU's powers that resulted in the Irish "No" vote, but rather the attempt to do so by way of a largely unintelligible Lisbon Treaty failing to clearly acknowledge the extension of these powers[52] and the obvious wish to override the democratic result of the French and Dutch "No" votes[53]. Such an approach encouraged an already skeptic Irish public to view the treaty with suspicion and to believe the wilder claims of "No" vote protagonists.

B. THE IRISH "NO" VOTE AND THE FUTURE DEVELOPMENT OF THE EUROPEAN UNION

It is now proposed to look more closely at the Irish "No" vote (1) and the effect it may have on the future development of the European Union (2)

The "No" Vote and Ireland

At the heart of the process of EU integration are two diametrically opposed forces. On one side is found the pro-European integrationist forces representing the majority of mainland Europe, its major industries, corporations and political elites[54]. For the integrationists, the only means for Europeans and European business to have any significance on world events is their increased integration at European level[55]. Pitted against the integrationists is a motley collection of mutually opposed groups[56], mainly made up of those on the political left[57], nationalists of all kinds and pro-US Atlanticists[58] (hereinafter, the anti-integrationist block).

The members of the anti-integrationist block had every interest in seeing the Lisbon Treaty rejected in Ireland. Indeed, the Irish referendum represented their only chance of defeating the treaty given that national parliaments were in the process of ratifying it in all the remaining EU member states. Well organized and funded[59] they began the campaign over a year before the actual vote. The "Yes" vote campaign on the other hand was slow to begin and remarkably over-confident, especially given that Irish voters had already rejected the Nice Treaty. Moreover, they failed to really address any of the arguments made by the anti-integrationist block. Instead, their campaign was fought on the grounds that the EU has been so good for Ireland economically that it would be unwise to now vote against the treaty. This in reality was a negative argument, although phrased in a positive context and it failed to address any of the wilder claims of the anti-EU group or put forward any positive arguments supporting further EU integration. Afraid of opening up a can of worms and of having to clearly admit that the treaty did indeed represent a forward step towards the development of a more federal Europe, they decided to try and side-step the "No" vote campaign, by mostly ignoring what they had to say[60]. However, this left the disparate and frequently mutually antagonistic anti-integrationist block free to make scaremongering contradictory claims that were sometimes incorrect or dangerously over-simplified to the point of being incorrect.

The collective position of the Irish "No" vote campaign can be summarized as follows[61]:

- *The Lisbon treaty would lead to Brussels driven fiscal harmonization.* This is untrue and indeed, the Lisbon treaty did not address the issue at all and thus represented no direct threat to the competitiveness of Irish business. However, it could be argued that the increased federalist character of the Union, post-treaty would create the necessary momentum to facilitate the removal of the national veto on this issue; however, this is unlikely[62]. The question of tax harmonization is a key issue of contention between integrationists and anti-integration block and the ratification or non-ratification of the Lisbon Treaty will do nothing to change this. Indeed, it could be argued that the loss of Irish influence resulting from the "No" vote has, if anything weakened those in favour of fiscal diversification;
- *Loss of Irish sovereignty and a threat to Irish neutrality.* This claim was based on the extension of QVM and the loss of an automatic Irish Commissioner in the European Commission. This argument although true failed to address the converse argument, that without greater QMV and a reduction in the size of the Commission, the EU would be unable to work efficiently. It was presented as an end to Irish sovereignty when perhaps it should probably have been identified as an evolution; sovereignty has, by definition of Irish membership of the Union, already been compromised. On the issue of neutrality, the argument of the "No" vote campaign was that the increased militarization of the EU under the heading of the development of a common defense policy would necessarily impact negatively on Ireland's policy of military neutrality to such a degree that it would no longer exist. It is true that some in the EU would

like to see the establishment of a European Army and that the Lisbon Treaty provisions on common defense and security is probably a step towards its eventual creation[63]. The reality of this argument is however, that Irish neutrality has long ago been compromised and that the Lisbon treaty has no real further direct impact on this[64]. Certainly, the Lisbon Treaty and the greater cooperation it ushers in the field of common defense would not result in the EU being able to order the insignificant and poorly armed Irish troops onto the military battle field, if for some reason they would want to. However, increased integration and the resulting shared interests might well mean that Irish military ambitions and those of the EU might well be one and the same, were the latter to develop a true military character. Again the argument is not about loss, as it was presented by the anti-integrationist block but rather about evolution, if even that[65].

- *Compromise of Christian values*. Here the argument was that the Lisbon Treaty was just one more attack of the Godless EU on Irish Christian values. Nothing in the Lisbon Treaty provides for the introduction of abortion or indeed euthanasia, as claimed by some fundamentalist Christian groups in Ireland. However, it is true that since Ireland's membership of the EU, social values in the country have changed enormously and for the worse as far as fundamentalist Christian groups are concerned. Whether this is a result of the modernization of EU in general or related to what is increasingly perceived as an overly influential Catholic Church in Ireland, or a combination of both, is hard to know. However, the Lisbon Treaty does not provide for abortion, gay marriages or euthanasia, although it does represent the continued advance of an organization that is fundamentally secular in nature.

The initial euphoria attached the success of the "No" vote campaign has over time evaporated into something more resembling a hangover. The disparate groups making up the anti-integrationist block have to a large extent melted back into the forests of their individual discontent leaving the government and the country to deal with the actual repercussions of their campaign. The "No" vote campaign was, as its name suggests, an exercise in negativity. Nothing was proposed as a real alternative to the adoption of the Lisbon Treaty apart from actually leaving the Union and this does not appear to reflect the wishes of the majority of Irish voters, who are actually the third most pro-EU member state in the Union[66]. It is suggested the "No" vote was not against the treaty but the manner of its introduction and more generally its incomprehensible nature.

The "No" Vote and the European Union

The problem of the Irish "No" vote is posed on two levels. On an immediate level, some plan will have to be conceived to try and get the Irish to vote again and this time to vote "Yes" (a). More importantly, given that only fortynine per cent of EU citizens now consider the EU a good thing when polled[67], the EU will have to reconnect with an increasingly disenchanted public (b).

(a) Dealing with the Irish "No"

The initial reaction of mainland European integrationist forces to the Irish "No" vote was one of disbelief. To a certain extent, Ireland, a country on the periphery of EU with a population of four million people, has always punched above its EU weight and been recognized as one of the EU's golden performers. Now it is seen as a pariah by the integrationist member states and with good reason. A major beneficiary of EU largesse, Ireland also was strategically placed to benefit from the creation of the Single Market and did so significantly. That the Irish would now "spit in their soup"[68], having already done so in the context of the Nice Treaty is considered a little excessive by many in mainland Europe and has to a certain extent left the country sidelined as the rest of the Union continues with the ratification process[69]. Could it be otherwise? Indeed, it is unconceivable that the wishes of one hundred thousand Irish voters should be allowed to stop the eventual desire of the majority to move forward.

Nonetheless, politicians, European and Irish, have fallen over themselves declaring that the Irish "No" vote will be respected, but this in reality is an empty formula and mere rhetoric. It is more likely, based on past experience that the Irish will simply be asked to vote again after being given assurances on the issues deemed most worrying to them[70]. Of course, in principle there is nothing wrong with this approach, given that there is no valid reason, as already mentioned, why a relatively small number of Irish voters should be able to hold up greater EU integration against the express wishes of the other twenty-six member states. However, is it really against their express wishes? Given that the French and Dutch people already voted "No" to a similar document and that probably, if given a referendum, the people of Britain, Poland, the Czech Republic[71] or some other member state would have also returned a majority "No" vote, then we are not in a situation where Ireland alone holding up EU integration. Rather we are in a situation where the citizens of Ireland, France and the Netherlands rejected the treaty in one form or other, and where the democratic vote of other member state citizens was side-stepped. It is in this very important distinction that the democratic deficit referred to above is found[72].

(b) Reconnecting with its Public—Dealing with the Issue of a Democratic Deficit at EU Level

When considering the nature of the democratic deficit at the heart of EU, it is proposed to first identify the nature of the deficit (i) before going on to identify the manner in which this issue can be best addressed by EU (ii).

(i) The Democratic Deficit at the Heart of EU

The approach of denying the quasi-majority of EU citizens to vote on the Lisbon Treaty may very well work and eventually allow passage of the Lisbon Treaty into EU law. However, it does not change the fact that the majority of the citizens in some of the other member states may also have voted "No" to the Treaty, had they been given the chance and that the French, Dutch and Irish voters will have effectively been ignored.

Indeed, by the manner in which it has approached the issue of institutional reform, the EU has done little else than shoot itself in its democratic foot repeatedly. It has left itself open to a claim of non-respect of democratic outcome, which unfortunately to some extent is true and consequently indefensible[73]. The original draft constitutional document was not a constitution and perhaps legally, under French and Dutch national law did not require a vote by way of referendum. However, having submitted the document to referendum, presumably because it was considered appropriate, it is now incumbent on politicians in both countries to then respect that vote. Instead, the vote was ignored, the treaty's name but not its content changed, to facilitate the circumvention of the democratic will of French and Dutch voters and instead ratification by the national parliaments[74]. This, it is contended smacks of short-term *gombeen* fix-it politics and will never provide the Union with the democratic foundations it requires if it is to prosper in the new millennium. Moreover, not content with this, it is now proposed to ignore the result of a subsequent third referendum, the Irish "No" vote and to probably instead require a second referendum; held in the context of an implicit threat– 'to choose the Lisbon Treaty or leave the Union'. Such behaviour gives proof to what should be the lie of the anti-integrationist block, namely that the EU is a non-democratic organization. "Oh! What a tangled web we weave when first we practice to deceive"[75] immediately comes to mind. It would appear that sure of their destination, integrationists have decided that all means are fair to ensure their arrival; and, having started down this dangerous path, the EU machine does not quite know how to get out of the maze it has now created for itself.

Some basic points need to be made. Firstly, complicated legal treaties are not suitable subjects for national referenda. Indeed, the inadequacies of the policy of asking citizens to vote on large legalistic documents, incomprehensible to nearly all but those who drafted them has clearly been shown to be an unworkable method of having their provisions blessed with a democratic vote. Moreover, even if a "Yes" vote is obtained, allegations that people did not understand the document on which they voted will always taint any such result[76]. Secondly, and perhaps even more importantly from an EU point of view, given the recent French, Dutch and Irish "No" votes and past experiences with the Nice and Maastricht Treaties, the method does not work. Thirdly, the alternative, i.e., having no referendum at all on such treaties is an untenable position, no matter how the argument is sweetened by the contention that referenda prevent the adoption of "good" policies and that the Treaty of Rome or monetary union would have been rejected by Europe's citizens if put to a vote[77]. People have a right to vote on the transfer of their sovereignty from their national government to another institution. If they do not, the European Union cannot be considered to be a democratic institution as it will have usurped national powers in an undemocratic way[78]; but the Union's institutions do not appear to want to accept this[79]. It is here that the argument becomes serious, for if democracy is by-passed, and knowingly so, then any result must leave itself open to claims of a *coup d'état à l'Union européenne*[80].

In reality, the EU has, since the adoption of the TEU, been living on borrowed time. Its federalist aspirations, which were perhaps tenable in a six-member Community, became unfeasible in an increasingly enlarged Union. Despite this the Union increased its rate of enlargement and papered over the anti-federalist cracks with complicated treaties and sham referenda[81]. The latest debacle with the draft Constitution, which was then replaced by the Lisbon Treaty, is proof that this approach has failed. Instead of stopping to consider whether its *modus operandi* needs to be modified, the EU juggernaut refuses to pause. Instead, it presses on with parliamentary ratifications which will isolate the democratic "No" vote of the Irish people, ignore that of the Dutch and the French, then by political and economic arm twisting seek to secure another Irish vote and a "Yes" result; and by using the same heavy handed tactics ensure Polish and Czech ratification at Parliament level[82]. The plan might still work, but at what price? At some time, be it today, tomorrow or in five years time, the EU's integrationist forces will have to accept that some citizen of its member states, perhaps forming a majority in their own, do not share their integrationist dream, or at least require open discussion and debate to be convinced of its necessity. Failing to address this issue plays into the hands of the anti-integrationist block who can correctly claim that the wishes and votes of EU citizens are being ignored and that citizens of the member states are being denied the right to vote on the transfer of their own sovereignty.

(ii) What can be done?

Obviously the Union cannot continue indefinitely offering unintelligible treaties for referendum and then openly ignoring the results when it does not like them. In place of this, two new approaches need to be adopted. First, the Union will have to find a better way to communicate effectively with its citizens. At present, few EU citizens have a true understanding of what occurs at EU level: how the organization's institutions work, how legislation is formulated and adopted. The European Union is in reality a very impressive organization, which, with a limited bureaucracy has had a vast and positive influence on the life in its member states. At the time of its creation, post-war Europe was a burnt out collection of ex-colonial powers, which had engulfed the world in two world wars. What the Union has achieved in the past fifty years is nothing short of an economic and political miracle[83]. However, it has failed to communicate that success to a citizenry, which has come to take for granted the then undreamt of standard of living presently enjoyed. The European Union is a success, but its citizens need to be reminded of that fact and made a real part of it. If this means informing citizens of the true rate of legislation coming from Brussels and of the increasingly limited role of their national parliaments in the adoption of legislation, then so be it. If this then means having a straight-forward referendum about the future direction of the Union and recognition of the need for increased federacy, then also so be it.

However, in this context the Union must also accept that citizens of some member states still cherish their independence and do not wish to dilute it further than has already occurred and that these states may well vote "No" in any future referenda. The inclusion in the TA and later in the Lisbon treaty of an express policy allowing for enhanced cooperation is in fact recognition of this reality. Indeed, it is contended that only the establishment of a two-speed Europe will allow reconciliation between two conflicting groups at the heart of the European Union. Why indeed, should a member state be forced into an ever-greater integrated Europe and by the same token, why member states should be prevented from integrating further? Moreover, this basic point has, it appears, been conceded by integrationists[84]. Indeed, it could happen that those in what we have referred to as the anti-integrationist block might well, in a two-speed Europe increase integration between them in economic matters[85], whilst the integrationists would be free to institute greater political cooperation. Such an approach would allow member states and their citizens to move at their own pace and not feel that they were being forced into further integration against their wishes. Needless to say, the extent of any such enhanced cooperation would have to be curtailed if the Union was to retain any coherence and it is in this detail that many devils may be found. Obviously, it would be better and more efficient were all the member states able to move forward together. However, in an ever-larger Union this is unlikely to be the case and continued attempts by the EU to insist otherwise, will slowly rob the organization of its democratic foundations. The EU of the new millennium must demonstrate the same strength and confidence its founders did in 1952 and later in 1957, when they came together and created something so successful and irresistible that the quasi-remainder of Europe's states wanted and needed to join. Once again Europe finds itself at a crossroad and perhaps it is those states which took the lead in 1957 that must once again enter unchartered waters and show the rest of Europe the way forward.

NOTES AND REFERENCES

1. As regards the European Coal and Steel Community Treaty (1952) and later European Economic Community Treaty (1957, also known as the Treaty of Rome), the signatory states were France, Germany, Italy, Belgium, the Netherlands and Luxembourg. Later countries such as Ireland, United Kingdom and Denmark (1973), Greece (1981), Spain and Portugal (1985), Sweden, Austria and Finland (1995), Cyprus, Czech Rep., Slovakia, Hungary, Lithuania, Latvia, Estonia, Poland, Malta and Slovenia (2005), Bulgaria and Romania (2007) joined bringing its current membership to 27 states. Turkey and Croatia have officially begun membership negotiations, whilst other countries such as Serbia, Montenegro and Macedonia amongst others have varying hopes of becoming members at some future date. Significantly, European countries such as Switzerland, Russia and Norway are not members and at present do not appear interested. However, there appears to be an enlargement malaise amongst the twenty-seven and future enlargement, especially to states largely geographically located in Asia Minor appears unlikely at present. Moreover, recently the French and Germans have linked further expansion to the adoption of the Lisbon Treaty under a policy referred to as "linkage".
2. Also referred to as the Treaty of Paris.
3. The term Benelux refers to the nations of Belgium, Netherlands and Luxembourg.

4. Reference is made to the Treaty of Versailles, 1919 at the end of World War I, which, it is considered by some commentators, imposed overly severe conditions on Germany; so severe as to actually sow the seeds for World War II. Certainly, in the 1930's, Adolf Hitler, amongst other things, traded on this severity to justify German discontent and to create the notion that Germany was robbed and justified in rearming. However, in reality Germany failed to comply with many of the economic conditions of the Treaty, mainly the amount of reparations due to France and thus in reality the Treaty was less harsh than probably intended.
5. Signed in 1951 and entered into force the following year.
6. The European Coal and Steel Community, which was governed by an institution referred to as the High Authority was also assisted by an Assembly and a Court of Justice.
7. Also known as the Treaty of Rome.
8. Originally referred to as the European Economic Community, its name was changed pursuant to the provisions of the Treaty on European Union (TEU) to the European Community (EC), reflecting the increased scope of its activities beyond economic issues to issues of a more social character. For the sake of simplicity, it is proposed to refer to the EEC Treaty, pre and post TEU, as the EC Treaty.
9. See the Preamble to the EC Treaty.
10. The institutions were later merged with those created to manage the ECSC and Euratom.
11. Originally known as the Council of Ministers, its name was changed to the Council of the European Union under the Maastricht Treaty. The Council is made up of national ministers having responsibility for the area under discussion. Thus, if the question being discussed involves economic or financial affairs, the ECOFIN Council will meet comprised of the Finance Ministers of the different member states. The Council has a general duty to "ensure the coordination of the general economic policies of the member states". The Council can be considered as the more powerful upper house in the two chamber legislative process, the first house being the European Parliament. The Council of the European Union should not be confused with the European Council, which comprises the Heads of State of each of the member states, and which normally meet four times a year at what is described as summit meetings.
12. The Commission is the most supranational of the EU's institutions and has Union rather than national goals at its heart. Frequently referred to as the motor of the Union, it has power to propose legislation which is then adopted by the Council and Parliament acting together. Thus, it is considered as being the executive power of the Union. The Commission is composed of different Commissioners and acts on a collegiate basis. It plays an important role in the area of competition law and also has important powers under the heading of "Commitology", whereby it has been given quasi-decision-making powers implementing framework legislation adopted by the Council and the Parliament (see Commitology Decision D87/373).

13 Under the Treaty of Rome the Parliament was originally referred to as the Assembly, members were not elected by universal suffrage and in this form it played only a minor consultative role. However, with the expansion of the EC, the Parliament's role has grown and since 1979, members are elected by direct vote of the European citizens and it is for this reason it is referred to as the democratic face of the EU. The Parliament's powers can be divided into three main areas:

- *Legislative role*—The Parliament is the first house in the EU legislature enjoying a power of veto over some legislative proposals adopted by the Council. In other areas it plays a more consultative role. In all there are four different legislative procedures: Consultation procedure, Co-operation procedure, Co-decision procedure, and the Assent procedure;
- *Budgetary power*—Pursuant to Article 272 of the EC Treaty, the Parliament plays a major role in the annual adoption of the EU budget;
- Control of the Commission—The Parliament has the power to censure the entire Commission and has already done so on one occasion (Santer Commission, 1999). Less dramatically, it has the power to question the Commission on any area of its activities and the latter must respond publicly, publishing its answers in the Official Journal. It also holds hearings at the time of the appointment of the Commission and can influence appointment of the Commissioners.

14. Initially there was only one EC Court, the European Court of Justice (ECJ). However, due to an excessive case load, two supplementary courts have since been created, namely the Court of First Instance and the Civil Service Tribunal. As the EC Treaty is a framework treaty, it has been left to the EU courts to put meat on its bones and it can be said that they have not hesitated to do so. The ECJ has handed down numerous landmark decisions, for example establishing the supremacy of EU law over the national law of the member states (Van Gend en Loos C-26/62) or the principal of mutual recognition between member states as regards free movement within the Single Market (Cassis de Dijon C-120/78) etc. There are also secondary institutions referred to as "bodies", such as the:

- Economic and Social Committee, the members of which are appointed by the Council of the European Union and is made up of representative groups such as farmers, trade unionists, producers etc. It plays a consultative role and has only a power of influence;
- Court of Auditors, established in 1975 the function of which is to control and supervise the implementation of the EU budget;
- European Central Bank, the function of which is to manage the EU's single currency, the Euro. More particularly, the ECB has responsibility for monetary policy within the EU and controls the setting of interest rates for those countries participating in the single currency;
- Committee of Regions, the membership of which is drawn from local and regional bodies throughout the EU.

15. In the area of goods, this required the suppression of custom's duties and quantitative restrictions (quotas) and measures having equivalent effect between member states. The notion of a measure having an equivalent effect was defined

in *Procureur du Roi* v Dassonville (ECJ, C-8/74) as comprising: "*All trading rules enacted by member states which are capable of hindering directly or indirectly, actually or potentially, intra-Community trade are to be considered as measures having an effect equivalent to quantitative restrictions*". This definition was broad enough to usher in a presumption of mutual recognition as regards regulatory rules in place in each of the member states.

16. On 19 September 1945 in Zurich, Churchill outlined plans for the creation of a United States of Europe as a means of countering the threat of Soviet domination of Central and Eastern Europe. In this regard, he asked Charles de Gaulle to "take Germany by the hand and rally her to the West and European civilization". Interestingly, even then Churchill saw a separate fate for the United Kingdom, which, along with its dominions and colonies would constitute another complementary but individual block of influence. However, the United Kingdom soon lost its colonies and by the 1960's had to go cap in hand to de Gaulle asking to be allowed join the EC and initially suffered rejection.
17. Established on 3 May 1960, EFTA is a free trade block, which sought to provide an alternative to those European states that sought the advantages of economic cooperation without an actual surrender of sovereignty. EFTA now has only four member state (Liechtenstein, Norway, Switzerland and Iceland), the other original member states (UK, Denmark, Portugal, Sweden, Austria) choosing instead over time to join the EU. Indeed, EFTA can nearly be regarded as a nursery for the EU, given that it's most important members, starting with the UK, all subsequently sought and successfully obtained EU membership.
18. Earlier attempts had been made to alter the institutional distribution of power prior to the adoption of the SEA, notably the European Parliament's draft treaty on European Union which had been rejected as too federalist in character. The SEA arose out of a 1985 Commission White Paper issued by the European Commission which demonstrated that the Single Market project set out in the original Treaty of Rome had not been successfully achieved.
19. QMV is a system of voting whereby each member state, depending on its economic, geographical and population size is attributed a weighted number of votes at Council level. Thereafter, a specified number of votes are required to secure adoption of legislative measures by the Council.
20. EU legislative initiatives may take any one of the following forms:
    - Regulations, which apply directly in the law of the member states from the time of their coming into force;
    - Directives, which must be implemented by the member state into its national law;
    - Decisions, that apply specifically to one party(s);
    - Recommendations, which do not have the force of law.
21. For example, in the recent past Germany was forced to accept the adoption of the Takeover Directive (Directive 2004/25/EC; 21/04/2004), even though it opened up the German economy to the possibility of the takeover of key German industrial companies, for example, Volkswagen, by foreign companies.

22. Hence the name by which it is more commonly known, the Maastricht Treaty.
23. Intergovernmental as member states retained a right of veto and QMV did not apply.
24. More generally, the TEU provided for harmonization in the area of social policy, refugees and asylum, the strengthening of social cohesion, environmental and consumer protection. The Maastricht Treaty also introduced the principle of Subsidiarity, whereby the Community is required *"to act within the limits of its powers"* and as regards areas not falling within its exclusive competence, the Community *"shall take action, in accordance with the principle of Subsidiarity, only if and insofar as the objectives of the proposed action cannot be sufficiently achieved by the member states and can therefore, by reason of the scale or effects of the proposed action, be better achieved by the Community"*. Subsidiarity, introduced at the insistence of a Eurosceptic UK, sought to contain the power of the nascent European Union. However, much like its US equivalent, the tenth amendment of the US Constitution, it has failed in this task.
25. It was initially rejected by the citizens of Denmark, who when asked to vote again, having secured certain opt outs, voted in favor.
26. At referendum, the French populace accepted the adoption of the TEU by the slimmest of margins.
27. The Treaty of Amsterdam was signed in October 1997 and took effect on 1 May 1999.
28. Prior to this, the EU had expanded to take in the states of Sweden, Finland and Austria. Moreover, plans were afoot to take in member states coming from Central Europe.
29. It was Henry Kissinger who famously complained that when he wished to talk to Europe he did not know who to ring.
30. More specifically, the TA committed the Union to respecting, *inter alia*, principles of:
    - *Transparency*: EU citizens are expressly given a right of access to documentation coming from any of the EU's institutions subject to the protection of public and private interests;
    - *Environmental protection*: The TA required member states to integrate their environmental protection policies and to promote sustainable development where possible;
    - *Enhanced cooperation*: Under this policy, designed to overcome the paralysis resulting from a minority member state(s) blocking a policy proposal, eight or more member states could move forward implementing the policy themselves in certain restricted conditions, namely, they must have the permission of the Commission and the area to be the subject of the enhanced cooperation must not involve defense matters;
    - *Human rights*: The Treaty specifically provides that the Union is required to respect human rights as set out in the European Convention on Human Rights and Fundamental Freedoms (ECHR) and as guaranteed by the constitutional traditions of each of the member state;
    - *Non-discrimination*: Under the provisions of the TA, the Council may act

to combat discrimination "based on sex, racial or ethnic origin, religion or belief, disability, age or sexual orientation".

31. Here we refer to the countries of Cyprus, Czech Rep., Slovakia, Hungary, Lithuania, Latvia, Estonia, Poland, Malta and Slovenia (2005), Bulgaria and Romania (2007) the membership of which brought the current membership of the EU to 27.
32. Germany increased her voting powers but new members under enlargement, in particular Poland, disagreed and the result was further compromise. Similarly, the question concerning a reduction in the size of the Commission, already fudged in the TA was only half dealt with. The member states agreed to a reduction in the number of Commissioners, but failed to actually agree on the number.
33. Irish Referendum, June 2001. Only 34 per cent of voters turned out to vote as it was generally presumed that Irish voters would vote yes. Many Irish voters criticized the Treaty's content believing that it marginalized smaller states such as Ireland. Others felt that its provisions on foreign policy and defense compromised the long cherished shibboleth of Irish neutrality. More generally, Irish voters were suspicious of "big government" from "Europe" and probably used their "No" vote as a way of signaling to a European leadership, perceived as arrogant, that Irish compliance was not *un fait accompli*.
34. 60 per cent of the population voted "Yes" and the percentage turn-out increased by 150.
35. See the Seville Declaration whereby the status of Irish military neutrality was copper-fastened through a guarantee that Ireland would not be forced to participate in any future European Union common defense policy. Further, it was confirmed that any Irish involvement in future policies adopted under the heading of enhanced cooperation would first require the agreement of the Irish Houses of Parliament (Seville Summit 2002).
36. Officially named as the "Draft Treaty establishing a Constitution for Europe".
37. Like the Lisbon Treaty, the proposed draft Constitution was an enormously complicated document running to hundreds of pages. Written in Eurospeak, it was difficult to understand and so complicated to summarize. Instead of the simple short six-page document that was the original US Constitution, the length and complexity of the draft European Constitution is to a certain extent a reflection of the disaccord at the heart of the EU as regards its present and future development. Its opening preamble spoke of a Union *unified in diversity*; which could be considered an attempt to put a positive spin on what is in fact the main problem of the European Union, namely, diversity in opinion as regards its role, function and future. The task for the drafters of the Constitution was to define a common vision in the face of such diversity. To help them do this, one of the primary purposes of the constitution was to codify in a single document the many treaties making-up the EU, thereby supposedly simplifying EU citizen's understanding of the functioning of the Union. In this context, it specifically sought to:
    - — improve and render more efficient the functioning of the principal EU institutions;
    - — provide for more clarity in EU foreign policy and extend its military character;

— better define the relationship between Union powers and those retained by the Member States;
— clearly outline the of civil rights of the Union's citizen;
— reinforce a European Union identity;
— increase the role of national parliaments.

38. 15 December 2001.
39. Reference is made to the process of drafting the US Constitution in Philadelphia 1787.
40. A constitution is the name given to a rulebook that defines the relationship between powers. In public law, a constitution describes the relationship between different powers of state (Aristotle has defined a constitution as "the arrangement of the offices in a state" (See Aristotle, *The Constitution of Athens*, Loeb Classical Library, Harvard University Press)). Can the EU be characterized as a state? If we define a state as an organized political community occupying a definite territory, having an organized government, and possessing internal and external sovereignty, the EU would appear to only partly fit the bill as it does not possess all the attributes necessary. For example, it has no tax raising powers of its own, nor does it possess an army or have the right to declare war, fundamental characteristics normally associated with a state entity. Consequently, use of the word *constitution* to describe the set of proposals, although maybe not technically wrong (as the treaty had constitutional significance), did definitely give off the wrong signal at a moment of particular national sensitivity in a number of member states, in particular France and the Netherlands. What the EU does need and what the Lisbon Treaty attempts to provide is a more transparent and efficient legislative framework as regards the organization of a 27-member Union.
41. The history of the Lisbon Treaty is as follows: in March 2007, the Heads of State met in Berlin at the Berlin Summit and fiftieth birthday celebrations of the EU and adopted a Declaration where they confirmed their intention in placing "the European Union on a renewed common basis before the European Parliament elections in 2009". Pursuant to this, a new IGC was established to draw up a new treaty without "constitutional characteristics" and the new Treaty was presented in October 2007 and formally signed in December.
42. This process has not yet been fully terminated at the time of writing and indeed, the Irish vote has made other Eurosceptic member states such as the Czech Rep. braver as regards their possible opposition to the Treaty, however, it is expected that over time the draft treaty will be ratified by all twenty-six member states leaving Ireland somewhat out on a limb.
43. Both the undemocratic nature of changing the name of the constitution as a means of avoiding a referendum and the fact that the document fundamentally remained the same can be seen from quotes below:
    — "The good thing about not calling it a Constitution is that no one can ask for a referendum on it"—Giuliano Amato, speech at London School of Economics, 21 February 2007;
    — "The substance of the constitution is preserved. That is a fact"—German Chancellor Angela Merkel, speech in the European Parliament, 27 June 2007;

— "The substance of what was agreed in 2004 has been retained. What is gone is the term 'constitution'"—Dermot Ahern, Irish Foreign Minister, *Daily Mail*, Ireland, 25 June 2007;

— "The difference between the original Constitution and the present Lisbon Treaty is one of approach, rather than content ... The proposals in the original constitutional treaty are practically unchanged. They have simply been dispersed through the old treaties in the form of amendments. Why this subtle change? Above all, to head off any threat of referenda by avoiding any form of constitutional vocabulary ... But lift the lid and look in the toolbox: all the same innovative and effective tools are there, just as they were carefully crafted by the European Convention"—Giscard D'Estaing, former French President and Chairman of the Convention which drew up the EU Constitution, *The Independent*, London, 30 October 2007;

— "The most striking change (between the EU Constitution in its older and newer version) is perhaps that in order to enable some governments to reassure their electorates that the changes will have no constitutional implications, the idea of a new and simpler treaty containing all the provisions governing the Union has now been dropped in favour of a huge series of individual amendments to two existing treaties. Virtual incomprehensibility has thus replaced simplicity as the key approach to EU reform. As for the changes now proposed to be made to the constitutional treaty, most are presentational changes that have no practical effect. They have simply been designed to enable certain Heads of Government to sell to their people the idea of ratification by parliamentary action rather than by referendum"—Dr Garret FitzGerald, former Irish Taoiseach, *Irish Times*, 30 June 2007;

— "The good thing is that all the symbolic elements are gone, and that which really matters—the core—is left"—Anders Fogh Rasmussen, Danish Prime Minister, *Jyllands-Posten*, 25 June 2007;

— "90 per cent of it is still there... These changes haven't made any dramatic change to the substance of what was agreed back in 2004"—Irish Taoiseach Bertie Ahern, *Irish Independent*, 24 June 2007;

— "The aim of the Constitutional Treaty was to be more readable; the aim of this treaty is to be unreadable ... The Constitution aimed to be clear, whereas this treaty had to be unclear. It is a success"—Karel de Gucht, Belgian Foreign Minister, *Flandre Info*, 23 June 2007.

44. The actual differences between the draft Constitution document and the Lisbon Treaty are as follows: the Lisbon Treaty does not seek to consolidate the previous treaties into a single constitutional treaty; all reference to a European flag and European national anthem have been dropped; the Charter of Human Rights is not included in the treaty although it remains binding; clauses on the primacy of EU law have been dropped although the EU case law confirming this point remains valid; the objectives of the EU do not include a clause promoting competition; enhanced cooperation will now require at least nine member states.
45. Member states such as Poland, the United Kingdom, the Czech Rep. and Denmark all have significant anti-integrationist blocks making up their voting populations.

However, the Euro-sceptic nature of Europe's citizens should not be over-exaggerated; prior to the French and Dutch "No", Austria, Germany, Greece, Hungary, Cyprus, Malta, Bulgaria, Romania, Italy, Lithuania, Latvia, Slovakia, Slovenia and Spain had all approved the Constitution, thus, it is not as if there was no support for it in the Union.

46. See the comments of Roman Herzog in this regard: "Most people have a fundamentally positive attitude to European integration. But at the same time, they have an ever increasing feeling that something is going wrong, that an un-transparent, complex, intricate, mammoth institution has evolved, divorced from the factual problems and national traditions, grabbing ever greater competencies and areas of power; that the democratic control mechanisms are failing: in brief, that it cannot go on like this"—Former German President Roman Herzog and former president of the German Constitutional Court, article on the EU Constitution, *Welt Am Sonntag*, 14 January 2007.
47. The EU's powers which are recognized as coming from the member states, can be considered under the heading of exclusive powers (customs union, competition policy, monetary policy, common fisheries policy, common agricultural policy, conclusion of international treaties) and shared powers which means that member states can act in these areas only if the EU fails to act (*inter alia*, internal market, social policy coming within the Lisbon Treaty), environment, consumer protection, trans-European networks, security and justice (as defined in the treaties)).
48. As the currency prepares to be extended to member states each with their own specific economic characteristics, the need for such control becomes all the more necessary.
49. The European Parliament is elected by the direct vote of European citizens.
50. Although it is possible that the power of the national parliaments under the proposed treaty may prove to be as illusory as the supposed application of the principle of Subsidiarity which it develops.
51. The comments of EU Commission President Barroso are interesting in this regard: "Sometimes I like to compare the EU as a creation to the organization of empires. We have the dimension of Empire but there is a great difference. Empires were usually made with force with a centre imposing diktat, a will on the others. Now what we have is the first non-imperial empire"—Commission President J-M Barroso, *The Brussels Journal*, 11 July 2007.
52. "They decided that the document should be unreadable. If it is unreadable, it is not constitutional, that was the sort of perception. Where they got this perception from is a mystery to me. In order to make our citizens happy, to produce a document that they will never understand! But, there is some truth [in it]. Because if this is the kind of document that the IGC will produce, any Prime Minister—imagine the UK Prime Minister—can go to the Commons and say 'Look, you see, it's absolutely unreadable, it's the typical Brussels treaty, nothing new, no need for a referendum.' Should you succeed in understanding it at first sight there might be some reason for a referendum, because it would mean that there is something new"—Giuliano Amato, former Italian Prime Minister and Vice-Chairman of the Convention which drew up the EU Constitution, recorded by

Open Europe, The Centre for European Reform, London, 12 July 2007. The Irish Taoiseach (Prime Minister) admitted that he had not read the document as he could not understand it; the Irish Commissioner also made the same admission.

53. The comments of Nicolas Sarkozy on this issue are revealing: "France was just ahead of all the other countries in voting No. It would happen in all Member States if they have a referendum. There is a cleavage between people and governments… A referendum now would bring Europe into danger. There will be no Treaty if we had a referendum in France, which would again be followed by a referendum in the UK"—French President Nicolas Sarkozy, at meeting of senior MEPs, *EU Observer*, 14 November 2007.
54. This power especially concentrated in founding member states and Europe's industrial heartland—France, Germany, the Benelux countries and Northern Italy.
55. See the comments of ex-Commission President Prodi: "Are we all clear that we want to build something that can aspire to be a world power? In other words, not just a trading bloc but a political entity. Do we realize that our nation states, taken individually, would find it far more difficult to assert their existence and their identity on the world stage"—Commission President Romano Prodi, European Parliament, 13 February 2001.
56. This group comprises, Marxists, neo-liberals, corporatists, fundamental Christian groups and nationalists and so although unified in their opposition to the EU, they are not unified in much else.
57. Here the author is not referring to the traditional socialist parties of Europe who have for the most part made their peace with European integration and the economic liberalism that it partly promotes; rather one is referring to the "real" left, made up of anti-liberal forces and pro-Communist groups.
58. Atlanticists are made up of:
    — supporters of the financial services industry in London, which with their links to tax havens in many ex-colonies (Cayman Islands, British Virgin Islands, Bermuda etc.) receive investment from many who would/should otherwise be paying taxes to continental European governments. A fiscally integrated EU would shut these havens down and effectively deprive the City of London of much of its funding and financial dominance;
    — US corporatists who secure Single Market access to continental European markets from low tax Atlanticist states such as Ireland, the UK and indeed newly enlarged member states such as the Baltic Republics all of whom have low corporate tax rates;
    — Pro-NATO activists who representing US military dominance support common defense planning as long as occurs within a NATO context but who are opposed to political integration as they perceive that the latter will have a negative impact on their influence over any European common defense programme.
59. Allegations have been made in many quarters but not proved that one of the main groups behind the Irish "No" vote, Liberals, was funded from the US.
60. The Treaty probably does represent a step towards the creation of a federalist Europe, indeed the following comment would seem to support this: "The

Constitution is the capstone of a European Federal State"—Guy Verhofstadt, Belgian Prime Minister, *Financial Times*, 21 June 2004.

61. The diverse, disparate and sometimes bizarre nature of some of the "No" vote campaign arguments means that the author can only provide a summary of some of the main claims of the "No" vote campaign and the following list in no way claims to be exhaustive.
62. Low fiscal regimes represent the only way that member states on the periphery of Europe can possibly hope to compete with their mainland brethren and so it can be supposed that they would fight tooth and nail to hold on to such policies. Moreover, it is the economies of mainland Europe who are actually dropping their fiscal levels and so if there is movement and momentum in this area, it would seem to favour the low tax entities.
63. Significant steps towards military cooperation between the UK, France and Germany have already been put in place independent of NATO.
64. Indeed, the Seville Declaration referred to above confirms this.
65. It should be recalled that at this moment Irish troops are in Chad operating with the French under the heading of EU military intervention and that prior to this Ireland has had one of the most impressive pro-US voting policies at UN level sending frequently troops in support of UN backed peace keeping missions. This is hardly military neutrality!
66. In a recent Eurobarometer Study (http://ec.europa.eu/public_opinion/archives/ebs/ebs_251_en.pdf) crucially, 68 per cent of Irish people said that they considered the EU to be a "good thing". Moreover, polls taken immediately after the « No » vote would appear to support this interpretation with the majority of people who voted "No" citing the fact that they did not understand fully the document they were asked to vote on as a reason for voting "No"—poll results in *Irish Times*, 18 June 2008.
67. In a recent Eurobarometer Study only 49 per cent of EU citizens consider it to be a "good thing". Now that is not to say that the other 51 per cent consider it to be a "bad thing", but the figures are worrying and should signal to the EU powers that they are losing public support and that if integration is going to work, they will have to take the time out to convince the EU public of its necessity and even more accept that the public do not want it if that is the case.
68. A French expression describing someone who is ungrateful.
69. See for example the comments of Bernard Kouchner, "The most likely victims of a potential 'no'—which I don't believe will happen—are the Irish … it would however be a huge obstacle to honest thinking if we couldn't count on the Irish who have counted so heavily on financing from Europe" (source http://www.cafebabel.com/fre/article/25255/france-reaction-irelans-vote-lisbon-treaty.html).
70. Moves are already been made in this direction with certain Irish government ministers urging a second vote whilst being careful to say that in this regard they are only expressing a personal opinion. For example European Affairs Minister Dick Roche commented recently "My personal view is that second referendum is the appropriate response to the position we are in. (…) If we want

to retain our position as a constructive EU member state, we cannot simply sit on our hands, as some would have us do and keep saying that "No" means "No"', (*Irish Times*, 25 August 2008). However, it could be legitimately asked of the Minister if "No" does not mean "No", what exactly does it mean. Moreover, and perhaps of more relevance, it is by no means guaranteed that the Irish would vote "yes" a second time. According to polls a second Irish vote on the Lisbon Treaty would be defeated by 62 per cent to 38 per cent. The findings show that opposition to the Lisbon Treaty has strengthened since the referendum on June 12 when the "No" vote was carried by 53.4 per cent to 46.6 per cent. When the 16 per cent of "don't knows" are included, the poll shows the "No side" holding a 52 per cent to 32 per cent lead over the "Yes side"; *Sunday Times*, 27 July 2008.

71. Moreover, both the Czech and Polish governments have expressed some doubt on the question of ratification only to be told that any further enlargement is dependent on the adoption of the Lisbon Treaty (see speech of Nicolas Sarkozy to the European Parliament—4 July 2008). This policy, referred to as "linkage" has been approved of by German Chancellor Angela Merkel. This could be interpreted as an example of arm-twisting as newer member states such as Poland and the Czech Rep. are known to be in favour of further enlargement. However, in his speech to the European Parliament, President Sarkozy commented that "linkage" was not about "blackmail" but coherence. Commenting that the reform policy of the Lisbon treaty should have been adopted prior to enlargement, he considered that there could not be further enlargement without prior reform. In a clear dig at his predecessor, he considered there was no use in repeating the mistakes of the past.
72. See the comments of Sarkozy: "There will be no Treaty if we had a referendum in France, which would again be followed by a referendum in the UK"—French President Nicolas Sarkozy, at meeting of senior MEPs, *EU Observer*, 14 November 2007;
73. The comments of the former Irish Taoiseach are interesting in this respect: "I think it's a bit upsetting... to see so many countries running away from giving their people an opportunity", Irish Prime Minister Bertie Ahern said on Sunday 21 October, "If you believe in something ...why not let your people have a say in it. I think the Irish people should take the opportunity to show the rest of Europe that they believe in the cause, and perhaps others shouldn't be so afraid of it" he added—Taoiseach Bertie Ahern, *EU Observer*, Brussels, 22 October 2007;
74. It should be recalled that the French Socialist party, the countries second largest party, boycotted the procedure whereby the Lisbon treaty was ratified in France. French President, Nicolas Sarkozy defends the ratification by the French Parliament of the Lisbon Treaty by stating that his intention to do so was clearly stated in his manifesto at the time of his election to his present exalted position. This is a valid point; however, it could be argued and it is the opinion of this author, that any question of a transfer of national sovereignty to another body is far more important than a mere Presidential election and that consequently it is inappropriate to have linkage in this way and can be likened to giving a car

away with every sale of a pack of cigarettes. As every schoolboy is taught, sovereignty does not belong to the national parliaments, it belongs or ought to belong to the people and this is the primary principle of democracy. Thus, especially in circumstances where a "No" vote has already been recorded, it is arguable that the people should be directly consulted on this question and not have it diluted with a more general question of presidential choice.

75. Sir Walter Scott, *Marmion*, Canto IV, Stanza 17.
76. The converse is also true by which it can be claimed that "No" votes campaigns highjack and distort the issues involved and that consequently any "No" vote does not represent the true sentiment of the voting public.
77. The argument of President Barroso does not convince: "Referendums make the process of approval of European treaties much more complicated and less predictable ... If a referendum had to be held on the creation of the European Community or the introduction of the euro, do you think these would have passed?"—Commission President Jose M. Barroso, *Irish Times*, 8 February 2007.
78. The author is not for a second suggesting that the EU has any undemocratic aims as such, rather that the organization is laying itself open to accusations of using undemocratic methods to achieve what might very well be democratic aims.
79. The reaction of the Speaker of European Parliament on this question is interesting (Hans-Gert Pottering): "It is of course a great disappointment for all those who wanted to achieve greater democracy, greater political effectiveness and greater clarity and transparency in decision-making in the European Union that the majority of the Irish could not be convinced of the need for these reforms of the European Union." Here we have the Head of the EU's only real elected body effectively saying the voters were wrong! That Mr. Pottering does not apparently see the obvious contradiction here, is perhaps proof, if any were needed, of a certain loss of contact at Brussels level with the real situation on the ground in Europe and an understanding of how, given the obvious tunnel vision existing in Brussels, that forcing people to vote on the same issue again and again until they get it "right" cannot in any way be considered democratic.
80. See the comments of Valerie Giscard D'Estaing, responsible for drafting the rejected European Constitution: "Public opinion will be led to adopt, without knowing it, the proposals that we dare not present to them directly ... All the earlier proposals will be in the new text, but will be hidden and disguised in some way"—V. Giscard D'Estaing, *Le Monde*, 14 June 2007, and *Sunday Telegraph*, 1 July 2007. Publicly, the architects of the reform accept that they are hoodwinking their public: Is this the way to construct a democratic future for Europe? The comments of Roman Herzog are also interesting in this regard and confirm that the ever greater expansion of the EU does involve a significant transfer of sovereignty from the national parliaments to the EU and justifies use of the word "*coup d'état*": "It is true that we are experiencing an ever greater, inappropriate centralization of powers away from the Member States and towards the EU. The German Ministry of Justice has compared the legal acts adopted by the Federal Republic of Germany between 1998 and 2004 with those adopted

by the European Union in the same period. Results: 84 per cent come from Brussels, with only 16 per cent coming originally from Berlin ... Against the fundamental principle of the separation of powers, the essential European legislative functions lie with the members of the executive ... The figures stated by the German Ministry of Justice make it quite clear. By far the large majority of legislation valid in Germany is adopted by the German Government in the Council of Ministers, and not by the German Parliament ... And so the question arises whether Germany can still be referred to unconditionally as a parliamentary democracy at all, because the separation of powers as a fundamental constituting principle of the constitutional order in Germany has been cancelled out for large sections of the legislation applying to this country ... The proposed draft Constitution does not contain the possibility of restoring individual competencies to the national level as a centralization brake. Instead, it counts on the same one-way street as before, heading towards ever greater centralization".

81. Sham, because when the result is not pleasing, the vote is simply ignored and the legislation introduced in another way, or if not possible, this having already been done, the population is asked to vote again with an economic gun held to its head. The comments of Jean Claude Juncker are interesting in this regard: "If it's a Yes, we will say 'On we go", and if it's a No we will say 'We continue.'"—Jean-Claude Juncker, Luxembourg Prime Minister and holder of the EU Presidency, *Daily Telegraph*, 26 May 2005.
82. As an example of pressure being put on Poland and the Czech Rep, Polish President Lech Kaczynski in early July confirmed to French President Nicolas Sarkozy that Poland would not block the ratification process, only days after saying that it would be pointless for Poland to ratify the Treaty after the Irish "No" vote. (*Financial Times*, 5-6 July, 2008). What, one wonders, triggered such a public and hurried about-face?
83. The world's largest economic block has been created, for the most part operating with a single currency. Moreover, its successes are not limited to economic affairs, it has also established a passport free travel zone throughout most of Europe, developed integrated policies on questions as diverse as criminal justice to environmental and social protection and it has also laid the foundations for a future common foreign policy and a European Army.
84. French President, Nicolas Sarkozy recently commented in a speech before the European Parliament that "Perhaps one day, unfortunately, we will have that multi-speed or multi-tier Europe"; speech to the European Parliament in July 2008 at the moment of France's accession to the presidency of the European Union.
85. For example, in a multi-speed Europe certain member states might come together and apply a more liberalized version of the recently adopted Bolkestein Directive, further freeing up the Single Market in services between them. These Member States would be free to create the extended Single Market between them on the basis of mutual recognition without any harmonization of the social framework of rules governing the presentation of such services, as is presently wished for by other Member States.

9

European Common Foreign and Security Policy: *In Perception and in Action*

B. KRISHNAMURTHY

> CFSP is about Europe making a difference in international politics; it is about the EU being able to project its values and its interest—the core of its political identity—effectively beyond its own borders.[1]
>
> —Javier Solana, Mr. CFSP

The main objective of the European integration programme is to secure peace and prosperity in Europe, by averting war among the European countries in general and between France and Germany in particular. Initially, the European Community (EC) at the individual member state level as well as at the collective level, concentrated on international economic policy and relations, through the establishment of common market and common external tariff.

Soon, the member states of the Community understood that international politics and economics could not be dealt with in isolation, as both influence and affect each other. So, the EC tried to promote political cooperation among the member states so as to present itself as "a United Europe", which would be in a position to assume "its responsibilities in the world of tomorrow" and "to make a contribution commensurate with its traditions and mission". As such, *L'Europe puissance* project represented basically the quest for a separate political space for Europe free from the domination of non-European superpowers. This political and economic integration or the «Euro-voluntarism» was supported by European, mainly French, politicians of all hue and cries.[2] De Gaulle's "Grand Design", to use Alfred Grosser's expression, was built around the pre-eminence of the political, the quest for a Concert of Europe system, adapted to the twentieth century. The French sincerely believed that a European concert alone could prevent the consolidation of the American-Soviet monopoly over the affairs of the world.[3]

Early Efforts towards Political Cooperation and Common Foreign Policy

In early 1950s, through Plevan Plan the French proposed to create the European Defence Community with the idea of keeping the re-armed Germany under control. Any how in 1954, the French National Assembly killed the proposal on the ground that such a step would lead to loss of sovereignty on the part of France and it may lead to a «Europe of Generals». Consequent plan to achieve European Political Community too failed. Subsequently, in 1961, the French Government published the Fouchet Plan, which proposed an intergovernmental European Political Union to coordinate foreign policy through the European Political Commission to be based in Paris. This proposal was perceived by other powers as Gaullist ploy to undermine the EC and in turn, to impose the French control over the external relations of other countries and was thus rejected.

In 1969, in their meeting at The Hague, the European leaders called for member states to cooperate on foreign policy in a procedure known as European Political Cooperation (EPC). The launch of *ostpolitik,* German policy of establishing relations with the countries of Soviet bloc, by this time, provided a strong impetus for member states to coordinate their policies with Central European countries and Soviet Union. The Davignon Report (October 1970) was the founding text of EPC. This report defined its goals—harmonisation of its positions, consultation and, where necessary, joint action and its instruments—meetings for foreign ministers twice a year, meetings for political directors, representing each member state, in the Political Committee four times a year and a range of specialised Working Groups composed of Foreign Ministry officials. It was an intergovernmental process with no institutional base. It aimed to provide mechanism for foreign policy cooperation/coordination to give political direction to the EC's external relations. Cooperation between member state missions in third countries was also envisaged. Consultation between Foreign Ministers and officials of the member states became routine at all levels, the Coreu telex system which directly linked EC Foreign Ministries facilitating instantaneous communication. However, the Coreu transmissions tended to be confined to relatively insignificant matters, due to the concerns of the member states about the security of the system.[4]

At the 1972 Paris Summit, the Six, founder-members of the EC, openly declared that political cooperation among them would enable Europe "to establish its position in world affairs as a distinct entity". The 1973 Middle East war and subsequent Euro-Arab dialogue had given further impetus to the EPC. In December 1973, the Nine (with the addition of Britain, Denmark and

Ireland) adopted their document on European Identity which sought to define their relations as a collectivity with the non-member states as well as their stand in international affairs. It was also decided that in their bilateral relations with third countries, they were to increasingly act on the basis of agreed common positions so as to strengthen their cohesion and "the framing of a genuinely European foreign policy". In 1974, at the Paris Summit, the Nine reiterated their "determination gradually to adopt common positions and coordinate their diplomatic action in all areas of international affairs which affect the interests of the European Community".[5] While rejecting the "power politics", the Nine adopted the "civilian power" approach, which stressed more on Europe's economic and cultural influences on the rest of the World.

In spite of these policy pronouncements and Galtung's prediction in the early 1970s that the EC was in the process of becoming a Super Power, the EPC was an exercise in low-profile politics. Its functioning based on consensus among the Nine, was hardly suitable or an ideal instrument for building up a "pax-Bruxelliana". The confused and bewildered reaction of the third countries to what was brewing in the Community on the name of common position and coordinated action is well reflected in Henry Kissinger's query: «Who speaks for Europe?»

In the early 1980s, the achievements claimed by the Community in its external relations during the earlier decade, were questioned by scholars like Hedley Bull and Kahler, who were skeptical about them. In turn, they argued that the Europeans would need to develop a military capacity through the Western European Union (WEU), if they were ever to be taken seriously on the great issues of international politics, where "hard" power is involved. This critique led to the advent of the security paradigm into the domain of EPC. The opinion that the EC as a civilian power had been rendered obsolete by the international developments of the early 80s and the belief that the EC could no longer "dissociate itself from the power politics of the contemporary world" gained currency.[6]

The Single European Act (SEA) of 1986 codified the EPC in an international treaty and placed it as a part of EC's central legal instrument. It provided treaty base for EPC, which remained till then an intergovernmental process between High Contracting Parties. Though the EPC Secretariat was established in Brussels, it was not provided with the status of a Community institution and was staffed by seconded member state officials.[7] The SEA confirmed the goals of EPC and also extended it to the security domain. Article 30(6) of the SEA states that closer cooperation on questions of European security "would contribute in an essential way to the development of a European identity in external policy matters" and confirms the High

Contracting Parties' readiness to "coordinate their positions more closely on the political and economic aspects of security". Though direct reference to military aspects was deliberately avoided, they were implicit in the form of words chosen and were subsequently made explicit. Thus, the SEA actually provided legal base to the EPC and maintained continuity of its goals.

However, the processes of EPC and the consequent external relations of the EC have been criticised for lack of coherent, independent common foreign policy initiatives and for its apparent preoccupation with simple rhetoric than any meaningful action. It was also pointed out that it represented a reflexive foreign policy style.[8] The challenge behind Kissinger's question of the early 70s continued to remain unanswered.

However, momentous developments of the late 1980s and early 90s, which witnessed the collapse of the erstwhile Soviet Union and heralded the end of Cold War, had left the EC bewildered. During the Yugoslavian crisis of early 90s, the European Union (EU) remained a mute observer, an economic giant, but, a political pigmy and a military worm incapable of punching collective weight politically. An inescapable urge was felt among the European leaders and decision-makers «to move from a foreign policy of communiqués and declarations full of strong nouns and weak verbs to something more substantive, more muscular, more focused that can have more impact».[9] The momentum gained by the establishment of the European Single Market too boosted the need for the development of a more coherent external political face, commensurate with the EC's, external commercial strength. All these resulted in the formulation of a common foreign policy.

Common Foreign and Security Policy

The Treaty on European Union (TEU) or the Maastricht Treaty of February 1992 which came into force on November 11,1993, in its earnestness to provide a single worldwide system of cooperation among the member states of the EC in international political affairs, projected the Common Foreign and Security Policy (CFSP) as the second pillar of the EU. In an era of global interdependence, the CFSP was considered as a vital means to protect the interests of individual member states that form the Union. While marking a new stage in the process of «creating an ever closer union among the people of Europe», the Maastricht treaty projected the main objective of the EU in its external relations would be «to assert its identity on the international scene, in particular through the implementation of a common foreign and security policy including the eventual framing of a common defence policy, which might in time lead to a common defence» (Article B).[10]

The CFSP named the WEU, a previously independent, little-known forum for defense consultations, as the nascent defense arm of the EU. Mention of the WEU in the Maastricht Treaty seemed to finally break down a long-standing taboo against linking defense cooperation to European economic integration.[11] The WEU was expected to elaborate and implement decisions and actions of the Union which have defence implications.

Human Rights Dimensions of CFSP

Since its inception, the EC tried to keep the issue of human rights at the centre stage. Article 177 of the Treaty establishing the European Community (TEC) or the Treaty of Rome of 1957 states: «community policy ... shall contribute to the general objective of developing and consolidating democracy and the rule of law and to that of respecting human rights and fundamental freedoms». Again, Article 6 of the TEU of 1992 maintains: «The Union is founded on the principles of liberty, democracy, respect for human rights and fundamental freedoms, and the rule of law, principles which are common to the Member States». It adds: «The Union shall respect fundamental rights, as guaranteed by the European Convention for the Protection of Human Rights and Fundamental Freedoms signed in Rome on November 4, 1950 and as they result from the constitutional traditions common to the Member States, as general principles of Community law».[12]

The TEU projects the main objective of the EU in its external relations as safe-guarding «the common value, fundamental value and independence of the Union» and also to «develop and consolidate democracy and the rule of law, and respect for human rights and fundamental freedom»(Article J.1). Again, as per Article J. 1(2) of the TEU, one of the objectives of the CFSP is to develop and consolidate democracy and the rule of law, and respect for human rights and for freedom. EU had taken a stand in Vienna in 1993 that human rights, democracy and development are interdependent and mutually reinforcing and that the promotion of human rights also improves the prospects of peace and security. In its earnestness to see that the third countries respect human rights and democracy, EU had deliberately linked the development and cooperation policy with the human rights record of the recipient country.

As such, the EU has given to the protection, promotion and defence of human rights, democracy, rule of law and good governance a prominent place in its external policy and relations. It is trying to convert the good will and the hold it has earned on third parties through its development and cooperation policies and programmes into their compliance of international human rights standards.[13]

Institutionalization of CFSP

While dealing with the issue of institutional framework of the EU with regard to its external relations, Article C of the TEU maintained that the Union shall be served by a single institutional framework so as to «ensure the consistency and the continuity of the activities ...». It added that the Union shall ensure «the consistency of its external activities as a whole in the context of its external relations, security, economic and development policies». The Council and the European Commission were expected to ensure such consistency and to implement these policies, each in accordance with its respective powers.

The European Council consists of the Heads of State or of Government of the member states and the President of the Commission, assisted by the Ministers of Foreign Affairs of the member states and by a member of the Commission, who is in charge of external relations. It occupies a position of the highest rank in the CFSP as it determines its principles and general guidelines (Article J.8.1), including those relating to matters with defence implications. The Council also decides on the common strategies which are implemented by the Union in areas where the member states have important common interests. This body is to meet at least twice a year and to initiate and express common positions vis-à-vis the outside world.

At the second stage, the CFSP matters are to be dealt with by the Foreign Affairs Ministers of the member states in the General Affairs Council of the Council of the European Union which has to take necessary decisions concerning the formulation and implementation of the CFSP on the basis of the general guidelines or common strategies laid down by the European Council. Actually, it adopts common positions and joint actions as well as decisions and is responsible for ensuring that the Union's action is unified, consistent and effective (Article J.8.2). Subsequently, CFSP Secretariat was incorporated into Council Secretariat.

Article J.8.5 provides for Political Committee, consisting of the Heads of Political Departments of Foreign Ministries of the member states. It was expected to monitor the international situation in the areas covered by CFSP and to contribute to the definition of policies by delivering opinions to the Council at its request or on its own initiative. A new Permanent Representative Committee (Coreper), an ambassadorial body, to be staffed by high-ranking representatives of the member states, was given the responsibility of preparing and finalising the Council's work regarding the CFSP affairs. Both these bodies were expected to compliment each other and while the Political Committee takes care of the content of the CFSP, the Coreper acts as a technical coordinator or looks after Community-related aspects. Over two dozen expert groups assist them in their activities. Meetings among the ambassadors of the member states to non-member countries and international organizations and conferences, which are normally held every month, provide useful inputs to the Union's activities in the sphere of CFSP.[14]

Article J.5 reposes the responsibility of representing the EU in matters of CFSP on the Presidency, which is held by each member state in turn for six months in accordance with the *rota* laid down in Article 146 of the TEC. It is also made responsible for the implementation of the common measures and to present the position of the Union in International organizations and conferences. In these activities, the current Presidency could seek the assistance of the previous and successive member states to hold the Presidency and this arrangement has come to be known as "Troika".

As mentioned earlier, the European Commission shares with the Presidency the responsibility of ensuring the consistency and implementation of the external activities of the EU. Article J.9 maintains that «the Commission shall be fully associated with all the work carried out in the sphere of CFSP». Moreover, in the G-8 summit meetings, the Commission is expected to represent the non-member Member States of the Union. Article J.7 provides for the considerations of the views of the European Parliament (EP) on the main aspects and basic choices of the CFSP. The EP is consulted by the Presidency of the Council and the Commission on the fundamental choices of the CFSP and is briefed in how it is developing. The EP is allowed to ask questions and make recommendations to the Council and to hold an annual debate on the progress in the implementation of the CFSP. However, the Parliament was effectively shut out of the EU's intergovernmental pillars and so, its influence on the CFSP turned out to be quite minimal.

Relating to the collective role to be played by the member states of the EU in other international organizations like the UN Security Council in which a couple of them alone are members and majority of them are not, the TEA has offered a solution. Article J.2 of the Maastricht Treaty takes care of this discrepancy and maintains that in "international organizations and at international conferences where not all member states participate, those which do take part shall uphold the common positions". Article J.5.4 specifies that the member states, which are permanent members of the UN Security Council, in the execution of their function, will "ensure the defence of the positions and the interests of the Union ...".

In its earnestness to wipe out the image of the EC as lacking unity, being too reactive and passive against the developments in international political scenario and that its internal decision-making procedures were too cumbersome and so, ineffective, the TEU opted for the abandonment of the consensus principle. It was decided to establish a new instrument of "concerted and convergent action" (Article J.2). Majority decisions are specifically confined to the implementation of joint actions and the Council has to determine whether the unanimity or majority rule applies in each case.

The Council struggled for months to reach a basic decision on how to meet the cost of the CFSP which are described in Article J.11 as "operational expenditure". Finally, it was decided to charge them to the budget of the European Communities or to the Member States on case by case basis and the Council was expected to take such a decision. Not surprisingly, member states preferred to draw on the EU budget rather than spending themselves.

Treaty of Amsterdam

The Treaty of Amsterdam of 1997, which aimed at giving Europe a clear message and a stronger voice in world affairs, tried to help the EU to overcome the contradictions that were affecting it in its CFSP goals. The new treaty provided for the appointment of a Secretary-General for Foreign Affairs to assist the President of the Council. It was also stipulated that the Secretary-General of the Council shall also be the High Representative for the CFSP. He was to assist the Council by contributing in particular to the formulation, drawing up and implementation of political decisions and, where necessary by acting on behalf of the Council at the request of the Presidency and conducting political dialogue with third parties. Regarding the issue of financing the CFSP operational expenses the member states resolved that these expenditures were to be charged to the EU budget, except those with military implications. This development invariably acknowledged the role of EP in the CFSP as the members of Parliament got an opportunity to scrutinize its operational expenses and consequently the activities of the Union in the external front. Moreover, the Amsterdam Treaty provided for the establishment of a Policy Planning and Early Warning Unit (PPEWU) in the Council Secretariat. However, neither the tasks nor the composition of the unit were made clear and consequently, the PPEWU failed to fulfill the more strategic policy role that its title would imply.[15]

EU High Representative for Foreign and Security Policy

The Treaty of Amsterdam came into force in 1999. In June of the same year, Javier Solana Madariga, former Chief of North Atlantic Treaty Organization (NATO), had been appointed as EU High Representative for Foreign and Security Policy and as such, the representative of the Foreign Ministers of the EU member states, thus having their political authority.[16] Solana was appointed as the Foreign Policy Czar, with the hope that this move would give the Union more clout, say and recognition on the international scene. This is also a move to project a person who should be approached if the leaders in Washington, New Delhi or other non-EU capitals want to find out the European stand on pressing international issues. With the appointment of Solana the Troika arrangement comprised up to four members—the Presidency, the future Presidency, the High Representative and a representative of the European Commission.[17] In terms of external representation, the Amsterdam Treaty provided a formal basis for the practice of appointing "Special Representatives" or envoys, with a mandate to represent the Union on particular issues. It was subsequently resolved that these Special Representatives should be responsible to the High Representative.[18]

European Security and Defence Policy

The Amsterdam Treaty laid the foundation for European Security and Defence Policy (ESDP), as an integral part of CFSP. The idea that European Union could have an autonomous defense policy was arrived at a meeting between the then British Prime Minister Tony Blair and President Jacques Chirac in St.Malo in December in 1998, in response to Europe's poor handling of the Balkan crisis and almost total dependence on Americans in Kosovo.[19] The Cologne European Council of June 1999 placed crisis management tasks at the core of the process of strengthening ESDP. A catalogue of missions, known as the Petersburg Tasks—humanitarian and rescue tasks, peacekeeping tasks and combat-force tasks in crisis management, including peacemaking—was set as a target for the European armed forces to be capable of conducting. It was resolved that «the Union must have the capacity for autonomous action, backed up by credible military forces, the means to decide to use them, and a readiness to do so, in order to respond to international crises ...». Subsequently, at the Helsinki European Council held in December, «headline goal» in terms of military capabilities was formulated. By this the Union would be able, by the year 2003, to deploy within sixty days and sustain for at least one year, up to 60,000 persons capable of carrying out the full range of Petersberg tasks. It was also resolved that this force should be militarily self-sustaining with the necessary command, control and intelligence capabilities, logistics, other combat support services, and additionally, as appropriate, air and naval elements. However, it was perceived, that this step would not lead to the establishment of a European army and the commitment to the deployment of national troops would be based on sovereign decisions taken by the member states.

The Nice European Council in December 2000, which came into force in 2003, codified developments in security sphere introduced at 1999 Cologne Council and took the decision to establish new permanent political and military structures within the Council to provide political control and strategic direction in a crisis. A political and Security Committee comprising Brussels-based national diplomats was established to meet twice weekly to monitor the development and implementation of CFSP. Moreover, a Military Committee was also created. The Council Secretariat now incorporates military staff composed of military experts seconded by the member states under the direction of the Military Committee which it is expected to assist. This could be described as a fundamental shift to the «corporate identity of the EU» as the Union used to display a thoroughly «civilian» attitude till then. Furthermore, permanent arrangements have been agreed upon for EU-NATO consultation and cooperation.

The EU also decided to develop mechanism for civilian aspects of crisis management in four priority areas: police, strengthening of the rule of law, strengthening civilian administration, and civil protection. As per the decision taken at the Göteborg summit in June 2001, member states were expected to provide 5000 officers by 2003 for international missions and to deploy 1000 of them within less than 30 days. Besides the European Council agreed that the EU should make a team of judges, prosecutors, and other legal experts; a group of civilian administrators; and rapid-response teams to assess emergency situations and to work for civilian crisis management. Discussions were on to define specific goals in connection with strengthening the rule of law and a Civilian Crisis Management Committee was established to oversee the development and required deployment of these resources. The EU took over most of the functions and bodies of the WEU in 2002, including the Satellite Centre and the old WEU think tank, located in Paris, which became an autonomous EU agency under the CFSP.[20]

In June 2003, Javier Solona presented a European Security Strategy to the EU leaders, in which he called for an assertive European foreign and security policy, including the use of military force, and identified three key threats to European security: terrorism, the proliferation of weapons of mass destruction and failed states. This security strategy was endorsed by the EU leaders by December 2003.[21] Moreover, in the same month, an agreement was reached on the establishment of an EU planning capability within NATO's military headquarters outside Brussels. To cap it all, in November 2004, Defence Ministers of the EU member states pledged up to 165,000 troops to make up a series of EU «battle groups», each consisting of about 1,500 troops from one or more member states, deployable within ten days to help quell or contain international conflicts. Thus, the EU has now developed its military muscle also, so as to enable the Union to play its due role in international politics.

Foreign Minister of the European Union

Still the confusing overlap between foreign policy Czardom of Solana and the Commission brief of Chris Patten and his successor, who were European Commission members in charge of External Relations had cropped up, which made Romano Prodi, the then President of the European Commission, to think of creating a single post of EU Foreign Minister with responsibilities similar to those of the US Secretary of State. His idea was to provide a European counterweight to the US, with matching clout and influence. Obviously, the US always remained the reference point in CFSP.

The European Draft Constitution which was signed on October 29, 2004 too envisioned certain key institutional changes in the foreign policy field. Now, the member states designated Solana to be the first Union Minister for Foreign Affairs. The minister will also be Vice-President of the Commission, by which it was meant that the current High Representative job will merge with the Commissioner for External Affairs. He will conduct the foreign and security policy and represent the Union in this sphere. He will chair the Foreign Affairs Council (regular meetings of EU Foreign Ministers). To support the EU Foreign Minister, a European External Action Service (EEAS) will be created, bringing together staff from relevant departments of the Commission and the Council Secretariat and integrating staff seconded from national diplomatic services. It was also resolved that at the level of Heads of State and Government, the EU will be represented by the President of the European Council, elected by the European Council for two and a half years, and the Commission President and at ministerial level, the EU Foreign Minister will represent the Union in contacts with third countries and conduct the political dialogue with them.

The Lisbon Reform Treaty reiterated that the functions of the EU High Representative for the CFSP and the European Commissioner in charge of External Relations will be merged into the new office of High Representative of the European Union for Foreign Affairs and Security Policy. It is believed that with the creation of the new office, EU foreign policy will be given a single profile for the first time and will reinforce the Union's cohesion in external affairs. Such an eventuality alone will answer the question raised by Kissinger in early 1970s, referred earlier. The choice of Solana, with his wide knowledge in diplomatic and security field and close contacts with most of the American and European leaders, clearly proves that EU is serious and mean business in this matter.

A new provision enables the European Council to decide, by unanimity, to extend the use of Qualified Majority Voting in the CFSP at a future date.

The Treaty specifically provides that this will not apply to matters having military or defence implications, which will continue to be taken unanimously. While the ESDP provides the Union with an operational capacity to use on missions outside the Union for «peacekeeping, conflict prevention and strengthening international security in accordance with the principles of the United Nations Charter», the Reform Treaty updates and expands these tasks to include disarmament operations, military advice and assistance tasks and post-conflict stabilisation. The Reform Treaty also addresses ways to improve the capabilities to be provided by member states to fulfill the civil and military crisis management tasks the Union may undertake any time in the future.

The institutional framework thus created has resulted in unprecedented coordination in the matter of foreign policy among the member states of the EU. Daily, governments across Europe are communicating, both electronically and in person, exchanging opinions, intelligence and proposals. Now, there is new scope and possibility for the EU to plan its foreign policy more strategically and to ensure that it is clearly articulated to partners worldwide.

CFSP and ESDP in Action

After studying the objectives and institutionalisation of the CFSP as well as ESDP, it is imperative to study and analyse how these policies were put into action as well as evaluate their successes and short comings.

(a) Successes

In October-November 1993, the member states of the EU reacted swiftly to the developments in former Yugoslavia and took a series of joint actions. At the face of problems of calamitous proportion in Bosnia-Herzegovina and later in Kosovo in the former Yugoslavia, the EU tried to formulate a common policy and to act decisively in unison, independent of the US, in its effort to preserve peace and stability in its own backyard.

As part of the strategy of stabilising the Russian political scene, European observers were sent to oversee the elections in Russia. Under the auspices of the Stability Pact which the EU signed with the Central and East European countries procedural proposals and conferences were held in an effort to channelise and resolve potential disputes among them. To maintain its presence in the Middle East, its traditional area of activities, the EU offered aid totaling around ECU 500 million to consolidate the agreement between Israel and the Palestine Liberation Organization. In its earnestness to help prepare the first elections in South Africa in 1994, a European election team of over 450 people were sent there to provide technical and organizational assistance. It was also decided to put an end to the economic sanctions; to resume Community aid programmes and to conclude a wide-ranging cooperation agreement, to nurture the nascent democracy in that region.[22] It is noteworthy that under the CFSP, the EU agreed on 163 policy statements in 1998 on issues ranging from the trial of the Lockerbie bomb suspects to the nuclear tests conducted by India and Pakistan.[23]

In 1990s, the CFSP enjoyed popular support. In a public opinion poll on the vision of "Europe of 2010", three out of five Europeans thought that the EU will have a common foreign policy by then.[24] Moreover, there has been unanimity amongst the member states of the EU on some of the guiding principles of the foreign, development aid and cooperation policies such as respect for democracy, rule of law as well as human rights and policy towards nuclear non-proliferation. Especially in the "third generation" agreements of the EU in the 1990s like the Fourth Lomé Convention, a deliberate attempt has been made to link aid with political reforms and human rights record of the recipient states. On December 19, 1994, the European Council approved a regulation to establish a Community regime for the control of the export of dual—use goods to non-member countries. In this regard, it was also decided to take joint action under the auspices of the CFSP. This tough and harmonised export control regime prescribes a unified list for the control of dual-use goods for all member states of the EU. Adoption of its all comprehensive and stringent «catch-all provision» prohibits firms from transferring equipment and technology to any country, even if there is scope for suspicion that the exported items or other products obtained thereof could be used to build up weapons of mass destruction.[25]

Role of EU in the UN

In recent years, EU member states are attempting to coordinate their positions in the UN General Assembly and related UN bodies, with considerable success. The reality that EU can muster 27 votes from member states and considerably more when candidate associate countries are persuaded to vote in its side, turned the EU into a power to be reckoned within the UN system and it is not surprising that the Union is recognised among the UN members as a formidable force. In the UNSC, where decisions are taken on key issues of international security, EU does not enjoy such prominence. However, since 1993 the practice of presenting written and verbal statements on behalf of the EU has developed, with both the Presidency and Javier Solana regularly addressing the Security Council.[26] In this context, it is significant to note that European Security Strategy of June 2003 identified UN Charter as the «fundamental framework» for international relations and prioritized its strengthening.[27] Under the framework of ESDP, the Union has developed operational capacity to use outside the Union on peacekeeping and conflict prevention missions in accordance with the principles of the United Nations Charter.

EU as a Benevolent Power

EU has developed the image of a soft, civilian power and purveyor of funds for development cooperation in international politics. In the South, EU is regarded as a relatively unbiased interlocutor, in that it has distanced from the colonial ties of individual member states.[28] Through the Lomé system, the Mediterranean preferences, and trade and commercial agreements with the regional organizations such as ASEAN and the Contadora countries, EU maintains institutionalized relations with most of the poorer countries of the World.[29] The countries in the developing world take to EU as a sober, benevolent power, which would be in their side in any eventualities. They have developed lot of expectations from EU, which the latter sometimes finds very difficult to fulfill.

ESDP in Action

In June 2003 the EU deployed a French-led peacekeeping mission, authorized by the UN Security Council, for three months to Bunia in the Democratic Republic of Congo. This was the first EU military mission undertaken without recourse to NATO, and the first mission outside Europe.[30] There are thirteen ESDP operations (civilian or military) currently under way. In the Western Balkans, in Bosnia-Herzegovina, where the European Union has been playing a key stabilizing role since the Dayton Accords were signed in 1995, two operations are under way: a military operation, EUFOR Althea, launched on December 2, 2004, with approximately 2,500 men. This operation contributes to the stability and security of Bosnia, mandated by the United Nations Security Council. Moreover, a police mission (EUPM), which, through monitoring, supervisory and inspection actions, aims to create a professional and multiethnic police force managed by Bosnia-Herzegovina. It has approximately 300 agents, 174 of whom are international. Again, in Kosovo, EULEX Kosovo is the biggest civilian mission in the history of the ESDP. Launched in 2008, its main objective is to assist and support the Kosovo government in issues of rule of law, specifically: police, justice and customs. It is a technical mission that is tasked primarily with monitoring and advising and will have only a limited number of executive powers. There are 330 agents deployed currently, and in the long run there should be 1,900 international agents and 1,100 local agents in the field. The assistance mission at the Moldavia-Ukraine border is tasked primarily with assisting the competent authorities of these two countries to improve their management of this border, by way of offering advice and training.[31]

(b) Shortcomings

However, all is not well with CFSP. After the initial activism, the member states of the EU displayed difference of opinion, which affected their action in the Balkan affairs. In the absence of much needed political integration, even limited military actions in Yugoslavia proved beyond the capacity of the Union.[32] The Americans had to intervene to bring some order, in the process discrediting the EU and its new initiatives towards common security at its own backyard. The failure of the EU in preventing the Balkan wars of the 1990s triggered by the disintegration of Yugoslavia was humiliating as the EU had to depend on the US to halt Serbia's aggression first in Bosnia and then in Kosovo. It was shameful to have done so little to avert the slaughter of thousands of Europeans in a far corner of the continent, which made Chris Patten to lament: «But 200,000 or more fellow Europeans died in Bosnia and Herzegovina alone. As Europeans we cannot avoid a heavy share of responsibility for what happened»[33].

On a whole range of issues, the EU as an entity is failing to make its voice heard in a coherent or persuasive way. Each of the member states retains ultimate responsibility for all aspects of its foreign policy. Moreover, some of the member states, especially the UK, want to resort to joint actions as restrictively as possible, as they could not reconcile themselves to the perceived loss of sovereignty in the sphere of foreign policy. As they are accustomed to take unilateral decisions, guided more by selfish national interest than by lofty principles or noble collective interests, the member states continue to do so, in spite of their commitment for common positions and policies. For instance, in 2001, on the issue of the American proposal for National Missile Defense, the EU failed to react with a single voice since the power to decide on issues, affecting territorial defense, is being jealously guarded by the member states. As such, it turned out to be virtually impossible for the EU to arrive at a consensus. For well—known reasons, Britain continued to resist a discussion on NMD at the EU platform and Robin Cook, the then British Foreign Minister, made it clear that the EU should not be a place for discussing territorial collective defense.[34] Again, in the issue of America's all-out war against terrorism, initially against Afghanistan and later extended to Iraq, EU failed to respond in unison.[35] On 30 January 2003, together with seven other European countries Poland signed the «Letter from Eight European Countries for a United Front against Iraq» which was to entail discord with the Paris-Brussels-Berlin axis, discredit the idea of a common external and defence policy. The impulsive reaction of the opposition camp led by France and Germany, along with Belgium and Luxembourg, to press ahead with their own plans for defence cooperation and to establish a military headquarters in the Brussels suburb of Tervuren further vitiated the atmosphere.[36] Simultaneous visit of Jack Straw, the then British Foreign Secretary and Chris Patten, the European Commissioner in charge of External Affairs, to India and Pakistan on similar mission during May-June 2002 to find a solution to the stand off between the two South Asian neighbours clearly shows that still the EU fails to speak and act collectively and convincingly on key international issues.[37] Solana puts this predicament in a nutshell: «Convergence has always been the goal, divergence was too often the reality»[38].

Limitations of EU in Regards to CFSP

As such, the viability and activities of CFSP turned out to be a "mixed bag" of achievement and fiasco. On many occasions, the EU failed miserably to fulfill the expectations of the member states as well as the third countries. This sorry state of affairs is due too several factors:

(a) Institutional and Structural Factors

EU is in many ways unpopular and its institutions are sometimes viewed as Byzantine in their complex interaction. This unpopularity is both domestic and external and as such the primary constraint of CFSP, since it is part of a single community institutional framework. However, the balance of power between the Council, the Parliament and the Commission in this field is different and implementation of the CFSP differs considerably from that of other community policies. For instance, the Commission is fully associated with the CFSP but does not have the exclusive right to submit initiatives. These come mainly from the Presidency, a Member State or the High Representative—all intergovernmental institutions. Lack of needed political will on the part of the member states leaves the policy formulation as well as implementation half-hearted and so half-baked.

Moreover, certain flaws in the decision-making process of the CFSP haunt the Union's external relations. Meeting only twice a year, the European Council is not the right tool to serve as a body for the day-to-day steering and coordination of the CFSP. Even the formulation of guiding principles of a foreign policy many a time proved difficult when sovereign representatives of the member states have to arrive at decisions unanimously. Again, the obvious drawback of this procedural requirement of the Council of the European Union is that the decisions are to be taken unanimously and unfortunately member states hold differing views on many questions resulting in the EU's inability to take quick and meaningful decisions and follow up action. This pathetic situation became apparent during the early 1990s when the member states were not in a position to agree on a unified stance concerning the civil war in Bosnia. The pressure tactics brought in by Germany to recognize Croatia and the hesitation on the part of other member states for such a move clearly brings out this predicament.

The fact that the EU High Representative on Foreign Policy is answerable to the Council of Ministers and his powers are limited and circumscribed by the national governments to whom he is expected to report, clearly shows the limitation of EU's ability to project a single figurehead in the foreign policy sphere. Solana-Patten combination has already made it a double-headed wonder. After the initial period of honeymoon, there were confusing overlaps between them, which led to the idea of creating a single post of EU Foreign Minister. Unless it is materialized, the presentation and projection of a single figurehead to represent EU in external relations will be a pipe dream. Again, the troika arrangement, which started with three members and further extended to four and subsequently five, further complicates the external representation of the Union

Other institutional shortcomings like the reorganization of the expert committees or the division of tasks between the Political Committee and the Permanent Representative Committee too created certain hurdles in the smooth functioning of the CFSP. Again, there were disputes over the demarcation of powers, which went beyond purely technical and legal aspects, reflecting the tension between supporters of Community orthodoxy, who apprehend "interference" of CFSP with the first pillar and those who find virtue in the traditional foreign policy line and believe that the CFSP must lay down comprehensive guidelines.[39]

(b) Capabilities—Expectation Gap

As in the case of any other institutional set up, there is always a gap between what the EU is expected to perform in the field of international politics and what its actual capabilities are, in terms of its ability to agree, its resources and the instruments at its disposal. The expectations from the EU, both from the member states as well as from the third countries, are multifarious and multifaceted. It was expected to play the role of a super state, a tamer of the US, a panacea for all the ills of present day international politics and economics, one of the predominant poles of the ensuing multipolar world, a champion of democracy, rule of law and human rights and a harbinger of new order. Unfortunately, the system on which the European political cooperation is based, severally and severely restricts the capabilities of the

EU. Not only in terms of substantive resources like financial and military power but also in terms of the ability to take decisions and stick to them, the EU is still far from being able to play the role expected of it from its *demandeurs.*[40] The failure of the EU in the Balkans, most notably in Bosnia and Kosovo, illustrates this «capabilities—expectation» gap.[41] As this is the case, the EU has to be realistic and try to bring this gap closer, either by self-restricting its expectations and making them clear to others or by enhancing its capabilities as required.[42]

(c) Military weakness and Limits of Soft Power

The Union has gradually acquired certain credibility and clout in international politics, which relies on the vast range of instruments that the European Union is likely to deploy in support of its diplomatic action and which no other regional organization in the world possesses, i.e. trade policy leading to the signing of preferential or free-trade agreements; policy on the facilitation of visa obtainment and on readmission; humanitarian action; development aid instruments that can mobilize about seven billion euros per annum, including European Development Fund contributions, in all regions of the world.[43]

However, Dinan rightly argues that the EU has only a limited foreign policy capacity and its political clout does not extend much beyond the power of the purse. Though the EU aid disbursements dwarf those of the United States, the big decisions, such as on military intention in trouble spots, remain the province of the nation-states and out of reach of EU, when it matters.[44] As a matter of fact, the soft power at the disposal of the EU fails to carry through the Union in difficult times. Again, in its ambitious policy of influencing the human rights record and democratic transformation of other countries, through judicious employment of its economic strength, EU could do substantial only when the recipient country is completely depend on it largesse or its economic management. Otherwise, with countries like China, the Europeans cut a sorry figure, as EU needs China as much as the latter needs EU.[45]

(d) Issue of Single Seat for EU in the UNSC

The issue of a single seat for EU in the UNSC illustrates the challenge of formulating and sustaining CFSP. If the EU wants to speak in single voice internationally, logically it should have a single seat in the UN Security Council. But Britain and France, who are permanent members in the present set up, are opposed to that idea, for fear of loosing their individual national prestige, if not clout. Others, who occupy the seats as non-permanent members, too do not want to loose the opportunity of occupying the UNSC seat temporarily for a couple of years once in a while. While Germany started pressing for a seat of its own, Italy opposes such a demand.[46] The charm of UNSC seat has turned EU a further divided house.

(e) Confusing Treaty Provisions

In case of CFSP provisions found in the EU treaties, whether it is Maastricht Treaty or otherwise, there was always an effort to satisfy all, leaving confusion behind. For instance, the text of the Maastricht Treaty was vague enough to satisfy both the maximalists, such as France, who wanted to see stronger integration in security and defence, and the minimalists, most importantly Britain, who wished to continue with status quo. The question of whether or not the EU could give direct instructions to the WEU was left particularly unclear. The 1996-97 Intergovernmental Conference, which resulted in the Amsterdam Treaty, was expected to clarify some of the uncertainty about the relationship between the WEU and the EU. Nonetheless, the result was seen as a victory for the Atlanticists. The independence of the WEU was maintained and the organization seemed more and more as a protection against a too independent security role for the EU rather than as a defence arm directly subordinated to the EU.[47]

(f) Presence of Neutral Member States

Another serious issue which influences adversely the common security policy and common defence is the presence of neutral countries as member states of the EU. In deference to the Ireland's traditional policy of military neutrality, the Lisbon Reform Treaty had to give several concessions to that country that fly on the face of the basic ideas of CFSP and EDSP. Accordingly, Ireland retains the sovereign right to decide on participation in any crisis management mission, in accordance with its national "triple lock" arrangements, which require a UN mandate to be in place. Ireland's position that under its Constitution it cannot participate in a common defence without the prior consent of the people in a referendum is accepted without murmur. The Treaty also states that if a member state is the victim of armed aggression on its territory, the other member states shall provide aid and assistance by all means in their power, in accordance with Article 51 of the United Nations Charter. However, it is made clear that this obligation "shall not prejudice the specific character of the security and defence policy of certain Member States". Ireland would therefore not be bound by any mutual defence commitment and would have the right to decide on whether and how to provide such assistance.

In its effort to cajole the Irish voters, who rejected the Nice Treaty in a referendum conducted earlier to vote positively in a subsequent popular consultation, the EU issued the Seville Declaration in 2002 whereby the status of Irish military neutrality was guaranteed through an undertaking that Ireland would not be forced to participate in any future European Union common defense policy. Further, it was assured that any Irish involvement in future policies adopted under the heading of enhanced cooperation would first require the agreement of the Irish Houses of Parliament.

In short, the neutral members like Ireland were allowed to maintain their neutrality even after becoming member states of the EU, which intends to have a common foreign and security policy and take common position and joint action on any single international issue of collective interest. The element of contradiction is quite disturbing.

How much 'Common' is CFSP?

In spite of the understanding that speaking in a single voice and acting in unison would strengthen their stand in the international political arena and best efforts to project the CFSP and the consequent common positions and cohesive actions, Europe still remains in realistic terms what de Gaulle willed, *l'Europe des patries* (Europe of States),[48] with separate sovereign states as central to its construction. This hybrid nature of the construction has been a ball and chain around the CFSP, which tends to make it impotent and ineffective. Even after creating EU mechanisms for conducting CFSP, there is a tendency to conduct a purely bilateral foreign policy. In the aftermath of September 11, the EU let the opportunity to present common purpose go waste, by indulging in an unseemly race to Washington to be the first to offer «unconditional solidarity» with the US.[49] Certain issues are still dealt with at the level of the member states. For instance, on the issue of India's claim for permanent seat in the UN Security Council, the EC has deliberately left it to the will and pleasure of the individual countries to support or maintain meaningful silence.[50] As this is the case, the third countries too try to deal with the EU member states individually, in stead of approaching the EU as a collectivity, since it has proved cumbersome and time-consuming.

Another outcome of this reality is the role played by the individual Member States in the formulation and modification of the EU's external policy. The lurking fear that the EU's policy may be dominated by or at least adversely influenced by big powers among the member states at the cost of smaller powers, seems to become a reality. The possibility of "constructive abstention" that was introduced in the Amsterdam Treaty does in practice allow a limited number of states to take initiatives in foreign policy without the full participation of all member states.[51] For instance, in 1997, France led the move in the European Union ministerial gathering to reject calls from the Foreign Minster of Holland to introduce a resolution condemning the human rights violations of China in the United Nations Human Rights Commission with the tacit support of Germany, Italy and Spain.[52] Likewise, France's policy towards nuclear India got translated into the EU's policy in due course.[53] In the same way, France's dream of building up a multipolar world with the strong and united Europe as the central pole, India being yet another, tends to move the EU towards that end.[54]

State sovereignty has always been defended with particular verve and the right and ability to conduct a foreign policy constitutes an important part of a nation's sense of purpose and identity.[55] As this is the case, it is quite natural that CFSP is to be pushed through the throat of the member states. It is rightly pointed out that many of the problems of the CFSP stem not only from the rules or institutions alone, but also from the member states' reluctance to "play by the rules of the game which they themselves established".

Conclusion

The protagonists of CFSP never hesitate to claim that it is the major global equilibria and is aimed at giving a cutting edge to EU in its external relations. The choice of Solana, who is well known for his diplomatic acumen and maintains excellent working relationship with most of the American and European leaders, as the High Representative of CFSP and subsequently as the Foreign Minister/Secretary of State of EU shows the seriousness of the Europeans regarding CFSP.

EU is a unique actor in international politics deriving power from the constituent states. As such, national sovereignty remains a formidable barrier to the development of a truly common foreign policy, let alone a common defence policy or a common army. In spite of the understanding and appreciation of the benefit of working as a collectivity, the idea to do it alone is still there. Likewise, a sort of reluctance on the part of EU to act as collectivity on certain occasions and issues is also perceived. The ground reality is that the EU is not even a mutual defense organization, since neutral member states are unwilling to make a collective defense commitment.

Moreover, the facts that it is not a sovereign state with an army but claims to have a foreign policy is unacceptable and incomprehensible to the neo-realists, who maintain that only a sovereign state can have foreign policy. As a natural corollary, the third countries are not ready to consider and treat EU as a global actor of influence and on the other hand, try to deal with the member states bilaterally. There is hesitation on the part of the Americans to take EU as partner in the hard ball game of international politics, especially when/where hard, military power matters.

Again, the CFSP suffers limitations as a result of several factors. Especially, the foreign policy decision-making process which works through consensus proved to be unsuitable for assuming and adopting swift and strong stand on ever-changing international political situation. Still there is competition among the member states in courting with third countries. On occasions, they take recourse to bilateral relations relegating the common institutions and policies painstakingly arrived at earlier. The most unfortunate thing for the CFSP is the prevalence of one-upmanship in stead of working in unison among the EU leadership.

However, the EU is successful in mustering soft power in abundance and tries to make good use of it to influence and impress on third countries. Especially, in spreading the idea of respect for human rights, democracy, rule of law and good governance in the developing world, EU is generally successful with its economic clout. Of late, the EU is developing its military might as well as civilian capabilities to handle any eventuality outside the EU area. This is especially a welcome development, since the EU is determined to not use military power for aggressive purposes, but, only for crisis management, war prevention and peace promotion. Moreover, this development may help erase the sad memory of the Union's failure in the Balkan region in the 1990s.

Successful European common foreign and defence policy is also welcome, especially among the developing countries, since it will represent a second Western voice, besides the US, which will be a moderating factor in international politics. The fact that the European Security Strategy of June 2003 identifies UN Charter as the «fundamental framework» for international relations and prioritized its strengthening clearly proves that EU has taken its role within the UN system seriously and its resolve to make multilateralism work. All these developments augur well not only for Europe but also for the world of tomorrow.

NOTES AND REFERENCES

1. Javier Solana, «Where does the EU Stand on Common Foreign and Security Policy»? (Speech by Javier Solana at the Forschungsinstitut der Deutschen Gesellschaft Fuer Auswaertige Politik, Berlin, November 14, 2000). http://www.dgap.org/texte/solana.html
2. David S.Yost, «France in the New Europe», *Foreign Affairs*, Winter 1990/91, p. 124.

3. Philippe Moreau Defarges, «France and Europe» in Paul Godt, (ed.), *Policy-Making in France, from de Gaulle to Mitterrand*, Pinter Publishers, London, 1989, p.228.
4. Charlotte Bretherton and John Vogler, *The European Union as a Global Actor,* Routledge, London, 2006, Second Edition, pp.165-6.
5. Juliet Lodge, «European Political Cooperation: towards the 1990s», Juliet Lodge (ed.), *The European Community and the Challenge of the Future*, Pinter Publishers, London, 1989, pp.229-230.
6. Panos Tsakaloyannis, "The EC: from civilian power to military integration", Lodge, n. 5., pp.245-246.
7. Bretherton and Vogler, n. 4, p. 164
8. Lodge, n. 5, p.235.
9. http://europe.eu.int/comm/external_relationss/nfewss/patten/sp02_134.htm (14-06-02) Developing Europe's External Policy in the Age of Globalization (Speech by Chris Patten, the then European Commissioner for External Relations on April 4, 2002).
10. *Official Journal of the European Communities*, No.C224, 31-8-1992, pp. 5, 94-96. All the references to the Articles of the Maastricht Treaty are from this source.
11. Michael Smith, «Understanding Europe's «New» Common Foreign and Security Policy», Institute on Global Conflict and Cooperation (IGCC) Policy Paper No. 52, (University of California, Multi-Campus Research Unit), 2000. http://repositories.cdlib.org/igcc/PP/pp52
12. *EU Annual Report on Human Right 1999*, Published by the European Initiative for Democracy and Human Rights, p.5. The EU started publishing its Annual Report from 1999 onwards wherein interesting details are given on the aspirations and activities of the Union in the sphere of human rights.
13. B.Krishnamurthy, «Human Rights dimension of the European Common Foreign and Security Policy: The Case Study of EU-China Relations» in *Journal of Contemporary Asia & Europe*, vol.1, No.1, January-June 2004,pp. 26-44.
14. Werner Weidenfeld and Wolfgang Wessels, *Europe from A to Z Guide to European Integration, Institut fur Europaische Politik*, Publication of the European Commission, 1997, p.45.
15. Bretherton and Vogler, n. 4, p. 170.
16. *The Hindu*, Chennai, June 5, 1999.
17. Bretherton and Vogler, n. 4, p.170.
18. *Ibid.*, p. 246, n. 20.
19. Douglas Gould, «A European Common Defense Community in the Making?», *Behind the Headlines* (Canada),vol. 64, no. 32, 2007, p. 9.
20. Desmond Dinan, *Ever Closer Union—An Introduction to European Integration,* Palgrave Macmillan, 2005, p. 601.
21. *Ibid.*, 602-4.
22. Weidenfeld and Wessels, n. 14, p. 44.
23. Chris Richards, «Europe is a cul-de-sac», http://www.europaworld.org/issue50/europaacts28901.htm (04/12/01)
24. *Newsweek*, February 3, 1997, p. 22.

25. Rajendra K. Jain, «India and the European Union: Challenges and Opportunities», in R.K. Jain (ed.), *India and Europe in the New Millennium*, Radiant Publishers, New Delhi, 2000, p. 94.
26. K.V. Laatikainen, «Assessing the EU as an actor at the UN: authority, cohesion, recognition and autonomy», *CFSP Forum*, 2, 1, 2004, pp. 4-9.
27. Dinan, n. 20, p. 604.
28. Bretherton and Vogler, n. 4, p. 136.
29. Christopher Hill, «The Capability-Expectations Gap, or Conceptualizing Europe's International Role», in Simon Bulmer and Andrew Scott (eds.), *Economic and Political Integration in Europe—Internal Dynamics and global Context*, Blackwell Publishers, Oxford, 1994, p. 109.
30. Dinan, n. 20, pp. 603-4
31. http://www.diplomatie.gouv.fr/en/european-union_157/eu-in-the-world_1491/european-defence_6602/foreign-security-and-defence-policy-fsdp-operations_11970.html
32. Hill, n. 29, p. 124.
33. Chris Patten, «The Western Balkans: The Road to Europe», speech to European Affairs Committee of the Bundestag, Berlin, April 28, 2004, http://www.ear.eu.int/agency/main/agency-a1a2g3.htm.
34. Tomas Valasek, «Europe's Role in National Missile Defense», National Missile Defense, *What Does it all Mean? A CDI Issue Brief*, Centre for Defense Information, Washington DC, September 2000, www.cdi.org
35. «Chirac says extension of Afghan campaign is unlikely», Agence France-Presse (via ClariNet)/Sat,1 Dec 2001 14:20:09 PST http://clarinet:westnet.com/webnews/wed/dv/Qus-attacks-france-tunis.R4o0 BD1.html (04/12/01).
36. Dinan, n. 20, pp.602-603.
37. Simon Tisdall, «EU needs a decisive foreign policy», May 23, 2002. http:www.guardian.co.uk/elsewhere/journalist/story/0, 7792,720847,00.html (29/05/02).
38. Solana, n. 1.
39. Weidenfeld and Wessels, n.14, p. 44.
40. Hill, n. 29, pp. 113-116.
41. Georgi Kamov, «EU's role in Conflict Resolution: The Case of Eastern Enlargement and Neighborhood Policy Areas», June 2006.p.16 www.iehei.org/bibliotheque/memoires/2006/Kamov.pdf.
42. B.Krishnamurthy, «Common Foreign and Security Policies of European Union—Implication for Peace and Security in South Asia», in Nalini Kant Jha (ed.), *South Asia in 21st Century*—India, Her Neighbours and Great Powers», South Asian Publishers Pvt. Ltd., New Delhi, 2003, p.239.
43. http://www.diplomatie.gouv.fr/en/european-union_157/eu-in-the-world_1491/common-foreign-and-security-policy_5463/index.html
44. Dinan, n. 20, pp. 610-2.
45. Krishnamurthy, n. 13, pp. 42-44.
46. Dinan, n. 20, p. 560.
47. Helene Sjursen, «The Common Foreign and Security Policy: An Emerging New

Voice in International Politics?», [ARENA Working Paper series: 15.12.1999], http://www.arena.uio.no/publications/wp99_34.htm

48. H.S.Chopra, «India and the EU: Divergence in Regional Approaches», *Journal of Peace Studies*, vol.7, Issue 4, July-August 2000, p. 32.
49. Mark C Fischer, «The European Union in the Changing International System» in Rajendra K. Jain, *The Europan Unionin a Changing World,* Radiant Publishers, New Delhi, 2002, pp. 23-4.
50. *The Hindu*, June 23, 2000.
51. Sjursen, n. 47.
52. *The Hindu*, April 17, 1997.
53. B. Krishnamurthy, «French Response to Nuclear India—Shared Ambitions and Post-Cold War Compulsions» in A. Subramanyam Raju (ed.), *Nuclear India: Problems and Perspectives*, South Asian Publishers, New Delhi, 2000, pp. 127-138.
54. *Strategic Digest*, vol. XXX, No.3, March 2000, pp. 276-77. (Speech delivered by Hubert Vedrine, Minister for Foreign Affairs of the Republic of France at the concluding Session of the Seminar on India and France in a Multi-Polar World). Vedrine advocated the formation of a multi-polar world and while projecting 'a strong and united Europe' as one of the poles of the ensuing multi-polar world order, he suggested Russia, China, Japan and India as other prospective poles. He invited India to collaborate with France in her effort to design 'Cooperative multi-polarity' with an improved version of multilateralism that respects all members of the international community as expressed by the United Nations
55. Fischer, n. 49, p. 25.

10

A Brave New World:

German-American Relations in the 21st Century

SCOTT ERB

As Russian tanks rolled into the contested region of South Ossetia in Georgia on August 9, 2008, the latest challenge to the NATO alliance and European-American relations took form. The United States had pushed strongly in April 2008 for Georgia and Ukraine to be included in NATO. The argument was not only were these states willing to join the western alliance and embrace NATO values, but that this would preclude any efforts by Russia to alter the status quo with military force. The Europeans were not convinced. Not only is Georgian and Ukrainian culture more like that of Russia than the West, but with areas as volatile as South Ossetia and Abkhazia in play, Georgia had not proven itself ready for membership. Although this difference of opinion did not generate a lot of press at the time, it was notable in demonstrating the lack of agreement between the United States and especially the West European states about the nature of NATO's future role, as well as relations with Russia. The inability of the United States to shape a coherent NATO response to the crisis demonstrates a changed relationship between the US and Europe.

Despite recovering from the intense rift between the United States and Europe caused by the Iraq war, a new relationship has emerged which finds the Europeans willing to break with the United States in major policy dimensions. The relationship between the Merkel and Bush administrations since she came to power in 2005 demonstrates that despite how the US shifted diplomatic tone and re-engaged Europe with positive rhetoric and more cooperative ventures, Germany is charting a path in which Atlanticist rhetoric is combined with policies more independent of the United States, asserting European interests and values on the world stage. If the United States does not re-assess its ideas on the use of military power and national security, this could lead to a slow collapse of the Atlantic alliance.

Cold War Atlanticism

After World War II Germany quickly embraced a foreign policy ideal defined by *Atlanticism.* The idea is that the western alliance is not built on the basis of national self-interest of the traditional sort, but on common values. Alliances built on mutual interests, as in pre-World War II realism, are by definition viable only so long as nations share common interests. Realism is best reflected in the old maxim put forth by Lord Palmerston: Great Britain has no permanent friends, just permanent interests. The Atlantic alliance was different, built on a shared set of values, a commitment to democracy, individual rights, market economics and anti-communism. Thus, the union of the western states reflects a shared set of values coming from common cultural and philosophical traditions. After the searing damage of the first two world wars, Atlanticism was the recognition that the era of *realpolitik* was gone. Ideology had replaced national interest as a driving force of world politics, and the West shared ideological values, and was confronted by a foe who challenged those values.

Despite this close partnership, by the late seventies it was clear that Atlanticism was built on an untenable premise: American leadership. To call this untenable may seem strange especially since the beginning it was also unavoidable. Yet an alliance based on shared values can only have a clear leader if the leader is governed by those values. From early on it was clear that American policy was a mix of idealism and realism, with an inherent danger that power politics would be used to expand these ideals, perhaps with force. This was not shared by the Europeans. Charles de Gaulle broke from NATO because he feared American global interests might put Europe at risk. Yet Germans found that despite the divergence between US and German attitude towards power politics, Germany had more to gain from the Atlantic alliance than to lose. The US helped Germany recover economically and politically after World War II, and US military power was designed to provide deterrence, which meant to avoid war. As long as NATO could be portrayed as an organization designed primarily to prevent rather than fight wars, the Germans found it palatable. An incident well before the end of the Cold War, however, shows that this was starting to change even before the Soviet Union collapsed, and illustrates some of the underlying long term issues shaping the German-American relationship.

When Ronald Reagan became President in 1981 he inherited a NATO decision called the «dual track» approach, in which NATO would respond to the Soviet introduction of SS-20 intermediate nuclear weapons by first negotiating to have the SS-20s removed (track one), and if that failed, then deploying Pershing and Cruise missiles in Western Europe (track two). This was seen as necessary because the SS-20's altered the nuclear balance of power in the region in favour of the USSR, and was strongly supported by the then German Chancellor Helmut Schmidt (SPD).[1] However, within Germany the decision was controversial from the start. Alfred Dregger (CDU) put it best: «the shorter the range, the deader the Germans».[2] There was contradiction between German security interests and expanding NATO's capacity to fight a limited nuclear war. Even the most limited nuclear exchange would certainly devastate both German states. Ronald Reagan's hawkishness and the Soviet invasion of Afghanistan added to the fears and the issue brought the tension in German-American foreign policy perspectives out in the open.

Not only had a new party, the Greens, emerged espousing anti-NATO rhetoric and a call for German neutrality, but many in Helmut Schmidt's own SPD were opposed to missile modernization.[3] Socialist Youth (*Juso*) leader and future Chancellor Gerhard Schröder took a strong stand against it and argued that the SS-20s were not a threat to Germany.[4] After Schmidt's government collapsed and Helmut Kohl (CDU) took over in late 1982, the SPD party voted 389-5 against missile modernization.[5] Indeed, 70 per cent Germans and even a majority of the conservative CDU opposed the NATO plans.[6]

In October 1983, 500,000 protested in Bonn, and a four city protest garnered a total of 1,000,000 demonstrators, as well as a human chain linking 400,000 people against missile deployment.[7] This was not a fringe movement. Nonetheless Kohl stuck with the Atlanticist policy, though with a twist. He focused on improving relations with the USSR and East Germany while accepting the new missiles. In essence, he rejected Reagan's rhetorical hard line, and moved at the same time to improve bilateral relations with France, agreeing to a Franco-German rapid reaction force of 47,000.[8] By rejecting Reagan's «Cold War II», Kohl was able to save German Atlanticism.

The missile modernization crisis, while now all but forgotten, is an important indicator that even during the Cold War Atlanticism had its limits. The limits were rooted in both national interest, and an emerging political culture which eschewed power politics and embraced a strong anti-militarist perspective. As Germany became more self-sufficient, and as the European Union emerged as a true actor on the world stage, the German people became increasingly predisposed to criticize and even oppose American policy. The end of the Cold War would make these disputes unavoidable, and force a rethinking of German-American relations.

Atlanticism under Pressure

After the end of Cold War two trends tore US and German policy makers apart. Germany no longer feared assault from the Soviet Union and German unification was the achievement of Germany's most significant post-war policy goal. That is not to say the United States became irrelevant; Germans recognized that the rise of globalization increased the importance of international cooperation. However, Germany did not support the US as much as before. At the same time, however, US policy became more willing to embrace military action than during the Cold War, since war no longer meant a nuclear exchange. This meant that the US could find ways to use its military power as a policy tool, in direct contradiction to the anti-militarist norms among the German public. This problem came out in the open in January 1991, when the US attacked Iraq in response to its invasion of Kuwait. While approval for the action neared 90 per cent in the US, Germans were divided, and 100,000 protested the war in Bonn.[9] Both the Social Democrats and the Greens opposed the war, and Helmut Kohl, citing German constitutional issues prohibiting active participation, paid $12 billion and offered non-combat support as Germany's contribution.

This created an intense debate within both Germany and the US about the role united Germany is expected to play within NATO. That debate became even more complex later that year, when Germany pushed for and got recognition of Croatian and Slovenian independence from Yugoslavia. The US, Great Britain, France, and Russia had all urged that Yugoslavia not split up, and Germany's pro-Croat attitude irritated many and alarmed some, who realized that with the pro-Croatian countries being Italy, Austria and Germany, this looked remarkably like pre-World War II alliance structures. Perhaps François Mitterrand, former President of France, was right when he warned that a united Germany might lead to pre-World War I conditions.[10]

As war in the Balkans spread to Bosnia, the German Government made legal changes which would make it possible for Germans to be more active in international peace keeping operations, as well as NATO and UN peace making missions, and the atrocities in Bosnia (1993-95) convinced even many Greens to give up the visceral anti-war pacifism that defined the movement in the eighties. By 1999 an SPD-Green coalition led by Gerhard Schröder would actively support a NATO decision for military action against Serbia in order to stop ethnic violence in Kosovo. This war would have been unthinkable less than a decade earlier, when the left was opposed to any NATO military action, and even Helmut Kohl had said that due to historical compulsions Germany could not send a military force to the Balkans. By the end of the decade, it appeared that the unified Germany was maintaining a true Atlanticist foreign policy. Germany had been a willing partner in Kosovo, a fact more poignant given that the previously skeptical left had embraced a NATO military operation under the US leadership.

When President George W. Bush took office, however, things became difficult again. The new Administration injected ideology into foreign policy by cutting aid to international agencies that allowed abortion.[11] The Bush Administration then repudiated the Anti-Ballistic Missile Treaty (ABM), a move opposed by most in Germany.[12] Rather unenthusiastically the Germans joined the effort to create a missile defense system once it was clear it would happen anyway.[13] The most divisive pre- 9-11 issue was the Kyoto Accords, which committed industrialized states to reducing their green house gas emissions to 1990 levels by 2012. Chancellor Schröder decided this was an issue where the world had to move forward with or without the United States, even though National Security Advisor Condoleezza Rice made it clear to European leaders that Kyoto was dead, and they needed to develop something which the United States could support.[14] Schröder responded by pushing forward with the Bonn Conference and winning enough support for Kyoto to put the accords into effect. This first tussle was an indication of personal rivalry between the President and Chancellor in coming years.[15] Nonetheless, it was not just personality; personality was also a factor during the Cold War with the poor relationship between Jimmy Carter and Helmut Schmidt as an example. Rather, this was a clash of norms; the Bush Administration's quest for a stronger American leadership role against Germany's hope for a true multilateralism.

An issue of contention that existed both before and after 9-11 involved the International Criminal Court (ICC). The US opposed this institution meant to be able to punish dictators, warlords and others who commit war crimes without having to enact a special tribunal or going through national legal systems. This was an important issue for Germans, who saw it as a move to enforce human rights through multilateralism. Yet when the US got involved in Afghanistan and then contemplated war in Iraq, they did not want to risk possible suits in the ICC involving American soldiers or leaders. The US and Europeans fought over the issue of immunity for American soldiers. The US wanted blanket immunity, but got only the right to negotiate limited immunity with EU Member States, a result that satisfied neither side, especially as Germany and France refused to consider any immunity.[16] The US rejected many treaties and initiatives supported by the Germans including not only the ICC and the Kyoto Accords, but also the Biological Weapons Convention, the Comprehensive Test Ban Treaty, the Chemical Weapons Convention and the Treaty to Ban Landmines.[17] Common to all of these was the US rejection of multilateral norm building in favour of unilateral protection of US rights to defend its national interest as it saw fit. When 9-11 occurred the future of the Atlantic alliance had been already called into question.

German-American Relations in Crisis

When terrorists attacked the United States on 9-11, Chancellor Schröder promised «*uneingeschränkte Solidarität*» (infinite solidarity) with the United States. The German Parliament quickly passed a resolution promising full solidarity with the United States with 611 of 666 votes (the former Communist PDS was the only party opposed.)[18] Still, unlike in the US, most Germans did not believe it was necessary to attack Afghanistan. German military experts criticized the scope of the bombing and many Germans thought the terrorists should be treated as criminals.[19] When Schröder announced that Germany would participate in Afghanistan, there was open rebellion amongst the Greens and within the SPD, causing Schröder to put his government on the line with a vote of trust which, if he failed, would have meant the end of the Red-Green coalition.[20] Although tight, the Chancellor got the 334 votes needed, with the motion passing 336-326. Two things can be noted in this episode. First, it's clear that while in the US and much of the world it was not very controversial to attack the Taliban regime that gave refugee to Osama Bin Laden and Al Qaeda, in Germany the public opinion was split. Second, Schröder, despite his problems with President Bush, was willing to put his job on the line for the US and NATO. Although the Iraq crisis would obscure this act, it's clear that as with the Kosovo war, the Schröder government tried to maintain the Atlanticist commitment.

By 2002 it became obvious that the neo-conservative argument for regime change in Iraq as a prelude to a restructuring of the Mideast to spread democracy and thus counteract terrorism was becoming the central tenet of the Bush Administration's foreign policy. This not only contradicted German policy norms completely, but Schröder was caught in a tough re-election campaign, behind in the polls. Whether motivated by electoral politics or conviction, Schröder gave up the usual balancing act between Paris and Washington to side fully with French President Chirac, questioning whether Iraq really posed a threat and worrying a war might only aid terrorists.[21] When the Chancellor told the New York Times that he thought the war would be misguided and wrong, the Americans started to notice the vehemence of Germany's refusal to support war in Iraq.[22] Schröder was supported by former Chancellor Helmut Schmidt, who publicly argued that the Europeans had to confront America's «nationalist, egocentric and imperialistic» approach, echoing British philosopher Edmund Burke's warning of the «hubris of superpower».[23] Others argued that the US was rejecting the very values of Atlanticism, and that Germany had to take a stand for these values—it was the US threatening the Atlantic partnership, not Germany.[24]

The Washington Post got into the fray, and reflecting the views of the US foreign policy elite, it criticized Schröder's argument as simply an effort to get re-elected. In an editorial «Schröder Ducks», the Post claimed that the Chancellor was sacrificing Germany's long term interest to be involved in removing Saddam and being part of Iraqi reconstruction in favour of simply winning an election.[25] Schröder won a very narrow victory to remain in power. After his victory, a chill in German-American relations set in, which lasted over a year as German diplomats were given the "cold shoulder" by Americans, and some voices inside the Bush administration hinted regime change might be necessary in Germany.[26] Despite hope that things would improve, the relationship soured further in the run up to the American led invasion of Iraq on March 20, 2003. Germany, France and Russia conferred with each other and worked within the United Nations Security Council to try to find someway to stop a war they were convinced was a potential disaster. American Defense Secretary Donald Rumsfeld even listed Germany together with Libya as states not cooperating with the US.[27] America's ambassador in Berlin, Daniel Coats, bluntly asserted that Germans should be worried about American anger over Germany's position.[28] But the anger went two ways, as both Schröder and Chirac vehemently rejected the attempt by Rumsfeld to divide Europe by labeling France and Germany as «old Europe», less important as East European states could now support American efforts.[29]

Throughout Europe, protests against the war reverberated, cheering the stance of Schröder and Chirac, and reflecting opposition to the war by nearly 80 per cent of Europeans surveyed, including those in Spain and Italy, whose governments supported the war. The European view was summed up by a bit in the German newsweekly *Der Spiegel*: «The United States is militarily, economically and culturally the undisputed number one in the world. But the superpower is beginning to suffer the illness of all empires in history: over-confidence and over-commitment. Will the Iraq war possibly lead to a downfall»?[30]

At this juncture transatlantic relations reached a new low. Historian Heinrich August Winkler pointed out that neo-conservatives such as Robert Kagan were dismissive of European desires for a «Kantian dream» of world order in a Hobbesian world. Yet that notion of a multilateral world order is precisely what motivates European policy, a desire to avoid the kind of power politics that poisoned Europe in the 20th century.[31] Clearly, the Europeans were focused on terrorism and Afghanistan as problems that needed to be taken care of, while the US thought a bold stroke starting in Iraq would solve the problem by expanding democracy and altering the make up of the region. Lothar Rühl labeled this a "transatlantic malaise," which could become a crisis.[32] These were two divergent views which threatened to break up the alliance completely.

Building a New Partnership

By the time Angela Merkel took office, the Bush White House had already recognized that Iraq had not gone as planned, and had shifted from the «cowboy diplomacy» of the first term to a more conciliatory tone. The emergence of a conservative like Merkel as the new German Chancellor made it easier for President Bush to create a new atmosphere, the bad blood that developed between the President and Schröder was no longer an obstacle. However, the Iraq war had exposed new realities in world affairs, and the Atlantic alliance would have to adjust:

1. *The World is Multi-Polar*: The end of the Cold War brought a brief period of unipolarity or United States dominance. The neo-conservative effort to use this moment to boldly use that power to shape international system in a way reflective of American interests failed in Afghanistan and Iraq. The second Bush Administration's change in both personnel and tone reflected recognition of this change. Major actors now include the US, Russia, the EU (though not usually speaking with one voice), India, China, and a number of regional powers such as Iran, Brazil, and Japan. Without a forced marriage due to bipolarity, the Europeans are free to make their own arrangements with other actors, regardless of Washington's approval.
2. *The Nation-State and sovereignty are weakened*: Globalization means that economic performance and political choices are no longer primarily driven by decisions made by state governments. This minimizes the role and scope of military power as a driving force in world affairs, allowing states like India and China to emerge as possible superpowers, despite having relatively modest military capacities. The United States, suffering economic problems with a severe current accounts deficit and high debt, is finding that its economic weakness is becoming more of a factor than its military prowess. For Germany, this supports its goal of multilateralism, and hence accentuates the major foreign policy dispute with the United States.
3. *Ideological conflict has given way to local disputes*: In the Cold War the «West» as a «community of values» had special meaning as it was seen as representing freedom and individualism against Communism and totalitarianism. Yet the US had few qualms about

supporting authoritarians who would work with it in opposition to Communism. Replacing the broad ideological conflict are a number of local points of contention, ranging from Islamic extremism (the closest thing to a globalized "ideology"), ethnic disputes, and fight for resources. These kinds of conflicts do not fit into clear categories and thus there is more disagreement about the level of danger posed by different disputes, how best to handle the threat (for instance, does one fight Islamic extremism by focusing on military action, or does one work to support Islamic moderates with aid and outreach?)

4. *The Europeans, especially the Germans, are developing a set of "values" different from those of the Americans*: Perhaps most importantly, the "community of values" defining the West is now under contention. While the essential differences are similar to those during the missile modernization crisis, changing world conditions noted above make it harder to sweep them under common rhetoric about human rights, freedom, democracy and cooperation. For Germans, western values entail a multilateral approach, and a rejection of national interest in favour of principle. For Americans the national interest and American values are inherently linked, and thus a multilateralism that weakens the US or western abilities to act quickly and decisively is dangerous.

Given the above, there are two general paths one could expect. First, the Germans could follow Schröder's model of promoting «the German Way», and chart a separate path, trying to steer the EU towards becoming a major, independent actor. German-American relations would likely be rocky in such a case, and it would also raise divisions within the EU, as did the Iraq war. Germany would build separate relations with countries like China and Russia to secure its position, and there would be a decoupling of Europe and the US. Second, the Germans could try to revive Atlanticism, deciding that American military power is still needed in a dangerous world, the US economy remains vibrant even if beaten down, and the two sides of the Atlantic need each other. In such a case Germany would soften criticisms of the US and do more to help the US in its foreign policy concerns, but the US would have to meet Germany half way and embrace a less militarist and more multilateral foreign policy. Merkel is clearly following the second path in rhetoric, but actions lean more towards the first. At the same time, the United States is playing nice; despite the reputation of the Bush Administration, since 2005 the Bush team under Secretary of State Rice and Secretary of Defense Gates has focused on multilateralism and diplomacy, a marked change of focus from the policies early on.[33] Four issues shed light on how the relationship is evolving:

(1) *Afghanistan*: European participation in "Operation Enduring Freedom" was welcomed by the Bush Administration both as a sign that the alliance remained strong, and with the Europeans taking over in Afghanistan it would free the US to devote more of its forces to Iraq. However, while the public statements of Chancellor Merkel and President Bush praise this cooperation, the reality is that extension of German participation in the Afghan mission has always been controversial, and it would create a political crisis in Germany if German troops were to move from relatively safe regions of the country to actively engage the Taliban. That riskier task remains the work of British and American soldiers. When the situation started to deteriorate in Afghanistan in late 2006, there was intense debate in the German Parliament about whether or not to continue to support 2900 troops there. They agreed, but without increasing funding or allowing combat operations.[34] In November 2006 this was causing tension, with open US criticism of Germany's refusal to go farther.[35] By February 2008 the situation was no better. With Germany at 3200 troops, remaining in Northern Afghanistan, NATO estimated that the alliance needed to add at least 7500 more combat troops. Secretary of Defense Robert Gates sent a «stern» letter to Germany concerning their unwillingness to do more to advance the effort. Germany rebuffed these demands and insisted they would stay in the north.[36] Finally by June 2008 Germany agreed to increase the troop level to 4500, but insisted these would remain in the relatively safe north; even that is subject to Bundestag approval, which is likely, but not certain given the increasingly defiant mood of the Social Dcmocrats.[37]

During this two year period conditions in Afghanistan had gotten progressively worse, as the Taliban expanded their power and increased attacks. Yet while the increase in troops to 4500 helps, it is at base a rejection of American calls for more combat ready troops to take on the Taliban.

(2) *NATO Expansion*: For the most part, there has been agreement on NATO expansion eastward. However, in April 2008 there was tension due to the US desire to expand NATO to two countries with difficult relations with Russia: Ukraine and Georgia. Since Madeline Albright tried to promote NATO as a force for peace in out of area affairs a decade earlier, Germans and the rest of Europe have resisted. While the rhetoric remains friendly, there is little reason to believe that NATO is going to emerge as an organization with an active, coherent policy on the world stage.

Former Chancellor Schröder speaking after the Russian incursion into Georgia, praised the decision by the French and German governments in April to resist NATO expansion and argued:

«Imagine if we were forced to intervene militarily on behalf of Georgia as a NATO country, on behalf of an obvious gambler, which is clearly the way one ought to characterize Saakashvili. Georgia and Ukraine must first resolve their domestic political problems and they are still a long way off. I see the chances of Georgian accession becoming even more remote as a result of the recent events in the Caucasus and, in this connection I have great difficulties following the rather ostentatious promises made by the NATO secretary general a few days ago».[38]

Although not accepting the Russian act, Schröder and others in Europe refuse to go along with the strident hard line taken by the Americans. Chancellor Merkel raised eyebrows by stating that Georgia would be allowed in NATO—though her office clarified that this was no different than the April decision to agree to someday include Ukraine and Georgia, but that neither country was yet ready. While in the US many believe the Russian invasion was a result of a mistaken decision not to admit Georgia earlier in the year, Europeans not only express relief at the earlier decision, but sound bearish on any kind of quick NATO entry for Georgia. If anything, Georgia's debacle weakened American interests in NATO and showed strategic weakness in issues involving Russia's near abroad.

(3) *Missile Defense Shield*: While most Europeans had decided not to oppose American efforts to expand its missile defense shield to Poland and the Czech Republics, Germans were divided. Social Democrat spokesman Kurt Beck argued that this could risk a new arms race with Russia, while Merkel warned Germans not to go "back to 2002," when Germany and America were divided on the Iraq war.[39] The government would prefer missile defense systems for Poland and the Czech Republic be a NATO effort rather than bilateral agreements between the US and those two countries.[40] This suggests that the German cultural trend towards maintaining pacifist norms is deeply held.[41] Nonetheless, there is a strong belief that some kind of MEADS (Medium Extended Air Defense System) is inevitable in Europe, and that Germany should continue its work with the US and Italy on such a system.[42] The Konrad Adenauer

Stiftung (CDU) goes further, noting that missile defense is not only important to Europe, but could revitalize NATO.[43]

(4) *The on-going war in Iraq*: Although German and European criticism of President Bush declined dramatically after the elections of Merkel in Germany and Sarkozy in France, the improvement was based on a tacit understanding that the Europeans would cease harping on Iraq, and the US would recognize that they cannot expect and will not seek more help for Iraq efforts. In essence, each realized they could not go back and change the past, so they decided to focus their energies elsewhere. Nonetheless, tensions remain. While Schröder was still Chancellor the prisoner abuse case at Abu Ghraib led Foreign Minister Fischer to again call for the United States to join the International Criminal Court to assure trust.[44] There was press buzz over an effort by some Germans to press charges against Secretary Rumsfeld for war crimes, though this was ultimately rejected by the German government. Guantanamo Bay also remains intensely controversial, as German political leaders often demand its closer. Germans also spoke out against the «surge» and urged the United States to accept the Iraqi Study Group proposals to open negotiations with neighbours such as Iran and Syria.

Nonetheless many Germans felt that Schröder's approach had been too assertive, noting that Germany had «dangerously deserted» its role as balancer between NATO and the EU, something which is important for transatlantic cooperation.[45] It is clear that the Iraq war is something Germans not only continue to oppose, but believe that time has proven their position to have been correct. There is unease over the way in which Schröder challenged the US in some quarters, and a hope that the United States has learned its lesson and will not engage in such adventures again. This, combined with the unwillingness of Europeans to increase combat troop levels in Afghanistan are enough to convince the Americans that NATO is not about to become a strong force for military action in out of area conflicts. Given this and the way the Iraq war has overstretched the US military, there is a good chance that Germany and the US will move closer together on these issues, despite the tension which lingers on over Iraq.

(5) *Economic policy*: The Europeans entertain considerable concern over the level of the US current accounts deficit, and the weakness of the dollar. A weak dollar also means a strong Euro, and given the size of the US current accounts deficit, the dollar could potentially fall much

> lower. At the same time, the two sides bicker over various economic policies. In response to European desires that the European Aeronautic Defence and Space Company (EADS) receive some preferences from the US, former US Ambassador John C. Kornblum, now at Lazard and Company, was dismissive, telling the Europeans to "get real," arguing that the Europeans have opposed US security policy and that «defense is not a market, defense is a politically controlled industrial operation».[46]

The fear in the future is even more profound, since at some point oil and gas will run low, and if there is not enough to go around, the only way to avoid dangerous resource wars will be to have effective cooperation between Europe and the US.[47] Moreover, as the world economy develops, the Europeans have far greater opportunities to make partnerships in India, China, and other markets, often to the detriment of the United States. India and China's rise has to be taken seriously and this could have implications for the transatlantic alliance.[48] However, since NATO relations have been defined primarily on security terms, and the US ideologically holds to a strong free market neo-liberal perspective, it's hard to see a coherent argument being made against German or EU economic diversification, unless it seems to directly contradict US security interests (Russia, Iran, etc.) At the same time, this may practically weaken the long term links between Europe and the US, especially if the US economy weakens further or resource needs require Europe make closer ties with US rivals.

New Values

Ultimately, it appears that the early 21st century will not see the kind of acrimony between the United States and Europe that appeared in 2002-03. In part, this is because most Europeans believe the United States is still an important partner with whom they share numerous values. Indeed, while most Germans dislike the policies of the Bush Administration (41 per cent favourable, 54 per cent unfavourable), Pew reports a generally favourable view of Americans (65 per cent favourable, 24 per cent unfavourable).[49] If the US can embrace multilateralism, it could do considerable good in promoting the kind of values embraced by German and European foreign policy elite. Moreover, given divisions within Europe, there is no clear European alternative to having a strong United States active on the world stage, supporting if not leading the West. However, the post-Cold War era of globalization will not see a return to the kind of American leadership of the alliance.

The German embrace of multilaterialism and an intense *Friedenspolitik* or "policy of peace" remains at odds with US foreign policy norms of both major American political parties. This is especially likely to continue because European culture on foreign policy is closer to the German view, pressuring the Atlantic alliance to embrace stronger multilateralism and anti-militarism.[50] Germans do not want to give up the partnership, but argue that there needs to be a new definition of partnership, one that cannot be like the last century, one that recognizes inevitable rivalries and has a pragmatic core.[51] The focus on multilateralism, cooperative institutions, international law, and military interventions as a last resort, primarily for humanitarian goals, reflects a strong Kantian or even Wilsonian ideal, which could be labeled as *post-sovereign identity.*

Post-Sovereign Attributes

- The West as a community of common values;
- Identity reflects values and value fulfillment, rather than power maximization;
- Military intervention should only be legal, through multilateral institutions;
- Primary values include human rights, liberty, and the construction of international law;
- Most current problems such as environmental crisis and poverty cannot be solved except through multilateral cooperation; and
- Subsidiarity replaces sovereignty as a fundamental principle of international organization.

Post-sovereignty puts principle over power overtly, in that Germans see force as something to be used primarily for support of human rights and international law, only when approved by the UN or an international legal authority, and not for raw national interest. This stands the traditional notion of foreign policy on its head, as common values and value fulfillment replaces power politics. This, combined with recognition that most problems are now transnational, and that destinies are linked through complex interdependence, makes traditional military power increasingly counter productive, even for states which use it. Thus, the goal must be to build a system of international norms that can work to solve conflicts and promote cooperation, avoiding a dangerous and inherently counter productive move towards militarization. Subsidiarity is the European Union concept that decisions should be made at the most decentralized unit possible for policy functionality. Thus, some issues are local, some state, some regional (including regions that cross borders) and major issues such as trade and monetary policy being determined at the

EU level. This essentially replaces true sovereignty with a more complex structure of authority. This also inherently weakens the likelihood of a strong European security stance, since the state is weakened in this approach, with economic issues taking precedence.

In the short term, the Atlantic alliance can survive with rhetorical solidarity along with increased differences on policy specifics. Ultimately, however, as economic ties globalize Europe, the connection to the United States will decrease in importance. As this happens, it will be easier for the Europeans to abandon the Atlantic alliance, following much the same logic that Chancellor Schröder and many still in the SPD use to critique American policy. The US doesn't really act on the values of the western alliance, but on its own interest. Hence, the conflict in Georgia was seen by Europeans, who strongly condemned Russian actions, as indicative of the difficulties of ethnic tensions and questions of self-determination. While the US saw Georgia as a «western» ally who was helping in Iraq and thus deserved support, the European goal is to avoid a West vs. Russia dynamic, and find a way to work towards settling the dispute. Although many Americans thought that weak, the US no longer truly led the alliance, and had to search for some common ground. There was really no other option.

The future may depend on whether or not the United States, perhaps learning the lessons of Iraq, Afghanistan, and the inability to stop countries like Russia and Iran from pursuing their national interests, will see the futility of focusing on military power and realist policies, and embrace a more wholly multilateral approach. In that case the western alliance might continue to remain a community of shared cultural values, playing a positive role in developing cooperation globally. If not, then the Atlantic alliance might well be seen as primarily a twentieth century Cold War phenomenon which slowly crumbled as the global economy transformed the world in the twenty first century.

NOTES AND REFERENCES

1. François de Rose, «Nulclear Forces and Alliance Relations: Updating Deterrence in Europe—Inflexible Response»? in Robert Nurick (ed.), *Nuclear Weapons and European Security,* New York: St. Martin's, pp. 123-137.
2. Hans Georg Betz, «Mitteleuropa and Post-Modern European Identity», *New German Critique*, No. 50, Spring/Summer 1990, p. 182.
3. Jörg Brechtefeld, *Mitteleuropa and German Politics*, New York: St. Martin's Press, 1996, p. 85
4. William E. Paterson, «The Chancellor and Foreign Policy» in Stephen Padget (ed.), *Adenauer to Kohl*, Washington DC: Georgetown University Press, 1994, p. 151.

5. David Gress, *Peace and Survival*, Stanford: Hoover Institution Press, 1985, p. 27.
6. «Nachrüstung ohne Historische Parallele», *Der Spiegel*, June 13, 1983, p. 29; and «Heißer Herbst: Diesmal wollen wir nicht schweigen», *Der Spiegel*, August 29, 1983, p. 25.
7. Alice Cooper, *Paradoxes of Peace: German Peace Movements since 1945*, Ann Arbor: University of Michigan Press, 1996, p. 213.
8. Philip Gordon, «The Franco-German Security Partnership» in Patrick McCarthy (ed.), *France-Germany 1983-1993: The Struggle to Cooperate*, New York: St. Martin's Press, 1993, p. 144.
9. Cooper, n. 7, p. 252.
10. Philip Zelikow and Condoleezza Rice, *Germany Unified and Europe Transformed*, Harvard University Press, 1997, p. xiii.
11. Malte Lehming, «*Gleiche Praxis, neuer Sound*», *Der Tagesspiegel*, January 24, 2001.
12. Herald Mueller, «Germany Hopes it Will Go Away», *Bulletin of Atomic Scientists*, 57, No. 6 (November/December 2001), p. 32.
13. Josef Joffe, «Raketen und Reflexe», *Die Zeit*, 6/2001; Robert von Rimscha, "Absurd aber erfolgreich», *Der Tagesspiegel*, March 2, 2001.
14. Malte Lehming, «Berlin—Texas: Die Distanz wächs», *Der Tagesspiegel*, March 31, 2001.
15. «Freund oder Feind», *Der Spiegel*, September 30, 2002, pp. 112-119.
16. John Chalmers, «EU Says Members may Negotiate with US on Court», *The Wahsington Post*, October 1, 2002, p. A17.
17. Harald Mueller, «Germany Hopes it will Go Away», *Bulletin of Atomic Scientists*, 57, No. 6 (November/December 2001), pp. 31-34.
18. For the full statement approved by the Bundestag see: «Das Parlament stellt sich hinter die Regierung», *Der Tagesspiegel,* September 20, 2001.
19. «Deutscher Ex-General kritisiert US-Stratege», *Die Welt*, October 31, 2001.
20. «Kanzler erhöht den Druck», *Westfalen-Blatt*, November 14, 2001, p. 1.
21. Matthias Nass, «Krieg gegen Saddam? Nicht ohne bessere Gründe», *Die Zeit*, 33/2002.
22. Steven Erlanger, «German Leader's Warning: War Plan is a Huge Mistake», *New York Times*, September 5, 2002.
23. Helmut Schmidt, «Europa braucht keinen Vormund», *Die Zeit*, 32/2002.
24. Richard Herzinger, «Die besseren Amerikaner sind wir», *Die Zeit*, 41/2002.
25. «Mr. Schroeder Ducks», *Washington Post*, September 17, 2002, p. A20.
26. «Auf dem Sonderweg», *Tageszeitung*, September 29, 2002.
27. «Rumsfeld stellt Deutschland mit Libyen auf eine Stufe», *Handelsblatt*, February 13, 2003.
28. Gerold Büchner, «Die Deutschen sollten sich Sorgen machen», *Berliner Zeitung*, February 6, 2003.
29. Andreas Middel, «Unmut in der EU über den Aufruf der Acht», *Die Welt*, February 13, 2003; and Jachim Fritz Vannahme and Petra Pinzler, «Die gefallenen Stern», *Die Zeit*, 12, February 13, 2003.

30. «Der entfesselte Gulliver», *Der Spiegel,* 12, March 17, 2003.
31. Heinrich August Winkler, «NATO am Scheideweg», *Der Spiegel*, September 30, 2002, pp. 126-27.
32. Lothar Rühl, «Das Kriegsproblem der Nato am Gulf», *Neue Zürcher Zeitung*, October 9, 2002.
33. Daniel W. Drezner, «The New New World Order», *Foreign Affairs*, March/April 2007, Vol. 86, No. 2.
34. *Deutsche Welle News*, September 28, 2006: http://www.dw-world.de/dw/article/0,2144,2188183,00.html
35. *Deutsche Welle News*, November 20, 2006: http://www.dw-world.de/dw/article/0,2144,2243473,00.html
36. Craig Whitlock, «Germany Rebuffs US Demands for Troops in Afghanistan», *Washington Post*, February 2, 2008, p. A10.
37. Judy Dempsey and Allen Cowell, «More German Troops to Afghanistan», *International Herald Tribune,* June 25, 2008.
38. Gerhard Schröder, interview with *Der Spiegel*, August 18, 2008, 34/2008, pp. 90-96.
39. Judy Dempsey, «Merkel Seeks Common Front on US Missile Plans», *International Herald Tribune*, March 21, 2008.
40. Thomas Bauer and Florian Baumann, «Missiles for Europe: US Plans Expose Europe's Strategic Weakness», *CAP Bertelsman Gruppe Politik*, No. 3, July 2007, pp. 9-10.
41. Thomas U. Berger, *Cultures of Anti-Militarism*, Baltimore: Johns Hopkins University Press, 1998.
42. Thomas Bauer and Martin Aguera, «MEADS ist unverzichtbar», CAPS Working Paper, *Centrum für Angewandte Politikforschung, München*, February 2006.
43. Raketenabwehr, «NATO und die Verteidigung Europas, Analysen und Argumenteu», *Aufgabe* 40, March 2007.
44. Fischer, «US Should Join International Criminal Court», German Embassy Washington, May 14, 2004, http://www.germany-info.org.
45 Björn Conrad and Mario Stumm, «German Strategic Culture and Institutional Choice», *Trierer Arbeitspapiere zur Internationalen Politik*, No. 9, December 2004, p 62.
46. Anita Hurrel, ed., German Council on Foreign Relations High Level Conference, *DGAP Bericht*, No. 10, Nov. 15-16, 2007, Berlin, p. 10.
47. Florian Baumann, *CAP Policy Analysis*, February 2007, pp. 12-14.
48. Thomas Bauer, «The CHINDIA Connection and its Implications for the Transatlantic Partnership», *CAP Aktuell*, Number 6, August 2006.
49. Clay Ramsay, «In Search of Anti-Americanism in European Publics» in *German American Issues, American Institute for Contemporary German Studies*, Baltimore: Johns Hopkins University, 2005, p. 25.
50. Björn Conrad and Mario Stumm, «German Strategic Culture and Institutional Choice», *Trierer Arbeitspapiere zur Internationalen Politik*, No. 9, December 2004, pp. 6-7.
51. Thomas Bauer, *CAP Bertelsman Forschungsgruppe Politik Aktuell*, Vol. 7, May 2007, p. 5.

11

The Construction of the Union of India and the European Union:
A Comparative Perspective

GEETHA GANAPATHY-DORÉ

The comparative perspective sketched in this paper does not bear the stamp of authority and legitimacy that comes from a formal and specialized training in international relations, but stems from my experience as a cross-cultural agent and a postcolonial citizen. I learnt French in Pondicherry and live and work in France. The colour of my passport has changed from blue to brown in the course of the past twenty-five years. Everyday, my tongue tethered to Tamil and English volubly produces transmogrified consonants and vowels in the French language. It is in this capacity of "translated being" that my observations and analysis are grounded.

Introduction

If India and the US could be looked upon as "estranged democracies" as Dennis Cux[1] calls them in spite of their being respectively the largest and the oldest of postcolonial democracies, India and Europe were "intimate enemies" to use Ashish Nandy's words[2], who are currently close trading partners and are trying to become strategic partners in the 21st century[3]. America's disenchantment with India started when the non-aligned India did not maintain equidistance between the two superpowers. India's disenchantment was obvious when Kissinger (1971) used Pakistan as a base for US-China rapprochement, thus precipitating India in the race for nuclear weapons. Disenchantment persisted on both sides in spite of the good will of the Indo-American diaspora, Rajiv Gandhi's 1985 and 1987 visits to Washington, Manmohan Singh's 1991 free market reforms and the existence of the Congressional Caucus on India because of America's staunch and unfailing support for Pakistan whose Mujahideens were being recycled in Kashmir after the Soviet-Afghan war. The disenchantment had lately been exacerbated due to the stalling of the civil nuclear deal signed between India and US in 2005 owing to opposition from both America's law makers and the Communist Party of India (Marxist), a source of external support for the ruling United Progressive Alliance. The confidence vote in favour of Prime Minister Manmohan Singh by the Indian Parliament[4] on 22 July 2008 and Barrack Obama's choice of Joe Biden who supports the deal as running mate have changed the situation. The forty-five member Nuclear Suppliers Group which includes the 27 EU member states finally granted India the waiver that it needs, as a country not having signed the Nuclear Non—Proliferation Treaty, to finalize the deal. In an other development, Russian military intervention in Georgia has raised fears of resurgence of the Cold War. Nicolas Blarel who has studied the scope and limits of the rapprochement between India and US concludes: "India is not a loyal ally of Washington like the United Kingdom or Japan, but rather an 'Asian France', that is to say, a partner of the US in the pursuit of certain general goals, but one who maintains strategic sovereignty, free from any outside influence"[5]. In this context, the logic and stakes of European Union's recognition of India[6] as a key player having the potential to check, if not surpass, China's rise in the postcommunist multipolar world are crucial for India as well as the European Union as a civil power[7].

According to myth, Princess Europa, abducted by Zeus, who gave Europe its name is Phoenician[8], thus foreign and Oriental. Though the European Union, its institutions, its potential and policies constitute a new body of academic discipline both inside and outside the Union, its historical core is familiar to Indians. Indeed thanks to India's non-alignment policies and friendship with the Soviet Union, Indians know some of the Central and Eastern European countries which are now part of the European Union such as the Czech Republic or Poland better than even some of their Western counterparts. Similarly, a flight to India from European capitals may take hours and cost several hundred euros, while a dip in Indian culture very often comes at the price of a simple suburban train ticket.

Edward Said's 1978 book *Orientalism* laid bare the ideological underpinnings behind the unfillable gap that Kipling postulated between East and West. "The Orient is an idea that has a history and a tradition of thought, imagery, and vocabulary that have given it reality and presence in and for the West"[9]. Postcolonial writing back to the Empire has been viewed as Occidentalism or Orientalism-in-Reverse. An attempt at comparing the Union of India and the European Union might, on the surface of it, look like a reverse Orientalist project, a disconcerting enterprise like Lakshmi Mittal's taking over Arcelor, a blatant case of misplaced pride on the part of a third world intellectual having arrived in First World academe. Vasant Kaiwar has laid bare the assumptions underlying such comparative exercises built on "a set of antimonies that underpin European universalism and everybody else's particularisms"[10]. The purpose of my paper is not to sustain that the European Union can learn some lessons from the Indian experience, but rather highlight the difficulties inherent in shaping and stabilizing a modern form of statehood that is capable of securing the welfare of its citizens and making peace prevail in the world. My paper simply attempts to be a concrete manifestation of India de-exoticised and Europe provincialized. The very same Europe that "modern imperialism and (third world) nationalism have, by their collaborative venture and violence, made universal", according to Dipesh Chakrabarthy[11].

The idea for this comparison came to my mind while working on a text book on English for EU law with a French and Irish colleague. The former had internalized the Franco-German Social Democrat vision of Europe, while the latter the liberal Anglo-Saxon one. I was trying to understand both from my "third" point of view. Besides, the period of referendum in favour of or against the European constitution was one of intense political debate in France. Paradoxically, it reminded me of the Federalist versus Anti-Federalist discussions in the America of the late 18th Century. On the very next morning after the referendum on 29 May 2005, there was a panel discussion in our faculty on the "Neither Yes nor No" of the French vote in which Professor Monjal and I took part. I was indeed happy to be living in those interesting times. The European Union seems to have surmounted, temporarily at least, the difficulties of its ongoing construction thanks to the Lisbon Treaty, commonly known as the Reform Treaty, while the Union of India celebrated its 59th Republic Day with the President of France as its chief guest. President Sarkozy invited the newly re-elected Prime Minister of India Dr. Manmohan Singh to be the guest of honour on the 14 July 2009 National Day celebration in Paris with four hundred Indian troops parading on the French soil, a gesture that is highly symbolic of the recognition of the rising power of the Union of India.

Ground for Comparison

The European Commission's 'EU's relations with India' page[12] states that these go back to the early 1960s: India was amongst the first countries to set up diplomatic relations with the European Economic Community. Both the Union of India whose constitution was adopted in 1950[13] and the European Steel and Coal Community set up in 1951 thanks to the Treaty of Paris were different responses to the violence of the Second World War. One of the sub chapters of Nehru's *Discovery of India* written in 1946 entitled "India: Partition or Strong National State or Centre of Supra-National State?" shows his political acumen in discerning the shape of things to come[14]. The specific nature of India and the EEC, one a multiethnic, multi-religious and multilingual nation-state which draws its legitimacy from a constitution and the other, an alliance of economic interests which is slowly evolving into a supranational political community by virtue of successive treaties, cannot, of course, be ignored. The Union of India comprises twenty-eight states and seven union territories with a population of over one billion and a GDP measured in terms of purchasing power parity of 2.965 trillion dollars[15]. The European Union comprises twenty-seven member states with a population of roughly half the size and a GDP five times the size of India's (14.45 trillion dollars)[16]. However, what makes the comparison possible is a common source of inspiration consisting of the British Magna Carta, the French Declaration of Human Rights and the American Constitution and the dream of finding unity among diversity through an inclusive democracy that may remain infinitely deferred, always to come from an unanticipatable future, hovering between absence and presence, to quote Jacques Derrida. Derrida believed that democracy "perhaps also keeps the power of universalizing, beyond the State and the nation, the account taken of anonymous and irreducible singularities, infinitely different and thereby indifferent to particular differences, to the raging quest for identity corrupting the most indestructible desires of the idiom"[17].

The Ideas of India and Europe

The idea that upholds the Union of India and the European Union is worth serious consideration. In his book entitled *The Idea of India*, Oxford scholar Sunil Khilnani remarks that "India's own past, as well as the contingencies of its unity, prepared it very poorly for democracy. Huge, impoverished, crowded with cultural and religious distinctions, with a hierarchical social order almost deliberately designed to resist the idea of political equality, India had little prospective reason to expect it could operate as a democracy"[18]. In Ramachandra Guha's terms, India is an "unnatural nation" and an "unlikely democracy"[19]. Whether it was homegrown in the village Panchayats or imported by Britain, the fact is "the democratic idea has penetrated the Indian political imagination"[20] and "India appears as the third moment in the great democratic experiment launched at the end of the 18th century by the American and French revolutions"[21]. The miracle of elections and the noise of its debates keep it alive. However, the first Article of the Constitution of India that states "India, that is Bharat, shall be a union of states" makes the religious subtext appear as filigree in a modern secular text. A single shared sense of India as embodied in the allegory of the Bharat Mata was henceforth impossible. The nation seen as a meshed territorial and religious entity is permanently at war with the concept of nation as legal-territorial and political identity[22]. Hindu nationalists of the early 20th century dreamed of a grand Asiatic empire comprising India, China and Japan[23], compared to which today's SAARC would appear a mere trifle. "The only possible idea of India", Shashi Tharoor has argued "is that of a nation greater than the sum of its parts"[24]. Such a definition has the merit of encompassing the Indias of the mind carried by diasporic Indians spread out all over the world.

It is a well known fact that the idea for a United Europe was born out of the humanist-pacifist dream of Robert Schuman and Jean Monnet, Winston Churchill and Alcide de Gasperi, Konrad Adenauer and Paul Henri Spaak. After achieving economic and monetary union, it is looking for a mode of sharing sovereignty for the greater common good. "Europe is more than just a merger of economic giants; Europe has a cultural foundation on which its central political values and attitudes rest", insisted the German Federal Minister of the Interior, Dr Wolfgang Schäuble, at the conference "A Soul for Europe" in Berlin on 19 November 2006[25]. The Berlin Declaration of March 2007 specifies that the "European model unites economic success and social responsibility"[26]. Geographically, the European Union comprises seven ultra peripheral regions, i.e., the Guadeloupe, Guyana, Martinique, Reunion, Azores, the Canaries and Madeira. Overseas Countries and Territories of member states fall under a different legal regime[27]. The Treaty establishing a Constitution for Europe[28] (already ratified by eighteen member states out of twenty-seven) highlights the cultural, religious and humanist inheritance of Europe in its preamble. Its Article 1, Section 2 of Part I, states that the Union is founded on the values of respect for human dignity, freedom, democracy, equality, the rule of law and respect for human rights, including the rights of persons belonging to minorities. The cumulative legacy of Greek thought, Christianity, Renaissance and Enlightenment philosophy could be traced back in these few lines. The President of the Constitutional Convention, Valéry Giscard d'Estaing, did not explicitly use the term Christian. However, countries like Poland and Slovakia and religious leaders from Italy and Ireland openly regretted the omission of God and Christianity in the constitution[29]. Despite their religious diversity, both the Union of India and the European Union seem to put a premium on the cultural weight and continental reach of their dominant religions.

Secularism and Minority Rights

Logically, the next point of comparison between the Union of India and the European Union would be their commitment to secularism. The strict separation between the Church and the State is a bequest of the French revolution. In France, "*la laicité*" is a concept that is opposed to religion and connotes a neutral and impartial space of the Republic free from the fetters of religion. At concept borrowed from the West and acclimatized in India, secularism is understood in India as an equal respect for and mutual tolerance of all religions. Without a secular framework, the uplift of the scheduled castes and tribes would have been impossible. Nevertheless, the word secular did not appear in the preamble to the Constitution of India until 1976 when Indira Gandhi got enacted the Forty-second Amendment. But an attempt to define it precisely within the constitutional framework in 1978 failed. As late as 1994, A.M. Ahmadi, a former Chief Justice of India, came forth with the interpretation that "the term "secular" had advisedly not been defined presumably because it is a very elastic term not capable of a precise definition and perhaps best left undefined"[30]. Unimpressed by such rhetorical manoeuvres, critics like T.N. Madan, Ashish Nandy and Partha Chatterjee have voiced their doubts with regard to positive secularism as practised in India because it has failed to safeguard India from religious extremism[31]. Political scientist Rajeev Bhargava has underscored the particularities of Indian secularism that stems from both the tradition of religious reform that began in India prior to the advent of colonial modernity and a critical engagement with the latter. The civilizational resource from which India has retrieved the notion is *'sarva dharma samabhava'*. India has innovatively used it to transform British colonial legacy. Such a conception of secularism deals simultaneously with inter-religious and intra-religious domination, points out Bhargava. It has an explicit multi-value character. Indian secularism rejects separation understood as principled distance. Indian secularism does not imply respectful indifference or active hostility towards religion.[32] The Union of India recognizes the personal law of Hindus, Muslims and Christians, a provision that undermines the equality of its citizens before the law. The 1985 Shah Banu case[33] revealed the need for a Uniform civil code in India. The demolition of Babri Masjid in 1992 and the consequent eruption of communal violence in different parts of the country at different times have unhinged Indian secularism from its position as practical arrangement in a multi-faith environment and put it on a more doctrinal path.

Article II-70 of the Constitutional Treaty for Europe guarantees freedom of religion: "in public or in private, to manifest religion or belief in worship, teaching, practice and observance". But the term "secular" is not literally mentioned in the treaty, though the spirit is clearly there. Within the European Union, the attitude towards secularism is not uniform. The monarch is the head of the Church of England. There are two readings of the controversies surrounding the Rushdie affair in 1986, the murder of Theo Van Gogh in 2004 and the Danish cartoons of the Prophet in 2005. The freedom of expression is inviolable in European Union member states. The Muslim minorities view the recourse to secularism as a façade to resist Islam. Besides, Pope Benedict XVI opined that the liberal consensus of secularism has, in the course of history, become an aggressive ideology in Europe. The Archbishop of Canterbury Dr Rowan Williams recently scandalized the British public by suggesting that the adoption of certain aspects of Sharia law in the UK "seems unavoidable". He felt that Muslims should not have to choose between "the stark alternatives of cultural loyalty or state loyalty"[34]. Muslim Sharia courts and Orthodox Jewish courts called Beth Din already operate in England. Europe thus seems to be converging towards an accommodative[35] definition of secularism resembling the Indian acception of the term. Let us note that the Union of India, wielding the host-guest rhetoric that one gets to hear often in Europe, offered only temporary asylum in the form of an entry visa to Bangladeshi writer Taslima Nasreen, recipient of the Simone de Beauvoir Prize for the liberty of women, while France, a EU member state is ready to welcome her at any time.

In the Indian constitution, minority rights are expressly protected in Article 29. The political process has paved the way for the integration of these minorities in the form of political parties. Though huge efforts in the social and economic uplift of the Dalits, the Other Backward Classes, Scheduled Castes and Tribes are yet to be made, the riots conducted by the Gujjar caste in May 2008[36] to be downgraded show that the constitutional provision for positive discrimination remains attractive. Civil society actors and religious organizations also play a role in protecting minorities within the nation state. The early treaties of the European Community did not mention minority rights. However, protection of minorities formed part of the 1993 Copenhagen criteria[37]. The other binding texts on EU members are Protocol 12, Article 14 of the European Convention on Human Rights and Article 13 of the Treaty on the European Union. Civil society actors such as the Minority Rights Group International or EUMAP in the UK independently monitor minority protection in the EU. The integration of Bulgaria and Romania brought the question of the Roma to the fore. There is also a debate on the definition of "minorities", a term which must include not only ethnic, linguistic, religious minorities but also homosexuals and the physically disabled.

Federalist or Anti-Federalist Model?

India's attitude towards Taslima Nasreen translates the power struggle between the Union Minister for External Affairs and the West Bengal State's Chief Minister[38]. At the time of independence, Gandhi wanted a united India. Unlike Mohammad Iqbal who advocated a confederation where provinces with Muslim majority could have their rights guaranteed through a high degree of autonomy, Mohammed Ali Jinnah preferred the two nation theory. The Constituent Assembly was left with the task of finding the right form of sovereignty for the Indian people. The president of the constituent assembly Dr. Ambedkar who was himself trained in Columbia adopted the American model of classical federalism into a co-operative one to suit the needs of India. The republic was not called "The United States of India" but rather "The Union of India". The passivity of the past participle 'united' fixes the political entity as an object from the outside, while the noun form 'union' is more dynamic and voluntary. The term 'Union' may also hark back to the Soviet Union. Nehru believed that state intervention and central planning were necessary to achieve self-reliance. Hence, he championed a strong central government. The seventh schedule of the constitution gives the list of ninety-seven competences belonging to the Union, sixty-seven belonging to the state and forty-seven concurrent competences. Legislation by parliament prevails over legislation by state legislature. In the wielding of concurrent powers, the central government takes precedence over the states. Besides, the constitution gives the president right to dismiss a state government and impose president's rule. Coordination between states is ensured by the interstate council much like intergovernmental conferences in the European Union. The sharing of fiscal resources between the centre and states has always been problematic. Indian type of federalism worked well when the Congress Party had majority at the centre and in the states. With the rise of regional parties, it is less the case.

Concerning the European Union, there exist two sides: one wanting genuine federalism, a sort of United States of Europe, with a directly elected President and more powers granted to the European Parliament. This emerging superpower could thus challenge American preponderance. The other side consists of people who resent the pervasive presence of the European Union regulations in their daily lives. Indeed, there are rules that lay down how a cucumber should curve. The hyper or transnational, not to mention the bureaucratic and technocratic nature of the European Union sovereignty frightens them. The treaty establishing a constitution proposed to allay their fears by including the principles of conferral, subsidiarity and proportionality which put limits on the extent of European Union competences. When French farmers or fishermen protest against the European Commission restrictions, one could not but hear echoes of Tamil Nadu protesting against the centre in the Kavery water issue[39].

Territorial Consolidation

Lord Mountbatten decided to partition the British Indian Empire to avoid the Balkanization of India. In spite of the trauma that presided at the birth of independent India, the pattern of nation building in India was one of progressive territorial integration. Both the former colonial provinces and princely states were invited to sign the treaty of accession to the Union of India, the official name of the Republic that only lawyers, diplomats and scholars use. Students of Indian history know how the accession of Junagadh, Hyderabad and Kashmir proved difficult. India's armed forces intervened in each of these three states. Bhutan chose to be independent. The Constitution of India distinguished between nine Part A states, eight Part B states and ten Part C states. The State Reorganization Act of 1956 took into consideration the aspiration of people for language based states and abolished these distinctions in favour of a single type of state. French possessions in India were transferred to the Union *de facto* in 1954 and *de jure* in 1962. Jammu and Kashmir enjoyed a special status till 1957. The Portuguese were forced to hand over Goa, Diu and Daman in 1961. Monarchy was abolished in Sikkim with the help of the Indian army in 1975 and Sikkim officially became the twenty second state of the Indian Union. Himachal Pradesh, Mizoram and Goa were granted statehood respectively in 1971, 1986 and 1987.

This territorial consolidation may be compared to the several waves of enlargement that brought the states that were once on the periphery of the original six member European Economic Community into the fold of the European Union[40]. Denmark, Ireland and the United Kingdom joined in 1973. Greece acceded to the Union in 1981, followed by Portugal and Spain in 1986. Austria, Finland and Sweden fulfilled the Copenhagen criteria of 1993 and joined the Union in 1995. The fifth enlargement that occurred in 2004 included ten new members from the Baltic, Central and Eastern Europe and the Mediterranean (Cyprus, the Czech Republic, Estonia, Hungary, Latvia, Lithuania, Malta, Poland, Slovakia, and Slovenia).Bulgaria and Romania were admitted in 2007. Croatia is expected to join the Union possibly around 2009 or 2010, Macedonia around 2012, with Albania, Bosnia and Herzegovina, Montenegro, Serbia, and Turkey hopefully following. However, the Indian pattern seems to be one of inward integration and redistribution, while the European model seems to radiate outword from a historical matrix.

Both the Indian Union and the European Union use the term accession in their official texts. India has not ruled out enlargement altogether because the constitution foresees territories that may be acquired. There is an enlargement fatigue in the European Union and the accession of Turkey is being perpetually postponed. The Treaty establishing a Constitution for Europe includes a mechanism for withdrawl, making the relationship between a member state and the Union contractual, while in the Indian constitutional framework, such a divorce between a state and the centre is not possible. The British Parliament, which is the model for Indian Parliament, has devolved power to the Scottish Parliament and Welsh Assembly prompting historians to speak about the disunited kingdom. The Indian Union, in the era of globalization and international terrorism, cannot afford to indulge in a costly experiment in disintegration. The danger is obviously fragmentation[41]. Then every individual could ask for a "selfistan" as Rushdie puts it in *Shalimar the Clown*[42].

Threats to Unity

As far as India is concerned, right from the beginning, there were some centrifugal forces that put the union at jeopardy, prompting critic Sarah Suleri to posit the theory of perpetual partition[43] as a paradoxical founding myth of the nation. The state of Andhrapradesh was carved out of the Telugu-speaking portions of Madras and Hyderabad states in 1956. Bombay State was split into the linguistic states of Gujarat and Maharashtra in 1960 by the Bombay Reorganization Act. Nagaland was split from Assam and made a state in 1963. The Punjab Reorganization Act of 1966 divided the Punjab along linguistic and religious lines, creating a new Hindu and Hindi-speaking state of Haryana. In 1969, Madras changed its name to Tamil Nadu to outwardly show its ethnic loyalty. In 1973, Mysore changed its name to Karnataka. In the year 2000, three new states Jharkhand, Chhattisgarh and Uttaranchal saw the light of day through a redesigning of the existing states of Bihar, Orissa and Uttar Pradesh.

Linguistic, religious, ethnic and tribal identities were the basis for separatist claims. The former union minister for commerce and industry Murasoli Maran had written a book on state autonomy, a devolution project conceived by the Dravidian movement. In 1984, the Sikhs wanted Khalistan. In Bihar there is a demand for a separate Maithili state for Maithili speakers. In West Bengal, the Gurkhas demand an autonomous Gurkhaland in north

Bengal. Naxalites or Maoist rebel groups in several states threaten the Indian state in a stealthy manner.

Though erosion of national sovereignty under the European Union preoccupies quite a few member states and Euroscepticism is as established a concept as Euroenthusiasm, the idea of seriously withdrawing from the union is not on the agenda of any member state. On the contrary, candidate countries are queuing up to accede to the European Union. However, some member states have sent signals of disapproval. United Kingdom, Denmark and Sweden are not part of the Eurozone. Britain has chosen to remain out of the Schengen agreement. France and Netherlands have said "No" to the constitutional treaty. Nationalist and separatist claims of the Basque people in Spain and Corsicans in France are causes for worry. The European Union has accepted twenty-three European languages as equally official languages. This has enabled it to avoid the struggle for supremacy of the national language over other languages and its ugly consequences that were witnessed in India. Leonard Orban was appointed European Commissioner for multilinguisim in January 2007 and his policy is to promote multilingualism through language learning, interpretation and translation in the fields of culture, education, communication and employment with a view to rendering European economy more competitive[44]. However, the recent crisis in Belgium between those who speak Dutch and those who speak French reminds us very much of the antagonism between the Marathi and Gujarati speaking people in Bombay that Rushdie recalls in *Midnight's Children*[45]. India recognizes twenty-two official languages. In spite of their equal status, cross translation from one Indian regional language to another is not as frequent or systematic as between one European Union language and another with the result that English functions as the lingua franca.

Both the Union of India and the European Union are confronted to the tricky issue of partition. Starting with the partition of Bengal in 1905, partition is a problem that has plagued India before and after independence. The 1947 ceasefire line dubbed Line of Control after the Simla Agreement in 1971 has virtually partitioned Kashmir. Pakistan is keen in reclaiming this territory as it forms part of its symbolic construction since Rahmat Ali invented the name of the nation in 1933[46]. If the criteria of religion of the majority of the population were to be applied as in Hyderabad, at least a part of Kashmir had to go to Pakistan. Pakistan is much keener on retrieving the Kashmiri territory after losing East Bengal. But India has spiritual bonds with Kashmir apart from economic and strategic interests. Jean Luc Racine has formulated the situation in Kashmir as one of improbable war and impossible peace[47]. Shared sovereignty rather than independence of Kashmir seems to be on the horizon.

In the European Union, divided Germany has become unified in 1990. The 1921 partition of Ireland by Britain is not likely to be ended through a plebiscite in Northern Ireland to know whether the people there want to be reunited with the Republic of Ireland. Kofi Annan's attempt to unify Cyprus in 2004 has failed. In this context, the unilateral declaration of independence by the Muslim majority in Kosovo on 17 February 2008 had divided the European Union members. France greeted this solution, while Serbs view Kosovo as the spiritual birthplace of the Serbian nation and have sworn to fight back. Greece and Germany were wary because they were afraid that recognition by them would somehow facilitate territorial disintegration at home[48]. The members of the European Union could sometimes be divided by foreign policy issues as in the case of the war on Iraq. The idea of a Mediterranean Union tossed around by the French President was initially viewed with suspicion as essentially a move to keep Muslim Turkey out of the European Union and give more prominence to Southern European states as opposed to the Council of the Baltic Sea States set up in 1992 after the fall of the Berlin wall.

Convergence and Divergence in Policies

The convergence between the Union of India and the European Union in their ways of functioning cannot make us forget the several areas of divergence that exist and which may be attributed to the rapidity of globalizing forces which are trying to overtake both the Unions. The agricultural subsidies paid by the European Union to its farmers have been denounced by India at the WTO[49]. India is opposed to European style humanitarian interventionism. There is an asymmetry in trade between India and the European Union. Trade with European Union matters more to India than to the former. EU is India's largest trading partner. The EU is also India's largest source of foreign direct investment. However, India accounts for just 1.8 per cent of total EU trade. India attracts only 1.3 per cent of the EU's worldwide investments. Also India is a major recipient of aid (470 million euros for 2007-2012) from Europe which makes India's position vulnerable vis à vis the European Union. At the same time, the Union of India is member of UN Human Rights Council, along with seven EU Member States. Both sides also encouraged the United Nations Peacebuilding Commission, which has India and seven EU Member States as well as the European Community among the members of its organizational committee. EU-India diplomacy is thus a milestone in the construction of the mutlipolar world.

Pre-Partition Map of India
AFGHANISTAN
North-West Frontier Province
Kashmir
Rawalpindi
Amritsar
Lahore
Multan
Quetta
Baluchistan
Indus
Sind
Karachi
Rajputana
Jaipur
Ajmer-Merwara
Meerut
Delhi
Bareilly
United Provinces
Lucknow
Gwalior
Kanpur
Allahabad
Banaras
Patna
Central India
Bihar
Jamshedpur
Cutch
Kathiawar
Indore
Baroda
Surat
Diu
Damao
Central Provinces
Berar
Nagpur
Orissa
Bombay
Poona
Hyderabad
Sholapur
Bastar
Goa
Krishna
Madras
Mysore
Bangalore
Pondicherry
Salem
Tiruchirapalli
Cochin
Travancore
Madurai
Amindivi Islands
Laccadive Islands
Arabian Sea
Princely States
Indian Provinces
Indian Ocean
N
BHUTAN
Sikkim
NEPAL
N.E.F.A.
Assam
Brahmaputra
Cooch Behar
Bengal
Khasi
Manipur
Dacca
Howrah
Calcutta
Chittagong
BURMA
Tripura
Bay of Bengal
Andaman Islands
Nicobar Islands

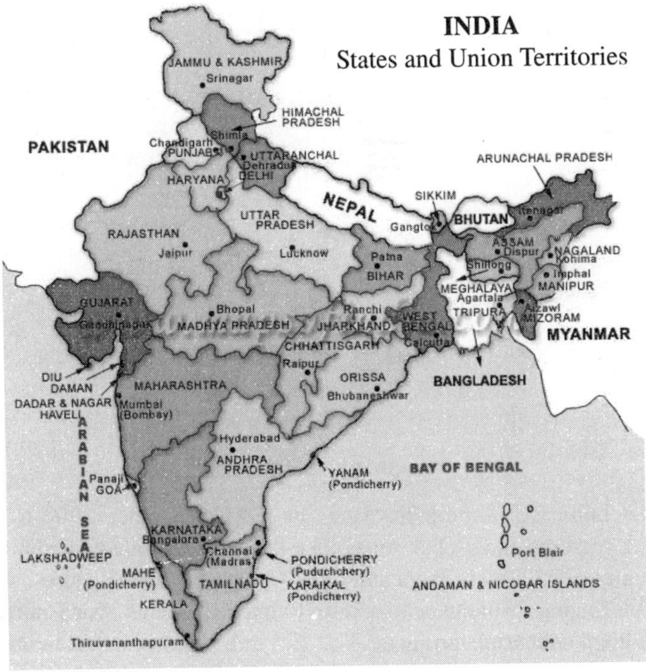
INDIA
States and Union Territories
JAMMU & KASHMIR
Srinagar
HIMACHAL PRADESH
Shimla
PAKISTAN
Chandigarh
PUNJAB
UTTARANCHAL
Dehradun
HARYANA
DELHI
ARUNACHAL PRADESH
Itanagar
SIKKIM
Gangtok
NEPAL
BHUTAN
UTTAR PRADESH
Lucknow
RAJASTHAN
Jaipur
Patna
BIHAR
ASSAM
Dispur
NAGALAND
Kohima
Shillong
Imphal
MANIPUR
MEGHALAYA
Agartala
TRIPURA
Aizawl
MIZORAM
MYANMAR
GUJARAT
Gandhinagar
Bhopal
MADHYA PRADESH
Ranchi
JHARKHAND
WEST BENGAL
Calcutta
CHHATTISGARH
Raipur
ORISSA
Bhubaneshwar
BANGLADESH
DIU
DAMAN
DADAR & NAGAR HAVELI
MAHARASHTRA
Mumbai (Bombay)
ARABIAN SEA
Hyderabad
ANDHRA PRADESH
YANAM (Pondicherry)
BAY OF BENGAL
Panaji
GOA
KARNATAKA
Bangalore
Chennai (Madras)
PONDICHERRY (Puducherry)
LAKSHADWEEP
MAHE (Pondicherry)
TAMILNADU
KARAIKAL (Pondicherry)
Port Blair
ANDAMAN & NICOBAR ISLANDS
KERALA
Thiruvananthapuram

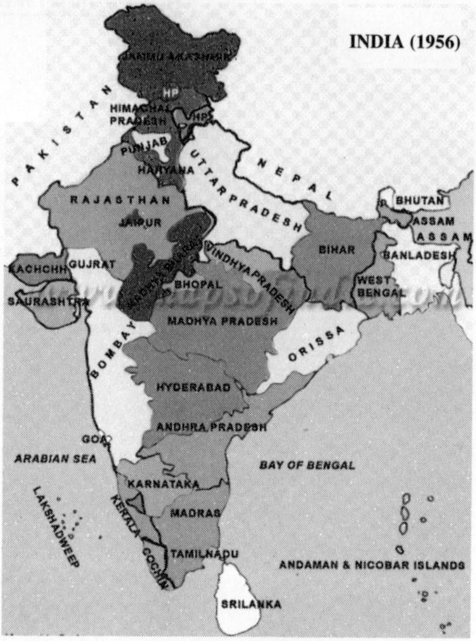

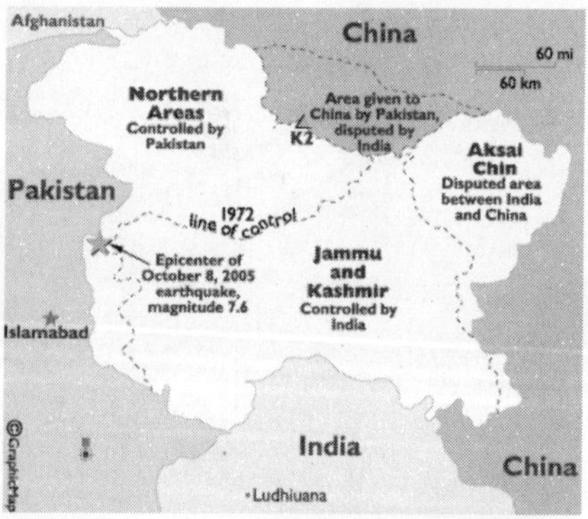

KASHMIR REGION MAP

The India-EU summit meetings have existed since 2000 to discuss bilateral, regional and global issues. The EU-India Economic Cross Cultural Programme (ECCP) was launched in 1997. The EU has set aside 30 million euros for Erasmus Mundus scholarships to Indian students. Asia Link supports joint higher education projects. The EU-India Cultural Declaration of 9 November 2004 recognizes "culture as an important instrument to foster close co-operation among States and to develop a better understanding among people"[50]. The EU-India action plan endorsed in 2005 aims to strengthen dialogue and consultation mechanisms with a view to ensuring internal and international security[51] by fighting against terrorism, promoting political dialogue and cooperation, bringing people and cultures together, fostering economic policy dialogue and cooperation and developing trade and investment[52]. Cooperation is being enforced in the field of science and technology. India is joining the Galileo satellite navigation project. The EU-India Energy panel is encouraging Indian participation in the ITER nuclear fusion reactor. The EU will fund the diffusion of green technologies in India through a joint initiative on clean development and climate change.

Conclusion

In January 2006 the United Kingdom proposed that India and the European Union enter into a Free Trade Agreement to counterbalance the weight of ASEAN + 3. The EU was associated with SAARC as an Observer State and attended the 14th SAARC Summit held in New Delhi in April 2007 in order to share experiences regarding the ongoing integration processes. However, it is not only by jumping into the bandwagon of economic prosperity but also by joining hands against the merciless onslaught of globalization as mercantile empire with the common objective of preserving human dignity, notably the dignity of their ageing citizens[53], and social justice and furthering sustainable development that the Union of India and the European Union[54] could make the world a better place. The EU-India summit held in Marseilles on 29 September 2008 included questions of food security and financial instability in the on-going dialogue between the two global partners and has drawn up a new action plan that puts the emphasis on the concept of comprehensive security and promotion of the diversity of cultural expressions.[55]

NOTES AND REFERENCES

1. Dennis Cux, *India and the United States 1941-1991: Estranged Democracies,* Washington: National Defence University Press, 1993.
2. Ashish Nandy, *The Intimate Enemy, Loss and Recovery of Self under Colonialism*, New Delhi: Oxford University Press, 1989.
3. Rajendra Jain, *India and the European Union: Building a Strategic Partnership*, New Delhi: Radiant Books, 2007.
4. The Economist called it «a tarnished triumph», Print Edition of 24 July 2008. Retrievable at http://www.economist.com/world/asia/displaystory.cfm?story_id=11792636
5. Nicolas Blarel, «New Delhi et Washington: portée et limites d'un rapprochement»

in Christophe Jaffrelot ed. *New Delhi et le monde, une puissance émergente entre realpolitik et soft power*, Paris: Autrement, 2008, p. 72 (translation mine).
6. Jean-Luc Racine (EHESS/CNRS): «Le rapprochement Inde/Etats-Unis: logique et enjeux», paper presented at the «Rencontres Internationales sur les Amériques Contemporaines» colloquium, 9 March 2007, University of Marne-la-Vallée.
7. Rajendra Jain, Hartmut Elsenhans and Amarjit S Narang eds. *The European Union in World Politics*. New Delhi: Radiant Publishers, 2006.
8. http://phoenicia.org/europa.html
9. Edward Said, *Orientalism*. New York: Vintage, 1979, p. 5.
10. Vasant Kaiwar and Mazumdar, "The Coordinates of Orientalism", *Mapping Difference: Asia, Europe and the Dialectic of Modernity*, Vasant Kaiwar, Sucheta Mazumdar and Thierry Labica eds., forthcoming, p. 2.
11. Dipesh Chakrabarty, *Provincializing Europe: Postcolonial Thought and Historical Difference*. Princeton: Princeton University Press. Reprinted 2007, p. 42.
12 http://ec.europa.eu/external_relations/india/intro/
13 Constitution of India, text in English http://lawmin.nic.in/coi.htm
14. Jawaharlal Nehru, *The Discovery of India.* New Delhi: OUP, reprinted 1995, p. 524.
15. Estimates for 2007. https://www.cia.gov/library/publications/the-world-factbook/geos/in.html#Econ
16. Estimates for 2007. https://www.cia.gov/library/publications/the-world-factbook/geos/ee.html#Econ
17. Jacques Derrida, *Politics of Friendship*, (George Collins translator), London: Verso, 2005, p. 106.
18. Sunil Khilnani, *The Idea of India.* New York: Farrar, Straus and Giroux, 1997, p. 2.
19. Ramachandra Guha, *India after Gandhi: The History of the World's Largest Democracy*. London: Picador, 2007, p.xi. See also his lecture entitled "The India of My Dreams" November 2, 2007 at the Foreign Service Institute, New Delhi. http://fsi.mea.gov.in/fsi/mystart.php?page=sp/2007/11/02sp01.htm
20. Khilnani, *Ibid*, p. 3.
21. Khilnani, *Ibid*, from front matter.
22. Juan J. Linz (Yale University), Alfred Stepan (Columbia University) and Yogendra Yadav (Center for the Study of Developing Societies, Delhi), "Nation State or State Nation, Comparative Reflections on Indian Democracy", draft paper, October 22, 2003 http://www.columbia.edu/~as48/Linz,%20Stepan,%20Yadav%20-%20Nation%20State%20or%20State% 20Nation.pdf
23. Alex Tickell, "The Discovery of Aryavarta: Hindu Nationalism and Early Indian Fiction in English" in *Alternative Indias*, Peter Morey and Alex Tickell eds, Amsterdam: Rodopi, 2007, p. 43.
24. Shashi Tharoor, *India: From Midnight to the Millennium and Beyond*. New York: Arcade Publishing. Reprinted 2007, p. 5.
25 http://www.eu2007.bmi.bund.de/nn_1050696/EU2007/EN/ServiceNavigation/Speeches/content__Reden/BM__BerlinerKonferenz__Europa__eine__Seele__geben__en.html
26. http://www.timesonline.co.uk/tol/news/world/europe/article1559376.ece

27. "The twenty-one overseas countries and Territories (OCTs) depend constitutionally on four of the European Union Member States: Denmark, France, the Netherlands, and the United Kingdom. OCT nationals are Union citizens. However, these countries do not form part of Community territory. Accordingly, Community law does not apply directly to them but they benefit from associate status conferred on them by the Treaty of Rome, which forms the basis for the current development policy". Cf. http://europa.eu/scadplus/leg/en/s05034.htm
28. Treaty establishing a Constitution for Europe http://eur-lex.europa.eu/JOHtml.do?uri=OJ%3AC%3A2004%3A310%3ASOM%3AEN%3AHTML
29. "*Do "God" and "Christianity" have a place in the European Union Constitution?*", http://www.religioustolerance.org/const_eu.htm
30. *S.R. Bommai v Union of India,* 1994, AIR SCW 2946, p. 2992.
31. T.N. Madan, «Secularism in its Place" in *Journal of Asian Studies,* 46, 4 (1987), 747-759.
    Ashish Nandy, "The Politics of Secularism and the Recovery of Religious Tolerance" in *Alternatives* 13-2 (1990), 177-194.
    Partha Chatterjee, «Secularism and Toleration» in *Economic and Political Weekly*, 29-28 (1994), pp. 1768-77.
32. Rajiv Bhargava, «La spécificité de la laïcité indienne» in *Critique internationale*. Paris: Presses de Sciences Po. 35-2 (2007), 121-147.
33. In this case the Supreme Court ordered the Muslim husband to maintain the divorced wife, till her death or remarriage. This went against the Muslim custom of maintaining the divorced wife only till the period of *iddat* (i.e., for three months or if she is pregnant, until the infant is two years old). Some Muslim organizations strongly protested against this judgement because it interfered with the Muslim Personal Law (*Shariat*) Application Act, 1937. Parliament hastily enacted the Muslim Women (Protection of Rights on Divorce) Act. 1986 to provide for some sort of maintenance to Muslim divorcees. It has the effect of neutralising the Supreme Court judgement. On April 1, 2008, a trial court in Lille (Northern France) set aside a marriage because the Muslim wife had concealed to her husband that she was not a virgin. This legal decision raised a hue and cry in France. The Public Prosecutor had to lodge an appeal against this decision.
34. Reported by the BBC, 7 January 2008. http://news.bbc.co.uk/1/hi/uk/7232661.stm
35. Rajendra Jain and Hartmut Elsenhans eds, *Multiculturalism in India and Europe*, New Delhi: Radiant Publishers, 2008 (forthcoming).
36. http://www.timesonline.co.uk/tol/news/world/asia/article4027974.ece
37. http://ue.eu.int/ueDocs/cms_Data/docs/pressdata/en/ec/72921.pdf
38. After violent riots in Kolkatta, Taslima Nasreen was taken to Jaipur in November 2007 and then to Jaipur House in New Delhi. She fled to Sweden in March 2008 and returned to India on 8th August to renew her visa.
39. See Rajendra Jain and Hartmut Elsenhans eds, *Political and Social Transition in India and Europe,* New Delhi: Radiant Publishers, 2008.
40. Please see the animated map of European enlargement at http://europa.eu/abc/history/animated_map/index_en.htm retrieved on 6th August 2009.

41. Cf the recent declaration of independence by South Ossetia and Abkhazia.
42. Salman Rushdie, *Shalimar the Clown*, London: Jonathan Cape, 2005, p. 102.
43. Sara Suleri, *The Rhetoric of English India*, Chicago: University of Chicago Press, 1993, p. 194.
44. http://ec.europa.eu/commission_barroso/orban/index_en.htm
45. Salman Rushdie, *Midnight's Children*, London: Picador, 1981, p. 191.
46. Rahmat Ali, *Now or Never*, Cambridge, 1933. This pamphlet can be retrieved at http://www.columbia.edu/itc/mealac/prichett/ooislamlinks/txt_rahmatali_1933.html, S.S. Pirzada, *Evoluation of Pakistan*, The All Pakistan Legal Decisions, Lahore, 1963, pp. 28-32. Pakistan or the land of the pure is an acronym formed by using the names of the following provinces: Punjab, Afghanistan, Kashmir, Sind and Baluchistan.
47. Jean Luc Racine, *Cachemire. Au péril de la guerre*. Paris: CERI/Autrement, 2002.
48. Germany recognized Kosovo on 20 February 2008, while Greece has not yet done so.
49. Rajendra Jain and Hartmut Elsenhans eds, *India, the European Union and the WTO*. New Delhi: Radiant Publishers, 2006.
50. http://ec.europa.eu/external_relations/india/sum11_04/joint_cultural.htm
51. Rajendra Jain and Hartmut Elsenhans eds, *India, Europe and the Changing Dimension of Security*. New Delhi: Radiant Publishers, 2006.
52. http://ec.europa.eu/external_relations/library/publications/25_india_brochure.pdf
53. Both Europe and India have to tackle the problem of aging. Cf. International Conference on "Multidisciplinary Approach to Healthy and Participatory Ageing" to be held from Jan 22nd to Jan 24th 2009 in Mumbai and organized by SVT College of Home Science. See also Hélène Thomas, «La promotion de la citoyenneté sociale et politique dans le grand âge à l'ère de la protection rapprochée», in *Gérontologie et sociétés*, no. 120, mars 2007, p. 99-114.
54. Rajendra Jain, *India and the European Union: Building a Strategic Partnership*. New Delhi: Radiant Publishers, 2007.
55. http://www.elysee.fr/documents/index.php?lang=fr&mode=view&cat_id=8&press_id=1847

12

Comparison of Indian Muslims and Muslims Living in the European Union Countries

SHAZIA AZIZ-WÜLBERS

The task of a comparison between Muslims living in Europe and Muslims living in India is an extremely difficult one. The reason behind this is the fact that their historical and political contexts are poles apart. Islam came to India probably in the seventh century through Arabic traders who came to the Malabar Coast in Kerala in the South of India. Most of Northern India came in contact with Islam thanks to its Muslim rulers.

On the other hand, Islam was uprooted from Spain, the only West-European country that was under Muslim rulers from the eighth to the fifteenth century and did not play a big role in its history from that time onwards. Since the time Spanish Muslim rulers were removed from the continent, Western Europe, most of which is now a part of the European Union, continued to remain predominantly Christian. After the Second World War, Western European countries brought in labourers to work for their reconstruction. They were supposed to be temporary workers who then stayed on. In Germany the term *Gastarbeiter*, meaning Guest Worker is still prevalent, although now steadily losing significance.

But some similarities do exist between the two. In India as well as the European Union countries, Muslims are the largest minority[1]: In India they form 12 per cent of the population and in the European Union there are about 15 million Muslims representing 3 per cent of European Union country citizens.

This article is an attempt to find convergences and divergences in the Muslim Community living in these two different parts of the world.

DIVERGENCES

Historical Context

Indian Muslims are either converted Muslims or a progeny of the Muslim immigrants from the time the Muslims ruled large parts of India. Conversions probably took place as a means of improving social standing or as a way of avoiding the special non-Muslim taxes called *Jizya*, levied on them during the Muslim rule. In addition to that Sufism played an important role in spreading the religion.

The Hindus were attracted to Islam since it resonates with a general Hindu way of life where meditation and non-voilence play a significant role. Untouchables and artisans were particularly interested in it and helped in bringing Islam closer to the indiginous traditions. During the Mughal Empire, large parts of India embraced Islam. Akbar, who was a liberal ruler, even established a new religon called *Din-i-Ilahi*, which included parts of the then prevalent religons like Hinduism, Islam, Buddhism, Jainism and Christianity. But his great grand son Aurangzeb was a fanatic under whom non-Muslims suffered.

The belief that Islam was propogated by such invaders like Mahmud Ghaznavi and the Muhammed Ghori is misplaced since Islam came to India much earlier and these invaders were only interested in plundering the enormous wealth and riches of India[2] and taking them to their home countries. They did not come to India to settle and rule it. Their objective was to plunder as much wealth as possible and transfer it to their capitals since it was crucial for them to maintain huge armed forces for their frequent military operations. However, it is probably true that the invading Sultans like Qutubuddin Aibak and Alauddin Khilji did practice forced conversions.

In the beginning of the twentieth century when India was under the British rule, Indian freedom struggle gained substantial momentum. During this time, Muhammad Ali Jinnah raised concerns that the Muslim populations would suffer under a united Hindu majority state. He managed to gain popular support for his ideas which eventually led to the formation of Pakistan on 14 August 1947. However, one third of the Muslims[3] remained in India while several millions migrated to Pakistan.

Thus, the history of Islam is almost a thousand years old. Since its advent in India, Islamic influences can be seen in the artistic, cultural, philosophical, social and political spheres. On the other hand, the Muslims of European Union countries have had no such history. Their presence dates back to the end of the Second World War. It was then that most European Union countries favoured the policy of bringing in workers from their erstwhile colonies to help rebuild a war-torn Europe. The United Kingdom had Pakistanis and Indians, Germany had Turks, France had North Africans, and the Netherlands had Indonesians and Surinamese, to name the major hosts. According to some estimates, 500,000 immigrants, primarily family reunion cases and 400,000 asylum seekers arrive in Western Europe each year[4], most of them being Muslims.

These immigrants usually lived on the margins of the European society and stayed poor. They always had in mind that they were only temporarily on European soil. Eventually, they stayed on and bred second and third generation Muslims who became European citizens. The amalgam and the mixing with Indian culture that remained a part and parcel of Indian Muslims through the centuries was not the case among European Muslims.

Political Context

Indian secularism is a special type of secularism which is more based on religious tolerance than separation of religious and state authorities. It means that officially there is no discrimination based on religion against any person professing any particular religious faith. Article 25 (1) of the Indian Constitution says "all persons are equally entitled to freedom of conscience and the right freely to profess, practice and propagate religion".[5]

In theory one can practice any religion that one wants. However, in the past half a century or more, Islam has been used to revive the nationalist sentiments by the right wing parties[6], trying to woo Hindu voters by declaring that India should be for Hindus and the rest of them can go where they came from.[7]

The site of the sixteenth century Babri Mosque has been a constant source of flaming nationalism. From 1985, Hindu nationalists have claimed with increasing persistence the site for building a Ram Temple[8]. In 1992, Hindu militants destroyed the mosque during a rally led by right wing political parties. Some three thousand people lost their lives in the ensuing communal violence.

Since then, this issue has been used by the right wing parties, to get votes from the majority Hindu population. Although the Hindu nationalists had only played a marginal role in politics since India's independence, after the Babri mosque was demolished, they slowly became India's main opposition party, thriving on opposing government benefits for Muslims and proposing to build a temple at the site of the destroyed mosque and finally winning elections with a landslide victory and forming government and staying in power from 1998 to 2004.

The nationalist parties instigate communal violence to polarise the elections and get votes by mobilising Hindus against Muslims[9]. They stir up fears in Hindu minds by arguing that Muslims have a higher birth rate and soon they will constitute 30 per cent of the population and will threaten the Hindu majority. Some even go to the extent of demanding Indian Muslims as well as Christians to reconvert to Hinduism.

The other issue that is also used for political purposes by nationalist parties is that of the Uniform Civil Code. Muslims in India are governed by the Sharia laws called the Muslim Personal Law[10], when it comes to marriage, divorce and inheritance. Article 44 of the Indian constitution recommends a uniform civil code[11]. This recommendation has also been used by successive political leadership in the country to stoke anti-Muslim sentiments, since Muslims consider it as an attempt by the state to dilute their cultural identity and the Hindu nationalists see it as the Muslims' refusal to integrate in the Indian society.

The major ruling party, the Congress Party, on the other hand, allegedly to keep its vote banks happy, has made some efforts to help in the upliftment of the downtrodden Muslim population. Nationalists or not, dealing with the Muslims of India has been a highly politicised and charged issue. And Muslims have always had a strong influence on and in Indian politics.

In the European context, the political dynamics are different. Only very recently, the European Union states have woken up to their angry 15 million fellow citizens[12]. For decades they had been neglected and suddenly due to riots of varied types in France, the Netherlands and Germany, the European Union countries have begun to notice them. But the violence has not aggravated to communal tensions level. The riots that take place are more against the state authorities and the police than against the general population and there is no authentic debate at present[13] about whether Sharia laws should be applied or not to the Muslim population in Europe.

Usually there is little talk about improving their plight and more talk about how Muslims do not integrate in mainstream European society[14]. The head scarf controversy is an example of the integration debate as well as the French brand of secularism of which they are very proud. Such a controversy probably cannot exist in India. Tolerance of religious symbols exists in India, since time immemorial. The debate on dress code which is the hot topic of public media is a non issue in India since the Indians have learnt to live with a permanent presence of such symbols, for example the turban of the Sikhs, the skull cap and the head scarf of the Muslims, the cross of the Christians, the bindi[15] of the Hindus etc.

Each country in the European Union has its own way of dealing with its Muslim minority: the French insist on laws of separation of religion and public life leading to the ban of head scarves; the Germans take steps to improve integration, by obliging German residence permit applicants to learn German through *Integrationskurs*; the Netherlands as well as the United Kingdom have traditionally favoured multiculturalism, involving the accommodation of different groups on equal terms; but this is swiftly in the process of changing in the aftermath of Theo Van Gogh's killing and the London bombings by terrorists born and brought up on European soil.

At the European level, the first time religion was ever mentioned in the European Union texts was in the Treaty of Amsterdam of 1997[16], where a brief mention was made of how the European Union respects religious associations and communities in the member states. The next reference to religion was in the white paper on European Governance of July 2001 which mentioned with reference to civil society that "churches and religious communities play an important role in voicing the concerns of the people.[17]

Another effort was made with the Lisbon Treaty which tried to introduce the idea of a dialogue between European institutions and religious communities, but it seems to be a half—hearted attempt although several other documents previously produced by the European Union have been more promising[18]. The treaty falls short of making any mention of its religious communities and the only "Religious Institutions and Organizations" it names are the "Churches".

> "1. The Union respects and does not prejudice the status under national law of churches and religious associations or communities in the Member States. 2. The Union equally respects the status under national law of philosophical and non-confessional organizations.3. Recognising their identity and their specific contribution, the Union shall maintain an open, transparent and regular dialogue with these churches and organizations".[19]

Thus, at the European Union level, the interaction between authorities and its minorities has just made a sputtering start.

Violence

"Violence between Hindus and Muslims is a structural given of Indian society."[20] In India, communal riots take away thousands of lives and bring about massive destruction of property. No single year goes by without them even if their numbers and intensity varies[21]. There is no agreement between researchers about when riots actually begun in India. Some researchers say that they took place even before the British came to India while others are of the opinion that they begun systematically only during the time of and after Indian independence[22]. But most of them agree that communal riots are based on factors other than religious animosity or social seclusion[23].

Some of the most violent events in recent times took place in Godhra, Gujarat. The riots began when some Muslims, allegedly, set fire to a train compartment which was bringing 50 Hindu nationalists belonging to the Vishwa Hindu Parishad (VHP) from the disputed site of the Babri Mosque. The riots that followed this incident were among the worst India had ever seen. These were not just Hindu-Muslim riots but in fact a state sponsored pogrom[24] nearing ethnic cleansing. But the fact that they were so rampant in nature shows that there were many Hindu sympathisers for it[25]. It was a systematic killing of Muslims at a large scale and that too with the state government ordering it and the central government just looking on without any semblance of action. Usually it is difficult to differentiate between riots and pogroms. According to Paul Brass,

> "Consider first the production of riots and pogroms. The first carries the appearance of spontaneous, intergroup mass action, the second of deliberately organized—and especially—state-supported killings and the destruction of property of a targeted group. In fact, however, no hard and fast distinction can be made between these supposedly distinct forms of violence, since pogroms masquerade as riots and many, if not most, large-scale riots display features supposedly special to pogroms".[26]

Such riots or pogroms against the Muslim population would probably not take place in the European Union countries. At least till the extreme right parties do not get too much power.

Thus riots may take place because of electoral competition[27], or the presence of an 'institutional riot system[28], or through the instigation of town level civic organizations and networks[29], they certainly do not take place because of the feeling of resentment of the Muslim population and as a direct consequence of their anger towards the society which has left them behind. This is more a trade mark of riots happening in some European Union countries like France and Germany. Social discrimination has alienated some French Muslims which has been the biggest factor in causing the riots in Paris area[30] in October 2005. This is the biggest point of divergence between the dynamics ruling the Muslims of India and the Muslims of Europe.

CONVERGENCES

The most important point of convergence between the two is that they form the poorest part of society.

Social Conditions

The Sachar Committee report[31] points out that Indian Muslims experience low literacy[32] and high poverty and unemployment rates. Although Islam came to India a thousand years ago, they still face prejudices and are mostly neglected by the mainstream society. For example, in the state of West Bengal where they make up to 27 per cent of the population, their employment in the government sector is below 3 per cent.[33]

The report also says that Muslims do not get loans from banks easily even if they are self-employed at a far higher rate than others. Muslims represent 13.4 per cent of the population but only 4 per cent of them can be found at the undergraduate level of elite universities and only 2 per cent of them are represented in the Indian Armed Forces. One cannot make straight-jacket statements about Muslims in India since Muslims living in Southern states like Kerala and Karnataka, are more educated, integrated and prosperous than the Muslims living in Northern states like Bihar and Uttar Pradesh, but one can safely say that when it comes to a national average, they form one of the most backward communities.

Some of the Hindu nationalists have called the Sachar Report yet another example of vote bank politics where the current UPA government is trying to attract votes from the Muslim vote bank. BJP President of Kerala, PK Krishnadas described the Sachar panel as "distorted, politically motivated and dangerous".[34] But the fact remains that India's booming economy has left out its largest minority group.

The Muslims living in the European Union countries face a similar situation. They are marginalised from mainstream European society. Their education levels are low, unemployment rates are high[35] and they have poor housing conditions. They face discrimination in daily life. This discrimination is the most apparent in the recruitment process and in their search for accommodation. A real life experience conducted by Canal+, the French channel, a two part series called, *Dans lapeau d'un noir*[36], one can really understand the experiences of the coloured community which is predominantly Muslim. In Germany, the unemployment rate of 'foreigners' around 20 per cent in 2004 was almost twice as high as the general average around 10 per cent.[37]

Also in the field of education, they are segregated and usually end up in schools that have a majority of people of foreign origin. Even if they wanted to, they could not get out of the ghetto since they are obliged to go to school in their locality. In Finland, for example, the highest educational level attained by most migrants was three years of vocational training at the secondary level.[38] According to the EUMC report some Muslim students in the Netherlands, were put on a waiting list to 'counterbalance any 'disproportion' in an individual schools' pupil numbers'.[39]

Due to discrimination their social conditions remain extremely precarious with exclusion from the main society, little money, little education and most importantly no future prospects. Be it Turks in Germany, Indonesians in the Netherlands, Pakistanis in the UK, they live in a parallel world within Europe.

Identity Issues

In India, Muslims have contributed in almost every field like sports, politics, arts, architecture, films, music, literature, to name just a few. There have been three Muslim presidents, Dr Zakir Hussain[40], Dr Fakhruddin Ali Ahmed and Dr APJ Abdul Kalam; several members of parliament; actors in

Bollywood like Shahrukh Khan and Amir Khan; sports persons like Sania Mirza and Irfan Pathan, and so on.

Although they have been in India for hundreds of years the Muslims are still considered by Hindu nationalists led by the Sangh Parivar, as foreigners who have extra territorial loyalties and a pro-Pakistan sentiment. The Hindu nationalists also insist that Islam is a threat and a foreign infliction brought to India through the invaders. The Indian Muslims are constantly blamed for terrorist activities[41]. And by doing so, the Hindu nationalist identify themselves as 'self' and the Muslims as the 'other' that have been forcefully imposed on them.

In European Union countries, the dynamics are a little different since Muslims have had a constant presence only for about 50 years. But needless to say, they are subjected to the same kind of treatment. They are identified by the rest of the Europeans with their Muslim identity. Granting a European identity to them seems too far-fetched since many of them live in ghettos, mix only within their own community and have almost nothing European about them, to the extent of not knowing the language of the host country. As a result they themselves have no idea where they belong and what their real identity is.

Because of being neglected by the mainstream European society, and having complicated identity issues, they seek solace within groups like those consisting of fundamentalist Islamists which give them the comfort of a strict identity, the identity of belonging to an Islamic group. The London Bombing is an example par excellence of this hypothesis where the terrorists involved were born and bred in Britain but harboured so much hatred in their hearts.

Moderate Muslims in the Netherlands were outraged by the killing of Theo Van Gogh, the filmmaker who made a documentary about conditions of Muslim women. Though Theo Van Gogh's murderer was a Dutch-Moroccan problem-youth belonging to the Hofstad terrorist network, several skirmishes were reported in which Muslims were indiscriminately held responsible. Such a situation, of course, increases their disillusionment and hopelessness further, especially since most of the Muslim population is under the age of 30—young, alienated, angry and easily influenced[42]. Many of them consider their primary identity as being Muslim instead of being Turk, Algerian or Moroccan.

And the mainstream society too, in European Union countries as well as in India, deals with their minority as if they had only one form of identity. Once they represent the 'other' as having only the Muslim identity, they bracket the entire Muslim population into one stereo type which is not a big help in interactions. While the self may have several layers of identities, every aspect of the 'other' is supposed to be determined by their Muslimness[43]. Amartya Sen's words are of particular relevance to this context.

> "The main hope of harmony in the contemporary world lies not in any imagined uniformity, but in the plurality of our identities, which cut across each other and work against sharp divisions around one uniquely hardened line of impenetrable division. The political leaders who dispute the clash of civilisations, but think and act in terms of a unique partitioning of humanity into 'the Western world," "the Muslim world," "the Hindu world," and so on, make the world not only more divisive, but also much more flammable. They also end up privileging the voice of religious authorities (who become the ex officio spokesmen), while muffling other voices and silencing other concerns".[44]

Conclusion

There is a widespread fear after the Madrid and London bombings and the cartoon controversy that Islam in Europe is getting more and more radicalised. This may be true to a certain extent. However, in spite of this fear, slowly there is a new kind of Islam emanating from the European Muslims, just as Indian Islam is different from other kinds of Islam by virtue of it mixing with Indian culture. The theory of Islam detaching from its own ethnic, linguistic and national roots[45] may not be completely convincing, but it is true that a new European Islam is emerging from the young third generation Muslims most of whom have not even been to the land of their ancestors.

Generally the European Union countries have tried to deal with their minorities in their own way: the French have banned head scarves in public insisting on the promotion of a secular identity for all its citizens, the Netherlands and Germany are working on integrating their new citizens by obliging them to learn their languages and the Danes are engaging in huge debates about freedom of speech and expression in democracy. These are all well—meaning steps but need to be combined by helping Muslims get out of the ghettos and find good jobs. Similarly, the Indian government needs to make sure that its largest minority gets to share India's economic boom.

The experiment of comparing the Muslim community living on two different continents has been a fruitful one. Bassam Tibi's Islam tinged with European values and Indian Islam having hues of traditional Indian values can be a reality if obstacles like feelings of alienation, complicated identity issues and unemployment are dealt with.

NOTES AND REFERENCES

1. Here one has to note that the influence of Muslims is much more on the Indian society and politics than in the European Union countries.

2. The cruellest looting took place at the Somnath Temple in 1024 by Mahmud Ghaznavi, which was well known for its riches in gold and precious stones.
3. Information extracted from Aminah Muhammad Arif, "L'Islam en Inde: ses origines et sa situation contemporaine", from the following website: http://www.clio.fr/bibliotheque/L_islam_en_Inde__ses_origines_et_sa_situation_contemporaine.asp
4. Timothy Savage, "Europe and Islam: Crescent Waxing, Cultures Clashing", *The Washington Quarterly,* vol. 27, no. 3, summer 2004, pp. 25-50, p.27.
5. Article 25 (1) of the Constitution of India can be consulted on the following government of India website: http://lawmin.nic.in/coi/coiason29july08.pdf
6. Most of these parties are part of the Sangh Parivar, Vishwa Hindu Parishad (VHP), Bajrang Dal, Shiv Sena, Rashtriya Swayam Sevak Sangh (RSS), and the Bharatiya Janata Party (BJP).
7. The Hindu nationalists do not target just the Muslims but also other minorities like Christians, Zoroastrians etc.
8. Christophe Jaffrelot, "Nationalisme hindou: le retour des radicaux", CERI, Sciences Po website. http://www.ceri-sciencespo.com/archive/mai03/artcj1.pdf
9. Christophe Jaffrelot, "Les violences entre hindous et musulmans au Gujarat (Inde) en 2002; Emeutes d'état pogromes et réactions anti-jihadiste", in *Revue Tiers monde*, no. 174, 2003, p. 346, pp. 345-367.
10. The organization "All India Muslim Personal Law Board" was set up in 1973 to see to the protection and continued applicability of Muslim Personal Law.
11. Article 44 of the Constitution of India "The State shall endeavour to secure for the citizens a uniform civil code throughout the territory of India", it can be consulted on the following government of India website: http://lawmin.nic.in/coi/coiason29july08.pdf
12. There have been very few Muslim members in European Parliament, though major political parties do field Muslim candidates. See http:/suffrage-universel.be/fr/frmieleu.htm
13. The BBC is an exception, which has telecasted several programmes and interviewed people on their ideas of Sharia laws for the UK. Please consult the following BBC website: http://news.bbc.co.uk/2/hi/uk_news/7232661.stm
14. This is not true in the banking sector where the first Islamic Bank of Britain, based on Sharia laws was opened in 2004 and the German province of Saxony Anhalt became the first in Europe to issue *sukuk*, an Islamic bond.
15. Coloured dot, usually red, on the forehead of Hindu women.
16. Treaty of Amsterdam amending the treaty on European Union, the treaties establishing the European Communities and certain related acts on the Europa website.
17. Commission of the European Communities, European Governance; A White Paper, COM(2001) 0428 final, July 2001.
18. Some of these documents are Commission of the European Communities, A Common Agenda for Integration Framework for the Integration of Third Country Nationals in the European Union, COM(2005) 389 Final, September 01 2005 and the Press Release, The Council of the European Union, Common Basic Principles on Integration, 14615/04, November 2004.

19. Article 17 of the Treaty of Lisbon: http://bookshop.europa.eu/eubookshop/FileCache/PUBPDF/FXAC08115ENC/FXAC08115ENC_002.pdf
20. Christophe Jaffrelot, "Communal Riots in Gujarat: The State at Risk?", Working Paper no. 17, South Asia Institute, Department of Political Science, University of Heidelberg, July 2003.
21. Asghar Ali Engineer, "Communal Riots", in *Islam and the Modern Age*, January 2003.
22. Bipin Chandra, *Communalism in Modern India*, New Delhi; Vikas Publishing House, 1984.
23. The ideas in this paper are interesting since the author explains that riots are not spontaneous nor have anything to do with religion. B Rajeshwari, "Communal Riots in India: A Chronology (1947-2003)", IPCS Research Papers, March 2004.
24. Ashutosh Varshney calls it as a "first full blooded pogrom" of India in his article. Ashutosh Varshney, "Understanding Gujarat Violence" in *Items and Issues,* vol. 4, no. 3, Winter 2002-2003, pp. 1-5.
25. Christophe Jaffrelot, *op. cit.*
26. Paul Brass, "On the Study of Riots, Pogroms and Genocide", Sawyer Seminar session on "Processes of Mass Killing" at the Centre for Advanced Study in the Behavioural Sciences, Stanford University), December 6-7 2002.
27. Steven I Wilkinson, "Communal Riots in India" in *Economic and Political Weekly*, October 29, 2005.
28. Paul Brass, *The Production of Hindu Muslim Violence in Contemporary India*, New Delhi: Oxford University Press, 2003.
29. Ashutosh Varshney, *Ethnic Conflict and Civic life, Hindus and Muslims in India*, Yale: Yale University Press, 2002.
30. Please refer to the following BBC website: http://news.bbc.co.uk/2/hi/europe/4375910.stm
31. It is named after Rajinder Sachar who was the President of the Committee that worked on the report. This committee was appointed by PM Manmohan Singh. This report is the first of its kind.
32. According the Sachar committee report, Muslim literacy ranks well below the national average.
33. Rajinder Sachar, *Social, Economic and Educational Status of the Muslim Community of India*, Prime Ministers High Level Committee, Government of India, November 2006.
34. "BJP leader criticises Sachar Report" in *The Hindu*, December 02, 2006.
35. Usually when employed, they occupy jobs that require low qualifications.
36. It was telecast in two series in February 2007 on Canal+
37. Quoted in *EUMC Report on Muslims in the European Union, Discrimination and Islamophobia*, 2006.
38. *Ibid.*
39. *Ibid.*
40. Another Muslim, Mr. Muhammad Hidayatullah had occupied the presidency from 20 July 1969 to 24 August 1969.

41. Though some Indian Muslims have participated in domestic terrorism, they have little sympathy with the global jihad. There are about 150 million Muslims in India but there doesn't seem to be a cell of Al Qaeda on Indian Territory. This does say a lot about Indian Muslim culture.
42. BBC's Islamic affairs analyst Roger Hardy brings home this point in his comprehensive report which can be consulted on the following website: http://news.bbc.co.uk/2/hi/europe/4781290.stm
43. This idea stems for the following article, "The Violence of Security: Hindu Nationalism and the Politics of Representing 'the Muslim' as a Danger", in *The Round table*, vol. 94, no. 379, April 2005, pp. 203-215.
44. Amartya Sen, "The Right to one's identity" in *The Frontline*, vol. 19, no. 1, January 05-18, 2002.
45. These ideas have been expressed in the following book. Stefano Allievi and Jorgen S Nielsen, eds, *Muslim Networks and Transnational Communities in and across Europe*, Leiden: Brill, 2003.

BIBLIOGRAPHY

Allievi, Stefano and Nielsen, Jorgen S., ed, *Muslim Networks and Transnational Communities in and across Europe*, Leiden: Brill, 2003.

Arif, Aminah Muhammad, "L'Islam en Inde: ses origines et sa situation contemporaine", from the following website:
http://www.clio.fr/bibliotheque/L_islam_en_Inde__ses_origines_et_sa_situation_contemporaine.asp

Brass, Paul, *The Production of Hindu Muslim Violence in Contemporary India*, New Delhi: Oxford University Press, 2003.

______, "On the Study of Riots, Pogroms and Genocide", Sawyer Seminar session on "Processes of Mass Killing," at the Centre for Advanced Study in the Behavioural Sciences, Stanford University, December 6-7, 2002.

Chandra, Bipin, *Communalism in Modern India*, New Delhi: Vikas Publishing House, 1984.

Engineer, Asghar Ali, "Communal Riots", in *Islam and the Modern Age*, January 2003.

Hardy Roger, Report on Islam in Europe, http://news.bbc.co.uk/2/hi/europe/4781290.stm

Jaffrelot, Christophe, "Communal Riots in Gujarat: The State at Risk?" Working Paper no 17, South Asia Institute, Department of Political Science, University of Heidelberg, July 2003.

________, "Les violences entre hindous et musulmans au Gujarat (Inde) en 2002 ; Emeutes d'état pogromes et réactions anti-jihadiste", in *Revue Tiers monde*, no. 174, 2003, pp. 345-367.

_______, "Nationalisme hindou: le retour des radicaux", CERI, Sciences Po website.

http://www.ceri-sciencespo.com/archive/mai03/artcj1.pdf

Rajeshwari, B., "Communal Riots in India: A Chronology-(1947-2003), *IPCS Research Papers*, March 2004.

Savage Timothy, "Europe and Islam: Crescent Waxing, Cultures Clashing", *The Washington Quarterly,* vol 27, no. 3, summer 2004, pp. 25-50, p.27.

Sen, Amartya, "The Right to one's identity", in *The Frontline*, vol. 19, no. 1, January 05-18, 2002.

Varshney, Ashutosh, "Understanding Gujarat Violence", in *Items and Issues,* vol 4, no. 3, Winter 2002-2003, pp. 1-5.

———*Ethnic Conflict and Civic life, Hindus and Muslims in India*, Yale; Yale University Press, 2002.

Wilkinson, Steven I, "Communal Riots in India", in *Economic and Political Weekly*, October 29, 2005.

Official Documents

Treaty of Lisbon Official Journal of the European Union, vol. 51, May 09, 2008.

Treaty of Amsterdam amending the treaty on European Union, the treaties establishing the European Communities and certain related acts on the Europa website.

Treaty of the European Union, Consolidated Version,

Commission of the European Communities, *European Governance; A White Paper*, COM(2001) 0428 final, July 2001.

Commission of the European Communities, *A Common Agenda for Integration Framework for the Integration of Third Country Nationals in the European Union*, COM(2005) 389 Final, September 01, 2005

Press Release, The Council of the European Union, *Common Basic Principles on Integration*, 14615/04, November 2004.

Sachar Report, Rajinder Sachar, *Social, Economic and Educational Status of the Muslim Community of India*, Prime Ministers High Level Committee, Government of India, November 2006.

EUMC Report, *Muslims in the European Union, Discrimination and Islamophobia*, 2006.

13

Is the Union for the Mediterranean a Postcolonial Political Contract?

GEETHA GANAPATHY-DORÉ

Theoreticians of World-systems like Janet Abu Lughod, Immanuel Wallerstein and Andre Gunder Frank see the world as a system of interacting hegemonies. Indeed Andre Gunder Frank contends that a global-scale world system that includes Asia, Europe and Africa has existed since the 4th millennium BC[1]. Old civilisations like the Egyptian and the Mesopotamian were considered the cradles of civilization. Modern Western civilization looked upon Africa[2] or India[3] as the mother of civilizations. Historian Fernand Braudel has underscored the penetrating influence of the Mediterranean in world history. "Mediterranean Latin culture was to Protestant Europe what Greece was to Rome"[4]. The Mediterranean civilization is accorded a privileged position as a connecting link between the East and West. In the words of Albert Camus[5],

> the one land among all others that joins great Oriental traditions of thought. For, it is not laid out in a classical and orderly manner, but looks diffuse and turbulent, like the Arab quarters or the ports of Genoa or Tunisia. The triumphant sense of life, the sense of crushing weight and boredom, the deserted places in Spain, the siesta—all this sum up the real Mediterranean and it is the Orient to which it is close. Not to Latin West. North Africa is the only land where the East and West cohabit. At this point of juncture, there is no difference between a Spaniard and an Italian from the platforms of Alger and the Arabs who throng there. What is most essential in the Mediterranean genius springs from this unique encounter between history and geography born out of the East meeting the West.

The recent buzz around the Union for the Mediterranean has resuscitated this myth. It is hard to believe that hardly seven years ago, in the very same

Grand Palais in Paris where the July 13, 2008 summit on the Union for the Mediterranean took place, an exhibition of paintings on the Mediterranean entitled "Méditerranée, de Courbet à Matisse"[6] was held in which the African side of the Mediterranean was totally forgotten. This article will first explore the birth of the idea of the Union for the Mediterranean and the motivations surrounding it, then study what the project actually consists in, analyse its benefits and shortcomings from the point of view of both the European and Mediterranean partners, and finally gather its implications for international relations and the global peace process.

The Birth of the Idea and Motivations Behind

It was the Roman Empire that brought unity to the region. Indeed the Romans considered the Mediterranean Sea as "*mare nostrum*" (our sea). They had almost domesticated it as if it were a swimming pool. During the course of history, others who tried to recreate the unity failed, even if in the 19th century, the Mediterranean was thought of as an "English lake".[7] In 1907, two «fringe» intellectuals[8], one French, Valentine de Saint-Point and one Italian, Ricciotto Canudo proposed that a "Mediterranean Confederation" be set up. They imagined it as "a spiritual federation of Mediterranean intelligences". Valentine de Saint-Point founded an "Elite College" in Ajaccio in 1921 to train the minds in Mediterranean thought. The idea was to reconcile the West which was using its sciences for the purposes of destruction and the East which lacked the precision of such sciences and was exhausting its energies without being able to renew itself. After the death of Canudo in 1923, Valentine de Saint-Point settled in Egypt and tried in vain to set the project on sail. In 1926, Mussolini launched in Tripoli the idea of a modern "*mare nostrum*" envisaging an Italian maritime dominance in the Mediterranean region. Strategically it was felt that "the one who controls the Mediterranean space could claim a hegemonic role in the international system"[9]. But the Second World War and the partition of Palestine led to the permanent postponement of the dream of unification.

If the end of the British Empire saw the birth of the Association of Commonwealth Nations[10], the end of French domination in Africa was followed by the Francophonie[11] and the so called African policy of the French government. The newly elected French President Nicolas Sarkozy wanted to decidedly mark his break with this time honoured French foreign policy line. His speech in Dakar in the capacity of President elect was the first step in this new turn. «The tragedy of Africa is that the African has not fully entered into history... They have never really launched themselves into the future [...] The African peasant only knew the eternal renewal of time, marked by the endless repetition of the same gestures and the same words», he intoned. «In this realm of fancy... there is neither room for human endeavour nor the idea of progress»[12]. His pro-American stand, his decision to join NATO's military command from which De Gaulle pulled out forty-two years ago and his determination to send troops to Afghanistan were the next defining steps of his pro-Atlanticist policy shift.

Earlier on 7 February, 2007 while he was campaigning for the presidential elections in Toulon, Sarkozy had announced the name of another project, a "Mediterranean Union... whose vocation will be to work closely with Europe"[13]. This electoral idea, inspired by an earlier call in 2005 by the Greek Pang Otis Roumentis and the French Jean-Louis Guigou for a Mediterranean Community[14], was put forward in support of Sarkozy's concept of chosen immigration and was tested ahead in view of the rotating presidency of the European Union that France would be taking over on 1 July 2008, for Sarkozy wanted his European partners to endorse his idea of a tighter immigration control. Perhaps the lessons of the North American Free Trade Area which had not solved the immigration issues between the US and Mexico were at the back of the French strategists' mind when a different model of co-operation was conceived. But it was packaged as a political will to reposition the Mediterranean in the world map. This "ideological back bone"[15] was supposed to nuance Sarkozy's portrait as an ultraliberal and Atlanticist. Thus, on 25 October 2007 President Sarkozy addressed the Mediterranean people "who are not able to get out of the cycle of vengeance and hatred". [...] "To all the Mediterranean people who are dreaming of peace and fraternity but only see the war of all against all, all the Mediterranean people who are imbued with tolerance and humanism and who are desperate about having to cope with intolerance and fundamentalism, I have come to say that the time has come to stop speaking and start acting"[16]. This was followed by the call from Rome on 20 December 2007 made together by Nicolas Sarkozy, Romano Prodi and Jose Luis Zapatero to countries bordering the Mediterranean to form a union of projects[17]. On 30 April 2008 in Tunis, Sarkozy explained his idea in detail to young students and promised that such a union will change the world[18].

The French President's sudden interest was interpreted by many as stemming from very personal reasons. Sarkozy's paternal grandfather was a Jew from Thessalonica and he had publicly rendered homage to his grandfather. His first wife Marie-Dominique Culioli is from Corsica. His second ex-wife Cécilia was born of a Jewish Russian father. His current wife Carla Bruni's Italian origin confirms his emotional links with the Mediterranean[19]. However, it is well-known that the idea of the Mediterranean Union was the brain child of the President's Special Adviser and speech writer

Henri Guaino. Some saw it as a deliberate attempt to stall Turkey's admission in the European Union as Sarkozy had remarked earlier during the campaign (Montpellier, 3 May 2007) that "Turkey does not have its place in the European Union because it is not a European country. But Turkey is a big Mediterranean country with which Mediterranean Europe could further the Unity of the Mediterranean"[20].

After President Sarkozy's attempt to rescue the Bulgarian nurses in an effort to bolster his image which was found to be overshadowing EU's diplomacy in the area, the French initiative for the Union for the Mediterranean was perceived as yet another gesture by the French government to assert itself within the European Union and the world at the expense of the Barcelona Process. The Barcelona Process[21], launched by Euro-Mediterranean Foreign Ministers in November 1995, defined the framework for a regional/multilateral alliance between the twenty-seven Members of the European Union and twelve Southern Mediterranean states (Albania, Algeria, Egypt, Israel, Jordan, Lebanon, Libya, Mauritania, Morocco, Occupied Palestinian territory, Syria, Tunisia, and Turkey). Though only fifteen kilometres separate Europe from Africa at Gibraltar, the gap in standard of living between them is so wide that a solution had to be found to attenuate the sense of despair that such a gap engenders[22]. Besides, the authoritarianism, lack of democracy and human rights, hastily built and terribly personalized nation states with weak institutions[23] prevailing in the Mediterranean had to be curbed. An economic partnership was thus set in motion as an instrument for that purpose. It was based on the principles of joint ownership, dialogue and co-operation. The main objectives of the partnership outlined in the Barcelona Declaration are: to build together an area of peace, security and shared prosperity. The economic/financial and the cultural/social sectors were the areas concerned by this policy. In 2005, migration was added as a fourth key sector. In 2005, the Barcelona Summit agreed on a five year work programme and a Euro-Mediterranean Code of Conduct for countering terrorism. The European Neighbourhood Policy (ENP) works to establish support programmes for economic transition and reform in the Mediterranean countries, taking into account each country's specific needs and characteristics. These actions are funded under the European Neighbourhood and Partnership Instrument (ENPI). The European Commission has supported the Barcelona Process with the provision of €16 billion from the Community budget since 1995. Loans from the European Investment Bank amount to approximately €2 billion per year.

The Barcelona Process tried to set right macroeconomic balances in the economies of North Africa and Middle East. Inflation in the region dropped from 20 per cent per year to less than 5 per cent. Budget deficit was reduced to 3 per cent of GDP compared to the earlier 5 per cent[24]. However, the Barcelona Process is widely considered to be a failure. The efforts made so far under the process have not contributed much in reducing immigration, containing radical Islam or promoting human rights. The foreign ministers of the fifteen EU member states and their twelve Mediterranean partners had agreed at the Stuttgart conference held in 1999 to draft a regional document on peace and stability called the "Euro-Med Charter" which was to include a long list of confidence-building measures and completed by late 2000. Its implementation was not easy primarily due to the failure of the Oslo peace process between Israel and Palestine. Morocco and Algeria are divided as to the Western Sahara issue. The Italian scholar Roberto Aliboni has argued that the charter proved inconclusive because "the priorities and contents assumed by the political and security partnership were incongruous with respect to objective political conditions and the organizational and institutional structure of the Partnership was unbalanced".[25] The free trade zone envisaged for 2010 is not likely to materialize either within that time frame.

German Chancellor Angela Merkel was not consulted in the first place about the Mediterranean Union. The German presidency was particularly hostile to the idea as Sarkozy originally meant to exclude European Countries which did not geographically border the Mediterranean from the project. It was felt that the French ambition for regional hegemony could endanger the unity of the European Union. The enlarged EU could split into two poles, one Northern and one Southern[26]. In all fairness, it should be pointed out that European Union's Baltic states, when they formed a neighbourhood alliance called Council of the Baltic Sea States in 1992 with twelve members—Germany, Denmark, Norway, Sweden, Finland, Russia, Estonia, Latvia, Lithuania, Poland, Iceland and the European Commission, did not include France or any other Southern state for that matter. Paradoxically, when the EU was trying to foster co-operation between the North and the South, the North-South tensions in the Union itself were coming to the fore. Sarkozy had to make concessions, accept the project to be called "Barcelona Process: Union for the Mediterranean"[27], include all EU member states to save the project, and reassure Turkey that its involvement will not undermine its chances of becoming a EU member state. For President Sarkozy, externally there was pressure to come up with a striking plan to mark the French Presidency. Internally, an attempt to embrace the Mediterranean people via this pact was a measure to control immigration and at the same time appease the migrant population by giving access to EU markets for non-European farm products. A new model for North-South co-operation had to be experimented that brought the benefits of the European model of regional integration to the mainly Muslim countries like Algeria, Morocco, Tunisia and even Libya to which Sarkozy had travelled. Besides, Sarkozy's contender for presidential elections, the socialist Ségolène Royale had advanced the very popular and postcolonial idea of co-development which attempted to do away with the idea of the third world perpetually depending on the first world and tried to bring a touch of dignity, equality, reciprocity and recognition in the French political discourse on Africa.

Strategically France was trying to stage a European come back in the oil-rich North Africa where new players such as China, India, Brazil and Russia were making a mark and where the United States was signing free trade agreements[28]. Sarkozy's move may also be seen as a French contribution to the Middle East peace process after the war in Lebanon. A rather original reading contends that the plan was conceived to precisely help the Americans.

> The plan, indeed, bears some resemblance to the "Greater Middle East" project favoured by the American neo-conservative strategists. Although the membership of the two proposed bodies is different (the Greater Middle East encompasses Arabia, Iran, Central Asian states and even Afghanistan and Pakistan) the ideology is the same: supranational and anti-national. The idea is to neutralise the Arab-Israeli conflict by "integrating" the Middle Eastern countries into a single political unit, rather as the Franco-German conflict was allegedly neutralised by the creation of the European Community. Given the fact that many Maghreb countries have signed partnership agreements with NATO, the Union for the Mediterranean would only be a political superstructure for a military structure that already exists. The ultimate goal was to consolidate the power of NATO and the United States over the Middle East. That is why Germany, America's senior partner in Europe, was determined to be involved[29].

The Roadmap of the Project—Institutions, Goals and Funding

The 13 July, 2008 Paris Summit brought together forty-two heads of states including the Israeli Prime Minister Ehud Olmert and the Syrian President Bachar Al Assad with the avowed purpose of promoting peace, though the much awaited symbolic handshake between the two did not occur. Syria has, however, agreed to open an Embassy in Lebanon. The Prime Minister of Turkey, Recep Tayyip Erdogan, the Lebanese President Michel Sleimane and Algerian President Abdel Aziz Bouteflika were notably present. The absence of the King of Morocco, Mohammed VI, reminded everyone of the tensions prevailing in the region. Apart from the twenty-seven EU member states, Albania, Algeria, Bosnia-Herzegovina, Croatia, Egypt, Israel, Jordan, Lebanon, Mauritania, Monaco, Montenegro, Syria, Tunisia, Turkey and the Palestinian Authority were represented.

With a population of 775 million people spread over 12.5 million kilometres and an estimated GDP of 18 000 billion dollars (in terms of purchasing power parity), the Union for the Mediterranean which has the legal status of an international organization will be heavier than the United States which has a 305 million strong population spread over 9.6 million kilometres and a GDP of 14 000 billion dollars per annum. But the income and population disparities are enormous between countries geographically bordering the Mediterranean and those which are not. Between the border countries themselves, there is a huge difference between the North (26 000 dollars GDP per capita) and the South (7000 dollars GDP per capita). But what is more significant is the fact is that the engine of the Union for the Mediterranean will be the EU which constitutes 64 per cent of the population and 86 per cent of GDP[30].

The summit adopted a declaration of nineteen pages (twenty in English)[31]. The administrative structure of the Union is rather light. Till the 31 December 2008 the French President Sarkozy and the Egyptian President Hosni Moubarek will copreside the Union. As far as the southern shoreline is concerned, the copresidence will be a term of two years. For the Northern shoreline, it will be the same rule as for the EU, i.e., rotating presidency of six months. However France will play a significant role during the next two presidencies which will be assumed by the Çzech Republic and Sweden. The copresidency is entrusted with the task of preparing the summits which will be held every two years.

The copresidence will be assisted by a secretariat comprising twenty members coming from the UPM member states and the secretariat of the Council of the European Union and the European Commission. There will be a secretary and a joint secretary whose term of office will be two years renewable once. The nature of their mission has not been clearly defined yet. The choice of the headquarters and the secretary general has not been made. However the names of cities like Marseille, Malta, Tunis and Barcelona have been floated.

The Paris Summit approved six projects. Cleaning up the Mediterranean has priority. Some one hundred and thirty sites have been identified and have to be cleaned up before 2020. The two billion euros needed, will be contributed by European Investment Bank, Agence française du développement and the World Bank. Issues like water management, access to drinking water and irrigation will be dealt with. The Solar Energy Plan comes next. Proposed by France with the awareness that only 10 per cent of the population living in the South of the Mediterranean Sea has access to energy, it aims at providing solar electricity to rural areas. Egyptians insisted on sea highways providing better connectivity along the Southern Mediterranean shore. Civil protection thanks to a better coordination of means to struggle against fire and natural catastrophes has also been foreseen. A Euro-Mediterranean university could be set up in Slovenia. The initiative in favour of SME is the last in the list[32].

The Copenhagen criteria such as respect of human rights and democracy or the promotion of the rights of women and minority, the struggle against racism and xenophobia were not laid down as prerequisites but as future goals. The approach was pragmatic and aimed at "creating a union of projects for the project of a union"[33] and insisted on the necessity to rely on concrete projects to weave solidarity among people. Another difference between the Barcelona Process and the UPM is, according to Guaino "not to heat-up Barcelona, but get rid of the bureaucracy and re-found Barcelona"[34].

There is optimism about financing the project. The sovereign states of the Arabic peninsula are supposed to contribute The regional banks as well as the European Bank for Reconstruction will be approached for help. President Sarkozy is planning to ask charities and private donors to step in. Nevertheless, the President of the European Parliament Hans-Gert Pöttering is asking for a financial audit of these projects.

Pros

The publicity around the summit is reinvigorating the Barcelona Process. Politically, the Union for the Mediterranean project goes further than the Barcelona Process and as such can help the Southern members come out of their isolation. It is also meant to dissuade the European Union from leaning too heavily on the Atlantic alliance. EU's Atlantic tilt occurred after the Iraq war when some of the new members of the enlarged EU supported the US whereas some old members such as France and Germany took a more prudent stand. The UMP project gives the EU the opportunity to show the world that it can build a truly unified European diplomacy and defence. For the time being, the United States is waiting and watching the European initiative in the area though it wants to keep the upper hand in the diplomatic and military game. If the project takes off substantially, then there might be some impatience.

The idea of joint ownership presupposes a two way relationship which means there is a give and take. The EU does not impose its agenda on them as it does with candidate countries. At the same time, it cannot put pressure on the Mediterranean countries to reform their economies and legal systems. The UPM project is inter-governmental and elite driven[35]. Jean Louis Guigou, a member of the aforementioned elite has this to say about the necessity for the two shores to meet: "Europe will otherwise become a big and old Switzerland and the Arab countries will be swept away by globalization as if they were mere confetti"[36].

Cons

The English language press reflected its anti-French sentiments when it called the UPM project Club-Med[37]. It was generally felt to be a grandiose French gesture with no real perspective of producing the expected outcome because of the huge diversity prevailing in the economies and societies of the members. On a very ordinary level, the protocolar difficulty in seating the members reflected the complexity of the task. Only the presidents of Egypt and Mauritania and the King of Jordan who maintained diplomatic relations with Israel could share the table with the Israeli Prime Minister at the summit.

The President of Senegal, Abdoulaye Wade was a very vocal critic of the project. "The UPM is an operation that aims at amputating the continent of its northern side"[38]. In other words, the EU was using North Africa to check the influx of immigrants from Black Africa. The Lybian President Mouammar Kaddafi was more explicit in his condemnation: "We are neither famished nor dogs for the Europeans to throw us some bones"[39]. The Arab Ligue for its part may lose its Mediterranean components which represent considerable demographic and economic weight. But Egypt has pointed out that there is no exclusion clause in either contract. Also Mauritania which is not strictly speaking a Mediterranean country has been invited to join by virtue of its cultural and economic links with the Maghrebi countries. However, Habib Boulares, ex-secretary of the *Union du Maghreb Arabe*, another regional organization, protested: "In diplomatic terms, it is signified to the *Union du Maghreb Arabe* countries, that you will only be our neighbours, a difficult suburb in a prosperous metropolis".[40]

Remarks on the timing were also made. "Africa has never been able to speak with one voice. One had to await the creation of the African Union to be able to do so. At the Lisbon EU-AU unity summit, we have managed to impose our strategic decision to have one sole representative: The AU Commission. This will be seriously challenged, if the UPM sees the light of day"[41].

The inherent difficulty of the project resides in the fact that it includes many well-known and conflict ridden areas such as Israel and Palestine, Syria and Lebanon, Greece and Turkey, North Cyprus and the Republic of Cyprus.

The unchecked progress of the UPM might alienate the Turkish population which has a choice between NATO and EU. It might indeed even turn to ultranationalism[42].

New memberships in NATO, EU or UPM might alter the geopolitical balance in the Balkans and isolate Serbia which might be tempted turn to Russia thus reproducing Cold War alignments[43]. As with Turkey, the problematic limits of a basis for adhesion based on geographical proximity can be discerned.

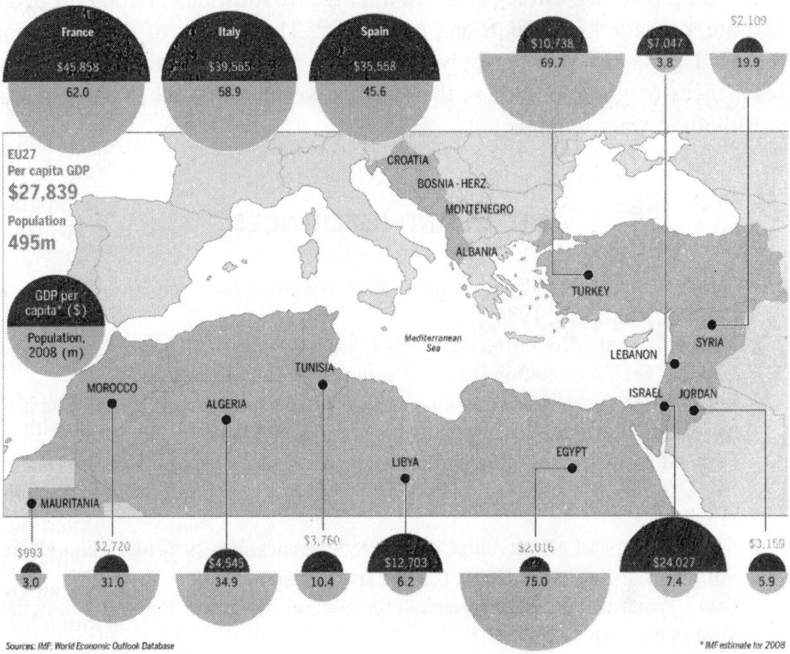

Figure under FT.com's copyright, used here as Quotation

Conclusion

International relations after the Second World War were determined by the balance of power principle. The Cold War led to an insidious nuclear arms race. The fall of communism gave rise to another paradigm—the West and the Islamic Other, prompting Samuel Huntington to predict civilizational clashes. Building regional blocs seemed to be one way of articulating solidarity far and above national allegiances. However, the inequitable distribution of the benefits of globalization and the more pressing need for environmental concerns have altered the picture. Future wars are going to be fought for access to water and energy. Environmental refugees are already rendering the substance of the Geneva Convention obsolete. In this context, trying to set up a Union for the Mediterranean with a view to pre-empting future conflicts and preventing natural catastrophes, amounts to common sense, if not to a grand political design. Albert Camus when he pleaded for the New Mediterranean Culture insisted on the fact that it should not become yet another form of imperialism. "We are here ... against Rome", he said before concluding that "the effort of human intelligence must be common property and not a source of conflicts and murders"[44]. The success of the Union for the Mediterranean will not only spell peace for the region but also send resonances of goodwill across the Muslim world which other parts of the world might want to emulate.

NOTES AND REFERENCES

1. Gunder Frank, *The World System: Five Hundred Years or Five Thousand*, London: Routledge, 1996.
2. Martin Bernal, *Black Athena: Afro-Asiatic Roots of Classical Civilization*, London: Free Association Books, 3 volumes reprinted 2004-06.
3. Max Müller, *India, What can it teach us?* New Delhi: Penguin, 2000. Can also be read on line at http://www.gutenberg.org/etext/20847
4. Fernand Braudel, Sian Reynolds. *The Mediterranean and the Mediterranean World in the age of Philip II*, Berkeley: University of California Press, 1996, Vol. 2, p. 826.
5. Albert Camus, «La Nouvelle Culture méditerranéenne» in *Œuvres complètes*, Vol.1, Paris: Gallimard, 2006, p. 569. Translation mine.
6. Jean Leymarie et al, *Méditerranée—De Courbet à Matisse*, Paris: Réunion des musées nationaux, 2001.
7. Interview of Bertrand Badie by Anthony Berginc, "Le projet de l'Union de la Méditerranée pourrait rééquilibrer le risque d'atlantisation de l'UE", *Le Monde*, 15th April 2008. http://www.lemonde.fr/web/chat/0,46-0@2-3214,55-1029964@51-1054225,0.html
8. Fawzia Zouari, «Il y a un siècle déjà » in *Jeune Afrique*, N°2478, 6-12 July 2008, p. 27.
9. Bertrand Badie interview in *Le Monde* cited above.
10. The Commonwealth of Nations has 53 members. http://www.thecommon wealth.org/
11. L'Organization internationale de la francophonie has 55 full members and 13 observors. http://www.francophonie.org/
12. This much criticized and controversial speech was written by Henri Guaino,

special adviser to Nicolas Sarkozy. The French original could be retrieved at http://www.afrik.com/article12199.html

13. http://www.u-m-p.org/site/index.php/s_informer/discours/nicolas_sarkozy_a_toulon
14. Mentioned in the entrée on "Union pour la Méditerrannée", Wikipedia. http://fr.wikipedia.org/wiki/Union_pour_la_M%C3%A9diterran%C3%A9e
15. Henri Guaino Interview by François Soudan & Pascal Airault, *Jeune Afrique*, N°2478, 6-12 July 2008, p.30.
16. http://www.fmes-france.net/IMG/pdf/union_de_la_mediterranee_prononce_1_.pdf
17. http://www.diplomatie.gouv.fr/fr/pays-zones-geo_833/afrique-du-nord-mediterranee_1062/appel-rome-pour-union-pour-mediterranee-france-italie-espagne-20.12.07_57998.html
18. http://www.diplomatie.gouv.fr/fr/europe_828/union-europeenne-monde_13399/relations-exterieures_853/union-pour-mediterranee_17975/discours-m.nicolas-sarkozy-devant-les-etudiants-institut-national-sciences-appliquees-technologie-30.04.2008_62792.html
19. John Laughland, "What Is Really Behind the Mediterranean Union?" in *Brussels Journal*, March 12, 2008. http://www.brusselsjournal.com/node/3083
20. http://sites.univ-provence.fr/veronis/Discours2007/transcript.php?n=Sarkozy&p=2007-05-03
21. http://ec.europa.eu/external_relations/euromed/index_en.htm
22. Alain Faujas, « Un processus de Barcelone anémique » in *Jeune Afrique*, N°2478, 6-12 July 2008, p. 24.
23. Bertrand Badie interview in *Le Monde* cited above.
24. Alain Faujas, *op. cit*., p. 25.
25. Roberto Aliboni, "The Charter for Peace and Stability in the Mediterranean", Instituto Affari Internazionali., March 1999.
26. Bertrand Badie interview in *Le Monde* cited above.
27. http://www.fmes-france.net/IMG/pdf/barcelona_process_union_for_the_mediterranean.pdf
28. US-Morocco Free Trade Agreement was signed on June 15, 2004. Trade and Investment Framework Agreements exist between US and Algeria (2001) and US and Tunisia (2002).
29. John Laughland, "What Is Really Behind the Mediterranean Union?" in *Brussels Journal*, March 12, 2008. http://www.brusselsjournal.com/node/3083
30. «L' Union pour la méditerranée dans tous ses états» in *Jeune Afrique*, N°2478, 6-12 July 2008, p. 35.
31. http://www.ue2008.fr/webdav/site/PFUE/shared/import/0713_declaration_de_paris/Joint_declaration_of_the_Paris_summit_for_the_Mediterranean-EN.pdf%20
32. Cécile Manciaux, «Des projets à la carte» in *Jeune Afrique*, N°2478, 6-12 July 2008, p. 25.
33. In the words of Ambassador Alain le Roy quoted in *Jeune Afrique*, N°2478, 6-12 July 2008, 28.

34. See Henri Guaino Interview by François Soudan & Pascal Airault in *Jeune Afrique* cited above, p. 31.
35. Tony Barber, "Scepticism abounds on Mediterranean club", *Financial Times*, July 10, 2008. http://www.ft.com/cms/s/0/d09b27cc-4e9a-11dd-ba7c-000077b07658.html
36. In the words of Jean-Louis Guigou, quoted in *Jeune Afrique*, N°2478, p. 28.
37. Stefan Simons, « Nicolas Sarkozy's New 'Club-Med'" in *Spiegel Online International*, 14 July 2008. http://www.spiegel.de/international/europe/0,1518,565667,00.html
38. Cherif Ouazani, « Une menace pour l'Afrique? » in *Jeune Afrique*, N°2478, p. 27.
39. Quoted in *Jeune Afrique*, N°2478, p.28.
40. Quoted in *Jeune Afrique*, N°2478, p.28.
41. Cherif Ouazani, «Une menace pour l'Afrique?» in *Jeune Afrique*, N°2478, p. 27.
42. Bertrand Badie interview in *Le Monde* cited above.
43. Bertrand Badie interview in *Le Monde* cited above.
44. Albert Camus, *op. cit*., p. 572. Translation mine.

14

Thou Shouldst be Living at this Hour! Milton as a Champion of Human Rights

P. MARUDANAYAGAM

That Milton is one of the greatest poets is common knowledge, but what is not so well known is that as an outstanding revolutionary genius in the form and content of his work, he was far ahead of his time in his championship of human rights. Being a child at once of the Renaissance and the Reformation, he combined in himself an intense love of art, music and literature and an extraordinary thirst for mental liberty. Though, in belief, he belonged to the extreme Puritans, called Separatists, Independents and Congregationalists, he was reluctant to identify himself with any particular sect and refused to be bound by any creed. His faith in the Puritan principles, the liberty of the individual soul before God, was so overwhelming that he rejected every form of external authority—secular or religious. Even at a very young age, he felt he was answerable to none but God and made it known to the world in his Sonnet «On His Having arrived at the Age of Twenty-Three»:

> All is, if I have grace to use it so,
> As ever in my great Task-Master's eye.[1]

Northrop Frye rightly observes that Milton will, «if society is relatively secure and at peace, devote himself to making poems out of the Christian vision of life; but, if society is in crisis, he will turn to prose and fight for liberty». (Frye: ix). It is true that the conception of liberty was the central theme of the vast corpus of his prose and emancipation from the tyranny of Kings and prelates, his major concern. Moreover, Milton was neither an armchair theologian breathing fire and brimstone nor a writer living in an ivory tower avoiding to take note of the unpleasant happenings in the lives of his countrymen. When, as a young man, he was travelling in Italy, which rekindled his old desire to leave an epic which posterity would not willingly let die, news reached him of the fight between King and Parliament in his motherland. Throwing caution to the winds and forgetting his dreams, he gave up his travels and rushed back to England to join the fight for human freedom. «For I thought it base», he writes, «to be travelling at my ease for intellectual culture while my fellow countrymen at home were fighting for liberty». During the next twenty years, most of what came from his pen was prose in the cause of freedom—violent denunciations of well-entrenched oppressors and powerful pleas for basic human rights. He did not participate in the civil war but engaged himself whole-heartedly in a service not less hazardous to himself and more beneficial to his fellow-citizens.

Later, when he was solicited to write a reply to Salmasius's *Defensio Regia Pro Carlo I*, praised by the Royalists as an invincible argument, he unhesitatingly undertook the task, though at the risk of losing the sight of his second eye.

> I would not have listened to the voice even of Esculapius himself from the shrine of Epidauris in preference to the suggestions of the heavenly monitor within my breast; my resolution was unshaken, though the alternative was either the loss of my sight, or the desertion of my duty. (p. 154)

Before the work was finished, he did become totally blind. This was not all. In the last part of his life, he could not enjoy his well-earned retirement but was relentlessly persecuted by the wicked monarch, Charles II and reduced to poverty. Though blind, disheartened, shamed, dishonoured and quelled, he did not fell frustrated but continued with missionary zeal the task of serving mankind by stressing, in immortal poems, the freedom of human will, a subject that had always been dear to his heart.

In one of his pamphlets, Milton divides liberty into three categories—religious, domestic and civil, relating the Church government, family and public life respectively. He was of the view that God wills liberty for man that if man submits himself to God he gains liberty and that none can love liberty heartily but good men. To Milton, the Church is a community in which all the members are made free and equal by their faith and spiritual authority has no power to coerce and cannot take the form of an institutional hierarchy. The Bible, designed to free man from a state of slavery, must be interpreted by the rule of charity; any passage in it, if it appears to approve the slavery of man, has only been wrongly interpreted. The core of Milton's theology is that God desires only the free love of man. This means that according to Milton, human creatures are extremely free to act. Those who speak of his «Turkish contempt for Women» should realise that in his conception God is female as well as male. Muse Urania, whom he invokes more than once, is presented as a specifically Christian inspiring power.

It is extremely unjust and totally wrong to view Milton's *Doctrine and Discipline of Divorce* as a work solely motivated by his unfortunate first marriage or as his selfish justification of his separation from his first wife. Milton felt compelled to chastise Churches for their uncharitable conceptions of scripture. In the doctrine of divorce, he was ready to fight for the right of any ill-starred couple against the law and the Church which insisted that man and wife are permanently joined altogether by God. Marshalling arguments from theology, scripture and history, he contended that no effect of tyranny can sit more heavily on the Commonwealth than that of this household unhappiness. Moses allowed for divorce in the marriage law but if Jesus declared marriage to be indissoluble it is because marriage as Jesus sees it is like the innocent love of Adam and Eve during the prelapsarian days. The law of marriage, on the contrary, relates only to a sexual union in the fallen world and, therefore, divorce must always be a part of marriage law. A divorce is necessary in the absence of the gospel marriage, the lifetime companionship. Milton attacks the ecclesiastical view of marriage and the Church as a force making for tyranny within the state:

> He who wisely would restrain the reasonable soul of man within due bounds, must first himself know perfectly, how far the territory and dominion extends of just and honest liberty. As little must he offer to find that which God hath loosened, as to loosen that which he hath bound. (p. 455)

Areopagitica, the most vigorous plea in English for the freedom of the writer to express his views on any subject of his choice, counters the licensing ordinance of a predominantly Presbyterian Parliament forbidding the publication of books until they were approved by the official censor, who, holding his office and salary by favour, would be naturally concerned with the divine right of Kings and bishops. Milton believed that education alone will enable man to preserve his freedom and that the individuals who have attained this state are duty bound to free others by their writings. In order to stress this idea, he begins his masterpiece with a poetic utterance by Euripides:

> This is true liberty, when free-born men, having to advise the public, may speak free, which he who can, and will, deserves praise; what can be given juster in a state than this? (p. 460)

Milton's defence of man's right to express what he desires to is strikingly modern and far-reaching in its consequences. Books are not dead things but do contain a potency of life in them; they can create as well as destroy. But he who kills a man kills a reasonable creature while he who destroys a book destroys reason itself. Just as the knowledge of good and evil cannot defile, if the will and conscience are not already defiled, no book, however wicked it may be, can contaminate the soul, if it is not already contaminated. A fugitive and cloistered virtue that does not know the utmost that vice promises to its adherents and rejects it is but a blank virtue, not a pure one. To all men, books are neither temptations nor vanities, but useful drugs with which to tamper and compose effective and strong medicines. God created passions within us, pleasures round about us so that rightly tempered they may be the very ingredients of virtue. If, by banning some books, a nation can become virtuous, what about Italy and Spain? Have they become, «one scruple the better, the honester, the wiser, the charter, since all the inquisitional rigour that hath been executed upon books»? (p. 482) What is the advantage of being a man over being a boy at school if we have only escaped the rod to come under the yoke of an Imprimatur? If a man believes something just because his pastor has said it or the Assembly has determined it, without caring for any other reason, even if his belief were true, it becomes his heresy. Where there is a desire to learn, there will be much arguing, much writing and many opinions and opinion of an intelligent man is but knowledge in the making.

Presenting his arguments with force, conviction and artistry, Milton tells the lords and commons that liberty is the nurse of all great wits and that it rarefies and enlightens our spirits like the influence of heaven. Hence, he appeals to them on behalf of the entire nation, on behalf of mankind:

> Give me the liberty to know, to utter, and to argue freely according to conscience, above all liberties. (p. 489)

If he is at his best in *Areopagitica*, he is fierce, vituperative, full of energy and conviction in his fight against monarchy, especially, in his defence of the execution of Charles I. Boldly rejecting the contemporary belief in the divine right theory, he contends that kings derive their authority from the people and are, like any other human being, subject to the eternal principle of law. It is lawful to call to account a tyrant or a wicked king and after due conviction, to depose and to put him to death. When a book entitled *Eikon Basilike* (Royal Image), presenting a rosy picture of the Kings' piety and condemning his Puritan enemies, attracted the attention of the public and threatened to become the gospel of the royalists, Milton rose to the occasion launching his *Eikonoklastes* (Image Breaker), which easily demolished all the claims of its rival.

It is in «The Second Defence of the People of England» written as a reply to an anonymous libel called «The Royal Blood Crying to Heaven for Vengeance on the English Parricides» that he convincingly vindicates the rights of the English nation and of liberty itself. Praising the English nation for its most courageous deed and identifying its honour with his own, he asks,

> And what can conduce more to the beauty or glory of one's country, than the recovery, not only of its civil but its religious liberty? And what nation or state ever obtained both, by more successful or more valorous exertion? (p. 507)

He expresses his hope that Britain, formerly styled the hot-bed of tyranny, now deserves to be glorified as a soil most congenial to the growth of liberty. Here a prophetic statement, which may now be read ironically, occurs:

> I now imagine that, from the columns of Hercules to the Indian Ocean, I behold the nations of the earth recovering that liberty which they so long had lost; and that the people of this island are transporting to other countries a plant of more beneficial qualities, and more noble growth, than that which Triptolemus is reported to have carried from region to region; that they are disseminating the blessings of civilization and freedom among cities, kingdoms and nations. (p. 510)

While generously acknowledging the services of Oliver Cromwell as the chief of the English army, as the leader of their councils and as the author, the guardian and the preserver of their liberties, Milton asks him to keep in mind what a dear pledge the beloved land of his nativity has entrusted to his care and to always remember that he cannot be free unless his country men are free too and that he who entrenches on the liberty of others is the first to lose his own and become a slave. Milton does not mince words while warning the Protector of the Commonwealth against taking a wrong step:

> But if you, who have hitherto been the patron and tutelary genius of liberty, if you, who are exceeded by no one in justice, in piety, and goodness, should hereafter invade that liberty which you have defended, your conduct must be fatally operative, not only against the cause of liberty, but the general interests of piety and virtue. Your integrity and virtue will appear to have evaporated, your faith in religion to have been small, your character with posterity will dwindle into insignificance, by which a most destructive blow will be levelled against the happiness of mankind. (p. 527)

When the Commonwealth began to totter after the death of Cromwell, Milton, in «The Ready and Easy Way to Establish a Free Commonwealth», spoke of the dreadful consequences if an Anglican monarchy was allowed to be restored. He insisted that the good old cause of the Republic would be undermined by Kings, who, never forgetting their former humiliation, would certainly strengthen and arm themselves for the future against all such attempts by the people. As an alternative, he recommended the establishment of a Grand Council of able men chosen by the public in order to safeguard both civil and religious liberty. He even had the courage of conviction and the foresight to propose the introduction of a kind of federalism based on county assemblies subordinate to a national parliament.

Though civil, religious and domestic rights are Milton's favourite themes in prose, they are not completely forgotten in his major and minor poems. During the early 1640s, he gathered a lot of material for an epic poem on ancient kingly heroism but was so upset by the sins of modern monarchs that he abandoned the idea and used most of it in his prose *History of Britain* which, actually, laments the miserable failure of Britons and Saxons to preserve their ancient liberties. Some of his Sonnets explicitly plead for religious liberty. When a group of clergymen submitted a brief to a parliamentary committee appointed by Cromwell to look into the state of the Church, the spirit of the appeal being in favour of intolerance and clerical censorship, Milton came out with a Sonnet addressed to «our chief of men», which, in the first part, praises Cromwell's faith, fortitude and famed military successes, but, the second part, demands civil action with a view to protecting the rights of dissenters to free themselves from the clutches of any established state Church:

> Peace hath her victories no less renowned than war; new foes arise, threatening to bind our souls with secular chains, help us to save free conscience from the paw of hireling wolves, whose gospel is their maw. (p. 368)

Another Sonnet, «On the Late Massacre in Piedmont», recaptures Milton's righteous indignation at the massacre of Waldensian Protestants by the Duke of Savoy on Easter Day, 1655 and calls for divine retribution on behalf of the Waldensians who had been in existence since the twelfth century and became Protestants at the Reformation:

> Avenge, O Lord, they slaughtered saints, whose bones Lie scattered on the Alpine mountains cold; Even them who kept thy truth so pure of old, When all our fathers worshipped stocks and stones. (p. 369)

Even though «Comus» is apparently about the temptation of a young lady by an evil spirit, the ultimate import of the poem is that ignorance is slavery and enlightenment emancipation. The lady's chastity, as some critic has explained, is the condition of life on the upper or spiritual level, enabling one to possess the joy and freedom that will satisfy a human being. The passion that Comus preaches is nothing but slavery to desire and lust. At the end of the masque, the attendant spirit emphasis the value of this kind of freedom to be cherished by every human being:

> Mortals, that would follow me, Love virtue, she alone is free. She can teach ye how to climb higher than the sphery chime; Or if virtue feeble were, Heaven itself would stoop to her. (p. 357)

Milton's magnum opus, *Paradise Lost* written during the days of his political disillusionment caused by the restoration of monarchy, is in one sense the story of how man lost his liberty and how he can regain it if only his will is in accordance with the will of God. After the fall, Adam is told that Satan will be reborn in every tyrant, every over reacher ambitious of earthly power. The poem presents Satan in such a way that the rebellion of the devil may be easily mistaken for a heroic fight for liberation. Some of his utterances do reflect the indomitable Puritan spirit, the Puritan love for liberty that sent the Pilgrim Fathers to a far-off place in the wilds of America to found a free Commonwealth:

> Here at least We shall be free; the Almighty hath not built Here for his envy will not drive us hence; Here we may reign secure; and in my choice to reign is worth ambition, though in Hell; Better to reign in Hell than serve in Heaven.

It has also been pointed out that the poem, though an epic, provides scope for a reader's unimpeded freedom of interpretation. He is permitted to exercise the principle of rational liberty and explore freely the meaning of religious experience. Though the narrator underlines certain assumptions, the epic voice does not attempt to narrowly enforce meaning. This has given rise to varied responses by readers. Though Milton would not have approved of some of them and would have been shocked by one or two, he would not have denied the right of any reader to interpret the poem the way he likes to.

Samson Agonistes, the list of Milton's major works, beautifully sums up his life and work. The great Israelite hero of the classical tragedy, enslaved by Philistines treacherously, cannot free himself but destroys the temple of his enemies, a symbol of ignorance and superstition. But before his tragic demise, Samson could successfully resist all the temptations—his father willing to offer ransom, his wife seeking reconciliation, a giant attempting to bully him. These only remind us of the poet's lifelong fight against domestic, religious and civil tyranny in all their diverse manifestations, urged by a disinterested passion for the extension of human rights

NOTES AND REFERENCES

1. All the citations are from Northrop Frye, ed. *John Milton and Selected Poetry and Prose*, New York: Holt, Rinehart and Winston, 1951.

15

Redefining the European Balance between Sovereignty and Human Rights in Kosovo

IVER B. NEUMANN

> Humanity does not gradually progress from combat to combat until it arrives at universal reciprocity, where the rule of law finally replaces warfare; humanity installs each of its violences in a system of rules and thus proceeds from domination to domination.
>
> —*Michel Foucault*

The Weberian principle of the state as possessing a legitimate monopoly on violence seems to be failing. Sovereigns no longer hold this monopoly; it now belongs to the international community. Basic human rights are being defined as universal principles that transcend sovereignty. If war is seen as the extension of politics by other means, then there are three crucial questions to be asked about its legitimacy. First, which actors are seen as legitimate wagers of war, and whom? Secondly, over which kinds of issues is it legitimate to intensify politics by going to war (*ius ad bellum*)? And thirdly, which are the legitimate ways of waging war? Expanding on a framework suggested by the Copenhagen School of International Relations, the article argues that the Kosovo war is a crucial part of two ongoing shifts. First, the actors going to war are increasingly states acting in alliance, and in the name of humanity. Secondly, war is legitimated less by reference to the safeguarding of state citizens and their well-being, and more in terms of infringements on human rights. It is further argued that one vital precondition for this shift is that, with the left-right divide which used to structure politics during the last two hundred years on the wane, there is only one camp left which has the resources legitimately to represent "humanity". In Kosovo, states going to war as NATO represented themselves as "humanity", the implication being that Serbia was cast as an enemy not only of human rights, but also of humanity as such.

There is an irony here, inasmuch as the kind of state infringement which NATO worked on Serbia by going to war over its internal politics was itself considered a *casus belli* only twenty years. In Kosovo, it was actually Serbia which embodied traditional thinking about the legitimacy of war, and NATO which embodied the break with that tradition. Serbia appears, therefore, as a living reminder of how that nation state which was considered normal not too long used to act. The abhorrence of Serbia to NATO states is partly an abhorrence of seeing a version of one's own state self.

The Copenhagen School and Violization

It is unlikely that war will disappear as a form of intensified conflicts between different human collectives. Sometimes such conflicts result in the use of violence, which is in turn met with violence. As a consequence war becomes a reality, and organised violence forces itself into our *repertoire* of social possibilities. War is a continuation of politics with other means.

Politics is, among other things, an ongoing negotiation of who 'we' are. Since a 'we' is untenable without a relationship to a group of 'theys,' the political question of who 'we' are is in fact a matter of separating 'us' from 'them.' To use Carl Schmitt's formulation, it is a question of separating friend from enemy.[1] In light of this, the question of war may be recast as one of how certain symbolic economies—certain packages of elements of a story of self as well as the relations between them—work to produce war as an outcome of ever more sharply defined friend/enemy relations. Over the last decade, the Copenhagen School has concentrated on expanding the referents of security from states and individuals to society, and on analysing how political concerns come to be treated as security concerns. As Ole Waever described in the published version of the 1988 paper that launched the concept of securitization, "State security has sovereignty as its ultimate criterion, and societal security has identity. Both usages imply survival. A state that loses its sovereignty does not survive as a state; a society that loses its identity fears that it will no longer be able to live as itself".[2] A major problem with this dichotomization, which I am quick to point out definitely has its uses in opening up the debate on the referents of security, is in fact detrimental effect on questions of war. The declaration of war, after all, is still an activity where states play a crucial role. While societies and society-level groups may continue to be active in a number of ways, both before and after the declaration of war, interesting gray areas emerge when a state's representation of self can no longer be easily represented.

The Copenhagen School argues that what it refers to as securitization can be thought of as an extension of politicization:

> [I]ssues become securitized when leaders (whether political, societal, or intellectual) begin to talk about them—and to gain the ear of the public and the state—in terms of existential threats against some valued referent object. Securitization can thus be seen as a more extreme version of politicization. It is the intersubjective establishment of an existential threat with a saliency sufficient to have substantial political effects. In theory, a public issue can be located on the spectrum ranging from non-politicized (meaning that the state doesn't deal with it, and it is not in any other way made an issue of public debate and decision); through politicized (meaning that the issue is part of public policy, requiring government decision and resource allocation or more rarely some other form of communal governance); to securitized (meaning that the issue is presented as an existential threat requiring emergency measures, and justifying actions outside the normal bounds of political procedure). In principle, the placement of issues on this spectrum is open; depending on circumstances, any issue can end up on any part of the spectrum (Buzan 1997:14).

Politicization is a matter of inscribing certain differences between self and other with meaning as the defining diacritics of self and other. That is, certain differences which have so far not been activated as part of the political, are being politicized, which makes it possible retrospectively to talk about them as having been "non-politicized" before they were "politicized".

Securitization, on the other hand, includes the added burden of defining what constitutes the security politics of a certain human collective in establishing political diacritics. Waever, who subscribes to a Schmittian definition of the political as a question of separating "friend" from "foe" (see above), tends to think about security as existential or ontological politics—that is, the political at its most political: the questions of telling friend from enemy, the defining of who "we" are and, functionally, the threats to who "we" are.

The theorem proposed is thus that issues can be non-politicized, politicized or securitized, and that there exist four processes known respectively as politicization, de-politicization, securitization, and de-securitization. An identity, for example, may be securitized by speech which inscribes the identity with meaning in terms of security politics, and may also be de-securitized by speech unsubscribing such a representation.

Emphasizing the importance of speech to the process of securitization, the Copenhagen School highlights the constructed, intrasubjective character of the concept of security and hence also of the *modus operandi* of security politics. Using the concept of discourse in order to de-differentiate words and action and analyze them separately, the School has advanced convincing work. The outbreak of war may, of course, also be conceptualized as a speech act, such as the case when the words "I hereby declare war" is indeed going to war (provided one's institutional station and preparations are appropriate). The actual waging of war, however, requires more than speech declaring war: it requires the use of force, or a violization of politics.[3] Waging war is, by definition, not only a question of speech, but also of actions. A crucial role in war involves the action of killing, and more generally, the acts of violence which literally inscribe the will of one collectively onto the physical bodies making up the body politic of another human collective. There is a reason why the number of people killed—be that 317 or 1000, almost always becomes the defining trait of what war is.[4]

Actually, there are intimations inside the Copenhagen School itself that a speech act perspective is hardly sufficient as a focus of political analysis. For example, Waever quotes Clausewitz to the effect that "War is an act of violence pushed to its utmost bounds" (quoted in Waever 1995: 53). When war-like activity does not include acts of violence, they are referred to by modifiers, such as "wars of position" and "cold wars." In order to link the work of the Copenhagen School to the outbreak of war, it may be useful to differentiate the concept of securitization, reserving that concept for those acts of speech which perform the tasks Buzan, Waever and others have assigned it, and subsequently adding a new category for cases where large-scale violence is actually in evidence.

We can best apply the Copenhagen School's framework to this question by defining the threshold between securitization and violization as the point of the outbreak of war itself (violence on a certain scale) rather than at the point where an individual dies. This is not to deny that a certain identity is already violized in situations such as an asylum center being arsonized, resulting in death, but simply to acknowledge that the question of scale must be addressed. It is not societal security and the identity/society nexus which is under consideration here, but identity and war, and I will argue that this question still implicates the state very directly. Thus, for this purpose, societal violence which is not intended to impinge on the question of state borders may be bracketed, and attention focused on cases where the issue is the representation of states. In this way, Clausewitz's formulation of war being the continuation of politics by other means can be directly classified, both directly and indirectly, within the Copenhagen School framework of politicization and securitization. If we add the category of "violized" to the three already in circulation in the Copenhagen School, and introduce the two corresponding processes of "violization" and "de-violization", we get the following extended continuum: Non-politicized—politicized—securitized—violized.

An obvious case to which the proposed extended continuum could be applied would be the war in Kosovo.[5] We have in this situation a number of cases where national identities became not only securitized, but also violized. Serb and Croatian national identities, Bosniak political identity and Muslim religious identity provide suitable examples. By contrast, Macedonian and Albanian ethnic identities were securitized but not violized (again, the suggested use of the term "violized" applying only when violence takes place on a certain scale). It would be interesting indeed if it can be demonstrated that the outbreaks and non-outbreaks of war can usefully be analyzed in terms of violization of identity. If it turns out that the structure of identities was not a crucial factor in the outbreaks of these wars, then this would also prove insightful.

War as Legitimate Violization of Politics

It is, however, a different aspect of the war in Kosovo which becomes a crucial concern when the problematique is who can *legitimately* wage war. For the last five hundred years or so, this function has fallen to states, and states have orchestrated a legal discourse which consecrates their going to war in certain circumstances, over certain issues. When fought by states in accordance with this *ius ad bello*, war has been a legitimate form of violization (inside the international law discourse). In Kosovo, however, two phenomena may be observed. First, although in accordance with the discourse of international law, states were still the actors to go to war, thc relevance of this discourse for the work of legitimation which was carried out by the instigators of war was not deemed to be wide ranging enough for it to stand alone. Additional legitimacy was sought by foregrounding how it was an *alliance* of states which went to war, and how the war itself should be seen as contributing to a *change* in the discoure of international law, and not simply as a case of following its rules. The war in Kosovo, that is, was represented as being constitutive of a new era. This change in *who* could legitimately wage war (alliances of states acting as self-proclaimed representatives of humanity), was intimately linked to the question of which *issues* it was legitimate to go to war for (alleged infringements of human rights, that is, the rights of the constituent members of humanity).

This constituted a breach with tradition of epochal character. In the seventeenth century Europe, the framework defining spiritual life—Protestant or Catholic—was central when defining military goals. In the eighteenth century wars evolved around disputes over inheritance and land, whereas the

Napoleonic wars added the type of regime—republican or monarchic—to them. An illustrative example of this tendency appears in the Yugoslavian communist Milovan Djilas' memoirs, in which he refers to a conversation held with Stalin in 1945.[6] This war is not like other wars, Stalin said to Djilas; the conqueror spreads his political system as far as his men can go. It cannot be any other way. The major point here for our purposes is the *plurality* of actors involved in constituting the major conflict line at any one time in the history of the European states system: two during the 17th century, many during the 18th and 19th centuries, again two during the 20th century. What has with reference to the US being the only superpower around been called the "unipolar moment", is also a unipolar moment when it comes to the number of systems-constituting identity projects available. There is only one: liberal globalization—and its negatives. This is an important condition for how human rights can emerge as a key legitimising resource, and so I will return to this problematique below.

The Kosova war defined the epoch exactly because it focused on the simultaneously existing conflict lines upon which politics are constituted. Since the end of the 17th century political life has centred around two great themes; the economic division between classes, and the question about which community in the nation the state rests upon. There is a tension between these two considerations. The existence of classes, understood as groups of people with different connections to the means of production, gave rise to divisions within the state. Today's European party system is still first and foremost the result of the previously existing struggle between classes about the economic distribution of wealth. The right-left axis was the political framework of industrial society. Conservative, liberal and socialist ideology spoke to a reality dominated by the agencies of social classes—understood as groups of individuals related to the means of production—clear enough that one could talk about a natural categorisation of people between "left" and "right". Politics needed this type of categorisation in order to operate. Politics is both a conflict and an arrangement to facilitate the solution to this conflict; the order is etymologically bound to the Greek *polemos*, war.

However, politics can also be traced to another Greek word, *polis*. In our context the point to retain is that politics turns itself around conflict, and the existence of the city state is dependent on the ability to restrict or apply this notion to the community. Therefore, it is not accidental that the emergence of industrial society had as its accompaniment the emergence of the nation. The industrial society established new social divisions casting worker against bourgeoisie, nationalism offering both groups a new community that they could attach themselves to, a community that bound them together and gave them a framework within which they could quarrel about material goods without experiencing the conflict as if they were two wholly different groups.

Between socialism and nationalism a connection was thereby established, one that served a complementary purpose. As we know this constellation of classes and nations gave rise to two different programmes for modernisation; communism which would solve the problem through the elimination of classes, and nationalism which would solve the problem by inserting political parenthesises around the classes. The Cold War was the end point for this development in two respects. Firstly, in "our" area of the world the connection between classes and the means of production dissolved. The struggle between socialism and capitalism, between east and west, was portrayed as a struggle between classes. In the modern west, however, the proletariat no longer exist as a production community, and the Soviet state as the kernel in the proletariats own international order has disappeared. The carpet has been taken away under the feet of the main principle of the organization of politics both at the national and international level.

This can of course be celebrated. It is potentially liberating for politics that the old order principles are disappearing. But, the end of the Cold War had another and less welcome consequence. As was earlier maintained, politics needs conflict in order to function—the Cold War evolved around the idea of conflict and conflict solution. Conflicts must be arranged in circumstances and around fundamental dividing lines that can be disputed for a long time. The right-left axis served as such a mechanism until lately, for both the national and international order. But what happens when this axis no longer exists in the same form as before? With the extinction of the right-left axis, nationalism once again stands alone. The historical nationalism was an ideology which worked as the political foundation of the right-left matrix, yet it is now about to become itself the matrix for political life. The political struggle which really caused problems was not formulated as an economic redistribution question, but as a question about who we are, and it is exactly this question that nationalism has an answer for. In this context it is not a coincidence that the Balkan War of the 1990s in the former Yugoslavia was fought out directly between ethnic groups, but the previous civil conflict, in the wake of the Second World War, was fought out between proletarian and middle class partisans. It follows that, in order to mediate between these ethnic tensions, one needs a multiethnic rhetoric, and no longer a class rhetoric. Therefore, resistance to war developed first and foremost as a programme in favour of a common multi-ethnic society and against nationalism (and not, as it did 50 years ago in the case of the communist partisans, as a class rhetoric).

This same pattern can be identified in the international context. The drama being enacted in the Maghreb lands can be portrayed as having the character of a struggle between land and town, between proletariat and town elite, but it is formed in principle as a struggle between the local and the global. To quote a book title, it is a case of *Jihad versus McWorld.*[7] And these two political powers work together, like all constellations, in order that politics may function. The so-called fundamentalist Islamic opposition in Maghreb and the politicians who mobilise ethnicity in the former Yugoslavia are, among other things, reacting to increasing globalization. And these reactions take above all a national identity. The *jihad*, at its starting point was inextricably connected to the concept of a universal religion, in itself a form of essentialism, which has evolved historically to take on key nationalist traits. Globalization has evolved as a threat against this nationalism, which is now arming itself to fight against "post nationalism". Here we have the new main axis which will order our political lives.

The reactions against globalization will of course vary. What they have in common, however, is the local support for the nation, which you find within certain groups. Nation states in Europe were similar, and its bearers thought of them as being of a kind, because they all adhered to a common idea, namely that those who shared a cultural community, should also share a political one. They had a project in common, even if they did not have a common project. The same may be said about today's opposition against integration and globalization in the name of the classic nation state. Furthermore, in Europe, given that the European Union is reality, the structural similarity between the traditional platforms from which the Union is being opposed make for a structurally conflict everywhere. Those who welcome globalization, also, as a rule, welcome integration, while those who oppose one generally oppose the other as well.

If national/post-national as a political main axis has replaced the right-left axis, then we will see immediate negative consequences influencing the possibility of constructing a consensus. As long as the right-left axis predominated, the main concern within politics was with economic distribution. And to handle such question there exists a medium which is eminently divisible; money. The so-called class compromises could be operationalized in the form of the redistribution of money. Furthermore, it was possible to operate with a far-reaching social mobility. The adherence to the notion of class may serve as a mechanism for manipulation. One could change the factors determining one's class: position, language, address etc. Ethnic belonging, however, is not so easy to change. The markers that define ethnic identity can be difficult to manipulate. They can, however, be acknowledged as more or less politically relevant. If nationalism is determining politics, and nationalism manifests itself in such a way, that people with one or another colour cannot be a member of that nation, then the outlook for social mobility is extremely marginal. And yet, at the same time, there is no obvious medium to be used so as to effect compromises between different ethnic groups, the same way as money could be used between classes. Money can change one's job, language and address, but not one's colour of skin. Classes used to be socially complementary: where purges took place within certain classes, as in the erstwhile Soviet Union, the whole society deteriorated as a result. Ethnic groups are not complementary in themselves. Ethnic cleansing can be carried out without the society immediately collapsing functionally (as the Czech example shows, however, ethnic cleansing can produce long term morally demolishing effects: one is still troubled after the purge of the Sudeten-Germans.)

To sum up: liberal globalization is left as the only political programme with a global appeal. It feeds opposition, but that opposition takes local forms and has so far taken the shape of negatives of globalization (ethnic and religious revivalism, nationalism etc.) What shape globalization will take and how effectively it will spread is not the issue here. The claim I want to push is that it constitutes a major precondition for NATO to easily represent itself as the guardian of human rights in the Kosovo war, and, in extension, to even pose as the representative of humanity as such. There simply was no major force around to issue a counter-claim.

The Ontologification of War

War is a matter of who we are, and how we are supposed to continue to exist. This aspect of war can be more or less central, possessing a radically different meaning for the two sides participating in a conflict. The stronger one side feels towards the fact that "we" can no longer be "we" if "we" loose the war, the more fundamental is the conflict perceived. We have, from the Ancient Greece, several examples of how defeat in war meant that women and children were taken as slaves and the men executed. The rationale in some wars is thereby still the physical existence of one of the combatants. It is rarely so radical, but the American tradition to demand the enemy's "unconditional surrender", is a reminder that such absolutism is still strongly evident in the thinking of our time. One can imagine a spectrum running from Hegel's way of approaching war—as a situation where right stands against right—to the (mainly) Catholic tradition about "just war", in which it is perceived that one side is fighting for the good, whilst the other often is cast as evil.[8] Developments in the 1990s indicate that we are moving towards this latter understanding of war. The notion of a just war was once again raised as a part of the discussion. This perspective has certain advantages to it; it furnishes an opportunity to talk about war in a way, in which the moral aspects are being emphasized. The danger, however, is that one can easily demonize the enemy. Just war becomes Holy war. Not least where legal discourse is concerned, Kosovo may entail that a large step will be taken in the direction of undermining the adversary head of state's legitimate position. Earlier, one looked upon a head of state as the symbolic head of the adversary. This was a person, if the surrender was not unconditional, who was to become an important negotiating partner. Whereas today, referring to the international order, it is possible to issue a warrant if the head of state does not seem symphathetic. War becomes more a question of good versus bad, and less of a way to settle disputes between two contradictory laws. Kosovo demonstrated this trend.

One could say a number of positive things about the moral commitment to a just war and to the evolution of humanitarian law on concerning war crimes. After Auschwitz, the Gulag and Srebrenica, it is difficult to defend a point of view saying that there is no evil in politics. There are situations, in which it is legitimate to talk about an evil opponent. But, although it is tempting to succumb to the temptation of passing such a judgment, the act must be postponed as long as possible. Even when it has been passed one must never cease to doubt whether the judgment is right, and how many individual members of the collective enemy it is legitimate to include. The moralization that takes place is not necessarily taking these circumstances into consideration, and induces great expense. What follows is an intensification of what is at stake. For both parts, war becomes, as a consequence of moralization, more a question of who we are, and concerns less specific war goals such as the territorial redistribution of material resources among different groups in society, or the securing of strategically important resources. It is more difficult to negotiate with an opponent about who "we" are, than about specific resources, for the simple reason that resources can be divided into smaller pieces, about which one can reach compromise. In contrast, one can not divide identities in the same way.

If war is going to be legitimated as a case of how humanity itself is emerging as a political community, then they are a case of good fighting evil, and it is of less interest to ask how the war goals are being perceived by the opponent, because he has already been cast in the subject position of evil itself. The thought behind a "just war" has the disadvantage, that one is not continuously evaluating the way in which the other side looks upon the world and its tactics. One knows the nature of the evil and knows that it is impossible to influence it by arguments, but, only with resolute action such as war.

The Other Side

A discourse which has no subject position for others than "humanity", is a totalizing discourse. It is always worth asking where the other is, and how the relationship is perceived. The case of Yugoslavia can be no exception. When one is to defend the old order, such a defence manifests itself in the purest form. Milosevic's Yugoslavia illustrates for us the ultimate consequences of the national doctrine that rejects everything and anyone who does not belong to the nation. Before we reject this as unfamiliar, we should remember that this was a creative part of the European political order for 200 years. It is *pathos* in the war in Kosovo. The old has no possibility of victory. As Karl Otto Hondrich stated in *Die Zeit* (27 May, 1999): the Serb military are not permitted to fight on equal terms, and thereby it is only by not retreating that they can win the respect and dignity that fighting embodies.

Milosevic is a classic sovereign. Indeed, the notions of sovereignty, the right of self-determination and the right to determine one's own internal affairs dominate Serb discourse. Milosevic can hardly be expected to enjoy the fading of that pivotal principle of the classic European states system: the immunity of sovereigns. In Serb discourse, the fading of that principle from the Second World War aftermath at the tribunals of Tokyo and Nuremberg via the formation of a body of humanitarian law to the founding of the International Criminal Court and beyond is doggedly discounted. NATO's policy is portrayed as that of an aggressor, culminating in the intrusion into other people's affairs. The main pillar in the Serbian national policy is the nation state, a state which they want to protect against interference and aggression from outside. There is, of course, a problem connected to where to draw the borders for this nation state: for many Serbs, the Serbian "we" are connected to Greater Serbia. But, aggression against areas outside Greater Serbia has never been on the agenda. The parallel often being drawn to Hitler, has therefore a fatal weakness, namely that it has never been a question of Serbia attacking the great powers of Europe or instituting a new regime type throughout Europe. On the contrary, Milosevic and most of the Serbs argue from a set of fundamental conceptions which have been common in Europe for the whole century, namely that political division in the world runs between "we" in one's own nation state on one side, and all the others outside on the other side.

As little as 20 years ago Vietnam intervened in the internal affairs of Cambodia, overthrowing Pol Pot and his regime and establishing their own man in his place. It did not matter that Pol Pot as ruling head had a couple million of human lives on his consciousness; the united West condemned Vietnam's conduct. The murder of his own citizens was therefore not accorded special political weight. This occurrence in Cambodia in 1979 serves as an example of the paucity of humanitarian intervention over the past century. The situation has thereby changed. The new NATO has appeared as the flag bearer, restricting violence and defining order in the world. This new order is post national, and must be understood as such. In opposition stands the old national state order, Milosevic and the old order proponents. One can perhaps even talk about this also in a social context, Yugoslavia standing for the old order and NATO and the West the new; all over Central and Eastern Europe people and state are deciding whether they want to submit to the post national order, global capitalism and multi-ethnic politics, or whether they will remain within the old nation state. Perhaps one of the reasons as to why Milosevic gained the support that he received was a result of the perception of the lifestyle that follows from the Western hegemony not necessarily appealing to the Serbian majority?

Legitimating Kinds of Warfare

If the subject which wages war is humanity, then a representation of that which is being fought as non-human lies close at hand. At least, it invites a dehumanizing gaze at the enemy. An enemy which may have to respond to such a gaze, may represent the stake of the conflict to be its humanity itself, or at the very least, to go out of business as a politcial entity of a legitimate kind. There are, furthermore, possible consequences for the gazer. If the enemy is defined by a dehumanizing gaze, it may have consequences for what means one considers legitimate in fighting that enemy. The less human the enemy, the less holds barred in picking your weapons and your strategy.

After Kosovo, the means employed in warfare has become an important issue. A so-called "revolution of military affairs", or rather a revolution in American military affairs, is taking place. New sorts of weapons have emerged, new constellations presented for the organization of military personnel. This debate has taken place in a field, in which every weapons system and every organizational model has its acronym. Therefore, there are few people who have the possibility to include this development in their comprehension of the world. This concerns not least politicians, who during the cold war also used to leave the military aspects of politics to the military. Thereby, they did not feel any urgent need for being up-dated in what was happening in the defence laboratories. As Kosovo shows, however, the development in areas such as aviation power came to play a crucial role for how the war developed. From the White House one could send a message to Pentagon, saying that one was going to bomb without loosing either personnel or planes. The military simulated several war operations to estimate the minimum height for planes in order not to be shot down by Serbian air defence. Thereby, 15,000 feet was estimated as the right value, an appraisal which turned out to be technically correct given the mission: even if one lost a plane, not a single soldier was lost.

During the Gulf war, in which also aviation power dominated, the French philosopher Jean Baudrillard wrote a set of controversial articles about war, saying that it had already taken place, or alternatively, it did not take place at all.[9] This was a familiar French provocation. Few people, particularly outside the Left bank, made an attempt to understand, what he actually meant. After Kosovo it may be easier. One aspect of characterising war nowadays is that it takes place in advance, as simulated exercises. There is, of course, nothing new about practising war. The planning in detail and the simulation of operations in advance, which is made possible by new communication technology, are, however, new. This new technology can easily lead to a planning hybris—the thought that the future can be predicted in detail. Even the air raids above Kosovo became simply a routine repetition of something one originally had done in a closed computer system in Pentagon. It was in Washington and not in the air above Kosovo, it was decided what sorts of bombs should be dropped, where and when. Consequently, one could argue that the war in Kosovo already had taken place—inside the Pentagon. It becomes really problematic, however, when one also can claim that the war between Yugoslavia and NATO in Kosovo never took place. This must be understood in the context that one protagonist used his superior technology to win a victory without getting involved in live warfare. The actions and battles which were fought did not happen between NATO and Yugoslavia, but between Yugoslavia and a third party. What went on the ground and the air war were, of course, closely connected. They were probably connected to such a degree, that the killings would not have been possible in such a form and to such a degree, were it not for the air war being so successful. And yet, they are two totally different phenomena.

The fact that the Americans had access to technology, which was so superior that they did not have to conduct war in the meaning of fighting, is problematic in a number of ways. It breaks in the first place with our conception of what kind of weapons is legitimate to use in war. In Europe, we have for a long time had several conceptions of which means are legitimate in particular circumstances. For example, in the late Medieval Age, it was good Latin that one could use squared bullets against infidels, whereas against a Christian enemy one should use a round bullet.[10] In this area, international law as (*ius in bello*) has played a crucial role. We have had a debate about which are the legitimate bombing targets. We have, not least in connection with the Vietnam war earlier had debates on which are legitimate bombs. We need another debate like this. The point is not to abolish bombing as such, but to restrict what kind of bombs one should be able to use. This should be done in such a way that aviation officers and those of us who find ourselves on the bombing side, can look at ourselves in the mirror the next day.

Bombs are technology. Approaches to the problem which consider what kind of technology is being used by the fighters, is a necessary part of our conversation on war. There is, however, another aspect to the way in which the war was conducted, which is causing even more anxiety. It is the question about when the politicians make their decisions. In Kosovo, it was asserted by politicians collectively that a loss of personnel could not be tolerated by public opinion. As a consequence of this, aircraft flew higher than the military would have preferred. The consequence of flying higher, was that the bombing was less precise, and causing more civilians death. This tendency to a larger and larger distance and the multiplication of standard procedures has reached new heights. How should one comprehend this? Is it possible to find a proportion, in such a way that one of 'our' pilots, for instance, should be worth 5000 civilian lives? This would be a way of thinking which totally would break with our fundamental conception about human worth. If one assumes, however, that politicians are elected and responsible to an electorate, which demands that war should be conducted without loss, this logic is sequitor.

The free exchange of views in our societies makes it, at least in this case, more difficult to reduce violence, not easier. When non-military personnel sometimes present the case in such a way, as it is the pilot's own will, or lack of such, to sacrifice their lives in operations, they grasp an important part of the problem. People who have chosen to become officers, have chosen a kind of lifestyle in which something—it can be a number of things, but something—is more important for them than this extra risk they expose themselves to by choosing a military way of living. The responsibility of politicians to their own officers and other volunteers is thereby associated with formulating clearly defined goals for military action and making it possible for the officers to execute these in a way which they see as professionally justifiable. It is not their responsibility to entirely exempt them from the possibility of dying. When politicians insist that their own personnel are not going to die, this can not be understood as some kind of concern for these people. Rather, it must be perceived as an attempt to avoid the political problems induced by a critical public opinion. And it is not only the meaning of loss as such, but also this concern, one has to measure against the responsibility politicians have to limit the amount of civilian losses.

More civilians died than if military action had not been conducted to accommodate the calculation that no losses were going to be suffered. The political reality is that the expense of suffering losses has become so high, that the temptation to let other people die instead is almost irresistible. In this case we are faced with two concrete questions, which have to be separated: whether it, in the first place, was immoral to start a war at all, and second, whether it was immoral to start a war the way in which it was done, namely without a ground invasion. In other words, in a way that clearly showed no intention to accept losses. To conduct a war without the willingness to sacrifice life seems especially problematic. And yet, nothing is easier to understand politically than politicians wanting to do everything to reduce losses on their own side among those who elect them. What we have here is an especially difficult case of a general problem, namely how do we balance our own citizen's rights against those rights which devolve on other parts of humanity. The old answer used to be that the nation state's sovereignty made it relatively easy to put the rights of the rest of the world to one side. In Kosovo, we were faced with the paradoxical situation that bombing was legitimized by breaking this logic. We would not define what happened as involving Yugoslav internal affairs, but human affairs. By choosing bombing, however, we opted, nevertheless, to save lives on 'our'side by killing even more of 'them'. What happens is thereby a bargaining game about how war after Kosovo should be comprehended. We do not agree with ourselves at this juncture. If we want to achieve a way of conducting war, in which use of violence is mostly restricted, the war in Kosovo does not seem to be much of an ideal. Those who triumph by the fact that no single American life was lost in Kosovo, contribute to the manifestation of an idea which asserts that war simply is a form of politics along with other forms, in the same way as economical aid, for instance. Air warfare becomes a policy option, which one can turn to whenever one fancies. And not only then, when all the other alternatives have been tried, and one feels like one really has to do something. If this is to become the place of war in the political, it is very unfortunate. In his *Discorsi*, Niccolò Machiavelli opposed the tendency to build quickly.[11] He argued that the bare existence of the fortresses could fool the prince to use this technology to keep the population in check. In the same way, one can nowadays make a specific warning to Western politicians and the military not to build too many of these advanced fighting planes, because the bare existence of these fighting planes opens the possibility to use them as an ordinary political tool. The wise prince restricts violence by choosing more indirect tools for ruling.

Conclusion

In conclusion, I offer the proposition that the problems concerning the questions of which actors are seen as legitimate wagers of war, of which kinds of issues is it legitimate to go to war, and of the legitimate ways of waging war have a common denominator. It is this: "humanity" may exist as a political notion and increasingly as a legal concept, but it is not (yet?) strong enough to carry the burden placed upon it by NATO countries, namely to legitimate the waging of war in Kosovo. As argued by Jean-François Lyotard,

> The "reason to die" always forms the bond of the we. The paradox of the order to die is that the name of its addressee, if he or she obeys the order, can never again gugure upon the addressor instance of subsequence, direct phrases, and in particular normative phrases like "I decree as a norm that..."[12]

States could pose as the legtimate wagers of war as long as that right had been conferred upon them by the community of states acting in unison, as legislators and guarantors of international law. Here is the link between the tension as to whether it was humanity acting through the security community of NATO which was waging war, or whether it was NATO members acting together as an alliance of states on the one hand, and the dogged unwillingness of the entities involved actually to suffer losses in the process. "Humanity" may be invoked as a legitimating speech act inside the discourse of international law, but it blatantly fails to legitimate the violence which follows its invocation. Serbia's attempts to legitimate its pose as that of a warring state defending the idea of state sovereignty was represented as an anachronism. Indeed, in Kosovo, the end of the legitimate warring state was at hand. Where is the political entity which may legitimately speak in the name of humanity?

NOTES AND REFERENCES

1. Carl Schmitt, *Der Begriff des Politischen: Text von 1932 mit einem Vorwort und drei Collarien*, Berlin: Duncker & Humblot, 1963.
2. In the piece, he also noted that 'Balkanization is a tool for legitimizing an international order *without* a named enemy'; Ole Wæver 'Securitization and Desecuritization' in Ronnie D. Lipschutz (ed.) *On Security* (New York, NY: Columbia University Press, 1995, p. 67. If so, then the Kosovo war debalkanised the Balkans and the world order both. For a general discussion, compare with

Barry Buzan (1997) 'Rethinking Security after the Cold War' in *Cooperation and Conflict*, 32 (1): 5-28.

3. See Iver B. Neumann 'Identity and the Outbreak of War' pp. 45-60 in Ho-Won Jeung (ed.) *The New Agenda for Peace Research*, Aldershot: Ashgate, 1999.
4. 317 is Richardson's suggestion, 1000 the Correlate of Wars project's, see Håkan Wiberg, *Konfliktteori och fredsforskning* Stockholm: Scandinavian University Books, 1976.
5. Compare with the discussion of Bosnia in Espen Barth Eide (1997), "Conflict entrepreneurship: A Few Post-Yugoslav Reflections on the «Art» of Waging Civil War" in *Engaging the Challenges of Tomorrow: Adjusting Humanitarian Interventions to the Character of Future Conflict*, Oslo: Norwegian Institute of International Affairs.
6. Milovan Djilas, *Memoirs of a Revolutionary,* New York, NY: Harcourt, Brae, Jovanovich, 1973.
7. Barber, Benjamin R, *Jihad vs. McWorld. How Globalism and Tribalism are Reshaping the World*, New York, NY: Ballantine, 1996.
8. Walzer, Michael, *Just and Unjust Wars: A Moral Argument with Historical Examples*, London: Penguin, 1980.
9. Reprinted in Jean Baudrillard, *La guerre du golfe n'a pas eu lieu,* Paris: Galilée, 1991. Baudrillard not only waged his campaign on the stratospheric level of phoilosophies, but also on empirical grounds: '*Les Presses de la Cité* invited me to go to the Gulf and cover the war. They were going to give me everything: money, documents, flights, etc. I live in the virtual. Send me into the real, and I don't know what to do. And, anyway, what more would I have seen? Those who went there saw nothing, only odds and ends'. Baudrillard in Mike Gane (ed.), *Baudrillard Live: Selected Interviews*, London: Routledge, 1991, p. 188.
10. R.J. Vincent, *Human Rights and International Relations*, Cambridge: Cambridge University Press, 1986.
11. Machiavelli, Niccolò, *The Discourses*, London: Penguin, 1970.
12. Jean-François Lyotard, *The Differend Phrases in Dispute*, Minneapolis, MN: University of Minnesota Press, 1988, p. 100 n. 156.

16

India, EU and US: *A Trialogue* *

B. KRISHNAMURTHY

> Another world is possible. But it is up to Europe to take the lead in achieving it.[1]
>
> —Joseph E. Stiglitz

"Dialogue" remains the very basis of relations between any two states in international politics and there were always dialogues, between India and the EU; India and the US and between the EU and the US, which has come to be termed as "transatlantic" relations. During the Cold War period the European leaders were constrained to take a stand on whether they were Atlanticists or Europeanists. Many a French leader took a stand that they could not be "Atlanticists" for obvious reasons. Jacques Chirac echoed the French dilemma when he said: «If being an Atlanticist means being one of the 500 million Westerners who hold a certain notion of freedom in common, then I am quite definitely an Atlanticist. If, on the other hand, an Atlanticist means being linked against one's will to a great power that tends to confuse an alliance of equals with casual hegemony, then, quite obviously, I cannot be an Atlanticist».[2]

Technically speaking, the transatlantic relations are within the West and within the NATO framework. As such, they are «exclusive» and «regional» in their scope and nature. Philip Bobbitt, well-known and influential American political philosopher, opines that the NATO has become irrelevant as it is quintessentially regional and calls for an alliance of world democracies in stead.[3] Robert Kagan, who served in the US State Department earlier and

* I am indebted to Dr. Geetha Ganapathy-Doré for her highly insightful comments and suggestions in the preparation of the epilogue.

is a senior associate at the Carnegie Endowment for International Peace, in his latest book, "The Return of History and the End of Dreams" perceives present times as «an age of divergence» and advocates an "axis of democracy" against the "club of autocrats", whose «rulers believe in the virtues of a strong central government and disdain the weaknesses of the democratic system».[4] In this context, let us discuss the rationale for a trialogue among the three democracies—India, EU and the US.

Why Trialogue and India as the Third Partner?

Contemporary *zeitgeist* in international politics is «inclusive» and «international» and the present day trends clearly point out towards the need to include Asia, as twenty-first century is said to be the «Asian Century». And within Asia, India calls for special attention and inclusion as it is an established democracy, an emerging economic power, a market equal to China, a knowledge power and an IT giant. Moreover, India is traditionally for engagement and for inclusiveness and is best suited to play a bridging role between the West and the East and also within the two pillars of the West—EU and the US. India could play a bigger role in convincing leading Western minds that they should stop seeing themselves as guardians of one leading civilization on the strength of its own time-honoured cultural traditions. Kishore Mahbubani believes that a great crusade is needed to convince the West that it is essentially no different from the rest and India may well play a leading role in this crusade.[5] Sunil Kilnani too suggests that to enhance its own power India needs to play the role of interlocutor between the most formidable power, the US and the most populated power, China.[6]

China Factor

Why to prefer India to China, to be "inclusive" and "international"? Since China is a competitor to all the three powers—India, EU and the US. It competes with India in attracting markets, investments and resources. Though the Chindia (China and India, as collaborators and not as competitors) theme was underscored in 2006, when China's Premier Wen Jiabao declared that both the countries would be a source of economic power in the 21st century and «Cooperation is just like two pagodas—one hardware and one software», Scott B. MacDonald is not very much off the mark when he maintains: «In a sense, China seems to desire that India remain a regional power that can be contained. For its part, India has greater aspirations, especially as its companies enjoy a period of global expansion. The aspirations of the two nations portend a future of growing rivalry, in which both countries will seek to advance their national interests generally by offering market and capital and through the projection of soft power, but with military power in the background».[7] While the Western countries have stopped treating India at par with Pakistan, China continues to follow the "two country policy" of equating India with Pakistan, to the great uneasiness and discomfort of India. Again, China tries to block India's ambitions to be an international player. It does not openly oppose the Indian claim for the UN Security Council permanent membership. At the same time, China is not forthcoming with its support also. It even tries to restrict India in its own backyard and challenges Indian leadership role in the Indian Ocean rim region through its growing transportation, trade, infrastructure building and defence links. On the issue of getting clearance for supply of nuclear materials and technology from the Nuclear Suppliers Group in 2008, initially China remained indifferent, but, at the crucial moment tried to block the deal with the connivance of fellow member countries who opposed the initiative. However, for obvious reasons, both India and China downplay their problematic relations. While China sermons on "peaceful rise", India talks about the historic relations between the two countries and on January 11, 2008, Premier Manmohan Singh emphatically declared: <India not part of any «contain China effort»>.

Noted economic historian Niall Ferguson has coined the term «Chimerica» to denote the close and growing interdependence and partnership between the US and China. Now, China is America's largest external creditor—with two-thirds of its $ 2 trillion foreign exchange reserves invested in US dollar-denominated financial instruments.[8] The member states of the EU vie with each other and with the US in courting China in their profit motive in spite of the hard fact that on the issues of democracy and human rights, China never hesitates to defy and challenge the West by pitching Europe against America and getting support of one against the other, whoever dares to speak and act against their interests.[9] The Europeans as well as the Americans are aghast with the system in China which combines an authoritarian political order with a highly dynamic capitalism, which they term as "Market Stalinism" or «Leninism with capitalist characteristics». The Western countries also envy China as their balance of trade is always in favour of the latter. Charles Krauthammer is forthright in pointing out that at the dawn of the twenty-first century, one of the two great geopolitical challenges on the horizon is the inexorable rise of China.[10] Actually, China poses a formidable challenge to the US, by being an "asymmetrical Super Power" which projects the example of its model in terms of the strength of its economic system and its robust defence of national sovereignty rather than by virtue of its brute military power or interventionism.[11] Perhaps the driving force in the new US-India relationship has been a shift in the perception of China in Washington, its metamorphosis from a strategic partner to a strategic rival.[12] Immanuel Wallerstein too clearly brings out this cat and mouse game when he points out that the U.S. government «sees China as an «emerging» power of growing importance in the economic, political, and military spheres. It likes the economic development, seeing China as an important trade partner, is dubious about the growing political strength, and fears the growing military strength». On the other hand, China «sees the United States as a giant in decline. It believes it needs to keep the giant unprovoked in the present, and merely bide its time, so that twenty years from now, when the U.S. star has dimmed, its own star will be shining brightly».[13] Though the EU does not come out openly against China, the Europeans too feel much uneasiness while dealing with China because of its poor human rights record, prevalence of death penalty, democratic deficit and so on.

However, the most serious challenge that the West—the US and its European allies—faces from China is in the developing world, where they could dangle big financial carrots to get countries to act in a certain way or turn the screws on those countries who held out. Of late, putting tough conditions on that money has become harder too, since poor countries turn to China and get cash with fewer strings attached. Peter Beinart, senior fellow at the American Council on Foreign Relations, points out that in this way China has been winning over friends and influencing people from Bangkok to Brazil.[14] This development has weakened the cutting edge of the Western soft power potential in its relations with the developing countries. All these clearly underline the need to take India as a partner by the other two powers in their effort to balance China.[15]

In any attempt to advocate trialogue among India, the EU and the US, it is imperative to find answers for five significant questions:

- What India, the EU and the US are actually?
- What are their self-perceptions? What these three powers think of themselves. Many a time, these self-images may be a bloated one or what they want to be in future rather than what they are *à present.*
- What are their perceptions of each others? One has to find out what India thinks that the EU and the US are/will be; what is the idea of the EU about India and the US and what are the images of India and the EU as perceived by the US?
- What are their perceptions on important international issues and how far do they converge or diverge? and
- What are their actions on the basis of these perceptions—self, of each other and of current international issues—and to what consequences?

What is India?

India's size, population, human as well as the natural resources and the consequent potentials remain its plus points. Its geo-strategic location in the middle of the Indian Ocean and its being located as a transit point between West Asia and the Far East, has given India a notable place in international politics. In terms of capabilities India is the fifth largest country in the world, second in population, fourth in armed forces, tenth in industrial potential (including defence industry), third largest pool of technical and scientific manpower, sixth nuclear power and fourth to launch its own satellite. While commenting on the promising demographic profile of India, Zakaria concludes: «If demography is destiny, India's future is secure».[16] While trying to answer the question, why India may be destined to overtake China?, Pete Engardio, senior writer, *Business Week*, points out to its «demographic dividend»—while India's workforce will keep growing for at least four more decades, its fertility rate is declining, meaning future families will have fewer children to support and more to spend on consumption.[17] India's soft power potential, especially as a cultural power, is something egregious.[18] The Indian educational, legal and judicial systems with English as medium and rooted in the western system give India an edge over other countries of the East.

Belying the calculations of "doubting Thomases", who pooh-poohed the very idea of India declaring itself a "Democratic Republic", India continues to remain a "functioning democracy" with well-established institutions, almost an oasis in the democracy-starved developing world. It is a regional heavyweight, with an aspiration to be an active player in international politics. India was fortunate enough to have a line of internationalist leadership, starting from Jawaharlal Nehru, its first Prime Minister who was his own Foreign Minister. «Father of the Indian Nation», Mahatma Gandhi, and his political philosophy based on non-violence, *satyagraha* and *sarvodaya* continues to hold considerable influence and following in the international community. India is enjoying the leadership of the Non-Aligned Movement and of the developing world, which turns to India for guidance and inspiration.[19] India remained the champion of the right to self-determination of the Afro-Asian countries against European imperialism-colonialism. It continues to be an ardent advocate of peaceful co-existence, disarmament and nuclear-weapon free world and an active participant in the United Nations system and the UN peacekeeping missions.

Over the past fifteen years, Indian has been the second-fastest-growing economy in the world, which grew at 6.9 per cent over the entire decade from 1997 and 8.5 per cent in the second-half of it. More Indians have moved out of poverty in the last decade than in the preceding fifty years and India's poverty rate is half what it was twenty years ago. *Incredible India!* was 'everywhere' in the World Economic Forum in Davos in 2006 and "captured the imagination of the conference and dominated the conversation".[20] India's economic potential is sound and in April 2007, India joined the trillion dollar economy club of 12 countries (among the developing countries China and Brazil are the other two members).

The scorching growth of India's software and IT-enabled services sector has given it a significant role in global business. From a $150 million industry in the early 1990s, the sector now stands to exceed $36 billion in revenues in 2006, two-thirds from exports. India's knowledge work has linked the country to American business in vital ways. In 2006 it became the fastest growing mobile phone market in the world, and its automobile sector is one of the fastest growing, too.[21] India remains a market of considerable size and depth and it has by experience realized that its market potential can very well be a good bargaining chip in international negotiations.

What is EU?

Castlereagh, former British Foreign Minister, while elaborating on the objectives of the Congress of Vienna and subsequent Concert of Europe, talked about the need «... to bring back the world to peaceful habits». Unfortunately for Europe and the World, the Europeans were not habituated to peace which resulted in perennial wars culminating in the two world wars, which resulted in heavy loss of human life and property. In the post-war world, Jean Monnet, Robert Schuman and others succeeded in establishing a new Concert of Europe which sought to bring about the «harmony» of people living together in peace. The driving motivation of the EU's founding fathers was long-lasting peace for the continent as well as for the world, which had spent more times in wars and crises than witnessed peace in the recorded history. Economic integration, it was hoped, would lead to greater understanding, underpinned by the myriad interactions that inevitably flow from commerce and increased interdependence would make conflict unthinkable. The EU has realized that dream. «The European project has been an enormous success not only for Europe but also for the world».[22]

The European Union is an association of sovereign states and is quite successful in establishing common institutions, policies, and programmes. Its real strength is institutional infrastructure including binding commitment to democracy and the vast array of laws and regulations that anyone too often takes for granted elsewhere. Though the EU is successful in developing an innovative democratic set up, often it is accused of suffering from "democratic deficit", by the disgruntled leaders of the member states as well as some sections of the people. In this context, Moutardier's suggestion (p. 64) that the redrafting of EC Regulation 1049/2001 for the sake of enhanced transparency in the EU institutions will help perhaps eradicate the growing tendency for Euroscepticism is quite appreciable.

Another issue that is always linked with the fortunes of the Union is the consensus among the member states with the forging ahead of the integration process. Some countries like France and Germany, which are considered as the "core" of Europe, are always ahead of other member states in their intentions to expedite the process, while England, due to the prejudices and predilections inbuilt into the system due to its "special" relationship with the US, proves to be the chief "laggard". This situation calls for the establishment of a two-speed or even multi-speed Europe, which will allow reconciliation between these two conflicting—pro and anti-European integrationist—groups at the heart of the European Union. Queries raised by Griffin (p. 152): «Why indeed, should a member state be forced into an ever-greater integrated Europe and by the same token, why member states should be prevented from integrating further?» are quite valid. He also argues that «the anti-integrationist block might well, in a two-speed Europe, increase integration between them in economic matters, whilst the integrationists would be free to institute greater political cooperation. Such an approach would allow member states and their citizens to move at their own pace and not feel that they were being forced into further integration against their wishes». His warning over «continued attempts by the EU to insist otherwise, will slowly rob the organization of its democratic foundations», needs to be taken seriously by those protagonists of EU who want to showcase European democratic model worth emulation.

A comprehensive and complex system has been created in EU which influences and guides the political, socio-economic and cultural life of each one of the member state and its citizen. Unfortunately, the «Byzantine» governing system appears to be «paralyzed now and then by antagonisms» of the member states. In spite of that drawback, the system continues to contribute to peace and prosperity of the region.

Generally, it is believed that the member states loose their sovereignty within the framework of the Union. Though it is generally true, there are occasional exceptions. For instance, as pointed out by Pouillaude (p. 94), Poland's accession to the European Union helps it assert its national sovereignty more than ever, though it appears paradoxical. Pouillaude's claim is substantiated by the facts that the Polish government had given active support to the Americans at the time of launching the war in Iraq in 2003; the Polish troops were involved on the field a few months before Poland's integration in the European Union. Again, Poland purchased military equipment from the United States in preference to those of other EU member states. All these prove beyond doubt that the member states gain rather than loose in the deal.

The Union is considered as a "privileged club", which bestows substantial political and economic benefits on the member states. This factor quite naturally continues to attract sovereign states to knock at the doors of EU for entry, even after getting imposed severe strictures and conditions. Moreover, they are ready to undertake political and economic reforms suggested, so as making themselves fit for inclusion. Turkey, for instance, introduced several constitutional, institutional and policy reforms to transform itself acceptable to the EU, but, still denied full membership.[23]

With $ 8 trillion economy, the EU is the largest trading bloc with a share of approximately 25 per cent of world trade. It is a market of about 500 million people. It is the largest investor and a generous purveyor of grants and aids, the fact that has given the Union considerable potential as a soft power with substantial political clout. Moreover, the economic integration helped achieve a broader set of goals in Europe and has saved the EU member countries and their people from the evil effects of economic globalization which «has contributed to widening the divide between rich and poor within countries and between rich and poor countries».

The EU has developed a distinctive approach to development policy that has been important in establishing the Union's role as a relatively benign "patron/mentor" in relation to the developing South. It has avoided the practice of tying aid to commercial interests. The European Community Humanitarian Office provides more than 25 per cent of all humanitarian assistance. EU member states' combined efforts contribute a further 25 per cent. As such, the Union as a whole provides more than half the world's emergency aid.[24] The Europeans are also sensible enough in realizing that we must live in harmony with our environment—the scarcest of all our resources. Europe has taken the lead, especially concerning global warming, showing that petty selfishness can be put aside to achieve a common good.

While the EU is a strong economic union, it has proved itself a weak political union and still remains "*Europe des patries*" (Europe of States) rather than the "United States of Europe". The tug-of-war between nationalism and internationalism continues unabated, jeopardizing the integration process occasionally. The EU is sitting on a demographic bomb. Nicholas Eberstadt, a scholar at the American Enterprise Institute, estimates that by 2030 the Europe will remain «virtually stagnant», and will have more than twice as many seniors older than 65 than children under 15, with drastic implications for future aging. The UN Population Division estimates that the ratio of working-age people to senior citizens in Western Europe will drop from 3.8:1 today to just 2.4:1 in 2030. This demographic problem is going to be a big headache for the European leaders in the years to come.

To put it in a nutshell, as pointed out by Monjal (p. 43), the Europeans "are inventing on a daily basis a unique and specific model which is legally an alloy, an alliance of governmental powers which are exercised on a revolutionary mode which is quite new and which consists in the common exercise of governmental powers detained by entities that are still sovereign... Peace was thus constructed in Europe around community law, free market economy and the political will of social democrat elite to do away with the most abject forms of political and economic nationalism—wars".

What is US?

The United States of America is celebrated as the most powerful democracy and the American President is considered as the most powerful man in the world with his fingers on the nuclear trigger, capable of devastating and destroying the universe, not once but thousands of times. The US plays a predominant role of the leading trend setter in international polity and economy. In international trade regime, the US dictates to dos and don'ts. For instance, as pointed by Reiplinger (pp. 72-80), the Foreign Corrupt Practices Act, which tries to curb corruptive practices in the sphere of trade and investment throughout the world, was initiated by the Americans, who set the ball rolling towards its rightful destination. The international financial market is centred on the US dollar. It is a power to be reckoned with in the field of science and technology, which are used systematically to achieve political and economic national interests.

The US is and will long remain the largest single aggregation of power and consequently the most powerful nation since imperial Rome, and the only one that was stronger than any likely combination of all other nations. It spends more than $500 billion annually on its military (more than $700 billion if the operations in Afghanistan and Iraq are included) and boasts land, air, and naval forces that are the world's most capable. Rumsfeld, the US Defence Secretary under Bush regime, initiated a programme to rapidly increase the lethal offensive military capacity called the "transformation of the American military". Washington's pursuit of the Revolution in Military Affairs (MTA), relying on GPS systems and information and electronic technology of all kinds, have given birth to an information technology-driven revolution in military affairs (IT-RMA) in the US.[25] This development has created a huge, unbridgeable gap between the US and other countries, both allies and rivals put together.

The US has combined both "hard" and "soft" versions of power as it remains not only the most important military power, but also the economic, technological as well as a "cultural" superpower. It is at the forefront of the techno-industrial revolution that is changing the world economy and dominates the content of the new channels of communication. These "intangible" assets are the key elements of its new and growing power structure. «From high culture to mass media, the US seems to have acquired a powerful grip on the minds of the people, throughout the world. ... its TV news programmes are watched by its enemies as well as its friends, its mass market entertainment products give flesh to the dreams of millions of people».[26] Richard Haass is quite right when he said: "U.S. power was unprecedented: above all, military—as seen in Kuwait, Kosovo and Afghanistan, among other places—but also economic, political and cultural. American primacy was a fact. The United States was demonstrably first among unequals".[27]

The US economy with a GDP of some $14 trillion is the world's largest. At the same time, it remains a major debtor country and at present its economy is in doldrums and the Americans who used to be ardent advocates of market economy and free enterprise, are going ahead with nationalisation programmes. The dollar is in downstream affecting not only the American economy and also having severe impacts on the global economy. Deregulated, American-style capitalism, which is the American prescription for prosperity, no longer looks as dominant now that Wall Street has blown up.

America is successful in creating the first universal nation, made up of all colours, races, and creeds, living and working together and developing its economy. It has constantly revitalizing by streams of people who are looking to make a new life in a new world. The immigrants have become the backbone of the American economy as the US has been able to tap this energy as a constant reinforcement, manage diversity, and assimilate the newcomers. Through this revitalization mechanism, America continued to possess a quality rare for a rich country—hunger to work hard and grow and energy to cope up with. Zakaria in his latest book, *The Post-American World* celebrates this American trait.[28]

Self-Perception of India

The Indians are quite proud of their great civilisational, art and architectural, literary and cultural achievements. Some even claim that it is a cultural super power. It is naturally proud of its democracy and democratic institutions and exercises like regular and periodical elections, which turn out to be "huge democratic celebration". In the absence of any co-equal power in the region, India is considered as a regional giant and some Indian scholars even term it as a regional unipolar power.[29] India considers itself fit to play a meaningful role in international politics and sincerely believes that on merit it deserves the seat of a permanent member in the UN Security Council with "veto" power. Again, India perceives that it is an economic power house with inordinate potential and the natural leader of the "developing world".

European Self-Perception

For Europeans, the integration process and the resultant EU is a break from its past, of wars and devastations towards a long peace and prosperity. Robert Cooper, a noted British diplomat, opines that the EU is the most developed example of a post-modern system as it represents security through transparency, and transparency through interdependence.[30] The EU is more a transnational than a supra-national system, a voluntary association of states rather than the subordination of states to a central power, he points out. Moreover, the European Union has become a highly developed system for mutual interference in each other's domestic affairs, right down to beer and sausages. The CFE Treaty, under which parties to the treaty have to notify the location of their heavy weapons and allow inspections, subject areas close to the core of sovereignty to international constraints. Cooper is forthright when he says: «Whereas in the modern world, following Clausewitz's dictum—war is an instrument of policy—was an accepted norm, in the postmodern world it is taken as a sign of policy failure». Incidentally, large majority of European public and elite indeed believe that they are living in post-modern times and interestingly considerable section of the American society too shares this point of view.

Cooper stretches his idea of post-modern state further and points out that while the members of the postmodern world may not represent a danger to one another, both the modern and pre-modern zones pose threats. As such, Cooper propounds a doctrine of liberal imperialism which claims that post-modern states have a right to intervene in the affairs of modern and pre-modern states if they pose a significant enough threat. In such a case, Cooper advocates: «Among ourselves, we operate on the basis of laws and open cooperative security. But when dealing with more old-fashioned kinds of states outside the postmodern continent of Europe, we need to revert to the rougher methods of an earlier era—force, pre-emptive attack, and deception, whatever is necessary to deal with those who still live in the nineteenth century world of every state for itself. Among ourselves, we keep the law but when we are operating in the jungle, we must also use the laws of the jungle». This argument is actually Cooper's effort to justify Tony Blair's support for the

US in its war with Iraq. However, Cooper's advocacy of following laws of jungle in a lawless world of jungles failed to find favour with majority of the French and the Germans and even with considerable sections of Britons.

From the beginning the Europeans consciously and deliberately projected the EU in its external relations as a "civilian power. Françoise Duchene, a strong exponent of the "civilian power" school defines this concept thus: «The European Community's interest as a civilian group of countries long on economic power and relatively short on armed force is as far as possible to domesticate relations between states, including those of its own members and those with states outside its frontiers. This means trying to bring to international problems the sense of responsibility and structures of contractual politics which have in the past been associated almost exclusively with "home" and not foreign, that is alien affairs».[31] As such, the Europeans aim at the domestication of their foreign policy and deliberately assume a non-military norm/approach in their external relations.

EU itself is the best example of institutionalized multilateralism, of the sharing of sovereignty for a common purpose, and it is but natural for the Union to preach and practice multilateralism, both in domestic and foreign fronts.[32] The Europeans insist that they approach and handle problems with greater nuance and sophistication as they try to influence others through subtlety and indirection. They claim that they are more tolerant of failure and more patient when solutions are not forthcoming instantly. Their preference is for peaceful responses to problems, through negotiation, diplomacy, and persuasion than coercion. They are for appeal to international law, international conventions, and international opinion to adjudicate disputes. They try to use commercial and economic ties to influence third countries in their effort to bind them together. They often emphasize process over result, believing that ultimately process can become substance.

The Europeans are especially proud of their democratic and liberal tradition, culture and value system. They sincerely believe that the concept of human rights originated in Europe and it is their legacy to the rest of the world. Interestingly, Marudanayagam (pp. 253-260) dwells deep into the English literature and comes out with the startling fact that John Milton, one of the gems of the English literature, was not only a proponent of human rights but also championed the cause through his literary works. In the issue of human rights protection and promotion, Europe deservedly occupies an exalted seat in the League table.

Moreover, the Europeans believe that their post-war experience is something worth emulating by third countries. «The genius of the founding fathers», European Commission President Romano Prodi commented in a speech at the *Institut d'Etudes Politiques* in Paris (May 29, 2001), «lay in translating extremely high political ambitions... into a series of more specific, almost technical decisions. This indirect approach made further action possible. Rapprochement took place gradually. From confrontation we moved to willingness to cooperate in the economic sphere and then on to integration». This historical lesson born out of their experience is what many Europeans believe they have to offer the world: not power, but the transcendence of power. The «essence» of the European Union is essentially all about subjecting inter-state relations to the rule of law. Europe's experience of successful multilateral governance has in turn produced an ambition to convert the world. Europe «has a role to play in world "governance"» adds Prodi, a role based on replicating the European experience on a global scale. In Europe «the rule of law has replaced the crude interplay of power... power politics have lost their influence» and by «making a success of integration we are demonstrating to the world that it is possible to create a method for peace». As such, the transmission of the European miracle to the rest of the world has become Europe's new *mission civilisatrice* (civilizing mission). The European ambition is to convert the world by their solid and laudable example. It is in this context, one has to appreciate when Geetha Ganapathy Doré claims (p. 250): «The success of the Union for the Mediterranean will not only spell peace for the region but also send resonances of goodwill across the Muslim world which other parts of the world might want to emulate».

The EU is a votary of 'multilateralism' and it stands for the UN, the international law and rule-bound international order. It also advocates a new and just multipolar world order with itself as a central pillar. The Europeans are secular in their outlook and are projecting themselves as champions for the cause of clean and green environment.

To sum up, the Europeans emphasize more on economics and how to use it as an instrument of integration of human beings and states at the regional as well as international levels. As a civilian power they tend to use foreign aid and development cooperation assistance to influence and to bring expected changes in the policies and attitudes of third countries.

Self Perception of the US

In his well-known book "The Shield of Achilles", Philip Bobbitt redefined the post-Cold War nation state as a vastly more complex, fluid and expansive entity that he called the «market state», and pointed out that the US is the foremost example of such an entity.[33] Bobbitt's thesis is that the nature of the state is changing, from nation state to market state. The purpose of the nation state was maximising the welfare of its members, while that of the market state is maximising their opportunity.[34] The threats to the market state, Bobbitt believes, are not nearly so perceptible, for they are not principally territorial. Vulnerability lies essentially in the market state's very means of maximising opportunity: privatisation, decentralisation, internationalisation etc. In his new book «Terror and Consent», Bobbitt posits a more or less permanent state of war between two types of market states—those of consent, such as the US, where power still flows from the governed and is used to defend their liberal democratic values, and those of terror, like Iraq, where control through fear is both the means and the end of the enemies of consent.

The Americans consider themselves as sole super power in the post Cold War era. They were quite proud of their achievements and Madeline Albright, former US Secretary of State under President Clinton's regime, deemed her country as an 'indispensable nation' in international politics. Charles Krauthammer, the truimphalist, claims that the US is a furiously concentrated unipolar power and «an unprecedentedly dominant United States ... is in the unique position of being able to fashion its own foreign policy. After a decade of Prometheus playing pygmy, the first task of the new [Bush] administration is precisely to reassert American freedom of action.[35] He also maintains that present day world is unipolar dominated by a single Super Power unchecked by any rival and with decisive reach in every corner of the globe".[36] The notion of disparity of power between the US and the rest of the world and that «nothing... no other nation comes close... no comparison», remains the domineering theme of his writings.

The Americans feel that they are quite idealistic and are for lofty principles like democracy, freedom, human rights and rule of law, in spite of the fact that they are quite powerful. They «sincerely believe that their country has been designated as custodian of the international system and that the eyes of every supplicant from East Timor to Afghanistan, from Iraq to Liberia; Arab and Israeli, Irish and British, North and South Korean are upon the US». They also believe that their country possesses laudable tradition and mission—the protection and promotion of freedom and peace—and are convinced of their moral leadership.[37] Bush administration's *National Security Strategy* of September 2002 puts it succinctly: 'The United States possesses unprecedented—unequaled—strength and influence in the world,' which it should use 'to promote a balance of power that favours freedom'[38] The Americans also claim that they want to work through the UN, though they are capable of unilateral action. Kagan claims: «Polls consistently show that Americans support multilateral action in principle—they even support acting under the rubric of the United Nations— ...but the fact remains that the United States can act unilaterally, and has done so many times with reasonable success. For Americans, who stand to lose at least some freedom of action, support for universal rules of behaviour really is a matter of idealism».[39]

As a power of preponderance and a country which is and will long remain the largest single aggregation of power, the US does not hesitate to use the predominant force at its disposal to achieve its national interests. This conviction enthused Kagan to claim that the Americans are from the 'Mars' and as such they are martial and are protagonists of war against their perceived antagonists. As a corollary, they perceive that they are 'good' and for 'good', in search of 'bad' guys. The Americans overemphasize on political and military issues and in particular they are in search of new potential enemies. This factor makes them to done the mantle of the 'international policeman'. The Americans generally see the world divided between good and evil, between friends and enemies and they tend to seek finality in international affairs: They want problems solved, threats eliminated and their stand vindicated.[40] While Kagan attributes this American tendency to their remaining «mired in history, exercising power in the anarchic Hobbesian world», Krauthammer justifies this in the name of «American exceptionalism».

Indian Perception of the EU

India is well aware of the fact that the EU is a large trading bloc and a huge market of considerable size and depth. It perceives the EU as a source of investment. EU is also seen as a source of high technology which is indispensable for the economic and industrial growth of India. Again, the developing world in general and India in particular perceives the EU as a 'positive influence' in international politics and a second western voice to balance the American bellicosity. There is overwhelming hope that the EU as a counter-hegemonic alternative will be able to restrain the all-powerful US, which is considered as a behemoth and a menace to world peace, through its unilateral actions.

Indian Perception of the US

In the Cold War era, India considered the US as a villain, especially because of its material and military support to Pakistan, its estranged neighbour and arch rival. Moreover, India sincerely believed that the Americans prop up Pakistan in order to contain and confine it to the South Asian region, thus preventing it from playing a meaningful role in international politics. The resultant anti-Americanism continued to be in vogue for a few decades and the Americans were blamed for all the Indian problems—domestic as well as international. Of late, India has shed its anti-Americanism and started moving closer with the US. While recognizing the US as a super power, India intends to take benefit of its friendship. Unlike the past, India started to positively react to the American overtures. The US is now perceived as a source of investment and a large trade partner. It is also considered as a source of technology, especially nuclear technology. The US is expected to restrain Pakistan from creating problems through abetting terrorists and their nefarious activities across the border. In short, India expects that as a fellow democratic power, which wants to see democracy thrive everywhere, the US should be a partner and supporter in its efforts to consolidate its economic growth rather than abet anti-Indian elements in their attempts to prevent India from achieving its political and economic targets.

European Perception of India

The Europeans try to balance the economic relations with India with a reinforced political dialogue through the EU-India Partnership Agreement of 1993. This partnership formulated a road plan for reinforcing the geo-political dialogue between the two largest democracies in terms of population in the present day world; aims to create a positive image of EU in India and of India in Europe, and is first of its kind involving the Union with any Asian country. By the end of 1999, the member states of the EU and the European Commission have decided to hold summit meetings with India and this development is quite significant for India in status as well as in substance.[41] EU holds such summit meetings with the US, Russia, Canada, China and Japan alone earlier and India has now become the sixth country. All these clearly show that the EU treats India differentially from her South Asian neighbours. In its 'concentric circle'[42] of external relations, India stands on par with China and Japan in Asia. During his visit to India in November 2001 to participate in the second India-EU summit meeting, Romano Prodi, the then President of the European Commission, insisted that both the parties should work as «poles of stability in an unstable world situation».

The Europeans are enamoured of the Indian cultural heritage. India is considered by the EU as the largest and most populous democracy. However,

Cooper is convinced that India still remains a 'traditional' modern state in the context of postmodern world. It is seen as a huge market of great opportunity. India, as perceived by the French scholar Dominique Moisi, «has stepped onto the world stage as both an independent and an important power. Cooperating diplomatically with the United States and making economic deals in Europe, the emerging Indian elites are displaying even more pride and optimism than their Chinese counterparts. The world's largest democracy will soon emerge as the most populous country, and it seems to know no limits».[43] In international political scenario India is perceived by the European leaders as one among the poles of the prospective multipolar world order.

European Perception of the US

In the post war period, most of the Western European countries had to depend on the American financial assistance under the Marshall Plan to tide over their economic problems and subsequent recovery. During the Cold War era, the Europeans had to tolerate the overbearing attitudes and activities of the US, since the Soviet threat was looming large over their heads and the Western European countries offered bases for the North Atlantic Treaty Organization (NATO) establishments. However, there was a feeling among the Europeans in general and the French n particular that Europe was treated as a foot-soldier of a US-dominated NATO.[44] In 1966, France withdrew from the NATO Joint Command and demanded the withdrawal of NATO establishments from its soil.

Moreover, there was uneasiness among the European powers on the militaristic orientation of the American foreign policy. They feared that the US would involve them into some wars, which would be nothing to do with their interests. As pointed out by Scott Erb (p. 195), even the Germans, who were generally considered as most reliable allies of the US in the continent, were quite often perturbed by the use of force by the Americans to achieve their perceived national interest, thereby shocking their non-military norm during Cold War era.

The EU and the US jointly represent 10 per cent of the world's population and account for roughly half of world trade and over 60 per cent of world GDP. As such, both the powers maintain close political and economic relations and the US is first among the six powers with which the EU maintains regular summit level meeting. The US was supportive of the integration process in Europe and during the Cold War period, as it provided Europe a security umbrella against the Soviet Union, which enabled the European countries to concentrate on peaceful regional economic consolidation.

However, in the post-Cold war period and especially under the Bush regime, the situation changed to worse. Now, many Europeans sincerely believe that the Americans are no more in favour and support of European integration and in stead, they plot to divide the Union and try to create a wedge between the member states. The American Defence Secretary Donald Rumsfeld's pronouncement of «old and new Europe» was considered by them as his attempt to divide Europe and to fish in the troubled waters. Griffin (p. 162 n. 59) refers about allegations that were in circulation in many quarters but not proved that one of the main groups behind the Irish "No" vote, liberals, was funded from the US.

Again, the Europeans believe that the Americans are for scaling down of their country's deals with the EU and lament that the US Congress doesn't care for maintaining close working relations with the European Parliament and it doesn't consider the EU as an 'entity' in international politics. The EU officials were especially irritated by the refusal of the Americans to acknowledge the EU as a serious political actor in the international political arena. Their grouse was that the US officials were either unwilling to see the EU as a political equal or prepared to comprehend the complexities of the CFSP. Their grievance was that the allies were not treated as partners but as satellites. The American efforts to deal with certain members of the EU directly and bilaterally and thereby bypass the EU decision-making structures so painstakingly developed through decades, was taken as the American slight on the EU rationale as well as achievements.[45]

In the context of postmodern world order, Cooper believes that the US is not a postmodern state, though he is hesitant to say so and if not, what it is then. As a corollary, the Europeans perceive that the US remains «military-minded and obsessed with rogue states and weapons of mass destruction».[46] Moisi sincerely believes that the demise and disintegration of the Soviet Union has given forth to America's Manichean view of itself and its role in the world and 9/11 reinforced it further.[47] Washington's pursuit of the Revolution in Military Affairs (MTA) appeared to most European observers driven by American industrial and defence lobbies rather than to face any clear cut external threat.

There are sharp differences between the US and the EU on the contentious issues like death penalty, gun culture, violence, health care, and preferential socio-economic models. The growing influence of religion has also been highlighted as a major cultural difference impinging on politics. Solana attributes widening gulf between the EU and US to a confrontation between the religious vision of world affairs in the White House and the secular vision of the Europeans. He states that «it is a sort of binary model, it is all or nothing. For us Europeans, it is difficult to deal with because we are secular. We do not see the world in such black and white terms».[48]

The European caricature at its most extreme depicts an America dominated by a «culture of death» both in its domestic and external fronts. They juxtapose their lower crime rates, far lower prison populations, the smaller income gap, safer cities and better-protected countryside, to the American domestic scenario which is being afflicted by higher levels of violent crime and wider gun availability. In this context, Europe perceives the US as a flawed superpower.[49]

Hubert Védrine, former French Foreign Minister under François Mitterrand, coined the term *hyperpuissance* (Hyper Power) to describe an American behemoth too worryingly powerful and so a cause of concern, to be designated merely a superpower. He also called the US as 'Omni—God-like, omnipotent, omnipresent and omniscient—Power». Védrine also envied at the soft power potential of the Americans.[50]

The European leaders as well as the public regret the fact that the US has become, especially under the Bush regime, one of the most unpopular in the world and self-certified pro-Americans among them like Nicolas Sarkozy, the current French President, believe that it presents overwhelming problems for the Americans as well as for their allies. As such, when he was asked by Condoleezza Rice, «What can I do for you?» Sarkozy is stated to have replied: «... do everything you can to improve the way you're perceived ...».[51]

There has always been a streak of anti-Americanism in Europe. Many an occasion, rampant anti-Americanism in Europe is a powerful force in EU identity building. Of late, staggering majorities in most European countries—as high as 80 per cent—oppose the American foreign policy and even believe that the US is the greatest threat to world peace.[52] Bush administration's indifference to European concerns, its plan to extend the war on terrorism to Iraq, its refusal to submit American citizens to the jurisdiction of the newly created International Criminal Court, its off-hand treatment to Kyoto Protocol and several other factors, which clearly proved that they want to be law unto themselves incensed most of the Europeans.[53] They were taken as the «hubris of superpower». and rejection of the very values of Atlanticism and of the West. The Europeans were determined to take a stand for the Western/Atlanticist values and to confront America's «nationalist, egocentric and imperialistic» approach to global affairs.

American Perception of India

India is taken by the Americans as a populous democracy and it is said that President Bush has taken a special liking for its 'diversifying' character and for President Obama, it is the land of Mahatma Gandhi. Its economic growth is well-appreciated and the Indian success story does not evince that much envy and uneasiness in the American mind as the economic success of the other Asian giant, China. On the other hand, India is taken as a big market equal to that of China and as such, an equalizer. Moreover, India is being taken as a partner of the US in international affairs. Haass cites 'The American National Security Strategy of 2006' which claims: «India now is poised to shoulder global obligations in cooperation with the United States in a way befitting a major power».[54]

At present, the distribution of power in the world is very different and in future it is going to be much more varied. The Goldman Sachs BRIC study projects that by 2015, India's economy will be equal to that of Italy's and will have caught up with Britain's within five more years. While by 2040, India will boast the third-largest economy of the world, its per capita income will have risen to twenty times its current level by mid-twenty first century.[55] It is also noticed by the American circle that though this widely cited study is the best source for projection of this kind, in actual terms, the BRICs have been growing at a faster rate than the Goldman economists assumed while finalizing their report. Chicago-based consultancy Keystone-India in their recent white paper titled «India Century» maintains that India is on track to surpass China in growth. Keystone Chief Economist William T. Wilson declares: «We believe this is India's moment». According to their projection, India's annual growth is projected to rise to around 7.3 per cent by 2010 and stay over 7 per cent until the mid-2030s, and still be in the 6 per cent range until 2050. They place their projections on the strength of following strong factors which are in favour of India: demographics, capital efficiency, investment growth, new entrepreneurs, higher productivity and manufacturing surge.[56] Drezner quotes the projection of The National Intelligence Council, a US government think tank, to the effect that by 2025, India will have the world's fourth-largest economy (China will be second).[57]

American Perception of the EU

Joseph S.Nye, a reputed American scholar on international relations, considers Europe's focus on law and institutions as an 'asset' not only for Europe but also for the world. Robert Kagan too talks highly about Europe's «entering a post-historical paradise of peace and relative prosperity, the realization of Kant's Perpetual Peace». Generally, both the American elite as well as common people are appreciative of Europe and its post-war peace and prosperity. Especially, Stiglitz has high hopes on Europe, which enthuses him to maintain: «Europe has succeeded because it recognizes that the rights of individuals are inalienable and universal and it has created institutions to protect those rights. Only Europe can speak with credibility on the subject of universal human rights. For the sake of all of us, Europe must continue to speak out—even more forcibly than it has in the past».[58]

The American Liberal Institutionalists stress on a Lockean world of nation-states which tend to pursue their national interests using both the hard and soft power at their disposal preferably within a multilateral framework of institutional cooperation, laws and rules. Naturally, they take into account the influence of unorthodox actors such as the EU and recognize the latter as a world player even though it is not a state with all its adjunct organs including armed forces. The liberal institutionalists sincerely believe that the EU has clout for what it is—an economic superpower with distinct social-democratic model and an example of interstate reconciliation and cooperation—, what it seems to be—an active influence in the international polity and economy, especially employing its soft power—and what it is likely to become—a union of about 35 states capable of making substantial contributions to international peace, stability and security—in the decades to come.

On the other hand, the Neorealists/Neoconservatives, who stress on a Hobbesian world of contending/competing great powers locked in perpetual conflict employing hard military power, tend to take little or no account of actors other than powerful nation-states, and as such, does not recognize the EU as an influential actor in international politics. They maintain that states alone can have foreign and security policies, thus stressing that the EU, which is not a state in the conventional sense, cannot claim to have foreign and security policies. Thus, they chide the Europeans for pretending to have a Common Foreign and Security Policy and question the very rationale of the EU—its objectives, activities and accomplishments—in its external relations. The most atrocious part of the prediction of the American realists is that Europe without the two controlling superpowers would dissolve into anarchy.

The European concept of Civilian Power, by which they intend to domesticate relations between states, is incomprehensible to the Americans. They have seen it as an effort to transform the international system from the Hobbesian universe into a Lockean universe; to turn the state of nature into a norm-driven community; to turn the law of the jungle into the rule of law—of treaties and contracts and UN resolutions and in short, to remake the international system in the image of domestic civil society. The American

Realists ridicule that the whole idea of the international system being modeled on domestic society as fundamental fallacy and point out: «The European conceit that relations with all nations—regardless of ideology, regardless of culture, regardless even of open hostility—should be transacted on the EU model of suasion and norms and negotiations and solemn contractual agreements is an illusion».[59] And they attribute this tendency of the Europeans not to their political sagacity but to economic rapacity and «see Europeans as pursuing economic advantage through trade with America's enemies while refusing to invest in military forces needed to confront hostile regimes».[60]

As such, the American scholars maintain that the Europeans continue to underinvest in their military capabilities to meet new post-post cold war threats to European homeland and international security and this is one of the key reasons why the Bush Administration is not taking the EU as seriously as it might have taken otherwise. Moreover, they ridicule the Europeans on their military weakness. For instance, Kagan maintains: «Europeans oppose unilateralism in part because they have no capacity for unilateralism... For Europeans, the appeal to multilateralism and international law has a real practical payoff, with little cost». He goes on to claim that the EU is a weak power, both militarily and morally and that they are from the 'Venus' and so, for a pacific policy.[61] As such, while the Europeans want to forget the backlog of about 500 years of war-infested history, they were reminded off by others, especially the Americans, whenever they want to tease the Europeans in the present day context of the American militarism and the European pacifism.

Krauthammer openly accuses the Europeans by maintaining that «the whole point of the multilateral enterprise (of the Europeans) is to reduce American freedom of action by making it subservient to, dependent on, constricted by the will and interests of other nations and it is an attempt to tie down Gulliver with a thousand strings. It is designed to domesticate the most undomesticated, most outsized, national interest on the planet of the Americans».[62]

Besides, the American State Department officials turn European criticism of American unilateralism on its head, by arguing that it is Europe and not US that has been acting in a unilateralist fashion of late. They complain that Brussels repeatedly presents Washington with non-negotiable policies precooked among the EU member states and allies, refusing to accommodate the unique role, considerations and responsibilities in the world or domestic compulsions of the US. In so doing, American officials charge, Europe is unilaterally defining new areas of international law with regard to climate change, biological weaponry, or whatever, without the international consensus that must necessarily include the US.[63] As such, they try to turn the table against the Europeans. The blame game continues.

Krauthammer maintains that the Bush administration followed democratic globalism, a foreign policy that defines the national interest not as power but as values and that identifies one supreme value, what John Kennedy called «the success of liberty». President Bush put this tendency in his speech at Whitehall in November 2003 thus: «The United States and Great Britain share a mission in the world beyond the balance of power or the simple pursuit of interest. We seek the advance of freedom and the peace that freedom brings». While elaborating on his idea of democratic globalism as pursued by Bush establishment, Krauthammer adds: «Beyond power. Beyond interest. Beyond interest defined as power. That is the credo of democratic globalism. Which explains its political appeal: America is a nation uniquely built not on blood, race or consanguinity, but on a proposition—to which its sacred honor has been pledged for two centuries. This American exceptionalism explains why non-Americans find this foreign policy so difficult to credit; why Blair has had more difficulty garnering support for it in his country; and why Europe, in particular, finds this kind of value-driven foreign policy hopelessly and irritatingly moralistic».[64]

In short, the US has taken the EU as a rival and there is a growing number of Americans who doubt whether European integration would be in the US interests. They point to the problems the US had to face whenever the EU had managed to speak with one voice (ICC, Kyoto, trade) and suggest the US should rather intensify its policy of divide and drive.[65] Many an American sincerely believes that the vision of the Europeans is always slightly ahead of reality.

Perceptions of India, EU and the US on Important International Issues—Convergences and Divergences

Democracy and Human Rights

India, EU and US are the largest, most innovative and most powerful democracies, respectively. As elaborated by Etien (p. 13-28), these three powers, in spite of the diverse contexts, cultures and traditions that have made them adopt different types of political regimes, benefit from a significantly historical experience in the functioning of democracy and protection of rights and fundamental liberties despite the difficulties faced. India since its independence has practised parliamentary democracy and remains an example for other emerging nations, even if the hurdles are still huge and minorities not completely integrated. Quite naturally, there is remarkable convergence of ideas over democratization, promotion of respect for human rights, rule of law and good governance among the three powers.

Both EU and the US consider promotion of the process of democratisation and human rights environment in the developing world as one of their foreign policy goals. They feel that their success in this front will ensure success in achieving their other objectives as well.

However, the Indian grievance is that in spite of its democratic credentials and comparatively better human rights record, its political and economic problems fail to receive due consideration from the other two powers. While the latter champion the cause of democratization of the developing world, India advocates democratization of the international system and especially, the UN Security Council, ultimate decision-making body in international politics and offers itself as a candidate for permanent seat with veto power.

Of late, some sort of convergence is emerging on the issue of the permanent seat for India and other aspirants in the UN Security Council, which was projected by India as a test case of democratization of international politics. While the individual member states of the EU harp on that for quite some time now, the American administration as well as the elite too reacted positively to such an eventuality, of late.[66] Again, there is some tacit understanding among the three powers to respect each others sentiments and limitations. This development has provided a better environment in which all the three powers may be able to work together in these areas, which is beneficial not only to them but also to the world.

In the human rights front, the Europeans have developed a system which is deservedly celebrated by those who are cautious and conscious of the protection and promotion of human rights, especially due to the enforcement mechanism that has come into being under the framework of European Convention on Human Rights and Fundamental Freedoms, signed and promulgated under the auspices of Council of Europe. Still, minority rights, and especially, the handling of the Muslim immigrant community leaves much to be desired. In this context, Shazia Wülber's contention (p. 235) that "Islam tinged with European values and Indian Islam having hues of traditional Indian values can be a reality if obstacles like feelings of alienation, complicated identity issues and unemployment are dealt with" holds some sense.

On certain occasions the Europeans criticize the Americans in the sphere of human rights. In the case of human rights violations that have occurred in Kosovo on the name of humanitarian intervention, quite rightly, scholars like Iver B. Neumann (pp. 275-6) points out: "By choosing bombing, however, we opted, nevertheless, to save lives on 'our'side by killing even more of 'them'. What happens is thereby a bargaining game about how war after Kosovo should be comprehended. We do not agree with ourselves at this juncture. If we want to achieve a way of conducting war, in which use of violence is mostly restricted, the war in Kosovo does not seem to be much of an ideal". By way of solution, Neumann offers "the proposition that the problems concerning the questions of which actors are seen as legitimate wagers of war, of which kinds of issues is it legitimate to go to war, and of the legitimate ways of waging war have a common denominator". His last, but not least important, salvo: "In Kosovo, the end of the legitimate warring state was at hand. Where is the political entity which may legitimately speak in the name of humanity?" deserves a sincere and truthful answer from the international community.

Market Economy and Globalization

Though most of the European countries and the US have adopted market economy model, there were difference of opinion in the details. On the economic side, the 'privileges of the dollar' in the international monetary system was highly resented by the European leaders like Charles de Gaulle.[67] In a way, the European activities towards the establishment of the Monetary Union in the 1970s were in response to the American unilateral measures in the international financial market. This process culminated in the introduction of 'Euro', the single European currency in late 1990s. On the face of continuing 'dollar dominance' in the international financial and stock markets, there is a conscious effort to project 'Euro' as a competitor and alternative to the 'dollar'. The French believe that the Euro is, more than likely, going to free not only Europe but also the world from its unilateral dependence on the dollar.[68]

On the issue of globalization process and its impacts also the Europeans and the Americans could not see eye to eye on all its dimensions. Generally, 'globalization' is identified with 'Americanisation' by the French, who termed it 'runaway globalization'.[69] They view that process with deep ambivalence as the bearer of the American way and are determined to defend the *exception française,* the French way. They detested its propensity to produce uniformity and disrespect for diversity, since the French have taken that "diversity in the cultural field is a factor of enrichment for our planet, and the basis of national identities." In stead, they advocated 'managed globalization', which would take care of their concerns over the developments related the process of globalization.

In the US, Liberalism seems to have triumphed in the 1990s as a political ideology. However, the US today is critical of European «continental corporatism» and appears «determined to demonstrate the superiority of its preferred market model over that of social democracy».[70] As such, the major French concern was to «cooperate without uncertainties with an omnipresent United States», without nonetheless «giving up our own ideas about the organization of the world». This made them to resolve «to be friends and allies» of the Americans, but not «aligned» with the US.[71]

India tried to maintain its own path of economic growth since independence till the end of 1970s. It took to liberalization of its economy in early 80s, which paved way for liberalization-privatization-globalization in the 90s, which hooked the Indian economy with a globalized world. Economic reforms were initiated and the process is still on, with certain hiccups on and off, with external pressure to open up further and internal compulsion to impress on 'enough is enough'.

In essence, both EU and India want to have their own choice and believe that while globalization has become inevitable it has also lead to many unwanted and unwarranted results, which calls for certain corrective measures. In this regard, Chris Patten maintains: «Europe sees an important part of its external role in helping to make globalization fairer and more acceptable to those who are presently marooned in misery. We cannot stop globalization. ... But we can make it more balanced».[72] Moreover, in his anxiety to tackle the problems born out of the dark side of globalization, Patten insists on the need for international agreements, rules and institutions, which can implement and police them. India too shares this optimism. As pointed out by Geetha Ganapathy Doré (p. 223) only «by joining hands against the merciless onslaught of globalization as mercantile empire with the common objective of preserving human dignity, notably the dignity of their ageing citizens, and social justice and furthering sustainable development», the Union of India and the European Union could make the world a better place.

Characteristics and Nature of International System

While recognizing the characteristics and nature of the present day world and the current international system also there is much difference of opinion among the three powers. In the early 1990s, there was a convergence in global opinion that the world was «unipolar» with the US as the sole super power and there is a general consensus that the unipolarity began in November of 1989—11/9, as it were—when the Berlin Wall fell. However, it was assumed that unipolarity was a passing phase, a «moment» and Krauthammer termed it America's «unipolar moment».[73] Others called it America's «Roman moment». There was also talk about the 'ensuing' multipolar world and some powers, especially France, attempted to challenge the then unipolar world dominated by the US. Samuel Huntington described the then international system in more accurate terms as «uni-multipolar». Some Chinese geopoliticians echoed this view by terming it «many powers and one superpower». However,

Krauthammer, subsequently, revised his calculations and claimed: «The unipolar moment has become the unipolar era» of prolonged duration.[74]

On the other hand, the European scholars like Moisi argue that the world is reverting to its pre-war multi-polar state. While acknowledging America's objective military superiority and the relative weakness of all others, Moisi labels it «asymmetrical multi-polarity».[75] Thereby, he indicates a tectonic shift in the international system: the shift from a unipolar to a multipolar world and maintains that America's unipolar 'moment', which began in 1991 with the collapse of the Soviet Empire, was over and it is no more Unipolar 'era' as claimed by Krauthammer. While recognising the fact that the US is more than a «normal Power», Moisi qualifies: «America no longer qualifies, if it ever did, as a «hyper power», to use Védrine's term, though it is still far from being a «normal» power».[76] Zakaria, while defining the current hybrid international system acknowledges the fact that the US remains by far the most powerful country, maintains: «... in a world with several other important great powers and with greater assertiveness and activity from all actors. ... It is easier to define what it is not than what it is, easier to describe the era it is moving away from than the era it is moving toward—hence the post-American World».[77]

Of late, Richard Haass maintains that the principal characteristic of twenty-first-century international relations is «turning out to be nonpolarity: a world dominated not by one or two or even several states but rather by dozens of actors possessing and exercising various kinds of power. This represents a tectonic shift from the past. In contrast to multipolarity—which involves several distinct poles or concentrations of power—a nonpolar international system is characterized by numerous centers with meaningful power».[78]

In the view of Haass, today's world differs in a fundamental way from one of classic multipolarity as there are many more power centers and quite a few of them are not nation-states. Indeed, one of the cardinal features of the contemporary international system is that nation-states have lost their monopoly on power and in some domains their preeminence as well. «States are being challenged from above, by regional and global organizations; from below, by militias; and from the side, by a variety of nongovernmental organizations (NGOs) and corporations. Power is now found in many hands and in many places» Haass points out.

International Law and Organization—Multilateralism

Regarding the role and usefulness of international institutions and multilateralism in the international politics there is a marked cleavage among the three powers. The soundness of obliging international law/rules and regulations too has become debatable. The Americans increasingly tend towards unilateralism in international affairs. They are less inclined to act through international institutions such as the United Nations, less intended to work cooperatively with other nations to pursue common goals, more skeptical about international law, and more willing to operate outside its framework when they deem it convenient.[79] The US refusal to play by the same rules as everyone else is considered as the root cause of the shattering of Atlnticism.[80]

The unipolar world pattern with a single model of culture, value concept and ideology, witnessed the steady weakening of the role of the United Nations and the Security Council. The 'global unilateralism' on the part of the US in its relationship with the rest of the world and its attempts to wield global hegemony was highly resented by the great, medium-sized and regional powers—member states of EU such as France and India. The French scholars like Pascal Boniface point out that a unipolar world is not a healthy situation, since the dominant power is bound to have a tendency to confuse its national interests with universal values. «Having embodied the fight for human rights over previous centuries, France today must take up another symbolic fight: the emergence of a multipolar world, a universally accepted principle, which meets the aspirations of the major part of humanity», Boniface argues.[81]

As such, the Europeans insist on multilateralism and on the need for international laws, agreements, rules and institutions, which can implement and police them. They emphasize on the need to ensure that the United Nations and the other institutions of global governance can operate as effectively as possible and on multilateral cooperation. Patten maintains: «The main role of the EU in international affairs must be to give teeth and bite to this multilateralism».[82] Moreover, the Europeans wish that the US should be ready to be bound by the rules and regulations and international law and not law unto itself.

On the other hand, the Americans view their international leadership in the war on terrorism and the containment of WMDs not as bullying unilateralism but as pragmatic necessity in a world where there is no other significant international leadership. Moreover, comparative military weakness of the Europeans and their alleged tolerance towards the international bullies were used by the Americans to justify their unilateral actions. American scholars like Haass argue that since the EU is preoccupied with its internal development, it falls on the United States to lead the international system, many a time unilaterally.

International Terrorism

On facing the new international scourge of global terrorism also there is certain difference of option, not in fighting against terrorism, but, in the manner in which it is to be tackled. Europe and India faced the terrorist problem for quite a few decades now.[83] The US has become its victim in due course. To the dismay and discomfiture of the Americans, 9/11 demonstrated how a little investment on the part of the technically-savvy terrorists could cause calculated, extra-ordinary, unprecedented and unpredictable levels of human and physical damage and many of the most costly, latest pieces of modern weaponry may not be of particular use in the surrogate warfare waged by non-state actors like terrorists in which traditional battlefields are replaced by urban combat zones. Weapons of the strong had no answer to the weapons of the weak. As such, September 11 is the definitive demonstration that the combination of modern technology and transnational primitivism has erased the barrier between "over here" and "over there" and now it is "any where" and "every where", "any time" and "every time" and to "any body" and "every body".

Though the Europeans rallied around the US in the wake of September 11 and were supportive of the US in its anti-terrorism ventures, they emphasized that «political response must accompany counterterrorism and preventive measures».[84] Moreover, majority of Europeans continue to believe that US foreign policy is partly to blame for the Al-Qaeda attacks. As such, there is a gulf between American and European perceptions of the sources/causes of international terrorism and on how to tackle the problem. India's grievance is that its terrorist problem aided and abetted by Pakistan fails to emanate positive response from the other two powers, who talk about all out war on terrorism elsewhere.

Later, in continuation with their war against terrorism, the Americans arrogated in claiming the right to attack any country it wants without credible pretext or without any international authorization.[85] This American behaviour was the outcome of its self-assumed role as international policeman in pursuit of bad elements in international politics with a bludgeon in hand and then to act as the judge as well as executioner. The international community is at a loss to understand and appreciate this logic.

President Bush's claim that "the world is safer today because our coalition ended a regime that cultivated ties to terror while it built weapons of mass destruction" was rejected with well-deserving contempt by Noam Chomsky, who points out that there is not the slightest evidence of any connection between Saddam Hussein and his bitter enemy, Osama bin Laden, and the idea of a connection is dismissed by every competent authority, including the intelligence agencies. On the other hand, he points out that the likely consequence of the Iraq invasion would be proliferation of weapons of mass destruction, and terror. "The Iraq war was a huge setback for the war on terror, led to a sharp spike in recruitment for Al Qaeda and other terrorist groups, and in fact Iraq itself turned into a haven for terrorists for the first time", Chomsky concludes.[86]

Power and Use of Power

Again, over the issue of concept of power and how to use it in international political arena too there are severe contentions. As mentioned earlier, the US sincerely believes that it is a power of preponderance as the 'sole' super power, 'uncontrolled and uncontrollable'. The unfortunate developments in the Western Balkans involving Serbia and the failure of the European Union to handle the situations at its own backyard, enthused the Americans to arrogate themselves to claim their right to intervene in Bosnia and then in Kosovo on the name of protection of human rights.

Chomsky is critical of the American claim for the right to humanitarian intervention and he points out that such a claim is just another expression of traditional imperialism. He always reminds his readers and audience on the World Court judgements passing strictures against the US that goes back to the Corfu case in 1949 and again in the Nicaragua case in 1980s.[87] Time and again, Chomsky has highlighted the world opinion against the claim of the US 'responsibility to protect' and humanitarian intervention in the case of Kosovo and points out that even the high power committee established to ponder over the need for the revision of the UN Charter in this regard has advised against such a measure.[88]

While questioning the claim of the US government over its right to preemption, Chomsky points out: «Preemptive war has a meaning in international law. It's kind of on the border of legality. If you think about the UN charter, it authorizes the use of force under one condition—two conditions, either the Security Council calls for it, or in self-defense against armed attack until the Security Council has a chance to act. And that has a sort of fringe of judgment. So, for example, if, say, Russian bombers were flying across the Atlantic with the obvious intent of bombing the United States it would be legitimate under—it would be interpreted as legitimate under Article 51 to shoot them down before they bomb. Maybe even to attack the base they were coming from. That's a preemptive strike. It's a military action taken against an imminent attack when no other possibility is open, and there's enough time to notify the Security Council».[89] He was highly critical about the US claim on preemptive strike on the name of self-defence and on the strength of Article 51 of the UN Charter.

Chomsky was quite successful in highlighting the hidden motives behind the American foreign policy and action. Bush administration declared Iran, North Korea and Iraq as rogue states, but attacked Iraq and not others. The attack on Iraq was projected as the exemplary action, of foreboding to others what is in store for them. «In part, that's because Iraq's just a lot more important. It's right in the center of the oil-producing region, but in part it's because Iraq was understood to be completely defenseless».

Europe in the past half-century has developed a genuinely different perspective on the role of power in international relations, a perspective that springs directly from its unique historical experience since the end of World War II. The modern European strategic culture represents a conscious rejection of their own past, a rejection of the evils of *machtpolitik*. Joschka Fischer, the then German Foreign Minister, presents this attitude succinctly in his speech outlining his vision of the 'Future Europe' at Humboldt University in Berlin on May 12, 2000, thus: «The core of the concept of Europe after 1945 was and still is a rejection of the European balance-of-power principle and the hegemonic ambitions of individual states that had emerged following the Peace of Westphalia in 1648». As is well appreciated the European Union is the positive reaction to awful centuries of European warfare. Most Europeans believe that it was the transformation of European politics, the deliberate abandonment and rejection of centuries of *machtpolitik*, that in the end made possible the «new order». They want to recreate it at the international level, by helping in the ushering of the «new world order». They have learnt from history and that is why wanted to abandon its backlog. Thus, the main plank of the European criticism of the U.S. is the overemphasis the Americans place on hard power, unilateral pursuit of interests and actions, and the under appreciation of the value of soft power. American reluctance to put their faith in multilateral solutions to the sources of threats to homeland security is perceived as the real danger to world peace and thus, the Europeans want to calibrate/restrain the US by multilateralizing it. They caution the US that possessing a superior resource may lead states to overuse it, or to attempt to use it for purposes for which it is not well-suited.

Threat Perception and on Facing the Threats

Even when Americans and Europeans agree on the kind of world order they would strive to build, they increasingly disagree about what constitutes a threat to that international endeavor. Indeed, Europeans and Americans differ most these days in their evaluation of what constitutes a tolerable versus an intolerable threat. This, too, is consistent with the disparity of power and its usage. The Americans claim that Europe's relative weakness results in its greater tolerance for threats. Kagan calls this as the 'psychology of weakness' of the Europeans and maintains: «The EU sees the world through the eyes of the weak, which constrains what the Europeans can do to face down threats to their security. Thus, it is in the European self-interest to stress on diplomacy and negotiation within multilateral contexts. The EU underestimates security threats from rogue states, WMDs and ballistic missiles, and international terrorism». By implication, he tries to impress that the Europeans do not want to endanger peace and prosperity that they enjoy by playing an active role (by using military power and thereby earn the wrath of rogue states) in international politics. Again, Kagan points out that it is also very much a realistic response in that Europe, precisely because it is weak, actually faces fewer threats than the far more powerful United States.[90]

EU seeks to differ more strongly with the US on certain fundamental issues, such as methods of dealing with «countries of concern»—North Korea, Cuba, Iran, Iraq and Libya. The Europeans feel that the Americans are preoccupied with discovering enemies and decide on the issue of who require a military response, on the basis of who among them are most vulnerable and where their economic and commercial priorities lies. Iraq was chosen since it was defenceless and rich in oil resources. Europe would perhaps expect the US «to invest in encouraging political accommodation or transition within authoritarian regimes», rather then adopt a military approach in dealing with these countries.[91]

Early in 2003 most Americans perceived themselves to live in a world in which Iraq appeared sufficiently threatening not only their beloved homeland but also the world and thus found enough reason to declare war with that country. The American establishment and media, both print and electronic, contributed to this sad spectacle. On the other hand, this was not the world most Europeans perceived. They saw a world in which US bombs and soldiers promised more harm than good, while multilateral diplomacy and application of international law promised the best hope of humane, effective maintenance of long-term security and prosperity. Accordingly, they voiced strong opposition to the US policy, which attempted «policy change» as well as «regime change» in Iraq simultaneously, as they felt that the American action was unnecessary, insensible, and morally indefensible.[92]

The United States, the Europeans argue, resorts to force more quickly and is less patient with diplomacy and that Americans have an unreasonable demand for «perfect» security, which they were used to enjoy for a couple of centuries as a result of their isolationist policy. The Americans, they claim, make far too much of the threats the so called 'rogue states' pose. In short, in international security issues, there is wholesale divergence, drawing no doubt on very different readings on the seriousness of threats to security and what to do about them.

Energy Security

Quest for resources always remain the hidden motive of all the laud-sounding rhetoric of the American foreign policy claims that they are for the propagation of democracy and for the protection and promotion of human rights every where. Especially, greed for other's energy resources and raw materials lies behind any American move. Imposition of American inspired/sponsored international system which would ensure uninterrupted access to resources remains the basis of all their foreign relations. To cater to their growing energy needs and to sustain their growth rate, the Americans are always in pursuit of having a control over those regions which are rich in energy resources and the routes through which energy resources could reach their country without any hindrance. While they intended to maintain direct assess to those resources, they were, on the other hand, interested in preventing their access to others, both allies as well as rivals. Moreover, the US is accused of wanton destruction of the productive resources of 'others' who dared to be 'against' them, by choosing different path of development. Critics maintain that the US invaded Iraq so as to have unhindered access to its oil. It was also intended to put its finger on the flow of oil to the Europeans, they point out.

Relations with Third Countries Especially Russia and China

The US intends to defy both Russia and China, while the Europeans want to be conciliatory and cooperative, rather than confront and alienate them. To slight Russia, the US flitters with Georgia, Ukraine and other former Soviet states, ready to offer them military assistance and membership in NATO and encourages them in their confrontationist postures against the Russians. The Europeans are not in favour of this divide and thrive policy. Regarding China, Europeans wanted to have constructive cooperation rather than confrontation and further alienation, while the Americans either cooperated with them or confronted them according to their national game plans. While in confrontation mood, they expected their allies and friends to side with them. This policy of blowing hot and cold whimsically is not taken lightly by other powers. In Iran's case while the Americans are hostile, the Europeans put a premium on negotiation and concession.

India does not want to be drawn into the controversies of the US making and that the new closeness between them would affect their friendly relations with Russia. Despite having definite problems with China, India is not prepared to come out open and be a party to the US in its 'Contain China' project. In the case of Iran as well, the Indians intend to maintain their time-tested cordial relations. In spite of the changed circumstances and new permutations and combinations, the Indian leaders are very particular about maintaining independence in foreign policy, which is very dear to them.

Environmental Issues

Approaches to the environmental degradation and new challenges like climate change and global warming as well as the ways and means through which they can be tackled too created divisions between the three powers. While EU puts its weight behind the Kyoto Protocol, the US is not serious about it. American intransigence on environmental issues is considered as irresponsible by the Europeans. The US insists that India and other developing countries should be restrained so that they would not cause further damage to the environment. On the other hand, India feels that the polluters, the developed countries, should pay and maintains that those developing countries which are on the path of economic growth should not be restricted in the name of environmental degradation.

On Some India-specific Issues

On certain India-specific issues like Kashmir and terrorism sponsored by Pakistan across the border, the EU and US reacts differently at different times. On the whole, there is a lingering feeling in India that both the powers have failed to approach the issue clinically on its own merit rather than viewing it from their point of view tinted by their selfish interests and motives. Comparatively, the EU's stand is found conciliatory, with occasional ruptures born out of unwanted gestures or statements emanating from certain member states. The American stand that Kashmir is a disputed territory irritates India and any effort to link Kashmir issue with terrorism is considered as unfriendly act. Any statement advocating international mediation in Kashmir is unacceptable to India, as it feels that it is a domestic issue or utmost bilateral to be sorted out with Pakistan.

On the issue of cross border terrorism emanating from Pakistan, especially in the wake of November 2008 terrorist attack in Mumbai, India feels that the international community has not done much to pressurize Pakistan. The

Indian leaders were singularly unhappy with the British Foreign Minister Miliband's attempt to link terrorist attack with Kashmir issue. On the other hand, the French stand which was conciliatory and supportive of the Indian point of view soothed their hurt feelings.

How these Perceptions (Self, of Each Other and on International Politics) Affect their Actions?

Democratization, Human Rights

As democratization and promotion of respect for human rights, rule of law and good governance in third countries remains one of the main objectives of foreign policy of both EU and the US, they are determined to use all the power at their disposal to achieve this goal. Again, both the powers lecture to other powers on the need to approach all the problems that they face, including the terrorist problem, with due respect for human rights and rule of law. The US is ready even to use force in democratising the developing world. For instance, the Bush administration claimed that its objective in Iraq was regime change and introduction of democracy in that country. The element of contradiction in this case is quite glaring—trying to achieve regime change and policy change simultaneously and also using unilateral force for that purpose.

What the Americans want to achieve through use of force, the Europeans try to accomplish through persuasion and platitude. The EU links its development and cooperation polices with the human rights record of the recipient country, in its effort to improve human rights situation and democratic profile of the latter. Benıta Ferrero-Waldner, European Commissioner for External Relations and European Neighbourhood Policy claims that in Afghanistan, the EU contributes substantially to improvements in rule of law through training of police, and reform of the justice system, infrastructure and basic services.[93] The EU is deeply engaged in supporting fledgling democracies in places like Ukraine and Lebanon, assisting the growth of democratic consciousness in Egypt and Georgia, she vouchsafes.

However, the success of the EU in the sphere of human rights promotion was sullied when it could not intervene and stop the catastrophe that overtook the Balkan region in the 1990s and subsequently in Kosovo. All the laments of Patten over the failure of the Europeans to prevent the genocide of millions of fellow Europeans in the Balkans could not wash away their sin.[94] The European inaction brought in the Americans into the fore. In the NATO bombings that ensued resulted in more civilian casualties as the Americans believed that one of their lives is superior to thousands of other 'lesser mortals'. Precisely, the Americans paid their compliments to the Serbians through their hearty imitations. The human rights violations that took place in the aftermath of 9/11 in the US and in Iraq and other places later betrays the huge gap between the American claims and actions in the human rights front and the European incapacity to rein in the US in this regard. Again, while in some cases of human rights violations they overact, in certain others they turn their blind eye. Many a times, they support autocracies and dictatorships in stead of fellow democracies, simply guided by their narrow political and economic national interests. As such, by their acts of omission and commission the Western powers, especially the US, do incalculable damage to the cause of human rights promotion and protection.

International Organization and Multilateralism

Through several of its unilateral actions, the US establishment under Bush displayed unashamedly its utter contempt for the UN system and other international initiatives to regulate the course of current developments. Europeans think the Americans are too quick to take unilateral security actions at the expense of negotiation and diplomacy. The decision of the Bush Administration to break with the 1972 ABM Treaty with Russia is a prime example of how an American decision, which went against European judgment, affected the vital security interest of the EU states. The unilateral declaration of war against Iraq without due sanction based on the UN Security Council resolution and without bothering to convince the allies on the issue of presence of WMDs, obliged the French and Germans to oppose the war.

Again, on the issues of International Criminal Court (ICC) and International Convention on the Use of Land Mines, the Americans showed marked indifference, which shocked the comity of nations in general. The Europeans were particularly offended when the Bush Administration acted unilaterally in utter disregard for their position. The American withdrawal from the UN peacekeeping mission in Bosnia, as a preventive mechanism and a challenge to the ICC's jurisdiction over American personnel serving in that operation, was viewed by the Europeans not only as unilateral but also as hostile to the emerging international norms, duly and deservedly supported by them.

Nuclear Non-Proliferation

All the five nuclear powers, the P-5, were united in one aspect—for maintaining their monopoly over the nuclear power and technology. Their aim was to prevent the nuclear threshold states like India from gate-crashing into their privileged club. The Americans were, especially, the protagonists and promoters of the nuclear non-proliferation regime, through which they tried to maintain control over the other nuclear 'haves' like France and to prevent the nuclear 'have-nots' like India as such, and they were quite successful in their attempt throughout 70s and 80s. That was why both France and India mainly opposed the Non-Proliferation Treaty (NPT) and refused to sign it, terming it discriminatory and unacceptable. Both the countries also collaborated in the nuclear field.[95] However, France signed the treaty in 1992 and then on joined the other nuclear powers to persuade/pressurize India to be a signatory to both NPT and Comprehensive Test Ban Treaty. Still, India persisted with its opposition to the nuclear restrictive regime. In the process, the nuclear powers and under their direction, the Nuclear Suppliers Group (NSG) introduced and implemented a nuclear denial regime on India, reducing it to the status of an untouchable in the nuclear field without access to civilian nuclear technology and materials.

Still, India kept the option open and in May 1998, detonated underground nuclear devices. The Clinton administration condemned New Delhi and imposed punitive sanctions, and indefinitely postponed the planned presidential visit. According to some estimate, the economic sanction cost India one per cent of GDP growth over the next year.[96] Subsequently, through Jaswant Singh—Strobe Talbot strategic dialogue, India could convince the Americans on the rationality of their nuclear stand and more importantly, it was an accomplished fact.

On the other hand, though the initial reaction of the EU to Indian nuclear test of May 1998 was 'furious', by October EU came out with a «common position' aimed at promoting non-proliferation and confidence-building in South Asia—offered «financial and conceptual contributions» to initiatives for enhancing confidence-building measures and technical assistance to implement and administer export control regulations.[97] For good, the EU had not towed the US policy of economic sanctions. As mentioned elsewhere, this shift in stand may be attributed to France's benevolent intervention in favour of India. France also argued India's case for civilian nuclear cooperation as an incentive for its abandoning nuclear weapons programme.

Through its strategic dialogue with France, India followed a peaceful and constructive nuclear diplomacy with EU and was successful in winning over major European states to its side. While addressing the Indo-EU Summit of June 2000, the Indian Premier Vajpayee tried to present the Indian Nuclear

Power status within the context of the ensuing multipolar world order. Taking the cue from the quest of the EU member states in general and of France in particular for achieving an effective multipolar world order, Vajpayee reiterated the Indian belief that for an effective multi-polarity, it was necessary to create a plural security order that accommodated and acknowledged the growing strength and confidence of the emerging economic and security players such as India, which intend to create and have a strategic space and independence in decision-making. "In an increasingly interdependent world, a plural security order alone can deal with the challenges of the new era. It is in this context that the development of our nuclear capability should be seen", he argued.[98]

In June 2005, India and the US concluded a bilateral agreement to cooperate on civilian nuclear energy—a *de facto* recognition by the United States that India is a nuclear weapons state. The agreement reinforces India's commitment to nonproliferation norms in its civilian nuclear programme, but it keeps India's military programme outside the orbit of inspections by the International Atomic Energy Agency. The US and majority member states of the EU have thus reconciled to the fact now that India is a nuclear power and still have every right to have access to the civilian nuclear energy as any other sovereign entity.

Critics of the deal warned that it threatens the NPT. Western advocates of nuclear non-proliferation regime felt that the Indo-US nuclear deal has weakened, if not, diluted that regime.[99] But the Bush administration justified its action by arguing that India «is emerging as a great power, the nuclear genie cannot be put back in the bottle, and because India is a democracy, the genie will do no harm».

Later, despite domestic opposition to the deal, the Indian Government went ahead with its effort to seek clearance from the International Atomic Energy Committee and subsequently from the Nuclear Supplier's Group for the sale of equipments and materials related to civilian nuclear programme. The US establishment put its weight behind these efforts and clinched the deal in favour of India. Though, some members of the EU opposed the deal, some others, especially France, whole-heartedly supported India and often reiterated their readiness to supply nuclear technology, especially to sell advanced nuclear reactors so as help India in meeting out its energy requirements. The American and French corporations in the nuclear field have already started negotiations with India in right earnestness in this regard. It is significant to note that the nuclear apartheid with regard to India came to an end when it signed its commercial nuclear deal with the French nuclear giant Areva for nuclear reactors and fuel supply.[100]

All out War against International Terrorism

In the aftermath of September 11, the EU reacted quickly and on September 21, the European Council was convened in an extraordinary meeting. An anti-terrorism action plan with 68 items encompassing ad hoc measures of enhancing police and judicial cooperation, the development of international legal instruments and the strengthening of European air security was agreed upon. EU also developed a Common Position on terrorism and introduced a European arrest warrant that supplanted the system of extradition between member states, allowing for wanted persons to be handed over directly from one judicial authority to another. Moreover, the EU agreed on a common definition of punishable terrorist activities and a common list of organizations, entities and groups engaged in terrorist activities. A specialist anti-terrorist team was set up with the Europewide police, Europol, cooperating closely with its US counterparts. A common position on air security regulations was also formulated.[101] The Counter-Terrorism Co-ordinator, Gijs de Vries, has been appointed to coordinate the European counter-terrorist measures and he is expected to directly report to Solana, the EU Foreign Policy Chief.

On the issue of combating international terrorism by organizing an international coalition, initially, the Europeans have collaborated with the Americans. They have taken several collective level measures to achieve control over the situation. In the American and NATO military action against the Taliban regime in Afghanistan, the Europeans whole-heartedly offered their might and money. They were part of the seventeen-strong coalition involved in the Afghan theatre.

In 2002-03, when the Americans tried to extend the scope and theatre of war against international terrorism to Iraq which they considered as part of 'axis of evil', the French and the Germans stuck to their guns by opposing the American move. This earned the wrath of Condoleezza Rice, the then American Secretary of State, who thundered that the US should "forgive Russia, ignore Germany and punish France".[102] In January 2003, Donald Rumsfeld, the then American Defence Secretary, issued a statement in which he singled out Europe's two largest countries, France and Germany, as «problems», and argued: «You are thinking of Europe as Germany and France. I don't. I think that's old Europe». At its inception, Rumsfeld's quip was meant to set apart the «coalition of the willing» (i.e. those countries that readily lined up behind the US in its war against Iraq) and the «axis of the sitting» (the «old Europe», the states that just would not follow Washington's lead). Rumsfeld's comments hit at the very heart of the entire EU political project in that it challenged the Union's backbone, the Franco-German axis. The gist of Rumsfeld's message was that while «old Europe» was not following the US's footsteps in Iraq and looked at Europe as a counterweight to Washington's military policies, the label «new Europe» should apply to those countries which were strongly Atlanticist at heart, recognised American power as the guardian of democracy and freedom and which thus readily joined the US-led «coalition of the willing» against Saddam Hussein. The Defence Secretary also noted that in Washington's view, the «centre of gravity [of NATO Europe] is shifting to the east».[103]

As a fall out, most Europeans distanced from the President's 'axis of evil' speech and the new openly proclaimed pre-emptive strike doctrine. They doubted whether military might alone could defeat terrorism or tackle the roots of terrorism. While the US talked of a 'war on terrorism'; Europeans talked of 'a fight against terrorism'. The Americans retorted that Europeans did not take defence seriously and pointed to the huge transatlantic gap in military capabilities. A related dispute concerned 'rogue states' with few Europeans even prepared to use the term and preferring a policy of conditional engagement rather than a policy of isolation and sanctions.[104]

Moreover, for good the Europeans rallied round and in September 2004, the Spanish Prime Minister José Luis Rodríguez Zapatero, representative of the 'New Europe' according to the Rumsfeld classification, declared that «the old Europe is brand new». Moreover, in a matter of two years, Rumsfeld's boast appeared to have got punctured as several members of his «new Europe» category—among them the Hungarians, the Czechs, the Poles and the Dutch—have decided to pack their bags and leave Iraq, upsetting the Defence Secretary's original paradigm. His «old Europe versus new Europe» division simply vanished into thin air, leaving EU intact.

India too extended its support to the US in its war against international terrorism, as it is the major victim of terrorism for a couple of decades by now. In turn, it expected unconditional and unrestricted support from the US and the EU, in its efforts to confront and checkmate the perpetrators of terrorist activities on its soil. Unfortunately, India got advice more than tangible assistance. The West liberally advised India that it should tackle terrorism without violating human rights. For quite some time, India and the EU are talking about common strategy against international terrorism. It is expected that at least in the wake of November 2008 terrorist attack in which some Europeans and the Americans too have lost their life may convince the EU and the US to the seriousness of the issue and goad them into some meaningful action.

Multipolar World

On the eve of his visit to India in February 2000, Védrine insisted on India's essential place in a multipolar world, on the need to establish with it the closest possible partnership and on the French support to its candidature, a legitimate one, for a permanent seat in the UN Security Council.[105] In New Delhi, while projecting 'a strong and united Europe' as one of the poles of the ensuing multipolar world order, Védrine suggested Russia, China, Japan and India as other prospective poles and invited India to collaborate with France in its effort to design 'Cooperative multi-polarity' with an improved version of multilateralism that respects all members of the international community as expressed by the United Nations.

Dominique de Villepin, French Foreign Minister, during his visit to India in September 2002, maintained: "France and India are two great powers which play an important role on the world stage, and they can both help to forge new strategic balance. Our two countries are concerned to build a world with a greater sense of solidarity, respectful of international law and attentive to the new social and environmental challenges."[106] Again, Paris insisted on injecting an element of multipolarity by inviting countries like India to have a dialogue with the G-8 countries prior to their summit meeting in Evian, France. India has been invited for the G-8 enlarged dialogue to discuss the questions of globalization and international governance. It must be taken note of that the decision to have enlarged dialogue was taken at the initiative of the French President Jacques Chirac.[107]

The Indian leaders too criticised the Uni-polarity by pointing out that it amounts to the assertion of political unreality. "For whereas uni-polarity asserts, at least ideologically freedom from bias, yet paradoxically, it denotes the very same intoxication of ideology—an intoxication that is born of precisely such an assertion of the relevance and centrality of the nation state and the sovereign interests of the one verses the many" the then Indian Foreign Minister Jaswant Singh asserted in February 2000.[108] While positively reacting to Védrine's call to build a different and better world of many power centers, Jaswant Singh called for «a concert of open societies» supported by an «overlapping network of institutions among governments and civil societies» to build a 'plural order' in the world.

To put it in a nutshell, the US judges the EU by its actions, not its rhetoric. The US officials are frustrated with the EU politically not because of the opacity of EU foreign policy making but because more often than not, EU action fails to match its rhetoric.[109] In frustration, the American establishment on several occasions sanctioned against European firms that deal with

American adversaries such as Cuba and Iran and accused the Europeans on their failure to understand the American domestic constraints.[110]

Dialogue in Danger and 'End of West'?

Divergence in perception and in action has resulted in cleavage between the US and the EU. These actions and counter-actions in turn created much bad blood, acrimony and divisions. It was assumed that a unilateral America is parting ways with a multilateral Europe. Kagan talks about widening and whooping gap in the Atlantic alliance and pronounces that no more West is a homogenous entity. «For along with these natural consequences of the transatlantic power gap, there has also opened a broad ideological gap. Europe, because of its unique historical experience of the past half-century—culminating in the past decade with the creation of the European Union—has developed a set of ideals and principles regarding the utility and morality of power different from the ideals and principles of Americans, who have not shared that experience. If the strategic chasm between the United States and Europe appears greater than ever today, and grows still wider at a worrying pace, it is because these material and ideological differences reinforce one another».[111]

Craig Smith also declares: «A dark cloud appears to have settled over the northern Atlantic. With regard to fostering international security, consensus-based cooperation between Europe and the United States seems overshadowed by tension, divisiveness, and uncertainty. This must dismay anyone who believes that even-handed cooperation would yield more peaceful prosperity than uncoordinated, competitive efforts».[112]

Efforts on their part to correct each other's actions further vitiated the atmosphere. Inevitable blame game followed and there was talk about irreparable damage and unbridgeable gap within the West. While some scholars foreseen 'end of Atlanticism', others even predicted 'end of West'. There was a marked loss of faith and understanding between the Americans and the Europeans. There were accusation and counter accusations—Europeans alleging that Americans are against the EU integration and the Americans returning the compliment with much more vigour. While Americans deplored the Spanish electorate's spinelessness in caving in to terrorism by voting the conservatives out of office after the Madrid bombings in March 2004, many Europeans decried the American electorate's stupidity in offering a second term for Bush in November 2004, in the wake of the disastrous war with Iraq that the latter plunged them into.[113]

Evil Effects of Divergence and Division

The US President's September 17, 2002 national security strategy does not refer to the EU as a partner of the U.S. in global affairs. It has not reiterated its support for the economic and political integration of Europe with the same quality of commitment of each of its predecessors since the founding of the EC in the 1950s. As such, it has thoroughly shaken the very foundation of the transatlantic relations. When EU and the US were divided, their failure in achieving the cherished common goals became imminent and inevitable. It is not an exaggeration, when Haass says: «No single country, no matter how powerful, can contend successfully on its own with transnational challenges. Any such effort will fail».[114] Due to their difference of opinion in the perception of threat and the way in which it is to be tackled, both the powers could not take a concerted and concrete action against international terrorism, countries holding WMDs and failed states, which threaten the world peace and well-being. In the international human rights regime they continued to fail miserably due to their working at cross purposes. The utter selfish manoeuvres and one-upmanship tricks as well as the divergence in political views and competition in the sphere of economic/trade relations between EU and the US is capitalized by China, as it could divide West in human rights issues by successfully playing Europe against the US and *vice versa*, by offering business contracts and trade opportunities. For instance, the European consortium Airbus Industrie and the American Boeing Industry, global rivals in the manufacture and sale of civilian aircrafts, were patronized with contracts to favour or tease the EU member states or the US, respectively.[115] Failure on this count is quite pronounced when the US had lost its seat in the Human Rights Commission in Geneva and on one occasion, Lebanon, with all its poor record on human rights, became the President of the Commission.

Call for Reconciliation and Strengthening of the Dialogue

For good, better sense continued to prevail on certain quarters of both sides of the Atlantic. Both American and the European leaders and scholars advocate restraint on the part of the Americans which will lead to restoration and further strengthening of the dialogue process. Chris Patten pleaded with the US to return to supporting the international «rule book» that it helped establish after 1945 to promote democracy, the rule of law and the opening of international markets. «The real future challenge for the US and EU, therefore, will be to try and better understand each other's interests and concerns; and to make the global «rule book» more successful», he advocated.[116] In his strategy paper of June 2003, Solana also emphasised on the importance of a solid transatlantic relationship to tackle the shared threats of terrorism and WMD.

There was conscious effort to impress upon the US that the Americans alone cannot manage or solve all the international problems and face various global challenges as they call for 'global solutions'. Cooperation and support from other like-minded partners are quite essential and indispensable. Globalization has unleashed economic, political and social forces that are not under the control of any one country, including the United States.[117] For instance, the U.S. cannot manage the terrorist threat by itself and it requires others to share intelligence, to coordinate law enforcement, to cooperate on homeland security. Some sort of a viable joint coordination and control mechanism is the need of the hour.

It was pointed out that there is a convergence on most transatlantic issues with the exceptions of diverging foreign policy reflexes (given different capabilities and habits) and elite opinion (European intellectuals on the left are particularly critical of U.S. policy and American intelligentsia on the right are natural bashers of EU policy). As this is the case there is a dire need to find ways to agree to disagree; to manage divergence and still to pull together.

Interestingly, Haass argues for bridging the gap and finding a solution to the transatlantic problem on a practical premise. He maintains: «But leadership requires followership, something that can only be engendered by a foreign policy that strives to get others to agree on the principles and rules of international relations and how they are to be enforced when they are violated.[118] Other scholars too concurred. Dinan was categorical when he says: «Despite their differences, the EU and the US are doomed to remain close collaborators, not only because of the importance of their bilateral relationship but also because of the need to defend their common interests and approaches in a world where democratic values and functioning market economies remain largely ideals rather than realities.[119] In reaction to the neo-conservative contention that US is a predominant power which cannot be contested by even the combination of all other powers, Zakaria quite rightly argues that they can complicate it, as it has happened in the case of the America's Iraqi venture.[120]

While extolling the transatlantic partnership the European Commission President José Manuel Barroso maintained on February 9, 2005: «The relationship between the United States and Europe constitutes the world's strongest, most comprehensive and strategically most important partnership». In the wake of the February 2005 Munich conference, the Commission went on record welcoming the signs of transatlantic reconciliation. Barroso reiterated that «more than ever, Europe needs the United States and the United States needs Europe [...] We must seize this opportunity with both hands. Today's international problems are too complex to go it alone».

President Bush echoed the sentiment by saying that «Today, security and justice and prosperity for our world depend on America and Europe working in common purpose. That makes our transatlantic ties as vital as they have ever been». Even Rumsfeld, while addressing the 41st Conference on European Security in Munich, Germany, on 11 February 2005, declared that «allies must cooperate» and that «we know that our collective security depends on our co-operation and mutual respect and understanding».[121] Since then there is talk of renewed partnership, a revitalised alliance and the US interest in a strong and united Europe.

While projecting the better image of EU and arguing for a better EU-US understanding, Benita Ferrero-Waldner, European Commissioner for External Relations and European Neighbourhood Policy, maintains: «The European Union is an increasingly mature partner for the US—capable of acting decisively on all the major issues of our day. With our 27 member states and our baffling institutions, we may be complex—but that complexity should not be confused with weakness. With few exceptions, we can and do speak with one voice on the issues that matter. And with very few exceptions indeed, we share the goals and values of the United States».[122] Dominique Moisi too insists that Europe, especially France, should not go against the US and maintains: «France cannot mistake its enemies. While the world is becoming ever more multipolar—with China and Russia's return as important actors and India's emergence on the international stage—it would be anachronistic and paradoxic to define oneself against or even in opposition to the United States».[123]

Again, while elaborating on the centrality of EU to the multipolarity in international politics, Moisi insists: «It is the EU that can make multi-polarity work if it plays its role positively. If the EU appears more concerned with the best ways to avoid the responsibilities that may befall it as a result of America's new and enforced modesty, then multi-polarity will result—by default, not by design—in a more chaotic world, rather than leading to greater stability». He adds: «Europe has a unique chance to demonstrate that it can make a difference in America's post-unipolar moment. It starts right now in the Middle-East. The world that Europe has called for is coming closer, and it can fail abysmally without the EU or improve at the margin thanks to it». He also emphasizes that in some ways, the end of a unipolar world could truly be the «Hour of Europe». But that can happen only if the EU regains its confidence and steps into a positive role—one that it must «play with, not against, the US».[124]

As such, there is a convergence of opinion among both the European and American scholars of repute like Dominique Moisi, Richard Haass and Joseph Nye on one significant point. All of them believe that the EU is the only natural American ally in terms of values. While analyzing the challenges faced by the international community in general and the US in particular, Joseph Nye points out: «The American military might is not adequate to deal with threats such as global pandemics, climate change, terrorism, and international crime. These issues require cooperation in the provision of global public goods and the soft power of attracting support. No part of the world shares more values or has a greater capacity to influence American attitudes and power than does Europe».[125]

While Kagan points out that a chasm has been developed in the transatlantic relations and with in the West, due to the unbridgeable gap between Europe and America on capabilities, preferences and performances, Nye maintains: «In their relations with each other, the use of force among advanced industrial democracies is virtually unthinkable and as such all of them are from Venus».[126] Richard Haass too says that it would be self-defeating for its foreign policy interests if the US ignores serious policy differences with the EU and NATO allies.

Besides arguing that nonpolarity will be difficult and dangerous and encouraging a greater degree of global integration alone will help promote stability, Haass advocates establishment of a core group of governments and others committed to cooperative multilateralism. «Call it «concerted nonpolarity». It would not eliminate nonpolarity, but it would help manage it and increase the odds that the international system will not deteriorate or disintegrate», he emphasizes.[127]

Supporting Huntington's contention of «uni-multipolarity» as well as Haass' prediction of a world with numerous power centres, both state and non-state, Zakaria foresees a broader diffusion of power across the world. The US continues to remain by far the most powerful country but in a world with several other important great powers, with great assertiveness and activity. The future world is likely to be more democratic, more dynamic, more open and more connected. The only way for the US to face the present day challenges like rogue states is to create a broad, durable coalition against them. It should allow other countries to become stakeholders in the new order, he maintains.[128]

Former Secretary of State Henry Kissinger, who, for a career-long proponent of international *realpolitik,* sounds surprisingly cautionary, in his recent book, «Does America Need a Foreign Policy? Towards a Diplomacy for the 21st Century». He suggests that U.S. policy makers must be careful to lead by example and not always by coercion. He concludes: «America's ultimate challenge is to transform its power into moral consensus, promoting its values not by imposition but by their willing acceptance in a world that, for all its seeming resistance, desperately needs enlightened leadership». Enlightened leadership must work towards enlightened national interest, which should form part of the common interest and not exclusive of it. «No matter how selfless America perceives its aims», Kissinger writes «an explicit insistence on predominance would gradually unite the world against the United States and force it into a position that would eventually leave it isolated and drained». Kissinger's warning calls for serious consideration of the present as well as future American leadership.

Rubin too exhorts that the new administration «should capitalize on this moment by declaring that the era of US unilateralism is over and that partnership with Europe is a central tenet of US foreign policy. Then, it should launch a diplomatic initiative to win closer cooperation from European allies in exchange for substantial changes in US policies toward Afghanistan and Iran and on issues such as climate change and the war on terrorism».[129]

Present environment is quite conducive for the EU-US rapprochement. The French President Nicolas Sarkozy is a self-proclaimed Atlanticist and a friend of the US. As such there is remarkable and positive change in the ground realities in Europe, since, France, usually the European pack leader in opposition to US global hegemony, in the words of Fraser Cameron, remains American-friendly. Bush, who was seen as one-man axis of evil by most Europeans, is no more at the helm of affairs and Barack Hussein Obama, who is for change, is at the helm of affairs in the other side of the Atlantic.[130] Unlike his immediate predecessor he is quite popular among the Europeans. Atmosphere is ripe for reconciliation!

Trialogue—Still Better Option

While advocating close EU-US relations and on the need on the part of Americans for adjusting their policies and priorities to the expectations of the Europeans, Volkmar Schultz, Bundestag member and the head of the German-American parliamentary exchange group points out: «But this doesn't have to be a Cain-and-Abel relationship» and further adds: «America is the bigger brother, but Europe is the older brother, and he wants to use that experience to protect our common interests. Right now, the Americans have no better friends and allies than the Europeans. And any nation that wants to be a global hegemon needs the trust of its many partners. That has nothing to do with power». There is a need for extending this logic in the relations of both EU and the US with India, which is still elder uncle—better to involve India to take benefit of its vast, varied and vivacious legacy as well.

Drezner suggests that the US should ensure the participation of India in international political and economic set ups and advocates that the Americans should keep «the old friends (the Europeans) close and its new friends closer».[131] This is the policy which the Europeans, especially the French, were following for the last couple of decades.[132] The Americans are the neo-converts to this cause.

While prescribing democratization to the developing world, the West may offer Indian model, as it may be more appropriate as well as palatable. After all, India's democratic experiment, with all its flaws, offers a better model to countries in Asia, Africa and South America than the much-touted and sanitized democracies of privileged Western Europe and North America. The EU and India must try to explore the possibility of galvanizing a new global democratic sentiment that rejects unipolarist assumptions without being antagonistic towards the US and a shift from unipolarity to a democratic multipolarity should be our common project of the 21st century.

In such circumstances, trialogue is the need of the hour for strengthening the transatlantic relations and to keep them on the track. It is necessary to develop a comparative perspective between EU-India and US-India relations with a focus on commonalities and differences of perceptions within India, EU and the US. For the good of all, the US and the EU should work together on common goals and for common good. India should be involved as it is a mature, reliable and useful partner. All the three countries should talk and negotiate with each other and with other powers. There is a compelling need to do away with the policy of confrontation, competition and exclusion, and to follow engagement, cooperation and inclusion. Such a policy and practice is good for all the three and good for the world as well. To be precise, a democratic and just new world is possible. It is for the EU to make it. India should lend its helping hand to make this happen and the US should facilitate and allow this happen.

NOTES AND REFERENCES

1. Joseph E. Stiglitz, «The EU's Global Mission», http://www.project-syndicate.org/print-commentry/stiglitz85/English. (18/6/2008).
2. Jacques Chirac, «France: Illusions, Temptations, Ambitions», *Foreign Affairs*, vol. 56, no. 3, April 1978, p. 494.

3. http://www.timesonline.co.uk/tol/news/world/us_and_americas/article3994910.ece
4. Robert Kagan, *The Return of History and the End of Dreams*, Knoob, 2008.
5. Kishore Mahbubani, India: Emerging as Eastern or Western Power? YaleGlobal, 19 December 2006, http://yaleglobal.yale.edu/display.article?id=8565
6. Sunil Kilnani, «India as a bridging power», in P.K. Basu et al., *India as a Global Leader*, London, The Foreign Policy Centre, 2005, p. 9. It is interesting to note that during the Cold War era France played successfully the role of the 'privileged' interlocutor in the context of the East-West as well as the North-South formulations. Refer Robert Aldrich and John Connell (eds.), *France in World Politics*, London, Routledge, 1989, p. 10.
7. Scott B. MacDonald, «China and India: Same Globalization Road, Different Destinies», Yale Global, October 24, 2007, http://yaleglobal.yale.edu/display.article?id=9871
8. Brahma Chellaney, «Increasing challenges to stability in Asia», *The Hindu* (Chennai), January 10, 2009.
9. B. Krishnamurthy, «Human Rights dimension of the European Common Foreign and Security Policy: The Case Study of EU-China Relations» in *Journal of Contemporary Asia & Europe*, vol.1, no. 1, January-June 2004, pp. 26-44.
10 Charles Krauthammer, 'An American Foreign Policy for a Unipolar World' http://www.aei.org/publications/pubID.19912, filter.all/pub_detail.asp. Posted: February 12, 2004. According to Krauthammer the other problem is coming demographic collapse of Europe and both will irrevocably disequilibrate the international system. In finding solutions for both the problems India can be of great help.
11. Fareed Zakaria, *The Post-American World,* Penguin-Viking, New Delhi, 2008, pp. 87-128. In the end of the chapter titled 'The Challenger' which deals with the Sino-US relations, Zakaria raises a slew of very pertinent and disturbing questions: «But what if China adheres to its asymmetrical strategy? What if it gradually expands its economic ties, acts calmly and moderately, and slowly enlarges its sphere of influence, seeking only greater weight, friendship, and influence in the world? What if it slowly pushes Washington onto the sidelines in Asia, in an effort to wear out America's patience and endurance? What if it quietly positions itself as the alternative to a hectoring and arrogant America? How will America cope with such a scenario—a kind of Cold War, ...? This is a new challenge for the United States, one it has not tackled before, and for which it is largely unprepared.
12. Alyssa Ayres, Is India Emerging as France of Asia?, Yale Global, 21 November 2006: http://yaleglobal.yale.edu/display.article?id=8452. Interestingly, Ayres argues: «The tango between Washington and New Delhi will resemble that of another problematic ally, France, a relationship of robust cooperation marked by disagreements and ideological bickerings» and suggests that the US should be prepared for it.
13. Immanuel Wallerstein, «The United States and China: Wary Rivals», Released: 1 May 2006. http://www.agenceglobal.com/article.asp?id=896;

14. Peter Beinart, «The Solvency Doctrine—*To restore American power, Obama needs foreign policy that recognizes its limits*», *Time*, February 2, 2009.
15. Immanuel Wallerstein, The United States and India: New Best Friends? Released: 15 Mar 2006, http://www.agenceglobal.com/article.asp?id=843. Wallerstein is very terse in saying: «It is said that the United States wants to build up India as a counterweight to China's potential military and political strength in Asia. Perhaps. And the United States gets a friendly nod from a major power, something in very short supply these years;
Zakaria (n. 10, pp. 129-166) appropriately titles his chapter on Indo-US relations as 'The Ally'.
16. Zakaria, n 11, pp. 132, 197.
17. Pete Engardio (ed.), *Chindia—How China and India are Revoutionizing Global Business*, Tata McGraw-Hill, New Delhi, 2008, p. 28. Development experts call this combination of a growing workforce and declining fertility rate a «demographic dividend» which helped power explosive economic growth in East Asia's Tiger economies from the 1960s through the early 1990s.
18. Jean-Luc Racine, «Quête de puissance, multipolarité et multilatéralisme», in Christophe Jafrelot (ed.), *New Delhi et le monde—Une puissance émergente entre realpolitik et soft power, Édition Autrement,* Paris, 2008, p. 52. Also refer p. 104. Incidentally, the biggest movie industry, in terms of both number of movies made and tickets sold, is Bollywood, not Hollywood. The former too enjoys wide market, due to the presence of the Indian Diaspora in every nook and corner of the world in great number.
19. Bal Gangadhar Tilak wrote to Clemenceau, the President of Paris Peace Conference, in 1918 that India with its large population, resources and area could «well aspire to be a leading power in Asia, if not in the world». (C.F. Andrews and Girija Mukerji, *The Rise and Growth of the Congress in India*, London, 1938, p. 272.) While reacting to the question of leading Asia or the developing World, Nehru said while delivering a speech at Indian Council of World Affairs, New Delhi on March 22, 1949: «... a certain special responsibility is cast on India. India realises it, and other countries realise it also. Responsibility is not necessarily for leadership but for taking the initiative sometimes and helping others to co-operate». (Jawaharlal Nehru, «Co-operation: Not Leadership», *United Asia*, vol.1, May-June 1948, p. 44).
20. Zakaria, n. 11, pp. 129-133. Zakaria sums up the Indian success story with a morale-boosting statement: «And India now has more billionaires than any other Asian country, and most of them are self-made».
21. Ayres, n. 12.
22. Stiglitz, n. 1.
23. B. Krishnamurthy, «Turkey's Membership in the European Union: Human Rights Factor», *Journal of the Institute for Research in Social Sciences and Humanities*, vol.2, no. 2, July 2007, pp. 247-264.
24. Charlotte Bretherton and John Vogler, *The European Union as a Global Actor,* Routledge, London, 2006, Second Edition, pp. 131, 136.

25. Chintamani Mahapatra, «US-EU Relations—Problems, Prospects and Implications» in Rajendra K. Jain, *The European Union in a Changing World*, Radiant Publishers, New Delhi, 2002, pp. 106-07.
26. J.M. Guehenno, «Multipolarity and Multilateralism», in *India and France in a Multipolar World*, Proceedings of the Seminar held on February 2000, *Centre de Sciences Humaines*, Manohar Publishers, New Delhi, 2001, p. 32. The former French Foreign Minister Hubert Védrine puts this fact bluntly: «The US could take on a hegemonic position. Almost 70 per cent of all pictures shown across the world are American». In 1998, the French government set up an agency to promote French higher education to foreigners. Vedrine at its launch said that the main motive was to counter America's «mega power» and to «disseminate our ideas». On the release of the French film «Astérix and Obélix against César» in early 1999, *Le Monde* declared that the film was «a symbol of Gallic resistance to the Hollywood invasion», the gritty small fighter against an imperial assault.
27. Richard N. Haass, "The end of the unipolar era", *Los Angeles Times*, July 18, 2005. http://articles.latimes.com/2005/jul/18/opinion/oe-haas18
28. Zakaria, n. 11, pp. 107-09
29. Subash Kapila, «South Asia Security—Divergence in United States and India's Perceptions: An Analysis». Paper No. 396. 22/01/2002. http://www.saag.org/papers4/paper 396.html
30. Robert Cooper Observer.co.uk, Sunday April 7 2002 http://www.guardian.co.uk/world/2002/apr/07/1.

    According to Cooper the main characteristics of the postmodern world are as follows:
    - The breaking down of the distinction between domestic and foreign affairs.
    - Mutual interference in (traditional) domestic affairs and mutual surveillance.
    - The rejection of force for resolving disputes and the consequent codification of self-enforced rules of behaviour.
    - The growing irrelevance of borders: this has come about both through the changing role of the state, but also through missiles, motor cars and satellites.
    - Security is based on transparency, mutual openness, interdependence and mutual vulnerability.

    Cooper also feels that the conception of an International Criminal Court is a striking example of the postmodern breakdown of the distinction between domestic and foreign affairs.
31. Françoise Duchene, «The European Community and the Uncertaintis of Interdependence», in K. Kohnstamm and W. Hager, *A Nation Writ Large? Foreign-policy Problems before the European Community*, London, Macmillan, 1973, pp. 19-20.
32. http://europe.eu.int/comm/external_relationss/nfewss/patten/sp02_134.htm (14-06-02) "Developing Europe's External Policy in the Age of Globalization" (Speech by Chris Patten, the then European Commissioner for External Relations on April 4, 2002).
33. While striking close consonance with Bobbitt's idea, Krauthammer calls the US as a 'commercial republic'.

34. http://www.timesonline.co.uk/tol/news/world/us_and_americas/article3994910.ece.
35. Charles Krauthammer, 'The New Unilateralism', *Washington Post*, June 8, 2001, p. A29.
36. Krauthammer, n. 10.
37. Dominique Moisi, *Financial Times*, 27 August, 2001.
38. *The National Security Strategy of the United States,* Washington: The White House, September 2002, p. 1.
39. Robert Kagan, «Power and Weakness—Why the United States and Europe see the world differently», http://www.hoover.org/publications/policyreview/3460246.html
40. *Ibid.*
41. *The Hindu*, June 20 and 23, 2000.
42. Christopher Hill, «The Capability-Expectations Gap, or Conceptualizing Europe's International Role» in Simon Bulmer and Andrew Scott (eds.), *Economic and Political Integration in Europe—Internal Dynamics and global Context*, Blackwell Publishers, Oxford, 1994, pp. 122-3. EU 's external relations is regulated by the concept of 'concentric circles' or the notion of the 'pyramid of privileges', whereby states like the US form the closest ring around the EU, followed by a belt including the CSCE, ASEAN, China, Japan and India, and then, another constituted by the African, Caribbean and Pacific and Asian and Latin American countries. The EU 's relations with these countries vary in warmth and intensity and while with some it is simple exchange relationship, in the case of some others, economic assistance and incentives are involved aiming at long-term patterns of friendship and stability. As of now, the EU has strategic partnership with the US, Russia, Canada, Japan, China and India, which makes the relationship maintained by the Union with these countries something 'special', more intensive and rigorous.
43. Dominique Moïsi, «The Clash of Emotions», *Foreign Affairs*, January/February 2007.
44. Jean François-Poncet, Introductory Speech, *India and France in a Multipolar World,* Proceedings of the Seminar held on February 2000, *Centre de Sciences Humaines*, Manohar Publishers, New Delhi, 2001, p. 21. The French always considered the NATO as a «tool of America».
45. Desmond Dinan, *Ever Closer Union—An Introduction to European Integration,* Palgrave Macmillan, 2005, p. 612.
46. Moisi, n. 37.
47. Dominique Moisi, "What Went Wrong with America", http://www.project-syndicate.org/commentary/moisi7
48. 'Solana fears widening gulf between EU and US', *Financial Times*, January 8, 2003.
49. William Wallace, «Europe, the Necessary Partner», *Foreign Affairs*, vol. 80, no. 3, May-June 2001, p. 28.
50. Hubert Védrine, *Les cartes de la France a l'heure de la mondialisation, Fayard,* 2000, pp. 9-12.

51. As recounted by Jean-David Levitte, Sarkozy's National Security Adviser, in Adam Gopnik, «The Human Bomb», *New Yorker,* August 27, 2007.
52. Zakaria, n. 11, p. 237.
53. Bruce Stokes, "A Long Marriage Ending?", *National Journal*, July 27, 2002. http://www.cfr.org/publication/4693/long_marriage_ending.html?breadcrumb=%2 Fpublication%2Fpublication_ list%3Fgroupby%3D0%26type%3Dop_ed%26 filter%3D368
54. Richard N. Haass, «The Age of Nonpolarity—What Will Follow U.S. Dominance», *Foreign Affairs*, May/June 2008.
55. Dominic Wilson and Roopa Purushothaman, *Dreaming with BRICs: The Path to 2050* (Goldman Sachs, Global Economics Paper no. 99, October 1, 2003).
56. Refer Engardio, no. 17, pp. 27-31.
57. Daniel W. Drezner, «The New New World Order», Foreign Affairs, March/April 2007, Vol. 86, No. 2. http://www.foreignaffairs.org/20070301faessay86203-p40/daniel-w-drezner/the-new-new-world-order.html
58. Stiglitz, n. 1.
59. Krauthammer, n. 35.
60. Wallace, n. 49, p. 20.
61. Kagan, n. 39.
62. Krauthammer, n. 10.
63. Stokes, n. 53.
64. Krauthammer, n. 10.
65. Fraser Cameron, «The EU and US: Friends or Rivals?», Paper presented in the seminar hosted by National Europe Centre & National Institute of Social Sciences and Law, 11 March 2004.
66. Karl F. Inderfurth, «The U.S. and India expanding engagement agenda», *The Hindu*, September 10, 2008.
67. Stanley Hoffmann, «Mitterrand 's Foreign Policy, or Gaullism by Any Other Name», in George Ross *et al., The Mitterrand Experiment: Continuity and Change in Modern France*, Polity Press, Cambridge, 1987, p. 294.
68. Poncet, n. 44., p. 22.
69. *Ibid.,* p. 20.
70. Wallace, n. 49, p. 28.
71. B. Krishnamurthy, «Ally, but not Aligned: French Quest for Multipolarism in an Unipolar World», in Vinay Kumar Malhotra (ed.), *The USA—Relations with India and Europe,* Wisdom House, India, 2002, pp. 134-37. The stand taken by the former French foreign minister Védrine was shared by many European leaders and people as well.
72. http://europe.eu.int/comm/external_relationss/nfewss/patten/sp02_134.htm (14-06-02) «Developing Europe's External Policy in the Age of Globalization» (Speech by Chris Patten, the then European Commissioner for External Relations on April 4, 2002).
73. Charles Krauthammer, 'The Unipolar Moment», *Foreign Affairs,* 70, no. 1 (1990/1991), pp. 23-33. Incidentally, Krauthammer believed that the unipolarity would

not last long and assumed that it would be in effect for a period of about fifteen to twenty years, which is really a 'moment' in international politics.

74. Charles Krauthammer, 'The Unipolar Moment Revisited,' *National Interest*, no. 70 (Winter 2003), p. 17.
75. Moisi, n. 47.
76. Dominique Moisi, «The Fall of the Hyper Power», http://www.project-syndicate.org/commentary/moisi12
77. Zakaria, n. 11, p. 43.
78. Haass, n. 54.
79. Kagan, n. 39.
80. Stokes, n. 53.
81. http://www.france.diplomatie.fr/label_france/ENGLISH/DOSSIER/2000/04puissance.html
82. http://europe.eu.int/comm/external_relationss/nfewss/patten/sp02_134.htm (14-06-02) "Developing Europe's External Policy in the Age of Globalization" (Speech by Chris Patten, the then European Commissioner for External Relations on April 4, 2002).
83. B. Krishnamurthy, «European Union's Response to Terrorism in Kashmir», in A. Subramanyam Raju (ed.), *Terrorism in South Asia: Views from India*, India Research Press, New Delhi, 2004, pp. 301-321.
84. Wallace, n. 49, p. 25.
85. Noam Chomsky, "On Hegemony or Survival", Lecture delivered at Illinois State University, October 7, 2003, http://www.chomsky.info/talks/20031007.htm
86. *Ibid.*
87. Chomsky, "Europe and America as Underwriters of the International Order", Lecture delivered at the Institute of European Affairs, January 19, 2006, http://www.chomsky.info/talks/20060119.htm
88. *Ibid.*
89. Chomsky, n. 85.
90. Kagan, n. 39.
91. Wallace, n. 49, p. 20.
92. Craig Smith, "New Transatlantic Tension and the Kagan Phenomenon: A Primer", *German Law Journal*, No. 9 (1 September 2003). http://www.germanlaw journal.com/article.php?id=306
93. Benita Ferrero-Waldner, «The EU and the US: meeting today's challenges together», Conference on «The US, Germany and Europe: towards a new global partnership», The American Council on Germany, Washington, DC, 30 April 2007.
94. Chris Patten, «The Western Balkans: The Road to Europe», Speech to European Affairs Committee of the Bundestag, Berlin, April 28, 2004, http://www.ear.eu.int/agency/main/agency-a la2g3.htm.
95. B.Krishnamurthy, *Indo-French Relations—Prospects and Perspectives*, Shipra Publications, New Delhi, 2005. Refer, especially Chapter 9 on Indo-French Nuclear Cooperation, pp. 109-125.

96. Zakaria, n. 11, p. 225.
97. B.Krishnamurthy, «Common Foreign and Security Policies of European Union—Implication for Peace and Security in South Asia», in Nalini Kant Jha (ed.), *South Asia in 21st Century*—India, Her Neighbours and Great Powers», South Asian Publishers Pvt. Ltd., New Delhi, 2003, p. 237.
98. *The Hindu*, June 29, 2000.
99. Several experts, including some Americans, share this point of view.
100. *The Hindu,* February 5, 2009.
101. Mark C Fischer, «The European Union in the Changing International System» in Rajendra K. Jain, *The European Union in a Changing World,* Radiant Publishers, New Delhi, 2002, p. 23.
102. «EU-US: Kiss and make up?», http://www.euractiv.com/en/security/eu-us-kiss/article-135513
103. *Ibid.*
104. Cameron, n. 65.
105. http://www.france.diplomatie.fr./actual/evenements/inde2/inde4.gb.html (Védrine's interview to Press Trust of India on April 12, 2000).
106. *The Hindu,* September 9, 2002. (Dominique de Villepin' s interview).
107. *Ibid.*, May 7 and June 1, 2003. François Mitterrand and Claude Cheysson visualised such a development in mid 1980s itself.
108. Jaswant Singh's Address to the Seminar on India and France in a Multipolar World, n. 26, p. 214.
109. Dinan, n. 45, p. 612.
110. Mahapatra, n. 25, pp. 104-5.
111. Kagan, n. 39.
112. Smith, n. 92.
113. Dinan, n. 45, p. 626.
114. Richard N. Haass, «The Opportunity: America's Moment to Alter History's Course», 2005, http://www.theglobalist.com/dbweb/StoryId.aspx?StoryId=4597
115. Krishnamurthy, n. 9, pp. 26-44.
116. Chris Patten during the course of his address at the Chicago Council on Foreign Relations, Chicago, on 3 October 2002 pleaded for bridging the gap between the partners of the Atlantic alliance and for reconciliation. He made it very clear to the Americans what the Europeans expected from them.
117. Ivo H. Daadler, «The End of Atlanticism», *Survival*, vol.45, no. 2, Summer 2003, p. 151.
118. Haass, n. 27.
119. Dinan, n. 45, p. 636.
120. Zakaria, n. 11, p. 228.
121. «EU-US: Kiss and make up?», http://www.euractiv.com/en/security/eu-us-kiss/article-135513.
122. Benita Ferrero-Waldner, «The EU and the US: meeting today's challenges together», Conference on «The US, Germany and Europe: towards a new global partnership», The American Council on Germany, Washington, DC, 30 April

2007. http://europa.eu/rapid/pressReleasesAction.do?reference=SPEECH/07/262&format=HTML&aged=1&language=EN&guiLanguage=en

123. Dominique Moisi, "What Is France's Place In The World?", September 24, 2007. http://www.atlantic- commmunity.org/index/Open_Think_Tank_Article/What_Is_France's_Place_In_The_World%3F
124. Dominique Moisi, «The Fall of the Hyper Power» http://www.project-syndicate.org/commentary/moisi12
125. Joseph S. Nye, «Europe's Power to Lead», February 2008, http://www.project-syndicate.org/commentary/nye54. Nye elaborates this theme in his book, *The Paradox of American Power: Why the World's Only Superpower Can't Go it Alone.*
126. *Ibid.*
127. Haass, n. 54.
128. Zakaria, n. 11, pp. 43-4.
129. James P. Rubin, «Building a New Atlantic Alliance—Restoring America's Partnership With Europe», *Foreign Affairs*, July/August 2008.
130. *Time,* November 17, 2008. On July 24, while speaking in Berlin, Senator Obama pledged to work with Europe in a spirit of «constant cooperation, strong institutions and shared sacrifice». Europe and the world expect President Obama to stick to this policy. Likewise, Obama referred to India as a natural ally and talked about cooperation between the two democracies in fighting against the common problems.
131. Drezner, n. 57.
132. Krishnamurthy, n. 95, p. 189.

Contributors

Robert Etien is currently Dean of the Faculty of Law, Political and Social Sciences of the University of Paris 13 which hosts four thousand students in the disciplines of Law, Economic and Social Administration, and Political Science, three research centres, more than hundred and fifty teachers and twenty-five members of administrative staff. He is Director of the Master's Degree in Business and International Trade with Emerging Nations. He heads the CERAL (Centre for Research on Local Action) research centre. He had previously served as Vice-President of the administrative board of the University of Paris 13 and is currently President of the University Statutes Commission.

Pierre-Yves Monjal is Professor of Public Law (holds a Ph.D) in the University of Paris 13. A specialist in Community Law, he has written numerous articles (more than hundred) on issues relating to the European Union and their repercussions on French law. He has authored five books and been legal adviser to the Ministry of Economy and Budget on questions involving Community law. He is an elected member of the Montrichard Municipal Council. He also teaches at the Institute of Political Studies, Paris. His current research interests centre on Public Procurement Law.

Claudine Moutardier holds a doctorate in Law from the University of Paris I-Sorbonne. She is currently Research Engineer in the University of Paris 13. She is also in charge of the Federal Centre for Research in Law and the European Documentation Centre. She regularly contributes to the chronicle «Questions of Interest to France» and «Conventions Concluded by France» in the *Annuaire français de droit international.*

Charles Reiplinger teaches public law, legal and political theory in Paris (Université de Paris 13). He is a member of the *Institut Michel Villey pour la culture juridique et la philosophie du droit (Université Paris II)* and of the *Centre de recherches administratives et politiques (Université de Paris 13).* He also works on contemporary public law, mostly constitutional, and takes interest in administrative and private (criminal) law. He believes legal concepts cannot be usefully understood without a philosophical and political point of view.

Hugo-Bernard Pouillaude has recently been appointed as Temporary Teaching and Research Assistant at the Faculty of Law, University of Paris 13. He has published several research papers on Social Law in specialized French journals. He has always been interested in Poland and visited it regularly.

Julien Sterck graduated from Bordeaux in Law and Political Science. He also holds an LL.B. from the University of Kent at Canterbury and a M. Phil. in Jurisprudence from Paris X Nanterre. He is currently Junior Lecturer in French Legal System at Trinity College, Dublin.

Dr. Patrick B Griffin is a solicitor (Ireland & United Kingdom) and works as a lecturer in the area of European Union law at Val de Marne University, Paris 12. After receiving a Ph.D from the University of Paris II, he has worked with some of the world's leading law firms, such as Baker & McKenzie, in the area of European Union commercial law. He is also the author of numerous articles and a number of books in the area of European law and has also been the editor of legal journals in this field.

B. Krishnamurthy is Doctor of Philosophy in History from the Maharaja Sayajirao University of Baroda, Vadodara. His post-doctoral work is on the freedom movement in the French Settlements in India and he has a couple of books on this subject to his credit. He has also authored a volume on Indo-French Relations—Prospects and Perspectives (2005). He has contributed numerous research articles on European Integration, European Human Rights Regime and French Foreign Policy. He is currently Associate Professor in the Department of Politics and International Studies, Pondicherry University, Puducherry, India. Currently he is working on the project: European Common Foreign and Security Policy—Implications for India.

Scott Erb is Professor of Political Science at the University of Maine Farmington, specializing in International Relations and European Politics. He graduated with a Ph.D. from the University of Minnesota (1994), and MA from Johns Hopkins School of Advanced International Studies (1984). His publications include *German Foreign Policy: Navigating a New Era* (Lynne Rienner, 2003), as well as articles on German economic policy, and scholarship on teaching, learning and assessment in the field of Political Science. He has served as Chair of the International Studies programme at Farmington and has been active in the American Political Science Association section on Political Science Education.

Geetha Ganapathy-Doré was born in India. A graduate of Annamalai University, she completed her postgraduate studies in Pondicherry. She started her career as Lecturer in French in Sri Venkateswara University, when she was awarded the French Government scholarship for doctoral studies. She completed her M.Phil in Comparative Literature and Ph.D in Semiotics at the University of Paris 7. After working as a free lance translator and as a temporary lecturer in the Universities of Paris X, Pontoise and Marne la Vallée, she got tenure as Senior Lecturer in English at the faculty of Law in the University of Paris XIII. She was an elected member of the Faculty Council from 2002-2006. She has published some seventy articles in English and French on Post Colonial Literature and Culture. She has also translated a few Tamil and Indian English short stories into French. She is a book reviews editor for *Post Colonial Text*, a peer reviewed on-line journal. She has co-authored a text book on *English for EU Law*.

Shazia Aziz-Wülbers is an affiliated researcher at the Bremen University and has just defended her doctoral thesis at the Sciences Po Paris. She has worked as a lecturer at Hamburg University and Bremen University. Her main areas of interests are EU India relations, contemporary Indian politics, theories of European integration and International Relations. She has published several articles and has recently edited the book *EU India Relations: A Critique* (New Delhi: Academic Foundations, 2008). She is a board member at the Euro India Centre.

P. Marudanayagam is former Professor and Head of the Department of English, Pondicherry University, Puducherry, India. At present, he is serving as Senior Fellow in the Centre for Classical Tamil, Chennai.

Iver B. Neumann (b. 1959), D. Phil. (Oxon), is Director of research at the Norwegian Institute of International Affairs and Professor at the Department for European Literature, Area Studies and Languages, Oslo University. H.S. major research interests are social theory, international relations theory, diplomacy, Russian and Norwegian foreign policy, European integration. He was the editor of Cooperation and Conflict. Nordic Journal of International Relations 1999-01. Among his twelve books are *Russia and Europe: A Study in Identity and International Relations* (Routledge, 1996) and *Uses of the Other: «The East» in European Identity Formation* (University of Minnesota Press, 1999).

Index